I'm Pregnant!

CANADIAN EDITION

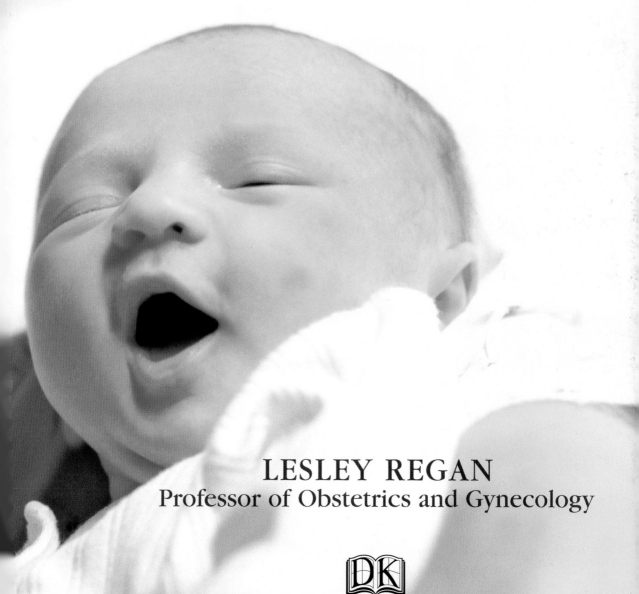

I'm Pregnant!

A week-by-week guide

LESLEY REGAN
Professor of Obstetrics and Gynecology

DK

CANADIAN EDITION
Project editor Ian Whitelaw
Editor Julia Roles
Production controller Rebecca Short

First Canadian edition 2007

Dorling Kindersley is represented in Canada by
Tourmaline Editions Inc.,
662 King Street West, Suite 304,
Toronto,
Ontario M5V 1M7

Library and Archives Canada Cataloguing in Publication

Regan, Lesley
I'm pregnant : a week-by-week guide / Lesley Regan.

Includes index.
ISBN 978-1-55363-077-7

1. Pregnancy--Popular works. I. Title.

RG525.R428 2007   618.2   C2006-905067-8

Reproduced by Colourscan, Singapore
Printed and bound in Singapore by Star Standard
07 08 09 10 5 4 3

Discover more at
www.dk.com

CONTENTS

Foreword 6
Introduction 7

YOUR JOURNEY THROUGH PREGNANCY

The Very Beginning 12
Conceiving a Baby **16**
Staying Safe in Pregnancy **26**
Diet and Exercise **38**
Work and Maternity Rights **58**

The First Trimester 64
Weeks 0–6 **68**
Prenatal Care and Birth Choices **84**
Weeks 6–10 **92**
Weeks 10–13 **106**
Prenatal tests **134**

The Second Trimester 148
Weeks 13–17 **152**
Weeks 17–21 **166**
Weeks 21–26 **180**

The Third Trimester 198
Weeks 26–30 **202**
Shopping for your Baby **224**
Weeks 30–35 **230**
Specialist Prenatal Monitoring **256**
Weeks 35–40 **260**

LABOR AND BIRTH

The Stages of Labor 280
The First Stage **282**
Pain Relief in Labor **308**
The Second & Third Stages **324**

When Help is Needed 336
Premature Labor **338**
Multiple Births **344**
Assisted Deliveries **350**
Cesarean Birth **360**

LIFE AFTER BIRTH
Your Newborn Baby 372
The Hours After Birth **374**

The First Six Weeks 382
Your Physical Recovery **384**
Your Emotional Recovery **390**
First Days and Weeks at Home **394**
Feeding Your Baby **396**
Family Adjustments **400**
The Six-week Postnatal Check **403**

CONCERNS AND COMPLICATIONS
Existing Medical Conditions **408**
Infections and Illnesses **411**
Fetal Abnormalities **415**
Problems in Pregnancy and Labor **422**
Concerns After Birth **432**

Useful Addresses **436**
Index **439**
Acknowledgments **447**

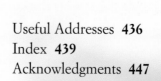

"Pregnancy is one of the most important journeys that you will ever embark upon..."

INTRODUCTION

There are plenty of pregnancy books on the market so why should I embark on writing another one? The reason is simple — the women I care for keep telling me that they would like more detailed answers to their questions about pregnancy and childbirth. Furthermore, they want a book that provides them with clear, comprehensive information, without any prescriptive or personal agenda.

I understand and sympathize with the request since, when I was expecting my twins, I remember feeling both astonished and intimidated by books that seem to suggest that there are right and wrong approaches to pregnancy and childbirth. I have no argument with the many different childbirth philosophies, but I do have a problem when they result in pregnant women feeling that they have failed in some way if they do not follow the advice to the last letter, or their pregnancy does not follow a textbook pattern.

So the agenda here is very simple — knowledge is key. My aim is to offer you a level of information about your prenatal care that is not always readily available. I want to ensure that you are fully aware of the extraordinary events in your baby's development and the remarkable adaptations your body will make. My belief is that the only way to be confident about the choices and decisions that you will need to make in pregnancy is to have a clear understanding of everything that may happen to you. I also believe that this is the best way to achieve the happiest outcome — a healthy mother and a beautiful take-home baby.

Lesley Ryan

ABOUT THIS BOOK

Pregnancy is one of the most important journeys that you will ever embark upon. To help you understand as much as possible about this eventful and exciting period of your life, this book is arranged chronologically. It takes you from the moment you conceive, through each week of your pregnancy to the day of delivery and then provides all the information you need to give birth and care for yourself and your baby afterward. This chronological arrangement makes it easier to find your way around the book smoothly. I also hope that you will be able to find the answers to your questions quickly and easily. Above all, I want to offer you clear, comprehensive, and up-to-date information to help you understand the medical jargon and the experiences you are likely to encounter in the next few months.

The journey section is divided into the three trimesters of pregnancy. Everyone seems to have her own idea about exactly which weeks fall in each trimester; the only important thing is that each one corresponds to an important and distinct phase of your baby's development. At the beginning of each trimester, there is a broad overview of the major milestones that occur, then it is broken down into three more detailed "through the weeks" guides. Each of these covers what routinely happens in pregnancy, including a description of your baby's development, how your own body changes, how you may be feeling both physically and emotionally, together with a section on the prenatal care you can expect and some

THE JOURNEY TIMELINE

The three trimesters are divided into 4–6 week sections offering detailed information that relates to your exact stage of pregnancy.

week 8 *week 12* *week 16* *week 20*

| 1 | 2 | 3 | 4 | 5 | 6 | 7 | 8 | 9 | 10 | 11 | 12 | 13 | 14 | 15 | 16 | 17 | 18 | 19 | 20 |

▶ WEEKS 0–6   ▶ WEEKS 6–10   ▶ WEEKS 10–13   ▶ WEEKS 13–17   ▶ WEEKS 17–21

▶ FIRST TRIMESTER   ▶ SECOND TRIMESTER

of the common concerns linked to that particular time. To keep things simple I define the age of your pregnancy and your baby as the number of weeks from your last menstrual period.

In this book, I have defined the first trimester as 0–13 weeks of pregnancy. Broadly speaking, the first trimester is the crucial period when all the organs, muscles, and bones are formed. During the first eight weeks, we refer to the baby as an embryo; subsequently, it is called a fetus. In the second trimester, all the basic structures that have developed are consolidated. During this period, the fetus grows rapidly and starts to make facial expressions, hear sounds, and can be felt kicking. In the third trimester the baby undergoes an important final phase of growth and maturation. Everything in the third trimester is based on the building blocks laid months before.

Although the vast majority of pregnancies are relatively problem-free, not every pregnancy is an entirely smooth journey. Whenever less common problems arise, you will be referred to the last section of the book for further explanation.

No two labors are alike. The summary of how normal labor progresses and the various pain-relief options will be all most readers need, but for those who may need more specialized treatment there is detailed information and advice on topics such as cesarean birth and premature delivery.

The Life after Birth chapter looks at the potential highs and lows after your baby is born. Delight in your new baby will be intermingled with anxiety about minor problems and your ability to cope with your new role. I hope my advice will help ease you and your baby through these first important weeks together.

	week 24			*week* 28			*week* 32			*week* 36			*week* 40

21	22	23	24	25	26	27	28	29	30	31	32	33	34	35	36	37	38	39	40

▶ WEEKS 21–26   ▶ WEEKS 26–30   ▶ WEEKS 30–35   ▶ WEEKS 35–40

▶ THIRD TRIMESTER

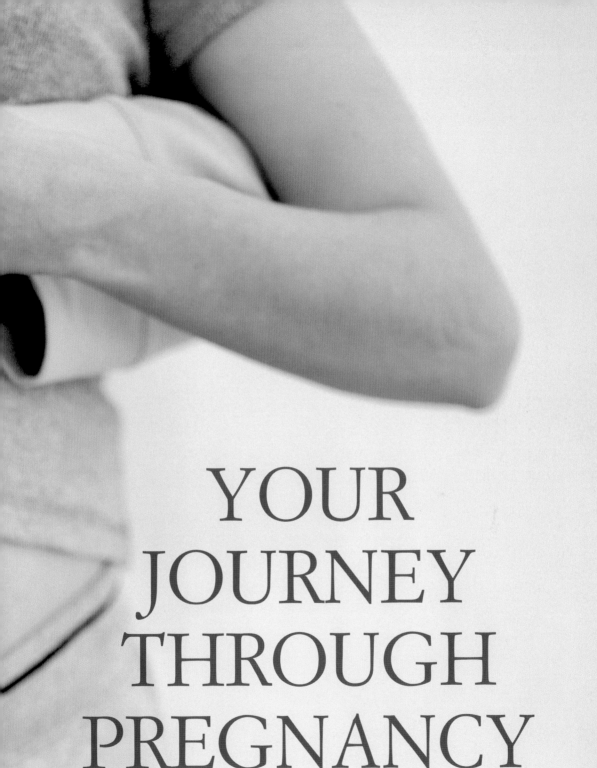

YOUR JOURNEY THROUGH PREGNANCY

THE VERY BEGINNING

Whether you are pregnant already or have simply made the decision to have a baby soon, this is the beginning of one of life's most exciting and, occasionally, daunting experiences. This section helps you lay the foundation for an enjoyable pregnancy — offering insights into conception and answering questions about what is safe in pregnancy; the best foods to eat; how to stay fit over the coming weeks, and how to negotiate your rights and benefits as a parent. These are your guidelines for the journey ahead....

CONTENTS

CONCEIVING
A BABY

22 Genes and inheritance

24 Confirming that
you are pregnant

STAYING SAFE
IN PREGNANCY

30 Environmental hazards

32 Illness during
pregnancy

36 Trouble-free travel

DIET AND EXERCISE

40 Healthy eating

43 The perfect pregnancy
diet

46 Essential vitamins and
minerals

53 Exercise in pregnancy

WORK AND
MATERNITY RIGHTS

60 Your rights and
benefits

THE ORIGINS OF LIFE

INSIDE THE UTERUS
THE LINING IS PERFECTLY
PRIMED FOR A LIFE TO BEGIN.
THE GRANULES OF MUCUS
(YELLOW) WILL PROVIDE
NUTRIENTS FOR A NEWLY
FERTILIZED EGG.

MATURING SPERM AS
SPERM PASS SLOWLY ALONG
THE EPIDIDYMIS — A COILED TUBE
THAT LIES BEHIND THE TESTES —
THEY MATURE UNTIL THEY ARE
READY TO BE EJACULATED.

JOURNEY'S END A SWARM OF
SURVIVING SPERM LOCK ONTO THE
THICK, INVITING SURFACE OF THE EGG
AFTER THEIR LONG JOURNEY UP THE
FALLOPIAN TUBE.

"A mature egg drifts in the fallopian tube... conditions are perfect for fertilization."

THE WINNER JUST ONE SPERM PENETRATES THE OVUM'S THICK OUTER LAYER, AND FERTILIZATION OCCURS.

SIX DAYS OLD THE TINY CLUSTER OF CELLS, NOW KNOWN AS A BLASTOCYST, EMBEDS IN THE WALL OF THE UTERUS — A PREGNANCY BEGINS.

CONCEIVING A BABY

When you consider the complex sequence of hormonal events that are necessary for you to become pregnant, and the hoops that your partner's sperm have to go through to fertilize an egg, you will begin to realize why the expression "the miracle of conception" is not an overstatement.

The series of events that occur during your menstrual cycle need to be carefully orchestrated if a pregnancy is to occur. Conception is a bit like a jigsaw puzzle — just one piece missing and the puzzle can't be completed.

As soon as your period ends, a hormone called follicle stimulating hormone (FSH) is secreted into your bloodstream by the pituitary gland, a small bean-sized gland that lies just behind your eyes in your brain. This hormone acts on your ovaries, which sit at the end of your fallopian tubes and contain many thousands of eggs. You were born with about three million eggs, but by puberty these will have degenerated to about 400,000. All of these eggs are exposed to FSH, and it is not clear why only a few are recruited to start developing. On average, a woman will release only 400 or fewer mature eggs during her reproductive lifespan.

ovary   fallopian tube

lining of uterus (endometrium)

uterus

cervix

vagina

FEMALE REPRODUCTIVE SYSTEM *The ovaries store and release eggs, which travel along the fallopian tube into the uterus. The narrow cervix connects the uterus to the vagina.*

OVULATION

Each ovary releases one egg (or occasionally more than one) in alternate menstrual cycles, so ovulation takes place from only one ovary at a time. Eggs that are selected to start to mature do so within a fluid-filled bubble called a follicle, which starts to enlarge under the influence of FSH. Every month about 20 eggs start this process, but usually only one "dominant" follicle becomes fully mature and ovulates; the others shrivel, and the eggs within them are lost. The egg grows to one side of the follicle, surrounded by special cells called granulosa cells, which feed it with nutrients and also produce estrogen. This hormone stimulates the growth of the lining of the uterus (endometrium) as well as breast tissues, which is why breast tenderness is a common premenstrual symptom.

◀ *A single sperm penetrates the outer layer of the comparatively huge ovum.*

"Conception is a bit like a jigsaw puzzle — just one piece missing and the puzzle can't be completed."

As the level of estrogen in your blood rises, it feeds back a message to the hypothalamus (a control center in the brain) telling it that the follicle is mature and ready to ovulate. In response, the hypothalamus informs the pituitary gland to release a short sharp burst of luteinizing hormone (LH), called a pulse, which triggers the release of the egg about 36 hours later. The egg bursts from the follicle, which has grown to about the size of a quarter coin. This is called ovulation and it usually occurs around the 14th day of the menstrual cycle.

The mature egg has developed several important features. It contains chromosomes (which carry genetic information) at the right stage for further development and it is capable of taking in a single sperm while blocking the entry of any other sperm surrounding it. The egg is swept into the fallopian tube by delicate wandlike projections called fimbria, which resemble the fronds of a sea anemone. Tiny hairlike strands, called cilia, line the fallopian tube and these help the newly released egg to pass down the tube toward the uterus.

Meanwhile, the remaining cells in the ruptured follicle form a swelling in the ovary called the corpus luteum, which starts to produce the hormone progesterone. Like estrogen, progesterone has an effect on the uterus, breasts, and the hypothalamus and pituitary glands in your brain. In the uterus, progesterone makes the cells receptive to pregnancy by producing the nutrients needed to support a developing embryo and by thickening the lining of the uterus.

If the egg is not fertilized after ovulation, your production of luteinizing hormone begins to fall and the corpus luteum withers away. When the levels of both estrogen and progesterone have fallen below the threshold needed to

THE RACE TO THE EGG

Ovulation occurs mid-menstrual cycle when the mature ovum (egg) bursts from its follicle.

Cohorts of sperm stream through the narrow opening of the cervix and into the uterus.

maintain the lining of the uterus in a receptive state for embryo implantation, the blood-filled lining starts to disintegrate and your menstrual period begins. In a normal cycle, this usually occurs around 14 days after ovulation. The onset of your menstrual period signals that a new cycle of follicle growth can begin again.

YOUR PARTNER'S ROLE IN CONCEPTION

This may seem to be the simpler part of the proposition, but the statistical probability of your partner's sperm meeting your egg is minute. On average a man ejaculates about 5ml (a teaspoonful) of semen containing 100 to 300 million sperm. Less than 100,000 make their way through the cervix; a mere 200 survive the journey up into the fallopian tubes to fertilize the egg.

Boys are not born with a full complement of sperm. Production starts around puberty and from this time onward, sperm are manufactured in the testes regularly at a rate of 1,500 per second. Each sperm has a lifespan of about 72 days. The testes deliver the sperm into the epididymis (a long coiled tube sitting at the top of each testis) and over the next two or three weeks they become capable of moving on their own and fertilizing an egg. From here the sperm move into the vas deferens. These tubes contract during male orgasm and transport the sperm out of the scrotum, past the seminal vesicles and the prostate gland (from which they collect seminal fluid) and into the urethra — the tube that travels between the bladder and the penis. During ejaculation, the opening to the bladder is shut off and the sperm are rapidly transported into the penis ready for their journey into the vagina.

A sperm negotiates the frond-filled lining of the fallopian tube on its way to the ovum.

Mission accomplished — the successful surviving sperm swarm over the mature ovum.

"It is amazing to reflect that, even before you realize you are pregnant, the design of your baby's body is being programed."

FIRST DIVISIONS *After fertilization, the zygote divides rapidly. Within 36 hours it is made up of 12 separate cells.*

Arriving in the vagina is not the end of the sperm's extraordinary obstacle race; they still need to navigate a considerable distance before they have an opportunity to fertilize an egg. The environment is fairly hostile to sperm: vaginal secretions are quite acidic to prevent bacteria and other organisms from reaching the uterus and fallopian tubes and causing damaging infections. However, once in the vagina, the semen coagulates rapidly and this helps keep the sperm in the right place and protect them from vaginal fluids.

Within 5 to 10 minutes after ejaculation some sperm have entered the uterus and are heading toward the fallopian tubes. During this journey the sperm become hyperactive and attain full fertilizing capacity so that when they get close to the egg they are able to shed their cap (acrosome) and fuse with the egg. For the next 72 hours, more sperm from the pool at the cervix continue to enter the uterus. Once in the fallopian tubes, the remaining sperm (by now reduced to about 200) swim upward aided by muscular contractions of the uterus and tubes. This in itself is an extraordinary feat, since at the same time the egg is being propelled down toward the uterine cavity.

FERTILIZATION

The process during which the sperm enters the egg, fuses with it, and the egg starts dividing takes about 24 hours to complete and usually takes place while the egg is still traveling down the fallopian tube.

Only the strongest cohort of sperm reaches the egg but it seems that the "winner" in the race is entirely random. Several sperm may bind to the surface of the egg and this stimulates them to lose their caps, exposing enzymes that digest their way through the outer membrane (the zona). However, only one sperm penetrates the oocyte, the innermost part of the egg, and fertilization occurs. The sperm tail, which has been so vital in propelling it to this point, is left outside and eventually disintegrates. The newly formed single cell that results is called a zygote and it now forms a thick wall around itself to prevent penetration by any other sperm. Your pregnancy has begun!

The zygote now begins to divide into further cells, called blastomeres, which number about a dozen by the third day. This tiny cluster of new life then takes about 60 hours to make its way to the uterus, by which time it is made up of about 50–60 cells and is called a blastocyst.

Already there are two distinct cell types — an outer layer of trophoblast cells, which will develop into the placenta, and an inner cell mass, which will eventually form the fetus. Two to three days later (about one week after fertilization) the blastocyst embeds itself in the lining of the uterus. It has now subdivided into approximately 100 cells and starts to produce the hormone human chorionic gonadotropin (HCG), which sends a signal to the corpus luteum to carry on producing progesterone. Having failed to do so, the lining of the uterus would begin to break down and menstrual bleeding would begin.

In the second week after conception, the trophoblast cells continue to enter the uterine lining and the inner cell mass develops into an embryo. It is only a dot, but has already started to differentiate into three different cell layers, called the germ layers, which will each become a different part of the baby's body. It is amazing to reflect that, even before you realize you are pregnant, the design of your baby's body is being programed.

HOW TWINS ARE CONCEIVED

Twins and triplets are conceived in two different ways:

▶ When two or more eggs are released and fertilized, the result is nonidentical twins.

▶ When one egg is fertilized by one sperm and then divides into two separate zygotes, the result is two separate embryos. These share identical genetic structures and will therefore become identical twins.

With both types of twin each baby develops surrounded by amniotic fluid, within its own amniotic sac. But because nonidentical twins are conceived from two separate eggs, each has its own placenta. Identical twins share one placenta, but each twin has a separate umbilical cord.

The number of twin pregnancies

IDENTICAL TWINS *share a placenta.*

NONIDENTICAL TWINS *have two placentas.*

 one fertilized egg divides

 two separate eggs are fertilized

has doubled compared to a generation ago. Twins now make up around two percent of all pregnancies — partly because of recent medical advances, such as in vitro fertilization (IVF) and fertility drugs (both of which carry an increased risk of multiple pregnancy), and partly because women are having

babies later in life. Women over 35 have a greater chance of conceiving nonidentical twins because they are more likely to release more than one egg per cycle. Nonidentical twins also run in families. However, there are no factors that increase the risk of conceiving identical twins.

GENES AND INHERITANCE

GENES CONTROL THE GROWTH AND REPAIR OF OUR BODIES AND ARE ALSO THE CODE BY WHICH WE PASS ON PHYSICAL AND MENTAL CHARACTERISTICS TO OUR CHILDREN. AT CONCEPTION, YOUR BABY INHERITS A UNIQUE PACKAGE OF GENES THAT WILL MAKE HIM OR HER DIFFERENT FROM ANY OTHER PERSON.

The 30–40,000 or so genes that make up the human genome are arranged in pairs along chromosomes, long strands of genetic material that are found in the nucleus of virtually all body cells. Individual genes are single units of information inherited from the parents and occupy a specific position on the chromosome. Genes contain numerous small segments of DNA (the genetic blueprint), which provide codes for specific traits such as blood type and also dictate the specialized function of cells. In some cases, the presence or absence of a gene can predispose a person to a disease or protect against it. Genes are also either dominant or recessive. In a pair made up of one dominant and one recessive gene, the dominant gene prevails and this has effects on inherited traits such as eye color (*see* opposite) and also in the development of some genetic diseases (*see* p.144).

When a baby is conceived, both the mother's egg and the father's sperm contribute a single set of 23 chromosomes to the embryo, making a total complement of 46. Each egg and sperm carries a different mix of genes, which is why, apart from identical twins (*see* p.21), every baby inherits a unique selection. However, because all cells are derived from this single fertilized egg, the same genetic material is duplicated in every cell of a baby's body.

BOY OR GIRL?

When an egg is fertilized by a sperm, the embryo that results has 23 pairs of chromosomes. The sex of your baby is determined by just one pair: chromosomes 45 and 46 (known as pair 23) are the sex chromosomes.

▶ **The sex chromosomes** are labeled the X (female) and Y (male) chromosomes. All eggs carry a single X chromosome, while sperm carry either a single X or a single Y in equal numbers. It is therefore the sperm that determines the sex of a child.

▶ **When a sperm carrying the X chromosome** fertilizes an egg, it forms an XX pair of chromosomes and the result is a girl.

▶ **When a sperm carrying the Y chromosome** fertilizes an egg, this results in an XY pair – a boy.

▶ **Methods that claim** to tip the balance in favor of a boy or girl rely on the fact that the Y-bearing sperm swim a little faster than the X-bearing sperm, but the latter survive a little longer. However, theories on the timing of conception to produce a boy or girl vary considerably. In spite of these methods, the ratio of boys to girls remains reassuringly normal.

BROWN EYES OR BLUE?

ONE OF THE MOST EASILY UNDERSTOOD EXAMPLES OF INHERITED TRAITS INVOLVING DOMINANT AND RECESSIVE GENES CONCERNS EYE COLOR. BECAUSE THE BROWN-EYE GENE IS DOMINANT AND THE BLUE-EYE GENE IS RECESSIVE, THE GENE FOR BROWN EYES ALWAYS PREVAILS.

Both you and your partner carry a pair of genes for eye color and this offers four possible combinations of genes in your own children. To work out your baby's chance of having blue or brown eyes you need to look at the eye-color genes you have inherited from your own parents. Even if you both have brown eyes, you may each have a blue-eyed parent and therefore be carrying recessive blue-eye genes. If these recessive genes combine, your baby will have blue eyes.

If you both have blue eyes, neither of you possess dominant brown-eye genes, so together you cannot have a child with brown eyes. (The brown-eye gene also covers hazel eyes, and the blue-eye gene includes gray and light-green eyes.)

Two brown-eyed parents In this example, the dominant brown-eye gene masks the recessive blue-eye gene so all children have brown eyes.

 PARENTS BR/BL + BR/BR

CHILD

BR+BR *child will have brown eyes*

BR+BR *child will have brown eyes*

BL+BR *child will have brown eyes*

BL+BR *child will have brown eyes*

One brown-eyed parent; one blue-eyed parent The dominant brown-eye gene will prevail or two recessive blue-eye genes will combine to produce blue eyes.

 PARENTS BR/BL + BL/BL

CHILD

BR+BL *child will have brown eyes*

BR+BL *child will have brown eyes*

BL+BL *child will have blue eyes*

BL+BL *child will have blue eyes*

Two brown-eyed parents In this example, both parents carry a recessive blue-eye gene from their own parents so have a 1 in 4 chance of a blue-eyed child.

 PARENTS BR/BL + BR/BL

CHILD

BR+BR *child will have brown eyes*

BR+BL *child will have brown eyes*

BL+BR *child will have brown eyes*

BL+BL *child will have blue eyes*

Two blue-eyed parents Blue-eyed parents both carry two copies of the recessive blue-eye gene so they cannot have a brown-eyed child.

 PARENTS BL/BL + BL/BL

CHILD

BL+BL *child will have blue eyes*

BL+BL *child will have blue eyes*

BL+BL *child will have blue eyes*

BL+BL *child will have blue eyes*

CONFIRMING THAT YOU ARE PREGNANT

AS SOON AS YOU BEGIN TO SUSPECT THAT YOU MIGHT BE PREGNANT, YOU CAN FIND OUT WITH CERTAINTY. NOW, TESTING IS QUICK AND EASY AND CAN GIVE A RELIABLE ANSWER AS SOON AS YOU HAVE MISSED A MENSTRUAL PERIOD.

HOME PREGNANCY TEST

Most kits are reliable and very easy to use.

Most women opt for a urine test, which measures rising levels of the hormone human chorionic gonadotropin (HCG), produced by the blastocyst about a week after fertilization has taken place. Your gynecologist or family planning clinic can perform the test for you or you can use a home pregnancy testing kit, available from your local pharmacy. These are accurate and simple to perform and offer the great advantages of speed, privacy, and convenience. The test strip or wand is packaged in a plastic container that looks like a tampon applicator; before you use it, check the sell-by date and read the instructions carefully. Most kits advise you to perform the test several days after your first missed period, although it may be positive earlier. The result may be negative if you take the test too early and there is too little HCG in your urine.

USING A PREGNANCY TESTING KIT

To use a kit all you have to do is use the toilet in order to pass fresh urine over the strip. The concentration of HCG is always highest in your early morning urine but newer test kits are sensitive enough to be used later in the day. When the HCG in your urine comes into contact with the test strip it causes a color change. At first a blue line or pink circle appears in the test window to confirm that the test kit is working. In a matter of minutes, a second blue line or a pink circle in the results window will indicate whether or not you are pregnant. The kits always provide a second test strip, so it is a good idea to check a borderline positive result with a follow-up test a week or so later. Sadly, some positive tests become negative later on because the embryo has not been able to implant successfully and will be followed shortly by your menstrual period.

OTHER WAYS OF TESTING

In some circumstances, a blood test may be used to detect the exact level of HCG in your body within the first month of pregnancy, before it is detectable in your urine. If you have been undergoing fertility treatment you may want to know if it has been successful even before your menstrual period is due.

Accurate measuring of HCG is also needed if an ectopic pregnancy (a pregnancy that develops outside the uterus) is suspected (*see* p.81).

Another method of diagnosing a pregnancy is using an ultrasound scan. Scans are not performed routinely in very early pregnancy, but they can be useful if you are unsure of your dates, have a history of miscarriage, or if you have symptoms or signs to suggest that you may have an ectopic pregnancy. Although there is little to see on the scan until about 10 days after your missed menstrual period, after this time it is usually possible to see the pregnancy sac in the uterus with a tiny fetal pole (a definite rectangular blob within the sac) and sometimes even a beating fetal heart.

Before the days of home pregnancy testing kits, most women had their pregnancy confirmed with an internal examination performed by a gynecologist after having missed one or two periods. An experienced doctor can diagnose a pregnancy by noting the bluish tinge of the vaginal skin and cervix, the fact that the uterus and cervix are softer than normal and, by six weeks, that the uterus is slightly larger. These changes are due to the increased blood supply to all the pelvic organs. Internal examinations are not performed routinely, but every now and again an unsuspected pregnancy is diagnosed this way.

YOUR EMOTIONAL RESPONSE

I have had many conversations with women who have just discovered they are pregnant and their reactions range from elation to mild panic. Here is a selection of the feelings that are expressed most frequently:

▶ I don't believe it.
▶ It's wonderful.
▶ I'm ecstatic.
▶ Help – I hadn't thought it would happen this quickly.
▶ What have I let myself in for?
▶ Can I afford a baby?
▶ I shouldn't have had that glass of wine after work.
▶ Will my job be safe?

▶ Why didn't I stop smoking last month, the way I planned to?
▶ Where will I have my baby?
▶ What can I do to help my baby?
▶ Will my baby be normal?

Not all of these are positive reactions and this is entirely normal, so don't feel guilty about any negative thoughts that you may be having. Even if you have been planning your pregnancy for some time, you may feel daunted as the consequences begin to sink in. Added to the reaction is a cocktail of pregnancy hormones coursing through your

bloodstream that is enough to make anyone feel emotionally unpredictable. There is no doubt that being pregnant and bringing a baby into the world will be one of the most eventful and unpredictable periods of your life and there will be times when the sheer magnitude of it leaves you feeling overwhelmed.

However, like every other important life event, pregnancy will be much more enjoyable if you feel confident and in control of the situation. The only way to achieve this is to find out everything you can about it – I hope this book will help you do just that.

STAYING SAFE IN PREGNANCY

Every worrying pregnancy statistic and media horror story comes into sharp focus as soon as you are pregnant, and you may be wondering just how much of your everyday life needs to be reevaluated. This section looks at some common concerns and will, I hope, help you weed out the myths and scares from the more sensible pregnancy precautions.

Of course it is impossible to eliminate risk from life, and pregnancy is no exception. In case you are feeling overwhelmed by worry, let's begin by getting things into perspective. About 4 in every 100 babies have an abnormality at birth (congenital abnormality). Most are due to genetic causes (*see* pp.144–45 and pp.415–18), with only a small proportion resulting from factors such as drugs, infections, and environmental hazards. Even if you are concerned that you have been exposed to something that may have harmed your baby (known as a teratogen), remember that you are more likely to be run down by the proverbial bus than to have a baby affected by one of these hazards in pregnancy.

"...it is impossible to eliminate risk from life, and pregnancy is no exception."

AN UNEXPECTED EVENT

If you find yourself pregnant unexpectedly or were not as prepared for it as you hoped you might be, you may be feeling a mixture of shock and disbelief coupled with anxiety about the kind of start your pregnancy might have had in the days and weeks when you were totally unaware of what was going on.

My first piece of advice to you is to stop worrying. Instead of dwelling on what you were meaning to do or might have done to prepare for a future pregnancy, start focusing on adopting a healthier lifestyle now. Promise yourself that you will eat a well-balanced daily diet (*see* pp.43–49). Keep your caffeine intake to a minimum, and if you are a cigarette smoker, stop today.

If you are still in the first trimester of your pregnancy, then start taking folic acid supplements (*see* p.51) immediately, because these will help protect your baby from neural tube defects such as spina bifida (*see* p.146 *and* p.418). Although women are advised to begin taking the supplement while they are trying to conceive, starting now and continuing until the 13th week is definitely worthwhile — so don't think that it's too late.

Another possible concern is that this unexpected baby may have been exposed to all sorts of potential damage when you did not know that you were pregnant. You might be worried, for example, that you had too much to drink at a party, or that you were taking medicines before you knew that you were pregnant. In practice, the most commonly prescribed drugs are antibiotics and fortunately there are very few that harm a developing embryo (*see* p.35). There is also the possibility that you were using contraceptives around the time of conception and you may now be wondering if this has the potential to cause problems. I've addressed these concerns below, but let me begin with some reassurance: the reality is that most tiny embryos destined to make it through pregnancy and become a live, take-home baby are very resilient.

IF YOUR CONTRACEPTION FAILED...

If you conceived your baby while you were using contraception, you are probably wondering if this is going to cause problems for your pregnancy. In most cases, there is nothing to worry about.

▶ **If you were taking hormonal contraception,** such as the combined pill, simply stop taking them because they are no longer useful. Oral contraceptives contain estrogen to inhibit ovulation, and progesterone, which makes the cervical mucus less penetrable by sperm and cells in the lining of the uterus less receptive to implantation by the tiny embryo. Progesterone-only contraceptives and three-monthly injections, such as Depo-Provera, have similar effects on the cervical mucus and lining of the uterus. Now that you have become pregnant these effects are no longer a consideration. There is no evidence that the hormones in modern-day preparations cause problems for the developing embryo and fetus.

▶ **Barrier methods of contraception** that involve spermicides are not harmful to a developing embryo, so there is no need to worry about them.

▶ **If you used postcoital contraception** such as the morning-after pill and are nonetheless pregnant, you may be distressed that the method has failed, but again, no harm will have come to the developing baby.

▶ **When pregnancy occurs with an intrauterine contraceptive device (IUD) in place** there is an increased risk of miscarriage because of the presence of a foreign body in the uterus; the inflammatory response that it causes; and the increasing risk of infection ascending along the IUD strings in the vagina. If the strings or the device are visible on vaginal examination, it is best to remove the IUD. This does not further increase the risk of miscarriage but it does reduce the risk of miscarriage at a later stage in the pregnancy due to infection.

However, if neither strings nor IUD are visible, then it is best left where it is. It is unlikely to cause problems in a pregnancy that progresses to term since the baby develops within the fluid-filled amniotic sac. The IUD will be outside the sac and is usually delivered with the placenta.

▶ **If you have been sterilized** (tubal ligation) and find that you are pregnant, you should consult your doctor promptly. Your tubes will have been damaged mechanically by the procedure, putting you at risk of an ectopic (tubal) pregnancy (*see* p.81 and p.422).

Smoking

If you are still smoking now that you are pregnant, you need to be aware of the problems that this can cause for your growing baby. During the first three months of pregnancy, smoking can directly reduce the ability of the developing placenta to invade the wall of the uterus and grow. If you continue to smoke in later pregnancy, you will be reducing the supply of oxygen and nutrients to your baby and increasing your risk of premature delivery, placental abruption (*see* p.427), and fetal growth retardation (*see* p.428). Quit now; your gynecologist can help you. Be aware too, that if you are exposed regularly to cigarette smoke you become a passive smoker with similar risks to your baby's health. If your partner smokes, encourage him to quit.

Alcohol

Any pregnant woman who has a heavy and regular alcohol intake is at increased risk of experiencing pregnancy complications. During the first few months of pregnancy, large quantities of alcohol can cause a distinctive pattern of abnormalities in the baby, known as the fetal alcohol syndrome (*see* p.434): these include failure to thrive after birth, damage to the nervous system, and poor childhood growth. Regular heavy consumption throughout pregnancy can have further toxic effects on the fetus. Because so much is yet to be known, the wisest choice is not to drink alcohol when you are pregnant.

If there were one or two occasions when you drank a bit too much in the weeks before you knew that you were pregnant, try not to worry unduly — just make sure that you stop drinking now.

Recreational drugs

I have no intention of preaching about the rights and wrongs of taking recreational drugs but I do want to pass on some facts: drugs such as cocaine, heroin, and ecstasy have the potential to be a serious problem for a developing fetus. They all cross the placenta and enter the baby's bloodstream, increasing the risk of miscarriage (*see* p.430), placental abruption, and premature delivery of a baby that is usually growth restricted (*see* p.428). After delivery, the baby may suffer serious withdrawal symptoms and possible brain damage, and will therefore inevitably be kept in the hospital under close observation for several weeks. So, if you want to have a trouble-free pregnancy and a healthy baby, avoid all recreational drugs.

"...the reality is that most tiny embryos destined to become a live, take-home baby are very resilient."

ENVIRONMENTAL HAZARDS

POTENTIAL HAZARDS IN THE ENVIRONMENT ARE OF PARTICULAR CONCERN IN EARLY

PREGNANCY WHEN YOUR BABY'S MAJOR ORGANS AND BODY SYSTEMS ARE DEVELOPING RAPIDLY.

MUCH OF WHAT YOU HEAR ON THIS TOPIC WILL BE ANECDOTAL, SO I'VE INCLUDED BELOW

EVIDENCE-BASED INFORMATION ON SOME OF THE MOST COMMON CONCERNS.

Although many environmental factors are blamed anecdotally for causing miscarriages and fetal abnormalities, most of them are not based on specific evidence. A brief summary of those that cause most anxiety is included here.

CONTACT WITH CHEMICALS

It is almost impossible to avoid all contact with chemicals in daily life, but you can try to minimize your exposure to them.

▶ **In your home:** Avoid inhaling vapors from gasoline, glue, cleaning fluids, volatile paints, household aerosols, and oven cleaners. Read the labels on any chemicals that you are thinking of using and if you are unsure about safety, don't use them. If you are stripping old paint and redecorating your house, keep the rooms well ventilated. If you think that the paint you are removing is so old that it may contain lead, delegate the decorating to someone else.

▶ **In the workplace:** A wide variety of solvents used in manufacturing industries can be the cause of problems to pregnant women who

SAFE DECORATING *Use low-odor paints and keep the room ventilated.*

are overly exposed to them during their work. Fat-soluble organic solvents, found in paints, pesticides, adhesives, lacquers, and cleaning agents, can cross the placenta and inhaling these compounds may lead to complications.

Women at risk are those working in factories, dry cleaners, pharmacies, laboratories, garages, funeral parlours, carpentry workshops, and artists' studios, to name but a few.

However, a recent study concluded that potential damage can be avoided if employers provide well-ventilated working premises and pregnant women are vigilant about wearing protective clothing and avoiding fume-filled areas.

One last point about chemicals: if your partner uses any of the above chemicals and/or vinyl chloride (found in plaster) in his work, avoid handling his clothing while you are pregnant. The same applies to clothes contaminated by pesticides.

X-RAYS

Large doses of ionizing radiation are known to cause problems in the fetus, and as a result, doctors are rightly concerned about the potential problems of X-rays during pregnancy. However, it is important to know that modern X-ray machines emit much less radiation than they used to and focus much more accurately on the part of the body being investigated.

The only risk of fetal abnormality would occur if you had undergone a series of abdominal or pelvic X-rays (at least eight) before week eight of pregnancy, and even then, the risk is only 0.1 percent (one in 1,000 cases). A single chest or abdominal X-ray will cause no harm, so even if you unwittingly had one when you were pregnant, rest assured that it will not have damaged your baby.

The other point to mention is that there are some problems in pregnancy that really do need to be investigated with X-rays. If this proves to be the case, it is highly unlikely that they will cause harm.

If you work in a hospital you will be required to wear a protective lead jacket whenever you are in contact with X-rays. Female radiographers are usually moved to other duties in their department while pregnant, although the risks to their baby are negligible because of the strict safety rules that apply at all times.

VIDEO DISPLAY TERMINALS

Even if your job demands that you work in front of a VDT screen for long periods of time each day, your baby is not at risk. Similarly, equipment that produces ultraviolet and infrared radiation, such as laser printers and photocopiers (and the microwave in the kitchen), is safe to use in pregnancy. There is also nothing to support the allegation that miscarriage and pregnancy problems are more common in women who live near electrical substations, electromagnetic fields, radio stations, and telephone masts. Ignore scary stories about them.

SAFETY OF ULTRASOUND

One of the questions I am asked most frequently by my patients is whether they should be concerned about ultrasound, particularly if they have early pregnancy problems that require repeated ultrasound examinations. Happily, I feel confident in stating that ultrasound causes no problems for mother or baby, thanks to several studies that have looked carefully at this issue.

Although it has been suggested that ultrasound waves might cause changes in the membranes of cells, theoretically affecting the development of the embryo and later growth of the fetus, there is no scientific evidence to support this claim. A recent Swedish study found no association between repeated pregnancy scans and childhood leukemia. Several other large studies followed up babies who had been scanned on many occasions during pregnancy and found no serious developmental abnormalities.

On a more functional level, many women worry that the vaginal ultrasound probes used to scan in early pregnancy may cause them to bleed, or aggravate a pregnancy that is threatening to miscarry. This is not the case, and avoiding a vaginal scan may mean missing out on vital information about your pregnancy.

ULTRASOUND *Even if you need repeated scans, they will not harm your baby.*

ILLNESS DURING PREGNANCY

STAYING WELL CAN NEVER BE ENTIRELY WITHIN YOUR CONTROL, BUT WHILE YOU ARE PREGNANT, YOU NEED TO BE EVEN MORE CAUTIOUS THAN USUAL ABOUT AVOIDING INFECTIONS — ESPECIALLY IN THE FIRST THREE MONTHS.

Of course, this is much easier said than done and as many as 1 in 20 pregnant women contract an infection during pregnancy. This may seem an alarming figure, but the majority of these infections are completely harmless. Only a small number are capable of causing damage to the fetus or the newborn baby.

Since the majority of viral infections are caught from other people, the only way to avoid them completely is to become a hermit — not a practical solution. Young children are the most common reservoirs of infection, so it is sensible to minimize your contact with any child who has a rash or unexplained fever. If you work with young children, the very least you can do is insist that any child with a fever is sent home promptly.

AVOIDING INFECTIONS *It is impossible to avoid all contact with infections, especially if you already have a child.*

CHILDHOOD INFECTIONS

The two serious viral infections for pregnant women are common childhood infections — chickenpox (*see* p.411) and rubella, also known as German measles, (*see* p.411). Chickenpox can cause miscarriage in the first eight weeks of pregnancy and carries a 1–2 percent risk of congenital abnormalities affecting the limbs, eyes, skin, and brain, together with growth problems in later pregnancy if it is contracted between eight and 20 weeks. Pregnant women exposed to chickenpox infection may be given varicella-zoster immune globin (within four days of exposure) to reduce the severity of the disease. If you are infected by the rubella virus for the first time when you are in early pregnancy, you are at risk of miscarrying; if the pregnancy continues, there can be severe effects on the fetus, including deafness, blindness, heart defects, and mental retardation. Fortunately, this is now rare, since almost all women of childbearing age have either had the infection or been immunized against it. Even so, your rubella status will be one of your first prenatal blood tests. If you are not immune, you will be advised to have a rubella vaccination as soon as you have delivered your baby. Meanwhile, you will need to take extra care to reduce your chances of becoming infected. Although rubella is a live vaccine and best administered to women before they become pregnant, I have met several patients who have become pregnant almost immediately after having the vaccination. Happily, I can tell you that no abnormalities have been detected in their babies. Mumps, measles, and polio are unlikely to be a problem for pregnant women thanks to the vaccination programs in Canada.

COLDS, FLU, AND STOMACH BUGS

Catching your work colleagues' cough, cold, and flu is inconvenient but it is highly unlikely that your baby will be affected unless you develop a very high fever, which is a recognized cause of miscarriage in early pregnancy. In Canada, we are exposed to a flu epidemic every couple of years and there is no doubt that these epidemics are responsible for a large number of deaths, both fetal and adult. If you develop a fever with a cold or flu, your doctor will advise you about safe drugs to help you reduce the fever quickly. Practical steps such as sponging with tepid water, tepid baths, and cooling fans are also effective.

If you are in a high-risk group for influenza, perhaps because you have diabetes or a heart condition, discuss with your doctor whether you should have an annual flu vaccination. Although they are not usually given in pregnancy, your risk of developing flu may be a more serious consideration.

An upset stomach or gastroenteritis is best treated with rest and plenty of clear fluids and is unlikely to cause problems to the pregnancy.

TOXOPLASMOSIS AND BRUCELLOSIS

Good hygiene around pets and other animals is especially important during the first trimester of pregnancy. The most serious potential problem is of contracting toxoplasmosis, a parasitic infection that is carried in the stools of infected animals, most commonly cats. About 80 percent of the population have already been infected but may not be aware of it because its flulike symptoms are usually mild. As a result, most women develop an immunity that also protects their fetus. However, if you become infected for the first time during pregnancy, there is a risk that the baby could miscarry or develop mental retardation and blindness.

Most people catch toxoplasmosis because they have inhaled eggs from cat stools or have eaten unwashed vegetables, salads, or poorly cooked, infected meat (*see* p.50). Even though there is a good chance that you are immune to the parasite (particularly if you have a cat), always wash your hands carefully after handling a cat and avoid contact with strays. Have your cats wormed regularly

RUBELLA *Virus particles are visible as pink spots in this blood sample.*

INFLUENZA *The pink fringe around the core of each virus attaches to host cells.*

TOXOPLASMOSIS *The single-cell, green parasites invade liver tissue (pink).*

"I am also anxious to impress on people that just because a herbal remedy is labeled 'natural', that does not make it safe."

and avoid contact with the litterbox. If you have to clean it yourself, wear gloves and wash the gloves and your hands afterward. You should also wear gloves to protect yourself from contaminated soil when gardening.

If you work on a farm or for a veterinarian, take precautions to reduce your risk of catching the bacterial infection brucellosis, which can cause miscarriage. Avoid work that involves lambing/calving or milking animals that have recently given birth, and wash your hands frequently.

OTHER MEDICAL CONDITIONS

If you have an existing medical condition (*see* pp.408–410), such as a heart problem or diabetes, you will need special care during your pregnancy and should see your doctor as soon as you know that you are pregnant (ideally, you should do this before you start trying to conceive). Do not on any account take it upon yourself to discontinue taking any prescribed medication.

If you had an operation before you discovered you were pregnant, you may be concerned about the effect of the anesthetic or the procedure on your baby. In the very early weeks the risk of miscarriage is quite high, particularly if you have a laparoscopy or similar procedure that involves placing instruments into the womb cavity or abdomen. This is why fertility specialists always take particular care to ensure that the woman is not pregnant when performing invasive tests or diagnostic procedures. An emergency appendectomy also increases the risk of miscarriage. That said, I have cared for many women who discovered they were pregnant after undergoing surgery and suffered no ill effects. If your pregnancy survived the operation, rest assured that your baby will not have been harmed by the anesthetic.

COMPLEMENTARY THERAPIES

Many of my patients ask me what I think of their using complementary therapies to treat some of the side effects of pregnancy and to ease pain during labor. On the whole, I don't have a strong view either for or against them. The problem is that many of them have not been rigorously tested in trials, so their benefits are not backed up by hard scientific evidence. This does not mean that they do not work, simply that it is impossible to have a clear picture of what their strengths and limitations can be. I am also anxious to impress on people that just because a herbal remedy is labeled "natural," that does not make it safe. Arsenic is natural — and can also be fatal. If you do decide to use a complementary therapy, make sure that you see a qualified practitioner (*see* p.436 for useful addresses), and tell your obstetrician or midwife about your treatment.

TAKING MEDICINES IN PREGNANCY

The list of drugs that can potentially cause problems for a pregnant woman and her unborn baby is lengthy and alarming. Fortunately, this fact is well understood by doctors and their patients. The information below can be used as a guide for treating a minor problem, but keep all medicines to a minimum and see your doctor if a problem does not respond to treatment promptly.

ANTIEMETICS If you need to take an antiemetic because morning sickness is severe, your doctor will advise about the safest types available.

ANTIHISTAMINES Some prescribed and common over-the-counter types are contraindicated in pregnancy. If you suffer from hay fever or another form of allergy, consult your doctor before taking antihistamines.

ANALGESICS Acetaminophen is probably the best option during pregnancy. Avoid aspirin (unless your doctor prescribes it for a specific reason), ibuprofen, and ergotamine (migraine remedy).

ANTIBIOTICS If you are prescribed antibiotics for an infection, the penicillin family of drugs will not endanger your baby. If you are allergic to penicillin, erythromycin is a safe alternative. The antibiotics below should be avoided because they can cause problems in early pregnancy.

▶ **Tetracyclines** can cause discoloration and deformity of a baby's teeth and bones.

▶ **Chloramphenicol** was a frequently prescribed antibiotic but is rarely used today, except to treat typhoid fever, because of potential abnormal blood reactions in the baby. The chloramphenicol contained in eye drops will not harm your pregnancy.

▶ **Streptomycin** should be avoided by pregnant women since it can cause hearing loss in the fetus.

▶ **Sulfonamides** are broad-spectrum antibiotics that can cause jaundice in newborn babies and severe allergic reactions in the mother.

LAXATIVES Constipation can be treated by adding fiber to your diet and by drinking plenty of water (see p.187). If you need to take a laxative, opt for the bulk-forming cellulose types such as Fybogel. Avoid senna-based laxatives: they irritate the gut, which has the potential to trigger uterine contractions.

ANTACIDS Most antacids are effective and safe to use to treat heartburn and indigestion (see p.187).

If you need iron tablets (see p.48), take them separately because antacids reduce their absorption.

DIURETICS Some fluid retention is to be expected in pregnancy and you should not take diuretics, including "natural" herbal types, in an attempt to deal with it. If your legs, feet, or fingers become very swollen this can be a sign of preeclampsia (see p.425); see your doctor right away.

COLD AND FLU REMEDIES Read the labels on cold and flu remedies carefully because most contain ingredients such as antihistamines and caffeine, which should be avoided in pregnancy. Taking acetaminophen and a hot drink is usually just as effective.

STEROIDS Creams containing steroids for eczema and other skin disorders should be used sparingly in pregnancy but are unlikely to cause problems. Steroid inhalers for asthma (see p.409) are similarly trouble-free. If you are taking oral steroids for a disorder such as Crohn's disease (see p.409), *do not* stop taking them, but see your doctor for advice. Anabolic (body-building) steroids should never be used in pregnancy because they can have a masculinizing effect on a female fetus.

TROUBLE-FREE TRAVEL

JUDGING BY THE NUMBER OF QUESTIONS I AM ASKED ABOUT THE SAFETY OF TRAVELING
WHEN PREGNANT, THIS IS AN ISSUE THAT IS AT THE TOP OF MOST WOMEN'S LIST OF CONCERNS.
HOWEVER, THERE IS NO EVIDENCE TO SUGGEST THAT TRAVEL INCREASES YOUR OWN
OR YOUR BABY'S RISK OF POTENTIAL COMPLICATIONS.

Whenever and however you travel, it makes sense to plan your trips. Long car journeys can be tiring, you should arrange regular stops to stretch your legs and get some fresh air.

Driving should not be a problem as long as you are well and feel comfortable behind the wheel. Please do not listen to scare stories about seat belts pressing on your uterus and unborn baby. I promise that you are both much safer behind a seat belt than not, should you be unlucky enough to be involved in an accident.

Your journey to and from work can sometimes turn out to be the most stressful of all, especially if you commute. If you have to stand during a long bus or train journey, ask for a seat. Even in early pregnancy, you may feel tired and nauseous and just as desperate to sit down as you will be later on in pregnancy.

AIR TRAVEL

Freak accidents and terrorist attacks aside, I do not think that air travel needs to be avoided in normal pregnancies. You may have heard that the reduced cabin pressure on long-haul flights can adversely affect a pregnancy, but this notion is difficult to explain scientifically. Your baby is surrounded by a thick muscular uterine wall and a pool of amniotic fluid, which protect it from any physical damage. Furthermore, the changes in your blood circulation and respiratory systems will ensure that your baby receives enough oxygen and nutrients, even if the oxygen supply in the outside world is a little lower than usual.

However, if you have had previous miscarriages, there are considerations about travel in general, and particularly air travel, to think about. Although I feel confident that traveling by air will not cause you to miscarry, you may not want to expose yourself to a situation where you would worry that you might be to blame should something go wrong. Miscarrying in the middle of a transatlantic flight, or in a foreign country where you do not speak the language, is something that needs to be avoided whenever possible.

BUYING FRUIT *Even the most enticing market fruits should be peeled or washed.*

Most airlines do not accept pregnant women after the 34th week of pregnancy but not, as is often assumed, because the mother's lower oxygen levels are likely to induce labor. It is because some 10 percent of women deliver prematurely, and airlines want to avoid the risk of dealing with this in midflight. (For more advice on travel in the third trimester, *see* p.251.)

FOREIGN TRIPS

If you are planning a trip, check with foreign embassies, the Public Health Agency of Canada, and other websites and helplines (*see* p.436), or ask your doctor whether or not you are at risk of endemic infections in the country or countries that you are visiting.

If at all possible, avoid traveling to countries where malaria is rife because the high fever that accompanies the infection increases the risk of miscarriage. During pregnancy, you are more likely to catch malaria, which will often be more severe and unpredictable than normal because your immune response alters in pregnancy.

If your trip to a malarial zone is unavoidable, make sure that you take antimalarial tablets and continue taking them after you leave the country and for as long as is recommended after your trip.

New antimalarial drugs are continually coming on the market so talk to your doctor about which drugs are safe in pregnancy. As a general rule of thumb:

▶ Chloroquine will not harm your baby, nor will proguanil if you take folate supplements at the same time.

▶ Mefloquin and pyrimethamine should be avoided in the first 12 weeks of pregnancy but if you have taken these drugs already, do not panic. A malarial infection is far more likely to cause problems in pregnancy than the drugs you have taken to prevent infection. For the latest advice on antimalarial drugs and immunization, contact Health Canada (*see* p.436).

TRAVEL IMMUNIZATION

You also need to check which, if any, immunizations are recommended for your destination and whether any of them should be avoided during pregnancy. Your altered immune response in pregnancy makes immunization more unpredictable;

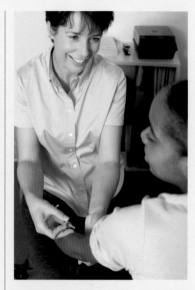

IMMUNIZATION *Your doctor will advise which travel vaccines are safe.*

as a rough rule of thumb, vaccines prepared with live viruses are best avoided, whereas non-live vaccines can be given without risk. Cholera, polio, rabies, and tetanus vaccinations are considered safe for pregnant women, but the safety of yellow fever and typhoid vaccinations is unclear.

TIPS FOR STAYING WELL ABROAD

▶ Be meticulous about washing your hands before you eat.

▶ Drink plenty of bottled water, particularly in hot climates.

▶ Avoid unpasteurized foods and shellfish.

▶ Resist the temptation to buy delicacies from market stalls (they may have been recycled or reheated and may contain harmful bacteria).

▶ Peel fruit and avoid watermelons, which are often spiked and then immersed in water to make them larger and juicier.

▶ Refuse ice in drinks — it may be made from contaminated water.

DIET AND EXERCISE

Like many women, you probably started to improve your diet and fitness levels while you were trying to conceive — but if that is not the case, this is the time to start. Both you and your baby will reap the benefits. Most of the information you need is included here, but there are also additional features on diet and exercise specific to your particular stage of pregnancy in the sections covering each trimester.

From the moment you conceive, your body provides all your baby's nutrients. From now until the birth, everything you eat will be broken down into molecules that pass from your own bloodstream into your baby's via the placenta. Until after the birth, you will breathe and eat for your baby so it is important that you try to do the very best that you can. This is a major responsibility and I am well aware that the subject of what you should be eating during your pregnancy can be a source of anxiety. Without becoming obsessive about amounts and portions, you need to know what to eat to meet all those basic requirements as well as which foods are better avoided. You should find most of the answers that you need in this section.

Being pregnant also raises a host of new questions about fitness. Whether you have an established exercise regime or whether you are not quite as committed to going to the gym or walking to work as you hoped that you might be, you are likely to be wondering what sort of physical activity you should be doing now and to what level. As with the diet question, all sorts of myths suddenly crawl out of the woodwork: don't get too hot — it harms the baby; don't jump around — you'll miscarry; don't do sit-ups — you'll cramp your baby's growth. Ideas such as these, based on a mixture of anecdote and misconception, used to be passed down through the generations without much questioning of the wisdom behind them. However, we are fortunate that our knowledge and thinking on the subject of exercise in the first trimester has evolved considerably in recent decades. So while in your mother's day, the idea of playing a game of tennis during early pregnancy would have raised eyebrows, today, doctors advise the majority of pregnant women that moderate exercise throughout the nine months will be good both for you and your baby.

"...all sorts of myths about diet and exercise suddenly crawl out of the woodwork."

HEALTHY EATING

AS WITH ALL PREGNANCY TOPICS, WELL-MEANING BUT UNSOUGHT ADVICE ON DIET WILL BE GIVEN TO YOU IN BUCKETFULS — MUCH OF IT CONFLICTING AND CONFUSING. THE ONE THING THAT IS CERTAIN IS THAT THIS IS A TIME IN YOUR LIFE WHEN YOU REALLY DO NEED TO EAT SENSIBLY AND HEALTHILY.

The first thing to understand is that the old adage of "eating for two" is a sure recipe for problems. Many pregnant women are urged to enjoy second helpings by well-meaning friends and family but being pregnant is not the green light to overeat. You really do not need to eat more than 2,000 calories a day (the same as any nonpregnant woman) in the first trimester of pregnancy, the reason being that as soon as your body recognizes you are pregnant, your metabolism changes in order to make the most efficient use of the food that you eat.

Extra calories will not benefit your developing baby and will simply be deposited as fat, which may prove hard to get rid of after your baby is born. In the last trimester you may need to increase your calorie intake, but by no more than 200–300 calories per day, which is the equivalent of a banana and a glass of milk.

At the other end of the scale, women who have spent most of their adult lives watching their weight and continuously dieting may require a major shift in their psychology during pregnancy. The Western obsession with body image can make it difficult for some women to accept that they will be putting on about 29 pounds (14kg) in weight over the next few months. Now that you are pregnant, fad diets are out, and proper meals and healthy portions of food are definitely in.

"Now that you are pregnant, fad diets are out, and proper meals and healthy portions are definitely in."

Studies of women with malnutrition during pregnancy and while breastfeeding in Africa have shown that babies born in these circumstances have an IQ that is significantly lower than normal. The evidence is enough to convince anyone that there is no place for vanity dieting in pregnancy. Let me reassure you: if you eat sensibly and exercise regularly, you can have your former body back very quickly after your baby is born.

YOUR IDEAL STARTING WEIGHT

Ideally, you should be of normal weight when you are trying to conceive, because being significantly under- or overweight can affect fertility. There are also good reasons for addressing a weight problem now that you are pregnant.

Underweight mother-to-be

Women who are significantly underweight often experience delays in becoming pregnant, because if a woman's body mass index (*see* right) falls below 17, her periods usually become irregular or cease altogether. During pregnancy, an underweight woman is at risk of becoming anemic (*see* p.423), delivering prematurely, or having a baby that is underweight or "small for dates" (*see* p.428). If you fall into this category, consult your doctor at the earliest opportunity for advice regarding your diet.

Overweight mother-to-be

If you are significantly overweight, you may also have suffered conception delays and are at greater risk of pregnancy complications such as miscarriage, high blood pressure, preeclampsia (*see* blood pressure problems, p.425), and gestational diabetes (*see* p.426). As your pregnancy progresses, you will find yourself becoming increasingly uncomfortable and unnecessarily tired. This puts you at a strong disadvantage: you need to be as fit and rested as possible in preparation for the huge physical demands you will make on your body during labor and the delivery of your baby. If you start off tired, you may find that giving birth leaves you feeling exhausted and distressed, instead of pleasantly tired and exhilarated.

These prenatal problems, together with the fact that your baby is more likely to be larger than average, may lead to an increased risk of complications developing at the time of delivery. These range from a cesarean section or forceps delivery to problems that develop after the birth, such as hemorrhage (heavy blood loss), wound infections, or thrombosis (blood clot) in the deep veins of your leg (*see* venous thromboembolism, p.423). Most importantly, the more overweight you are, the greater the risk, which reflects the fact that obesity results in a disordered metabolic state — for both you and your baby.

Having spelled out the problems, let's tackle the situation actively. If you are overweight, taking care with your diet from this point onward can leave you in good shape at the end of your pregnancy while still supplying all your baby's nutritional needs. The following guidelines will help, but your dietician will also provide you with a calorie-controlled, low-fat diet to follow during pregnancy.

YOUR BODY MASS INDEX

The best way of knowing if you are either underweight or overweight at the beginning of your pregnancy is to work out your body mass index (BMI).

▶ **This is calculated using a simple equation:** your weight in pounds divided by your height in inches squared, and then multiplied by 703. For measurements in kilograms and meters, your weight in kilograms divided by your height in meters squared will yield your BMI. For example, a woman who is 5'7" (1.7m) tall and weighs 143lb (65kg) will have a BMI of 703 x 143lb/(67 x 67in) = 22.4

▶ **Most doctors consider that a normal BMI is in the range 19–25.** Between 25 and 28 is overweight and over 28 is classified as obese. Over 40 is dangerously obese. At the lower end of the scale it is usually only when the BMI drops below 19 that a woman is considered to be significantly underweight.

YOUR WEIGHT GAIN OVER 40 WEEKS

ALTHOUGH EVERY WOMAN'S PREGNANCY IS DIFFERENT, THESE GUIDELINES FOR THE AMOUNT AND RATE OF WEIGHT GAIN OVER A NORMAL PREGNANCY WILL HELP YOU DETERMINE WHETHER YOU ARE PUTTING ON WEIGHT TOO SLOWLY OR TOO FAST IN EACH TRIMESTER.

If you are of average height and weight, you can be expected to gain about 22–33lb (10–15kg) during the 40 weeks of a normal pregnancy. As you can see from the chart, there will be times in your pregnancy when you put on weight faster than others. During the first trimester, your weight should change very little, and most of your weight gain will take place from the second trimester onward. Of course, the chart can only be used as a guide: allowances need to be made for individual variations between women and between pregnancies. For example, if you are expecting twins, you are likely to gain in the region of 35–40lb (16–18kg).

WHAT MAKES UP THE WEIGHT?

Your overall weight gain is roughly divided into two different strands:
▶ **the weight of your baby**, the placenta, and amniotic fluid
▶ **your own increased weight** to support the pregnancy. This includes the increasing weight of your uterus and breasts, the increase in your blood volume, and your increased stores of fat, together with a variable amount of water retention.

EXCESS FAT

All of the weight gain mentioned is governed (for the most part) by the natural needs of the pregnancy. However, the amount of fat that a pregnant woman deposits on her body depends on what and how much fat and carbohydrate she eats. Gaining 6lb (3kg) in body fat is to be expected – 90 percent of this will occur during the first 30 weeks and most of it will be shed during breastfeeding. However, if you lay down excess fat during pregnancy, breastfeeding will not reduce it – it will continue to sit there.

AVERAGE WEIGHT GAIN

Baby	7–9lb/3–4kg
Placenta	1½lb/0.7kg
Amniotic fluid	2lb/1kg
Maternal fat	5½lb/2.5kg
Increased blood + fluid	3lb/1.5kg
Water retention	5½lb/2.5kg
Breasts	1lb/0.5kg
Uterus	2lb/1kg
TOTAL	**28–30lb/12.7–13.7kg**

31lb/14kg
26lb/12kg
22lb/10kg
17½lb/8kg
13lb/6kg
9lb/4kg
4½lb/2kg

5 10 15 20 25 30 35

WEIGHT GAIN OVER 40 WEEKS *In a normal pregnancy, there is little gain in the first trimester. Most women then gain about 1½–2lb (0.7–1kg) a week until the last 1 or 2 weeks, when little further weight gain occurs.*

THE PERFECT PREGNANCY DIET

THE FIRST THING TO MAKE CLEAR IS THAT THERE ARE TWO SORTS OF PREGNANCY DIETS — THE TEXTBOOK DIET AND THE REALISTIC DIET THAT REFLECTS YOUR EVERYDAY LIFE. THIS SECTION IS ALL ABOUT THE SECOND KIND.

"...pregnant women are sometimes made to feel guilty and obsessive about what they eat."

A healthy diet in pregnancy contains the right balance of carbohydrates, protein, fats, vitamins, and minerals. In this section I have listed the foods that are the best source of these essentials and explained why they are important in building your baby's body and helping keep yours healthy. Having said that, I know that there will be times when there is some discrepancy between the ideal diet and what you actually eat, particularly in the early months when nausea and vomiting can make well-planned eating nigh on impossible. Pregnant women are sometimes made to feel guilty and obsessive about diet and it is not my intention to fuel those sentiments. Women are led to believe that they will be harming the health and intelligence of their unborn child if they eat too much chocolate or have a day when the most they can face is a scone, a shrimp cocktail sandwich, and a few pickled onions. I want to stress that if you try to eat as varied a diet as possible, you will be doing all that is necessary.

PROTEIN

From the very early weeks of pregnancy, your protein requirement will increase by 15–20 percent. Proteins are the essential building blocks for your own muscles, bones, connective tissues, and internal body organs and have the same key role in the healthy growth of your baby. They are made up of 20 different amino acids, 12 of which are produced within the body and so are termed non-essential amino acids. The other eight amino acids are referred to as essential amino acids because they have to be supplied from food. These are found in the right proportions in first-class proteins — such as meat, poultry, fish, eggs, and dairy products. Amino acids are also found in nuts, grains and legumes, soybeans and tofu; these are known as second-class proteins because they need to be eaten in combinations to supply the necessary amino acids. If you are vegan or lactose-intolerant you will need plenty of these.

Not all protein-rich foods have the same nutritional value: some are higher in fat than others and some have additional vitamins and minerals. So while red meat may be a first class source of protein, it contains much more fat than chicken. Fish is low in fat and high in vitamins, and oily fish, such as sardines, contains essential unsaturated fatty acids, which are particularly beneficial for your developing baby's brain. However, due to the danger posed by mercury to the developing fetus, Health Canada recommends that while you are pregnant you should limit your consumption of top predator fish such as swordfish, shark, and fresh or frozen tuna (excluding canned tuna) to one meal per month. You need 2–3 servings of protein-rich foods each day, a typical serving being 3oz (85g) of red meat or poultry; 5oz (150g) of fish; 1–2oz (30–60g) of hard cheese; or 4oz (125g) of legumes, grains, or cereals.

CARBOHYDRATES

There are two types of carbohydrates, simple and complex. Generally speaking, simple carbohydrates, as found in cookies and sodas, are high in sugar (sucrose) and of little nutritional value. They give you a quick burst of energy because they are absorbed quickly into your bloodstream but are of only short-term benefit. The only real exception is fructose in fruit. Since fruits are a good source of vitamins, minerals, and fiber, you should make sure you eat about five portions a day. Complex carbohydrates are found in starchy foods such as pasta, wholegrain bread, brown rice, potatoes, and legumes. They are the mainstay of a healthy diet, providing a slow and steady release of energy over a longer period because their starch has to be broken down into simple carbohydrates before it can be absorbed into your bloodstream. Unrefined wholegrain flour, rice, and pasta are good sources because they retain valuable vitamins and minerals and also have a high fiber content to help prevent constipation. Try to include 4–6 servings a day of any of the following: 1 slice of wholegrain bread; 2–4oz (60–125g) of wholewheat pasta, brown rice, and potatoes; 2oz (60g) of cereal.

RECOMMENDED PREGNANCY FOODS: HOW MUCH TO EAT EACH DAY

3–4 servings of vegetables such as broccoli and salad

4–6 servings of carbohydrates such as wholegrain bread

2–3 portions of protein — fish, chicken, red meat, and legumes

FATS

Although you should aim to limit your fat intake when you are pregnant, don't cut out fat completely. Fats have nutritional value in that they help build cell walls in the body and supply important vitamins needed by your growing baby. Broadly speaking, dietary fats divide into less healthy saturated fats, which come from animal sources, and healthier unsaturated fats, sourced from vegetable oils and fish, which are important for the development of your baby's nervous system. Typically, fried foods and fatty meats and meat products such as sausages and pastries are loaded with unhealthy saturated fats. Eat too many of these and you will pile on extra pounds as well as encourage the build-up of fat deposits on the lining of your blood vessels, which increases your risk of heart disease later in life. For a healthy fat intake, trim the fat off meat, use butter sparingly and choose low-fat varieties of dairy products and half-fat hard cheeses. Wherever possible choose foods that are rich in unsaturated fats.

DAIRY PRODUCTS

Eating dairy products provides you with a balanced mixture of protein, fats, calcium and vitamins A, B, and D. Milk is a great standby in pregnancy so if you enjoy milk-based drinks include plenty of the low-fat variety, which contains the same amount of calcium and vitamins as full-fat milk. Low-fat dairy products are preferable to the full-fat varieties, but some of the virtually no-fat varieties of yogurt are loaded with sugar and as a result are high in calories. Aim for 2–4 servings of dairy foods each day; typical portions are 1–2oz (30–60g) of hard cheese or ⅓ pint (200ml) of reduced-fat milk.

"Some of the virtually no-fat varieties of yogurt are loaded with sugar..."

2–4 servings of low-fat dairy products such as milk

1–2 servings of iron-rich foods such as eggs and fortified cereals

5 portions of fruit to provide fiber and vitamins

ESSENTIAL VITAMINS AND MINERALS

Your own health and that of your developing baby relies on a regular supply of vitamins and minerals, most of which have to be obtained from the food you eat. The chart below is a guide to the best sources. Vitamins and minerals tend to break down during cooking and processing so choose food that is as fresh as possible.

	BEST SOURCES	BENEFITS
VITAMIN A	orange fruit and vegetables — peaches, melons, mangoes, apricots, carrots, and peppers; green vegetables; egg yolk; oily fish such as herring	antioxidant properties; important for healthy eyes, hair, skin, and bones; helps fight infections; can be toxic in excess (do not take supplements or eat liver)
B VITAMINS	poultry, pork, beef, and lamb; cod; dairy products; eggs; brewer's yeast; green vegetables, such as Brussels sprouts and cabbage; nuts, especially pecans, peanuts, and walnuts; fortified cereals; wholegrain bread and pasta; oranges; mangos; bananas; avocados; figs; sesame seeds	helps energy production and protein release from food; maintains healthy skin, hair, and nails; essential for nervous system and brain function; assists in the production of antibodies to fight infection and of oxygen-carrying hemoglobin in red blood cells (B_{12} supplements may be needed if you don't eat meat or dairy food)
FOLIC ACID	green vegetables such as broccoli, spinach, and green beans; fortified cereals, legumes (peas and chick peas); and yeast extract such as Marmite	helps prevent neural tube defects in the fetus; aids red blood cell formation and protein break down in the body (400 mcg supplement recommended daily)
VITAMIN C	kiwi fruit, citrus fruit, sweet peppers, black currants, potatoes (especially the skins), and tomatoes	assists growth and repair of tissues (skin, teeth and bones); aids iron absorption; antioxidant properties

FOLIC ACID *Early in pregnancy, eat foods rich in folic acid such as green beans and legumes.*

FETUS *Folic acid helps prevent neural defects at a very early stage of fetal development.*

FOOD SOURCES *Vitamins and minerals are absorbed most effectively from food with little danger of overdose — any excess is eliminated naturally.*

	BEST SOURCES	BENEFITS
VITAMIN D	eggs; oily fish such as herring, salmon, and sardines; butter; margarine; cheese; also provided through exposure to natural light	enhances calcium absorption; increases the rate of mineral deposits in the bones; can be toxic if taken in excess (do not take supplements)
VITAMIN E	eggs; nuts, such as hazelnuts, pine nuts, and almonds; sunflower seeds; green vegetables such as broccoli and spinach; avocado; vegetable oils	maintains healthy skin, nerves, muscles, red blood cells, and heart; important antioxidant — protects against free radicals, which can damage body tissues
IRON	red meat; eggs; apricots, raisins, and prunes; tinned sardines, crab, and tuna in oil; fortified cereals; sesame seeds (liver and kidneys are rich in iron but should be avoided in pregnancy)	essential for oxygen-carrying hemoglobin production in red blood cells of mother and fetus; builds and maintains muscles
CALCIUM	dairy products; eggs; small bony fish such as sardines; soy products; most nuts; fortified cereals; leafy green vegetables, especially broccoli	essential for healthy bones, teeth, and muscles in mother and fetus; also helps with conduction of nerve impulses
ZINC	beef; seafood; nuts; onions; corn; bananas; wholegrain foods (iron-rich foods block absorption)	necessary for growth and energy; aids healing of wounds; supports the immune system

CALCIUM *Boost your intake of calcium-rich foods such as cheese in pregnancy.*

FETAL SKELETON *Calcium builds fetal bones and teeth and preserves the health of your own.*

VITAMINS

Vitamins are vital for good health, both yours and your baby's. There are five of them in total — vitamins A, B, C, D, and E and, with the exception of vitamin D, all have to be obtained from the food we eat. We need about 40 minutes of light (not necessarily sunlight) per day to produce sufficient vitamin D. Vitamins A, C, and E are antioxidants, which have an important role in protecting the body from the damaging effects of free radicals — chemicals produced from the waste products of the oxygen that we breathe. Antioxidants help mop up the chemicals and stop them injuring our body cells.

Some vitamins such as the B and C vitamins are not stored by the body, so you need to make a particular effort to ensure that you have an adequate daily intake when you are pregnant. Furthermore some vitamins, such as vitamin C, break down quickly when exposed to air and heat, which is why raw fruits or vegetables are preferable to the cooked variety in many instances. Similarly, frozen vegetables contain more vitamins than the canned variety, which lose most of their vitamins during processing.

MINERALS

"When it comes to minerals, your baby will behave like a parasite, taking everything it needs..."

Your diet also needs to include sufficient amounts of minerals and trace elements, the most important of which are iron, calcium, and zinc. These chemicals make an important contribution to the way our bodies function, but like vitamins, cannot be synthesized by the body, so have to be supplied from food. High levels of iron and calcium are particularly important during pregnancy because they help support your baby's development. When it comes to minerals, your baby will behave like a parasite, taking everything it needs from your body's reserves, so don't leave yourself feeling tired and unwell because they have been depleted by the demands of your developing baby.

Iron is essential for oxygen-carrying hemoglobin in red blood cells and also helps maintain healthy muscles. It clears from your body very quickly, so you need to eat iron-rich foods (*see* table p.47) on a daily basis. Although requirements vary from woman to woman (and the best way to boost iron supplies is a matter of debate), what is absolutely certain is that your blood volume will double during pregnancy, so you will need more than your usual level of iron to protect yourself from anemia (*see* p.423).

Animal sources of iron are better absorbed than the iron found in fruit and vegetables, although iron-rich food such as apricots and prunes have the advantage that they are also a good source of fiber, which helps prevent constipation. Pregnant women used to be advised to eat large amounts of liver because it is rich in iron, but it is now known that the high levels of vitamin A may cause birth defects. So avoid liver and liver products such as sausage and pâté.

An important point is that iron absorption is improved when iron is taken with acidic drinks that contain vitamin C, such as orange juice. On the other hand both milk and antacid drugs reduce the uptake of iron, so have your glass of milk between meals and increase your intake of iron-rich foods if you need to take antacids for indigestion.

You do not need to take over-the-counter or prescribed iron supplements unless you are anemic when you start your pregnancy or you develop iron deficiency during it. There is no need to expose yourself to the common side effects of iron — constipation or stomach upsets — unless a blood test establishes that you have a low blood count.

Zinc is a mineral that helps encourage growth and is also important in the immune system, wound healing, and digestion. Zinc absorption can be blocked by iron, especially supplements, so if you have to take these, try not to take them at the same time as zinc-rich foods (*see* table).

Calcium supplies are important for your bones and teeth and while you are pregnant, your baby will be drawing all its calcium from you. This process starts very early on — your baby's bones begin to develop from the fourth to sixth week — so ideally you should make sure that your calcium intake is high before pregnancy and remains so throughout. The old saying that "for every pregnancy, a mother loses a tooth" has its origins in the fact that low levels of calcium led to poor teeth in later years. Even if you think you are getting enough calcium, do see your dentist. All dairy products are good sources of calcium, as are nuts and leafy vegetables, particularly broccoli (*see* table, p.47). An increasing variety of cereals and juices are now fortified with calcium and you might consider switching to these while you are pregnant.

Salt is used in high quantities in many processed and prepared foods, since it acts as a natural flavor enhancer and preservative. You can add a little salt when you cook, but remember that too much can be harmful because it encourages fluid retention, which in turn may lead to high blood pressure.

VEGETARIANS & VEGANS

If you are vegetarian, vegan or allergic to dairy products, you need to discuss with your doctor the best way for you to obtain adequate levels of iron, calcium and vitamin B_{12}, in particular, as you may well be deficient in one or all of these elements. Vitamin B_{12} only exists naturally in animal products, although it is found in yeast extract spreads and fortified cereals. If you are a vegan, you may need to take supplements during pregnancy and while you are breastfeeding.

▶ **For a vegan diet** you can combine different plant proteins in order to receive your full complement of essential amino acids. For example, a handful of nuts or a portion of peas can be combined with a serving of rice or sweetcorn. To ensure you have enough iron, eat extra portions of haricot beans, cereals and dried fruits such as apricots, raisins and prunes.

▶ **If you are vegetarian,** you should eat more dairy products and eggs to ensure you keep up your intake of proteins, vitamin B_{12}, calcium and iron.

AVOIDING FOOD POISONING

WHEN COOKING INVOLVES LITTLE MORE THAN A READY MEAL AND A MICROWAVE, IT IS EASY TO BECOME RELAXED ABOUT HYGIENE. IN PREGNANCY YOU ARE MORE VULNERABLE TO INFECTIONS AND NEED TO BE MORE CAREFUL ABOUT WHAT YOU EAT AND HOW YOU PREPARE IT.

Much of what follows may seem excessively cautious and I want to emphasize that if you follow basic rules of hygiene, such as always checking sell-by dates on labels, and throwing away any suspect food, you would be very unlikely to be infected by any troublesome or potentially dangerous bacteria.

Having said that, some foods are known to carry bacteria that can be harmful to you, and sometimes to your baby as well. A severe episode of food poisoning can trigger a first-trimester miscarriage so it is worth being extra vigilant, especially during the first three months.

SALMONELLA BACTERIA

These bacteria are found primarily in eggs and chicken. Infection with salmonella causes vomiting, nausea, diarrhea, and fever — effects that usually kick in within 12–48 hours of eating the affected food. Your baby will not be affected, as the bacteria do not cross the placenta, but you should see a doctor as soon as you suspect an infection.

Salmonella bacteria are killed by heat, so cook chicken thoroughly and avoid dishes containing undercooked or raw eggs such as mayonnaise, ice cream, cheesecake, and chocolate mousse. When you cook eggs make sure the whites and the yolks are both solid.

Note that free-range chicken and eggs are not free of salmonella but a smaller percentage of them carry the bacteria than caged hens.

LISTERIA INFECTION

Although listeria infection is rare, it can have fatal effects on your unborn baby (see p.412). It is found occasionally in pâtés, unpasteurized soft cheeses, such as brie and camembert, and blue cheeses. It can also be found in other chilled foods that have not been stored to very high standards. I would advise you to avoid these foods in pregnancy and stick to hard cheeses and those made from pasteurized milk (the pasteurization process kills the bacteria). Cottage cheese and mozzarella are also safe. Drink only pasteurized and UHT milk. If you are in any doubt, boil milk before you drink it. Avoid unpasteurized goat's or sheep's milk and products.

E-COLI

This is another relatively rare bacteria that can be extremely dangerous to anyone who contracts it, since it can ultimately lead to kidney failure and death. It is primarily found in cooked meats and pâtés that have been stored at the wrong temperature. Again, I would advise you to avoid pâtés and to make sure that you buy cooked meats from hygienically proven sources. Always check sell-by dates and if you are in any doubt about the freshness of a particular food, throw it out.

TOXOPLASMOSIS

This is a relatively common infection, which produces only mild flulike symptoms but which can be highly dangerous for your unborn baby (see p.412). It is derived from a parasite that is present in animal stools, particularly cats' stools, and is also found in raw or undercooked meat. While you are pregnant, make sure that you cook your meat thoroughly and wash your hands after preparing it. You should also wash all vegetables and fruit thoroughly (see opposite).

SHOULD I TAKE VITAMIN SUPPLEMENTS?

The only vitamin supplement that you should be taking routinely during pregnancy is folic acid — one of the B vitamins that is particularly important during the first trimester of pregnancy because it reduces the risk of the fetus developing neural tube defects, such as spina bifida (*see* p.146 *and* p.418). There is some evidence that folic acid may also reduce the risk of other types of congenital abnormality and birth defects.

Start taking 400mcg tablets of folic acid (available from your pharmacist) as soon as you know you are pregnant; if your pregnancy was planned, you may have been taking this dose for three months or more. A normal diet of folate-rich foods (*see* table, p.46) will provide you with a further 200mcg of folate, bringing your total daily intake up to 600mcg. If you have had a previous pregnancy affected by a neural tube defect or you have epilepsy, a higher dose of 5mg a day is recommended while you are trying to conceive and for the first 12 weeks of your pregnancy. This dose is only available on prescription.

Two other supplements you might take (only on your doctor's advice) are calcium and iron. Do not rush off and buy other supplements "just to make sure"; if you eat a healthy diet you get all you need. If your diet lacks certain nutrients, your doctor may advise a prenatal vitamin. I should add that your body absorbs vitamins and minerals more effectively from food — folic acid being the only exception. By taking supplements you may overdose on certain vitamins, such as vitamin A, which can be harmful to the fetus in high doses.

> "If you eat a healthy diet you will be getting all the vitamins and minerals that you need."

FOOD HYGIENE BASICS

▶ **Wash your hands** before and after handling food; take extra care with raw meat and poultry.

▶ **Make sure that raw food**, especially raw meat, is stored separately from prepared food to avoid contamination.

▶ **Use separate chopping boards** and knives for raw meats and wash both with very hot water and detergent afterward.

▶ **Wash fruit carefully before eating.** Most fruit is treated with pesticides and ethylene oxide, which is used to ripen fruit,

has been shown to cause miscarriages.

▶ **Thoroughly wash** all vegetables and salads, peeling and topping carrots to remove all traces of soil. Wash your hands after picking fruit or gathering vegetables.

▶ **Take care to defrost frozen food.** In the microwave, turn the food around a few times so that it is fully defrosted.

▶ **When you are reheating** previously cooked food in the microwave ensure that it is piping hot everywhere. Do not reheat a frozen dish a second time.

HERBAL TEAS *These teas do not contain caffeine, which is best avoided in pregnancy, and many women find that they prefer the taste of them.*

WHAT TO DRINK

Pregnant women need to drink eight large glasses of water — the equivalent of 2 pints (1 liter) — every day. If you cannot bear the thought of drinking so much water, try herbal teas instead. Fruit juice and milk are also good but not as effective as water. The better hydrated you are, the less tired you will be, since dehydration causes muscle fatigue, which in turn leads to a general feeling of tiredness. You are also less likely to suffer from constipation. Think of your kidneys as a waterfall — the more water you flush down them the better.

Caffeine in tea, coffee and soft drinks is now on the list of substances "to be avoided in pregnancy," even though studies linking a moderate intake of caffeine to problems during pregnancy are, at best, inconclusive. However, a recent Italian study reported that more than six cups of coffee a day was accompanied by a higher rate of miscarriage. That said, so many women stop drinking coffee during their first trimester, they rarely need any encouragement to cut down their intake. The problem with caffeine is that it acts as a diuretic, draining you of much-needed fluid. It also interferes with the absorption of iron, calcium, and vitamin C, thus negating all your healthy eating habits. Chocolate also contains caffeine, and however much you tell yourself that it also contains high levels of brain-boosting magnesium, it also contains too much sugar and fats to make it a food you should eat in anything other than small quantities.

HOW MUCH ALCOHOL?

Many of us drink alcohol — albeit in small amounts — on a regular basis and one of the most common questions I am asked is whether it is safe to drink in pregnancy and if so, how much? Even though there is no definitive evidence to show that a few glasses of wine here and there increases the risk of miscarriage or damage to the fetus, I would advise you to limit alcohol consumption as much as possible during the first three months.

There is no doubt that drinking large quantities of alcohol during this period (especially binge drinking) can cause fetal abnormalities. Alcoholic mothers put their babies at risk of fetal alcohol syndrome (*see* p.434), the effects of which are numerous and severe: the main ones include intrauterine growth restriction (*see* p.428), followed by failure to thrive after birth. When the child is a little older, other neurological and behavioral problems come to light. This syndrome is more common than people think and serves to illustrate the point that alcohol and pregnancy (particularly in the first trimester) do not mix. Not surprisingly, nature has an unerring way of pointing us in the right direction in early pregnancy, and many women cannot face the taste or smell of alcohol.

EXERCISE IN PREGNANCY

THERE ARE PARTICULAR REASONS WHY BEING FIT DURING PREGNANCY IS A GOOD IDEA. THE NEXT NINE MONTHS ARE GOING TO BE A TESTING TIME FOR YOU PHYSICALLY SO IF YOU CAN BOOST YOUR GENERAL FITNESS NOW, YOU ARE LIKELY TO COPE MUCH BETTER WITH PREGNANCY, LABOR, AND BIRTH.

Why do we now advise women to keep fit during pregnancy and in what way do you and your developing baby benefit? It used to be thought that during exercise, blood flow to the uterus was reduced and this put the baby at risk, but many studies have shown that even strenuous exercise is of no risk to the baby, especially in the first half of pregnancy. Sufficient uterine blood flow is directed to the placenta during exercise and the uterine circulation is also able to increase the amount of oxygen it extracts from the mother's blood to compensate for the exercise requirements.

Female professional athletes who undertake endurance training at high levels during their pregnancy tend to have poor weight gain and low-birth-weight babies. They are usually advised to reduce their training schedules in later pregnancy. Studies that involve monitoring the fetal heart rate show that usually there is a short period after exercise when the fetal heart rate and temperature rise, but that in neither instance is this a danger to the baby. The conclusion is that in pregnancy you can exercise at up to 70 percent of your capacity (see box) without putting your baby's growth at risk.

Many women I meet are worried that if they continue to exercise in early pregnancy, they may precipitate a miscarriage. This concern has deep-rooted origins in the Western world: in the past it was generally assumed that strenuous exercise might disturb the implantation of a young embryo. The reality is that a pregnancy that is at risk of miscarrying will miscarry, even if the mother wraps herself in blankets or spends the day in bed. Similarly, a healthy pregnancy that is destined to be successful will continue to be so and it will take a lot more than a few bursts of physical exertion to dislodge it. So do remember that exercise is very unlikely to cause problems in the development of early pregnancy. If you doubt these words, then just

A SAFE HEART RATE

▶ **To calculate your personal safe heart rate** when exercising, subtract your age from 220 and then work out 70 percent of that figure. This will give you the rate of heartbeats per minute that you should be aiming for during exercise.

▶ **So, for example, if you are 30,** you will calculate 70 percent of 190 (220–30), giving you an exercising heart rate of 133 beats per minute.

▶ **To find your heart rate during exercise,** take your pulse for 20 seconds, then multiply by three. Alternatively, consider buying a heart rate monitor, available from most sporting goods stores.

"Worldwide, pregnant women are exposed to much more physical exertion in their day-to-day lives than the majority of Western women."

reflect on the fact that, worldwide, most pregnant women are exposed to much more physical exertion in their day-to-day lives than the majority of Western women. Furthermore, the population explosion continues in countries where pregnant women undertake hard physical labor in early pregnancy.

BENEFITS OF EXERCISE

As for the benefits of exercise in pregnancy, they are unquestionable. Doing any form of aerobic exercise, such as swimming, cycling, or brisk walking, makes the heart pump faster than normal and so increases stamina. This means that your heart muscle is able to pump blood round your body more efficiently and work less hard at times of physical stress. This will be of particular value in late pregnancy when you find yourself climbing stairs with a great deal of extra weight around your middle and also during labor.

Anaerobic activity, such as pilates, yoga, isometrics, or working with weights, is more resistance-based and is designed to exercise the muscles as well as improve flexibility. If you exercise in a gym, you probably do a mixture of aerobic and anaerobic exercises. The golden rule is that any sport you are already doing on a regular basis is safe to continue for the first three months, as long as there are no pregnancy complications such as pain or bleeding. You should aim to exercise regularly and make sure you warm up and cool down gradually and stop exercising if you experience any pain or discomfort. You are best placed to know how hard you can push your body and will instinctively know what your limits are. If you are feeling exhausted, it is your body's way of telling you to slow down.

WHAT KIND OF EXERCISE?

If you normally come out in a rash at the very thought of doing any exercise but feel that for once in your life you are prepared to give it a try, then do not be over-ambitious. If you stick to activities you will a) enjoy b) not become bored with after two months and c) be able to fit into your weekly schedule, you cannot go wrong. Be realistic and you will be much more likely to succeed. Obviously, you would not be advised to take up a strenuous or difficult sport at this stage, so consider some of the activities below, all of which are safe to pursue throughout pregnancy. Whether you exercise regularly or not, you should think about including one of them in your fitness schedule.

Yoga is excellent for flexibility and general well being (*see* opposite page). Choose a class that focuses on prenatal exercises rather than a general class. You will find yoga is a wonderful form of exercise in the latter stages of pregnancy

YOGA IN PREGNANCY

MANY OF MY PATIENTS EXTOL THE VIRTUES OF YOGA FOR ITS ALL-ROUND EFFECTS ON

STRENGTH AND FLEXIBILITY. BEFORE YOU START, ENSURE THAT THE YOGA CLASS OR BOOK YOU

CHOOSE IS SUITABLE FOR PREGNANT WOMEN. RELAXATION TECHNIQUES ARE QUITE SAFE TO DO.

One of the core components of all forms of prenatal exercise is relaxation. Learning a variety of comfortable positions and breathing exercises will enable you to recover your equilibrium when you feel overwhelmed by your pregnant state and will give you some strategies to help you deal with the more testing times during labor and birth.

BUTTERFLY POSE Put your feet together against the wall and drop your knees to each side without straining, as wide as feels comfortable.

The key elements of any form of relaxation exercise are these:

▶ Find a time and place where you will not be disturbed and lie down in a position in which you can remain comfortable for 5-10 minutes.

▶ Close your eyes, keep your head straight and your neck relaxed, and drop your lower jaw.

▶ Breathe evenly and effortlessly.

▶ Clear your mind of worrying thoughts or lists of things to do – this will take practice.

▶ Before you resume your activities, take a few deep breaths, roll on to your side and get up slowly.

BREATHING TOGETHER

The belief that different types of breathing can help women deal with the pain of labor is central to many childbirth philosophies (see pp.248–9).

Joined breathing (shown left) is a yoga exercise designed to foster harmony between you, your partner and your growing baby. Sit in a position where you can both place your hands comfortably over your baby and uterus. As you breathe together deeply and slowly, focus on the muscles of your uterus, taking care not to tense the muscles in the rest of your body.

KEEP WALKING *You can continue a brisk daily walk throughout pregnancy, although you may need to reduce the distance later on.*

when the delivery begins to loom closer and you are in need of relaxation. Yoga has the added benefit that it teaches you to control your breathing — a useful technique for the big day itself.

Swimming is the perfect three-in-one exercise, enabling you to develop stamina, flexibility, and muscle tone all at once. Like most women, you are likely to find swimming wonderfully relaxing in pregnancy, especially in the later stages when all of your extra weight is supported by water. Exercise in water has the added bonus of eliminating the possibility of overstraining any part of your body. The hardest bit is getting back onto dry land and feeling the full force of your pregnant weight again.

Walking is easy to fit in as part of your daily routine — walking an extra 10 minutes on your way to or from work, walking to the stores rather than automatically jumping into your car is a good way to start. You will find that your ability to walk longer distances reduces later on in your pregnancy.

Cycling is useful because your leg joints are not under excessive strain from your increased weight. It develops stamina and tones your lower body, so it is an activity that can be continued right through to the birth.

ADAPTING YOUR EXERCISE REGIME

During the first trimester, it are safe to do sit-ups, especially if you are used to doing them on a regular basis, although you should not do any more than usual. If you are not used to doing them, try gentle head and shoulder lifts:

• Lie flat on your back with your legs bent at the knees and your feet flat on the ground, shoulder-width apart. Your arms should be alongside your body.

• Raise your arms towards your knees while at the same time lifting your head and shoulders about 6in (15cm) off the ground. Do this exercise 10 times. If you have toned abdominal muscles they will help to support your bump, taking pressure off your back muscles and spine. The most usual advice is that you should stop sit-ups in the fourth month of pregnancy when your waistline begins to expand and the exercise may feel uncomfortable.

When you become pregnant, the level of the hormone relaxin begins to rise. The purpose of this hormone is to relax the ligaments, especially those in the pelvic area, in preparation for childbirth. Consequently, all your ligaments become looser, but this leaves you more prone to injury, should you put too much strain on them. Unlike muscles, which do regain their shape after the birth, your ligaments do not recover if you stretch them excessively. Bear this in mind if you do any exercise that involves lifting weights. After the first trimester, you should reduce the weights you lift to protect your pelvis and your lower spine to avoid putting any strain on your abdominal area. This advice also applies to any form of heavy lifting, whether it be of grocery bags or toddlers. Of course, at times this will be unavoidable, so make sure you adopt a safe way of doing it (*see* p.193).

AS YOUR PREGNANCY ADVANCES

There are certain activities, such as squash, skiing and horseback riding, which are not particularly advisable for women to continue beyond the sixth month of pregnancy, largely because they carry the risk of high impact injuries. However, if you are used to these sports and do not have a history of miscarriage, there is no reason why you shouldn't continue to do them during the first three months.

Sports such as tennis and golf can be continued as far into the pregnancy as you feel comfortable — you may have to stop when your enlarging tummy starts getting in the way but it won't be because of a potential risk to your baby.

Your ability to withstand the biggest physical upheaval that your body is ever likely to know — labor and childbirth — is certain to be enhanced if you are reasonably fit, as will your ability to return to your pre-pregancy shape. I hope you will not rush to the gym and work out until you are red in the face and aching all over, but rather will make a vow to keep active and fit during the months ahead. Remember, too, that although moderation and regularity are key, so is your enjoyment.

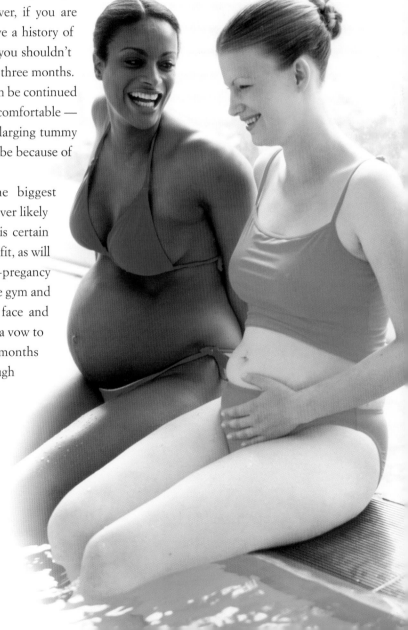

SWIMMING *Whether you exercise in the water, swim lengths, or float and relax, your buoyancy supports your extra weight and prevents damage to your ligaments and muscles.*

WORK AND MATERNITY RIGHTS

Before you inform your employer and colleagues at work that you are pregnant, you need to give some careful thought to the issue of your maternity rights. Now is the time to find out what benefits are available to you and make plans for working during your pregnancy, timing your departure, and adapting your life after your baby is born.

Many women are justifiably worried that they will be perceived differently at work from the moment they announce they are pregnant, whether this is a first or a subsequent pregnancy. Some employers assume that you will be less committed to your career from this point onward and caught up in the exciting developments of your pregnancy. As a result, you may have serious concerns about your current job security and about your future career.

Maternity rights and benefits in Canada are protected by federal law, such as the Employment Insurance Act. This legislation requires employers to allow leave for various family and medical reasons, including childbirth, and guarantees that you will return to the same position or one of equal seniority and salary when you return. Other legislation, such as Section III of the Canada Labour Code, protects your right to working conditions that are safe both for you and your unborn child. Canadian labor law also guarantees that your pregnancy must be treated as a medical condition for which you cannot be discriminated. For full details of the relevant legislation, visit the Department of Justice Canada website (http://canada.justice.gc.ca) or the Social Development Canada website (http://www.sdc.gc.ca). Further legislation has been enacted in various Provinces and Territories that extends the provisions of the federal legislation by varying degrees.

MAKING PLANS

If you are aiming to return to your job after the birth, work out some clear ideas about what you want to do and explain your plans to your employers or colleagues. It is entirely within your rights to say that you intend to return to

MAKING PLANS *Exploring options for your future working life will make you feel more secure and give your colleagues confidence in you.*

work after a certain period of maternity leave and subsequently change your mind. However, try not to vacillate between the two options — it won't inspire your employer to have long-term confidence in you.

Think through how long you would like to take off (you can always change the exact dates later on) and what you would like to happen to your job while you are away. There may be an established procedure in your workplace for maternity cover but if there is not, you can help by suggesting how best to achieve this cover. Does an additional outside individual need to be hired? Can an existing colleague switch roles for a while? Don't undersell yourself by suggesting that someone can fill in for a couple of days a week or a few hours a day while you are away. First, this begs the question of what on earth you are doing for a full five days. Second, you do not want to return after your leave to find an overflowing inbox or a catalog of things that have not been done.

If you are self-employed, the ground rules are much the same as they are for an employed woman: be clear about your future plans; tell people how long you are taking off; and inform them of any maternity cover that will be arranged.

PART-TIME AND FLEXIBLE WORK

You may have already started to think about whether you want to work full time, part time, or flextime after your baby is born. Many employers will now consider a request to work part-time or flexibly to enhance the work/life balance, but such policies do not give you an automatic right to do so. You may discover that a precedent for part-time or flexible work has already been established in your workplace, but even if your preferred working option has never been tried before, it does not mean that it is impractical. Present all the arguments in favor of your suggestion — most importantly, how it will benefit the employer as a whole — and draft a specific plan. Make sure that you have already thought out solutions for any problems that might be raised and be prepared to listen to any counter-offers that your employer might present. Also, bear in mind that both you and your partner are entitled to take a year's parental leave (unpaid) during your child's first five years if you've worked for your present employer for at least one year.

WHEN WORK IS A HAZARD

Although some women worry that their work is potentially harmful to their unborn child, hard evidence showing the link between certain occupations and a risk to an unborn child is scant. The few types of work that are potentially hazardous are strenuous jobs involving long hours; shift work; jobs that require a lot of lifting or standing for long periods of time; and work that exposes women to certain chemicals or harmful environmental factors (*see* pp. 30–31).

• If your job involves a great deal of standing, look for ways to reduce this in the second half of the pregnancy. This is not because long periods of standing will harm your baby, but they will exacerbate common pregnancy problems such as fatigue, backache, varicose veins, and swollen legs and ankles.

• If your work involves heavy lifting, make sure that you always lift correctly by bending your knees and keeping your back straight (*see* p.193). After the second trimester, try to reduce the weight of what you lift and the frequency. If that is not possible, request a switch to a less strenuous role until you stop work.

• Working long hours or shift work is not dangerous to either you or your baby, but both become increasingly tiring, which can affect you both. You need to conserve your energy, particularly in the third trimester, so if there is no alternative to your current job, consider stopping work a little earlier.

• Some jobs, such as those in dentistry, medicine, and certain industries, involve exposure to chemicals, X-rays, or other toxic substances. Your doctor or employer should be able to clarify whether your work is putting your baby at risk. If this is not possible, you have the right to be suspended at full pay.

LEAVING AND RETURNING TO WORK

▶ **How can I maximize my employee benefits?**
You should check with your employer to determine the company's maternity leave policies before you get pregnant. In some cases, you need to have worked for an employer for a set period before you become eligible for all benefits under the Employment Insurance Act.

▶ **How should I negotiate the best maternity-leave package possible?**
You should discuss your maternity-leave plans with your employer approximately 12 weeks before your baby is due. Make sure that you check whether you are covered by any local laws or collective bargaining agreements that expand upon or limit the provisions of the Employment Insurance Act .

▶ **How can I protect my rights under the Employment Insurance Act?**
You should inform your employer in writing of your intentions at least 30 days before you go on maternity leave.

▶ **When should I finalize the details of my maternity leave with my employer?**
You should give your employer a letter summarizing your plans and what you have agreed upon, about 10 weeks before your baby is due.

▶ **How can I maintain good relations with my employer and hold my job until I return?**
About 6–8 weeks after the birth, you should tell your employer whether you expect to return to work on the date anticipated.

WEEKS 0–13

THE FIRST TRIMESTER

During the first trimester, your baby will evolve from a cluster of cells into a recognizable fetus measuring about 3in (80mm). All the major organs, muscles, and bones will be formed. Until the placenta becomes mature enough to take over, your pregnancy is supported by maternal hormones, which also contribute to early symptoms such as nausea and fatigue. Although you may not look pregnant in the first trimester, you will almost certainly feel pregnant.

CONTENTS

WEEKS 0-6

68 The developing baby

71 Your changing body

73 How you may feel physically

75 Your emotional response

78 Your prenatal care

80 Common concerns

84 Prenatal care and birth choices

WEEKS 6–10

93 The developing baby

95 Your changing body

97 How you may feel physically

101 Your emotional response

102 Common concerns

104 Things to consider

WEEKS 10–13

107 The developing baby

112 Your changing body

113 How you may feel physically

114 Your emotional response

115 Your prenatal care

131 Common concerns

134 Prenatal tests

144 Congenital disorders

YOUR BABY
IN THE FIRST TRIMESTER

WEEK 3–4 THE BRAIN
DEVELOPS FROM SEPARATE
VESICLES—WITHIN DAYS
THESE WILL CLOSE TOGETHER.

WEEK 5 THE EMBRYO HAS THE
BEGINNINGS OF A PROFILE WITH
A BULGING NASAL REGION AND A
PRIMITIVE CAVITY FOR A MOUTH.

WEEK 6–7 THE FETAL HAND IS A SIMPLE PADDLE WITH RAYS OF CARTILAGE WHERE FINGERS WILL FORM.

WEEK 12 THE FINGERS ARE SEPARATING INTO INDIVIDUAL DIGITS AND TINY NAILS ARE VISIBLE.

"The embryo has tiny limb buds, which will develop into arms and legs. A balloonlike yolk sac (foreground) sustains its growth."

WEEKS 0-6
THE DEVELOPING BABY

THE FIRST SIX WEEKS OF PREGNANCY ARE AN EXTREMELY CREATIVE TIME. JUST THREE WEEKS AFTER YOUR LAST MENSTRUAL PERIOD, THE NEWLY FERTILIZED EGG DIVIDES REPEATEDLY TO FORM A CLUSTER OF CELLS CALLED A BLASTOCYST. IT FLOATS DOWN INTO THE UTERUS AND EMBEDS ITSELF IN THE LINING.

At this early stage when you do not even know that you are pregnant, many of the foundations of your pregnancy are being laid down. This tiny blastocyst produces chemical messengers that will send signals to your body to prevent your menstrual period from starting and prepare itself for the journey to come. At about the time of implantation, the clustered cells that will become your future baby have already become more specialized and have somehow acquired the capacity to know to which part of the body they have been assigned.

Three different layers of cells develop and each type will create different parts of your baby's body. The outer layer, or ectoderm, forms the skin, hair, nails, nipples, and tooth enamel together with the lenses of the eyes, the nervous system, and the brain. The middle layer, or mesoderm, will become the skeleton and muscles, the heart and blood vessels, together with the reproductive organs. The innermost layer, the endoderm, gives rise to the respiratory and digestive systems including the liver, pancreas, stomach, and bowel together with the urinary tract and bladder. Once a cell has been directed or programmed to have a specific function, it cannot change to become another type of cell.

By the beginning of week five, the cluster of cells is just recognizable as an embryo and is visible as a tiny nubbin of tissue on the ultrasound scan. Although little bigger than a nailhead, all the building blocks for your baby's vital organs are already in place. The primitive heart begins to form and starts to circulate blood. At this early stage, it is a simple tubelike structure.

The position of the spinal cord has been decided and a row of dark cells appears down the back of the embryo. These cells then fold lengthwise and as they close together, they become the neural tube. At the top of the row, two large lobes of tissue become visible, which will become the brain. A digestive system is in place, although it will be many months before it is capable of functioning. A tube now extends from the mouth to the tail of the embryo and from this tube the stomach, liver, pancreas, and bowels will develop. All of the above organs and tissues are covered by a thin layer of translucent skin.

◄ *A tiny four-week-old embryo rests on the huge orb of its yolk sac.*

WEEKS

FIRST TRIMESTER ▸ 1
▸ 2
▸ 3
▸ 4
▸ 5
10 x life size ▸ 6
▸ 7
▸ 8
▸ 9
▸ 10
▸ 11
▸ 12
▸ 13
SECOND TRIMESTER ▸ 14
▸ 15
▸ 16
▸ 17
▸ 18
▸ 19
▸ 20
▸ 21
▸ 22
▸ 23
▸ 24
▸ 25
▸ 26
THIRD TRIMESTER ▸ 27
▸ 28
▸ 29
▸ 30
▸ 31
▸ 32
▸ 33
▸ 34
▸ 35
▸ 36
▸ 37
▸ 38
▸ 39
▸ 40

10 x life size

At four weeks, the embryo measures about 0.078in (2mm), roughly the size of this dash –. By the end of this six-week period it will double to 0.15in (4mm) in length.

WHAT DOES THE EMBRYO LOOK LIKE?

This is the question that most women ask and thanks to modern ultrasound scan techniques, it is now possible to see the tiny embryo on screen and describe it. By week six, the ball of cells has changed dramatically and now resembles a tadpole or a rather odd-looking shrimp. At the large head end, gill-like folds are visible, which will later become the face and jaw. The embryo's rudimentary heart bulges out of the mid portion of the body and by the sixth week it can be seen beating, or rather fluttering, on a vaginal ultrasound scan, although it is not always possible to see this if you have an abdominal ultrasound performed. Little budlike protuberances start to appear on each side of the embryo, and these will become legs and arms. Very soon these limb buds will develop nodules at their ends and these will become hands and feet.

THE SUPPORT SYSTEM

As soon as the blastocyst starts to implant into your uterine wall, a support system for the embryo begins to develop. At this early stage, all its needs are met by the yolk sac, a balloonlike structure attached to the embryo by a stalk, which will continue to supply sustenance until the placenta is fully developed. The embryo floats in a fluid-filled bubble called the amniotic sac, which is covered by an outer protective sac called the chorion. The outer layer of the chorion will become the early placenta, and already little fingers of tissue called chorionic villi are starting to sprout and set up their future access to your circulation. Later on they will transfer nutrients and oxygen to your baby from your blood supply.

EMBRYO AT SIX WEEKS

By week six, the beginnings of a nose can be seen on a head that nods over the bulging heart.

Two sets of limb buds will later develop into arms and legs. The body ends with a prominent tail.

YOUR CHANGING BODY

FIVE WEEKS *The embryo looks rather like an oddly shaped prawn, floating in a fluid-filled bubble called the amniotic sac.*

IN THE FIRST SIX WEEKS OF YOUR PREGNANCY YOU WILL NOT LOOK PREGNANT AND YOU MAY NOT BE FEELING PREGNANT, YET YOUR BODY IS ALREADY UNDERGOING MAJOR CHANGES IN RESPONSE TO A MASSIVE SURGE IN PREGNANCY HORMONES THAT STARTED IMMEDIATELY AFTER CONCEPTION.

Even when your period is not due for another seven days or so and you are unlikely to have realized that you are pregnant, several changes are taking place inside you. Your body is producing a flood of pregnancy hormones. In particular the levels of the estrogen hormone are higher than normal to help thicken the uterine lining and provide a rich environment for the tiny implanting embryo. The hormones human chorionic gonadotropin (HCG) and progesterone help to keep the embryo embedded, and progesterone also ensures that your cervical mucus thickens and forms a protective plug, which will seal the uterus off from vaginal infections for the duration of the pregnancy.

NO EARLY SIGNS

Although some women know that they are pregnant even before their period is due, many others do not experience any early signs of pregnancy. Furthermore, if their periods are very irregular, they may not realize that they are pregnant for weeks or even months. When the embryo embeds further into the lining of the uterus between the eighth and tenth day after ovulation, there is sometimes a little bleeding; this can mislead a woman into thinking she is having a light period and is therefore not pregnant The same is true for those women who, for reasons that we do not fully understand, continue to have light periods throughout their pregnancy. I know that many women worry if they do not experience clearly recognizable symptoms of pregnancy in the first few weeks and think this means that their pregnancy is weaker or at risk. This is not the case. There is no right or wrong way to feel at this stage of pregnancy and no one symptom — or lack of — will have any bearing on your ability to carry a healthy baby to term. Signs and symptoms of pregnancy are very individual and, just as no two women will have an identical labor, no two women will have the same start to pregnancy or an identical journey through it.

PREGNANCY AFTER IVF TREATMENT

If you are undergoing invitro fertilization (IVF), the treatment cycle begins by stimulating your ovaries with hormones to produce multiple eggs. These eggs are collected on or around Day 13 and mixed with sperm in the laboratory (hence — in vitro). If fertilization is successful during the next 48 hours, two embryos will be transferred back into your uterus on about Day 16.

A blood test on Day 27 will check for raised levels of human chorionic gonadotropin (hCG) — the first sign that the IVF treatment may have been successful. However, it is possible to have a positive test, only to discover, in a few days time, that the hCG levels have fallen because the embryo has not implanted successfully.

Your first US scan usually takes place 5–6 weeks after the start of the treatment. All being well, there will be a small pregnancy sac visible in the uterine cavity. If no sac is present there is a risk that you have an ectopic pregnancy (see p.81 and p.422). Sometimes the scan reveals several sacs, suggesting twins or triplets, but quite frequently the extra sac(s) disappears (vanishing twin syndrome). Multiple pregnancies are at greater risk of miscarriage, congenital abnormalities, and prematurity, which is why IVF clinics are concerned to keep the number of embryos they transfer to the minimum.

A further scan at 6–7 weeks should show a fetal pole and beating fetal heart. Your pregnancy is under way!

FERTILIZATION *Intra-ctyoplasmic sperm injection (ICSI) involves injecting a single sperm into an egg.*

YOUR EMOTIONAL RESPONSE

UNDOUBTEDLY YOUR FEELINGS AT THE BEGINNING OF PREGNANCY ARE VERY MUCH DICTATED BY YOUR PERSONAL CIRCUMSTANCES BUT IF, LIKE MANY WOMEN, YOU ARE FEELING EMOTIONALLY UNPREDICTABLE, YOUR SURGING PREGNANCY HORMONES ARE ALMOST CERTAINLY PLAYING A PART.

As I described in my chapter on conception, the mix of panic and elation that you may be feeling from one moment to the next may not simply be a reaction to the new future that is about to unfold. Most pregnancy books explain that fragile emotions and tearfulness gradually settle down and become less troublesome but I am increasingly of the view that they continue, since they are hormonally linked. Basically, we get used to them and, practical creatures that we are, we learn to ignore or accommodate them.

If your pregnancy was planned or has been difficult to achieve, you may feel on an almost permanent high in these early days and bursting to pass on your exciting news. However, for some women the knowledge that they are pregnant is something very private that they want to share only with their partner, or closest family and friends in the early weeks. Others, particularly those who have miscarried in the past, do not want to tempt fate by declaring to the world at large that they are pregnant, just in case something goes wrong, and prefer to wait until the pregnancy has progressed to the second trimester before announcing their news.

Deciding whether you want to tell other people about your pregnancy at this stage is a very individual issue and there is no right or wrong way to deal with it. As we all know, family dynamics are complex and only you will know the best way to break the news to your partner, mother, sister, in-laws, or friends. The only piece of reassurance I can offer is that, by and large, most family members and friends will be thrilled by your news and the fact that you want to share it with them. Indeed, the only significant problem you are likely to meet, in my experience, is a deluge of well-meaning advice and offers of help.

Many women in early pregnancy tell me that they are concerned they will upset friends and family members who are having fertility problems, have lost a baby, or experienced a pregnancy complication in the past. I think it is practically impossible to protect everyone you know from their own raw emotions and sad memories. In any event, they will have to come to terms with the situation sooner or later. However, I must add here that I am repeatedly impressed by patients in my miscarriage clinic and how generous they can be

HIGH EMOTION *Some women are bursting to pass on their exciting news; others want to hug their secret to themselves for a little longer.*

toward other women who announce they are pregnant, even when the news must bring them personal heartache. On balance, I think it is best to be open about the news that you are pregnant. I suspect that you will feel pleasantly surprised by the warmth of the response that you receive.

HOW YOUR PARTNER MAY FEEL

Whatever your decision about when and how to reveal your pregnancy, if you are part of a couple, your partner is likely to be the first to share your news. Remember that it is not only women who have a mass of conflicting emotions at this time — many men feel much the same. Although most will be pleased at the thought of becoming a father, I think there is a fundamental difference in how men and women feel about pregnancy in the early stages. For a start, men have nothing tangible to relate to in the first few weeks. Until a baby can be visualized on an ultrasound scan or can be felt and seen moving inside you, your partner may find it hard to feel as involved as you might want him to be. Women on the other hand are already conscious of the fact that a live baby is growing inside their body, they feel physically and emotionally different and soon they will start to look different, too.

YOUR PARTNER Becoming a father may be the best news possible or something that he needs time to come to terms with.

I do feel it is important to talk to your partner about how you are feeling, but it is all too easy to make your pregnancy the sole topic of conversation. Try not to feel disappointed or resentful if you find he is less than fascinated by your early symptoms and prefers to settle down with a crime novel rather than the pregnancy book that you are finding irresistible.

Just like you, he may need time to come to terms with the news and how it will impact on your lives. Remember that he may be feeling very apprehensive about the responsibility that looms ahead, especially if you are considering living on his salary for a while. Although there are likely to be few noticeable changes in the next few months, he will be acutely aware that he is moving into another phase of life. Calm, relaxed discussions during which he can talk openly about his feelings will help to prevent any misunderstandings building up (on either side).

So much of the focus during pregnancy is on the mother-to-be that your partner's opinions can end up being overlooked. For example, it is generally assumed nowadays that fathers should be, and will want to be, present at the birth. For some men, nothing could be further from the truth. Similarly, partners are often actively encouraged to attend antenatal classes. Great, if he wants to be included and is keen to join you, but pressuring him to do things a certain way, or making him feel that he is letting you down if he does not immediately adopt the role of ideal prospective father, is likely to be the source of future conflicts. Having said that, don't worry if at this stage he swears that he is not coming to any prenatal classes and that you won't catch him anywhere near the delivery room. Believe me, most men do change their mind.

WHAT IS HE THINKING?

The thoughts going through your partner's head may well include some of the following:

▶ Will our relationship stay the same?

▶ Will I still be able to go out with my friends/watch football?

▶ What happens if one of us has to give up work?

▶ How much do I want to be involved in the pregnancy?

▶ Is she more fragile than she was before?

▶ What happens if something goes wrong?

▶ Do I want to be at the birth and what will I be expected to do?

▶ Will she give the baby all the attention?

▶ Will I be a good father?

HAVING A BABY ON YOUR OWN

Inevitably, much of the discussion in this book relates to women with partners with the general assumption that their partner is a man, but I'm conscious of the fact that society is a good deal more complex than this. Many readers will be embarking on their pregnancy alone and it is not my intention to make them feel excluded from this journey. If you have chosen to be a single parent, you have probably given plenty of thought to the way you will handle the next nine months and life with a baby. If lone parenting is something that has been forced on you by circumstances, you may be feeling overwhelmed by the the prospect as well as by practical and financial considerations. The only general advice I can offer is that you should start now to put in place a network of support. Ask a relative or friend to share your pregnancy and to be with you for key events, such as the first scan, and for the birth. If this is difficult, find out about local prenatal classes for single mothers and single-parent support groups (*see* Useful Addresses, pp.436–8). Having close friends who share similar experiences can make all the difference.

"Until a baby can be visualized on an ultrasound scan or can be felt and seen moving inside you, your partner may find it hard to feel as involved as you might want him to be."

YOUR PRENATAL CARE

AS SOON AS YOU KNOW THAT YOU ARE PREGNANT, MAKE AN APPOINTMENT
WITH YOUR GYNECOLOGIST OR FAMILY DOCTOR. IT'S A GOOD IDEA TO GET TO
KNOW YOUR DOCTOR AT THE BEGINNING OF YOUR PREGNANCY, ESPECIALLY IF,
LIKE MOST HEALTHY WOMEN, YOU RARELY SEE HIM OR HER NORMALLY.

The first thing the doctor will do is ask you for the date of your last menstrual
period so your estimated date of delivery (EDD) can be calculated. An average
pregnancy lasts from 37 to 40 weeks from the first day of your last period, so
your doctor will add 40 weeks on to that date using a chart or a pregnancy
wheel. Much confusion and potential distress can be avoided if you always use
weeks, rather than months, to measure the stage that your pregnancy has
reached. The accuracy of the EDD calculated in this way will depend on
whether you have a regular 28-day cycle. If yours is shorter, longer or irregular,
the doctor will aim to adjust the EDD accordingly and may well suggest that you
do not rely on this date until you have had your first scan, when the age of your
pregnancy and your future EDD can be decided very precisely.

Your doctor may also carry out a few basic tests such as testing your urine
for the presence of sugar or protein and measuring your blood pressure. More
detailed tests will be performed at your first formal prenatal visit, which will
take place a few weeks later.

ORGANIZING YOUR FIRST PRENATAL VISIT

"Even if you are hoping for a home birth, make sure that you attend a hospital or community prenatal booking visit."

Your initial meeting with your doctor will also give you the opportunity to
discuss the options for care during your pregnancy. If you have had a baby
before or have strongly held views on childbirth, you may know exactly what
type of prenatal care you want and where you want to receive it. However, if this
is your first baby, you will probably welcome a detailed explanation of what is
available and some guidance as to which option is best suited to your individual
needs. For this reason, I have included a comprehensive section on prenatal care
and birth choices at the end of this section (*see* pp.84–91)

Your first formal prenatal visit will probably take place about four weeks
later. This will take place at your doctor's office, health center, or hospital, and
you should attend this even if you are going to be cared for by a midwife and
intend to have subsequent prenatal visits in your own home. At this first formal
visit, you will be able to discuss your pregnancy and your preferred program of
prenatal care with midwives and doctors, and they will be able to offer you

YOUR ESTIMATED DELIVERY DATE

Look on the chart for the month and then the first day of your last menstrual period (printed in bold type). Directly below it is the date that your baby is due – your estimated delivery date.

Month	1	2	3	4	5	6	7	8	9	10	11	12	13	14	15	16	17	18	19	20	21	22	23	24	25	26	27	28	29	30	31
January	1	2	3	4	5	6	7	8	9	10	11	12	13	14	15	16	17	18	19	20	21	22	23	24	25	26	27	28	29	30	31
Oct/Nov	8	9	10	11	12	13	14	15	16	17	18	19	20	21	22	23	24	25	26	27	28	29	30	31	1	2	3	4	5	6	7
February	1	2	3	4	5	6	7	8	9	10	11	12	13	14	15	16	17	18	19	20	21	22	23	24	25	26	27	28			
Nov/Dec	8	9	10	11	12	13	14	15	16	17	18	19	20	21	22	23	24	25	26	27	28	29	30	1	2	3	4	5			
March	1	2	3	4	5	6	7	8	9	10	11	12	13	14	15	16	17	18	19	20	21	22	23	24	25	26	27	28	29	30	31
Dec/Jan	6	7	8	9	10	11	12	13	14	15	16	17	18	19	20	21	22	23	24	25	26	27	28	29	30	31	1	2	3	4	5
April	1	2	3	4	5	6	7	8	9	10	11	12	13	14	15	16	17	18	19	20	21	22	23	24	25	26	27	28	29	30	31
Jan/Feb	8	9	10	11	12	13	14	15	16	17	18	19	20	21	22	23	24	25	26	27	28	29	30	31	1	2	3	4	5	6	7
May	1	2	3	4	5	6	7	8	9	10	11	12	13	14	15	16	17	18	19	20	21	22	23	24	25	26	27	28	29	30	31
Feb/Mar	5	6	7	8	9	10	11	12	13	14	15	16	17	18	19	20	21	22	23	24	25	26	27	28	1	2	3	4	5	6	7
June	1	2	3	4	5	6	7	8	9	10	11	12	13	14	15	16	17	18	19	20	21	22	23	24	25	26	27	28	29	30	
Mar/Apr	8	9	10	11	12	13	14	15	16	17	18	19	20	21	22	23	24	25	26	27	28	29	30	31	1	2	3	4	5	6	
July	1	2	3	4	5	6	7	8	9	10	11	12	13	14	15	16	17	18	19	20	21	22	23	24	25	26	27	28	29	30	31
Apr/May	7	8	9	10	11	12	13	14	15	16	17	18	19	20	21	22	23	24	25	26	27	28	29	30	1	2	3	4	5	6	7
August	1	2	3	4	5	6	7	8	9	10	11	12	13	14	15	16	17	18	19	20	21	22	23	24	25	26	27	28	29	30	
May/Jun	8	9	10	11	12	13	14	15	16	17	18	19	20	21	22	23	24	25	26	27	28	29	30	1	2	3	4	5	6	7	
September	1	2	3	4	5	6	7	8	9	10	11	12	13	14	15	16	17	18	19	20	21	22	23	24	25	26	27	28	29	30	
Jun/Jul	8	9	10	11	12	13	14	15	16	17	18	19	20	21	22	23	24	25	26	27	28	29	30	1	2	3	4	5	6	7	
October	1	2	3	4	5	6	7	8	9	10	11	12	13	14	15	16	17	18	19	20	21	22	23	24	25	26	27	28	29	30	31
Jul/Aug	8	9	10	11	12	13	14	15	16	17	18	19	20	21	22	23	24	25	26	27	28	29	30	31	1	2	3	4	5	6	7
November	1	2	3	4	5	6	7	8	9	10	11	12	13	14	15	16	17	18	19	20	21	22	23	24	25	26	27	28	29	30	
Aug/Sep	8	9	10	11	12	13	14	15	16	17	18	19	20	21	22	23	24	25	26	27	28	29	30	31	1	2	3	4	5	6	
December	1	2	3	4	5	6	7	8	9	10	11	12	13	14	15	16	17	18	19	20	21	22	23	24	25	26	27	28	29	30	31
Sep/Oct	7	8	9	10	11	12	13	14	15	16	17	18	19	20	21	22	23	24	25	26	27	28	29	30	1	2	3	4	5	6	7

valuable advice as to how you can best achieve your aim. It is often presumed (wrongly) that all obstetricians and hospital midwives are against the idea of home deliveries. On the contrary, they just want to make very sure that both mother and baby are safe and that the prospective mother knows what action should be taken if problems arise.

At your first formal prenatal visit, you will also undergo a physical examination and a range of laboratory tests to establish your blood type and your general state of health. This visit usually takes place a few weeks after you notify your doctor that you are pregnant. The exceptions are women who have been unlucky enough to experience a previous pregnancy problem, such as a miscarriage or a late pregnancy complication. If this is the case for you, your doctor will probably arrange an immediate prenatal visit and possibly an early scan. If you have an existing medical condition, such as diabetes, your hospital prenatal care is also likely to start sooner rather than later.

Many women I talk to in the prenatal clinic tell me how disappointed they were that no one seemed very interested in their pregnancy until they attended their first prental visit. They also felt bewildered because there was no one to talk to about what to do and where to go to find out more about being pregnant. As one first-time mother said: "I am very grateful that I am just a normal pregnant woman with no medical problems, but this is all new to me. This is a special time for me and I am out of my depth."

This is one of the reasons why it is very important for pregnant women to be able to access as much information as possible both to reassure them and help them understand what is going to happen next. In an ideal world with limitless health care resources, we would be able to offer women instant access to the prenatal care they choose at the moment that their pregnancy test is positive. In the real world, the best solution I can offer is an informative book.

COMMON CONCERNS

YOU MAY ALREADY HAVE A FEW QUESTIONS ABOUT THE EARLY STAGES OF YOUR PREGNANCY AND ABOUT YOUR GENERAL HEALTH. THESE ARE DEFINITELY WORTH DISCUSSING WITH YOUR DOCTOR AT YOUR FIRST CONSULTATION.

I've included some common early pregnancy concerns below but if you cannot find your particular problem here, check the further examples in the next two sections of the first trimester: weeks 6–10 and weeks 10–13. Do not hesitate to bring up any others you may have with your doctor; it is always better to have advice on them sooner rather than later. It is important that you have all the reassurance you need to make the next few weeks as enjoyable as possible.

PREVIOUS PREGNANCY PROBLEMS

FETAL POLE *The tiny embryo is just visible as a white speck on the yolk sac, which is floating in the dark circle of the amniotic sac.*

If you had previous pregnancy problems, such as a miscarriage, an ectopic pregnancy (*see* p.81 *and* p.422), or complications in later pregnancy such as pre-eclampsia (*see* p.425), then your doctor will probably arrange for you to have an early ultrasound scan and/or an early appointment to see an obstetrician. For those women who have experienced miscarriages in the past, a scan is often very helpful in allaying fears that history is repeating itself. But do remember that all you need to see at this stage is a healthy sac in the uterine cavity. While a sophisticated scanner may detect a tiny fetal heart beat at 5–6 weeks, every pregnancy is unique and as long as a pregnancy sac can be seen in the uterus, the absence of a fetal pole (a tiny rectangular blob within the sac) or a heartbeat at this early stage, is common. The most likely explanation is that your embryo implanted a few days later than you had calculated or expected, so a little more time is needed to see these landmarks in your pregnancy. This may be the case if your menstrual cycle is irregular, or you are not sure exactly when you conceived.

Early ultrasound scans are also particularly valuable for women who have had a previous ectopic pregnancy, in which the embryo develops outside the uterus. The most common site is in the fallopian tube, although ectopic pregnancies are also found on an ovary or in the abdominal cavity. A scan establishes whether there is an early pregnancy sac in the right place inside the uterus. If there is no evidence of this, you will probably undergo a series of blood tests to establish your blood levels of hCG hormone. If these are raised and yet there is still no sign of an intrauterine sac on the scan, you may need to undergo laparoscopy or drug treatment to stop the ectopic pregnancy continuing and prevent further damage to the fallopian tube.

pregnancy sac with embryo

fallopian tube

uterus

ovary

cervix

ECTOPIC PREGNANCY

The sac and embryo have developed in the fallopian tube where there is insufficient room for them to grow.

OLDER MOTHERS-TO-BE

▶ **If you are over 35 years of age** and this is your first pregnancy, you may have heard someone describe you as an "elderly primigravida" – the medical term for an older first-time mother-to-be. This in spite of the fact that you may not be feeling a day older than 21. My advice is – don't worry too much about it. Even though the medical profession considers you to be a bit of a late starter, more and more women are bearing their first children successfully well beyond the age of 35.

Nevertheless, whether this is your first or your fourth pregnancy, there are some health risks in pregnancy that are linked to increasing age.

▶ **Genetic abnormalities** become more common as the mother's age increases because her eggs are older and more likely to be carrying a defective gene or chromosome. One example is the incidence of babies born with the most common fetal abnormality, Down syndrome (*see* p.147), which increases markedly from the age of 35 years. For this reason, women over the age of 35 are usually offered prenatal tests to diagnose possible fetal genetic and physical abnormalities (*see* pp.134–43).

The earlier you start your prenatal care, the better the opportunity to provide the best advice and the safest, most useful tests.

▶ **Several pregnancy complications** such as high blood pressure, preeclampsia, gestational diabetes, and premature births are also more common in older mothers. That said, most of these can be identified or predicted to minimize the consequences, and serious problems are still rare. There is no reason why your pregnancy should not be successful as long as you have regular prenatal checks.

URINARY INFECTIONS

Although it is normal for pregnant women to experience urinary frequency in the early weeks of pregnancy, the possibility of a urine infection should not be overlooked. If you feel tingling when you pass urine, the urgent need to urinate, lower abdominal pain or discomfort, or notice blood in the urine, you may have an infection and need prompt treatment with antibiotics.

Urinary infections are very common in pregnancy because progesterone makes the urinary tract more relaxed. This makes it easier for bacteria to enter the urethra and reach the bladder, where they cause inflammation or cystitis. Because the bladder is also relaxed in pregnancy, the infection can spread easily up the ureters and infect the kidneys, a condition known as pyelonephritis. The symptoms usually develop suddenly, and include a high temperature and shivering, pain over the bladder and kidneys, with severe discomfort in the abdominal region, which may radiate down to the groin. Antibiotic treatment will resolve the infection promptly. Left untreated, the infection can cause permanent scarring and damage to the kidney.

AN EXISTING CONDITION

If you have a general medical problem, however minor, you should discuss this with your doctor as soon as you know that you are pregnant. Your doctor will help you to decide on the best type of care for your needs, and if you are taking any medication, will also advise on whether the dosage needs to be altered. On no account should you stop taking prescribed drugs without first seeking advice.

In the final section of this book you will find details about existing medical conditions, such as diabetes, high blood pressure, thyroid disease, renal disease, heart disease, epilepsy, and inflammatory bowel disorders, which need specialist care during pregnancy (see pp.408–10). If you suffer from one of these (or a disorder that is not included in this list), your doctor may suggest prenatal care at a particular hospital that offers specialist expertise for your condition. You will be seen as quickly as possible, particularly if you are taking medications that may need to be altered. Throughout your pregnancy, you will be monitored by consultant obstetricians and, quite possibly, a physician with specialist knowledge of your particular condition. Your part of the bargain is to try to stay healthy and to follow their advice rigorously.

"I can guarantee you that, once the first three months of pregnancy are over, you are likely to feel a renewed vigor..."

DIET AND EXERCISE

I AM ALL TOO AWARE THAT TWO COMMON PROBLEMS IN THE FIRST TRIMESTER — NAUSEA
AND FATIGUE — CAN BE A SETBACK TO YOUR BEST-LAID PLANS TO EAT THE HEALTHIEST DIET
POSSIBLE AND STAY FIT AND SUPPLE DURING YOUR PREGNANCY.

HARD TO STOMACH

In the first trimester, what you eat
is particularly important because
during these weeks, your baby's
vital organs will be formed. The early
development of the heart, liver,
brain, and nervous system, for
example, takes place in this period.
Having said that, I know from
personal experience that nausea
and sickness in the early months of
pregnancy can make it impossible
to follow your ideal diet.

If you find yourself suffering from
extreme morning sickness during
the first few weeks or months
of pregnancy, remind yourself
that most pregnant women are
experiencing much of the same, and
the majority of pregnancies progress
without complications. As long as
you understand what you should
aim to be eating, even on particularly
nauseous days, and manage to
include a few of the most nutritious
items, you and your baby will be fine.

▶ Eat little and often. Small meals
and snacks are easier on the stomach
than three large meals per day. Try
nibbling on a piece of bread or some
plain toast early in the morning. Eat
at least some of your lunch and then
come back to it later in the evening.

▶ Keep healthy snack foods such
as fruit, nuts, and pieces of cheese
easily available, so that your blood
sugar level never gets too low.

▶ At the end of the day, eat small
portions of foods you enjoy.

▶ However little solid food you can
tolerate, try to remember to drink
plenty of fluids regularly.

TOO TIRED TO EXERCISE?

Even if you feel happier skipping
your daily exercise now that you are
pregnant, do remember that exercise
is very unlikely to cause any
problems in early pregnancy and, if
you maintain your exercise program,
it will help you keep fit and healthy.

Enrolling in an exercise class
targeted for pregnant women is
a good idea. These will focus on
flexibility and exercises to help you
prepare for labor. As a bonus, you
will meet other women who might
become part of your post-birth
network.

On the other hand, you may be
feeling so sick and/or exhausted that,
even if you are a regular exerciser,

LIGHT MEALS *Eat small portions of
foods you enjoy.*

you simply cannot face the idea of
working up a sweat. Again, do not
be too hard on yourself. There will be
some days when your body is telling
you that enough is enough and that
a rest is more beneficial than an
hour's worth of tennis.

I can guarantee that, once the first
three months are over, you are likely
to feel a renewed vigor that will
propel you back, if not to the tennis
court, at least to the pool for some
wonderfully relaxing and beneficial
swimming sessions.

PRENATAL CARE AND BIRTH CHOICES

Where you decide to have your prenatal care depends both on the type of birth you are hoping for and on where you live and what facilities are available to you. Choosing the right kind of care goes a long way toward making your pregnancy a pleasurable time in your life.

AN OPEN-MINDED APPROACH

When I was pregnant and looking for a book to read that would help me understand my special condition, I was struck by how polarized most books are on the particular issue of where I should have my baby. They divided roughly into two camps: those written by obstetricians who seemed to believe that the only place to have a baby is in a specialized hospital unit and those written by vehement supporters of natural childbirth and home births who suggest that hospital units are designed to make women feel lost and vulnerable by taking away control of their own bodies during childbirth. Like most readers, I was left with the feeling that I would have failed as a mother, missed out, or been cheated of something special if medical interventions were required. I concluded that both types of books were unrealistic and unhelpful because they did nothing to make me feel calm and confident about the potentially unpredictable journey I had just embarked upon. On reflection, that is when I decided another type of book was needed and that I should sit down and write it.

GOOD ADVICE *Your prenatal care team look after your health in pregnancy and offer advice and information.*

BEFORE YOU DECIDE

The main aim of prenatal care is to maintain your health during pregnancy and to help you produce a healthy baby, and this involves detecting any condition that may adversely affect either of you as early as possible. During your prenatal care, you will also be offered information and health education that will prepare you for labor and motherhood. These two major principles will be followed through wherever care is provided.

TYPES OF PRENATAL CAREGIVERS

The availability of various kinds of prenatal care differs from one region of the country to another, and in towns and cities there are more options than in rural areas. However, wherever you live you should have some choice in the type of care you receive. Your decision about the kind of care you want may depend on the hospital or birth center to which your healthcare provider is affiliated, on the recommendations of your doctor or friends, or your provider's flexibility about birthing options. Sometimes groups of healthcare professionals work together to provide care for pregnant women. Such groups may include combinations of family doctors, midwives, nurses, and obstetricians.

FAMILY PHYSICIAN

Your family doctor will probably be the first professional person involved in your pregnancy, and you may already have an idea about his or her views on birthing options, especially if you are already interested in the possibility of a home birth. The family physician may be able to provide continuity of care throughout the pregnancy and birth (although fewer family doctors are now providing maternity care). He or she can also provide medical care for the baby.

However, if you have a difficult pregnancy, or previous pregnancies or deliveries were not straightforward, your medical care is more likely to be supervised by an obstetrician.

MIDWIFE

While physicians and obstetricians tend to focus on the pathological, midwives focus on the normal process of pregnancy and birth, and are interested not only in your uterus and how it functions but also in your general well-being. A midwife is a specialist educated in childbirth, and he or she (not all midwives are female) is qualified to take responsibility for you before, during, and after the birth. In Canada, although not in all provinces, midwives are licensed independent healthcare professionals, paid by the provincial health system. Midwives may deliver babies at home, in the hospital, or in a birth center, but they must always have a physician on call in case of an unforeseen emergency. Midwives spend more time with you during labor than the average doctor, and may be more flexible about birthing options. If there is a problem during a home birth, the midwife will accompany you to the hospital and will stay with you throughout the delivery.

OBSTETRICIAN

An obstetrician is a physician who specializes in pregnancy and childbirth and possible associated medical problems. You may be referred to an obstetrician for complications during your pregnancy, but many obstetricians also follow uncomplicated pregnancies. The obstetrician is specially trained to perform cesarian sections, as well as forceps or vacuum-assisted births.

OTHER TEAM MEMBERS

Other healthcare professionals with whom your doctor may co-ordinate to meet your needs during and after your pregnancy include:

▶ **Nurses**, who assist the doctor by gathering information needed to diagnose and treat medical conditions.

▶ **Childbirth educators**, who teach prospective parents about conception, pregnancy, childbirth and family life.

▶ **Postpartum nurses**, who help care for the mother after birth.

▶ **Neonatal nurses**, who help care for the newborn.

▶ **Social workers**, who provide counseling and information.

▶ **Nutritionists**, who give advice and guidance on diet, nutrition, and any special dietary needs, both before and after the delivery.

A CHANGE IN APPROACH

THE ISSUE OF CHOICE IN CHILDBIRTH HAS BEEN A MATTER OF FIERCE DEBATE OVER THE
YEARS, MUCH OF IT PROMPTED BY THE DISSATISFACTION MANY PREGNANT WOMEN BEGAN
TO FEEL WITH THE MORE TRADITIONAL HOSPITAL-BASED PATTERNS OF CARE.

What is today perceived as a "medicalized" approach to childbirth developed over the last 50 years as a by-product of advances in the way labor and birth could be managed. As a result women began to protest that they were being treated as part of a baby production machine, rather than informed participants. These widespread feelings prompted Doris Haire to write her ground-breaking *The Cultural Warping of Childbirth* in 1972. Comparing birthing practices in developed countries around the world, she illustrated how childbirth had become over-medicalized in North America, and prompted women to educate themselves.

▶ It was no longer justified on the grounds of safety to encourage all women to give birth in the hospital.

▶ Many women wished to have continuity of care throughout pregnancy and childbirth, and midwives were likely to be best placed to provide this.

▶ Greater choice in the type of care for pregnant women was needed.

▶ Provision for home birth or birth in a small maternity unit was largely inadequate in North America, despite increasing demand.

▶ Some traditional interventions during labor and delivery such as continuous fetal monitoring, epidurals, chemical stimulation of labor, and episiotomy were unnecessary or not evidence-based.

▶ The hospital environment was leaving some women feeling that they had lost control of their bodies and disappointed by their labor and birthing experience.

▶ Within the hospital, women should be able to exercise choice in the personnel who care for them.

▶ The relationship between the woman and her caregiver was of fundamental importance and needed to be recognized.

Doris Haire's report did much to raise public awareness of these issues in the US, where two Congressional hearings have been held to discuss obstetric care and a law has been enacted in New York State requiring all New York hospitals to publish rates of cesarean sections, VBACs, forceps use, induced labor, augmentation of labor, and episiotomy, enabling women to compare hospitals.

Hospital maternity units have become friendlier, more comfortable, and less clinical places in which to give birth. Although the number of home deliveries has not increased dramatically, there has been a very significant change in the way that hospital units provide care for women at the time of delivery. The emphasis is now on flexibility, one-to-one midwifery care, and minimizing medical interventions wherever possible.

I believe that in the majority of cases, obstetricians should work in an advisory role to the midwife and only become the principal provider of care when a woman is at risk of medical and obstetric complications. The key to this is finding better ways of identifying the women who are at greatest risk and require medical intervention.

Even if you feel it is too early at this stage for you to know whether you would prefer to deliver your baby in the hospital, in a birthing center, or at home, your choice of prenatal care is a more pressing issue because your first appointment will take place at the end of the first trimester. So take some time to read through the various options on page 85 to see what might suit you best.

What is available in terms of prenatal care varies from one region to the next: some women have many different options available to them, while others have only a limited choice. Your physician will be able to tell you what is available and which services are provided by your physician's or obstetrician's office and nearby hospitals. Make sure that you understand the details so that you can consider all of the options in your own time. Explore other sources of information before coming to a decision — talk to friends and neighbors, pick up any information pamphlets in your physicians' offices, and contact your local health center as well as the Society of Obstetricians and Gynaecologists of Canada and your provincial college or association of midwives (*see* Useful Addresses, p. 436). There is also a bottomless pit of information on the internet, but remember that much of this is not backed by professional expertise. Lastly, remember that you can always change your mind at a later date.

CHILDBIRTH IN NORTH AMERICA

Although the figure is rising, the percentage of babies born at home or in birthing centers in North America remains very small — just two percent in the US in 2002 according to statistics. In 1972, in *The Cultural Warping of Childbirth*, Doris Haire noted that childbirth practices were relying on the so-called common sense of doctors rather than on scientific fact. Haire criticized a number of obstetrical practices that were common in the early 1970s, including routine induction of labor; depriving women of support during labor and delivery; and requiring them to give birth on their backs. Hospital birth wasn't actually safer but infant mortality rates had fallen dramatically in recent years, making hospital birth appear to be safer. Undoubtedly, the major reason for this fall was an overall improvement in prenatal care and general living standards.

Now that women are so well informed about pregnancy and their general health, and living standards have improved, there is the opportunity to offer greater choice in their prenatal care and place of birth. Although there will always be women who need high-tech medical care, the majority are likely to have straightforward pregnancies with a normal vaginal delivery. In view of this, many women and their maternal caregivers now feel that the option of a home delivery should at least be considered for low-risk pregnancies.

CHOOSING A BIRTHPLACE

Your choice of where you want to have your baby is likely to come down to one of the following options: in a hospital, in a gynecological unit, or in your own home. The two important factors to take into account when making a decision are personal preference and the safety of both you and your baby. Sometimes problems that arise in the pregnancy or previous complications make these factors incompatible, but it is usually possible to reach a compromise, as long as time is spent discussing the practicalities rather than either you or your medical caregivers sticking to a previously held bottom line.

In the hospital

If this is your first pregnancy, if you have current medical problems, or have experienced complications in a previous pregnancy, your obstetrician will probably recommend that you deliver your baby in the hospital. However, it is likely that you will still have prenatal care with your family practitioner or midwives. There may be more than one hospital in your area and if you can choose which to go to, try to find out about the facilities and prenatal care options each one offers. For example, if you want your midwife to deliver the baby, she will usually be based at one particular hospital, and this may influence your decision. In addition, many hospitals now have a limited number of birthing rooms, which are designed to be much less clinical; in fact, much more similar to your own home than the standard delivery room. Most of these birthing rooms have soft lighting, music, comfortable chairs, and large floor cushions, birthing balls, and stools, and some units also provide a birthing pool.

In a birthing center

Family practitioner and midwifery units are more common in rural areas and are located either within the main hospital maternity unit or as a separate stand-alone unit in the local district or community hospital. Staffed by doctors and midwives who can offer continuity of care throughout your pregnancy, labor, and delivery, birthing centers are designed to deal with normal pregnancies and deliveries in a low-tech and informal environment. Those hospital maternity units that include a birthing center are probably offering pregnant women the best of both worlds in that the surroundings are less formal, continuity of care can be maintained, but expert medical help is literally just around the next corner if any problems requiring specialist expertise arise during the birth, such as difficult presentations that may require a cesarean delivery.

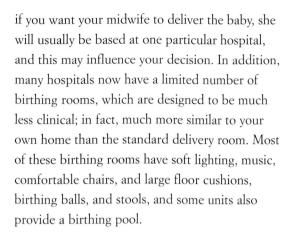

HOSPITAL BIRTH *If this is your first baby, your caregivers may recommend a hospital birth.*

At home

If you are considering having a home birth, the first thing to do is talk to your obstetrician and midwife. If this is your first baby, most will have concerns about the safety of a home delivery. No matter how well your pregnancy goes, no one can predict what will actually happen during labor. They will have similar concerns if you have had medical problems or previous pregnancy complications.

You may be a potential candidate for a home birth if you have had one or more previous pregnancies that were free of complications and that ended in straightforward vaginal deliveries. Even then, no two pregnancies can be guaranteed to follow the same pattern, so be prepared to change your plans if this pregnancy turns out differently.

It is within your right to have your baby at home, but it will be your responsibility to identify the people who will look after you, so find out whether your own obstetrician is prepared to care for you during pregnancy and home delivery. If he or she cannot help, there may be another local obstetrician that can. Your health insurer can give you the names of providers in your area with a special interest in pregnancy and childbirth and you can arrange to transfer your care to them.

Alternatively, you can contact the local supervisor of midwives at your nearest hospital who will arrange for a midwife to visit you at home to discuss your plans for a home delivery and possibly put you in touch with one of the midwifery teams prepared to come to your home and help you give birth. The Canadian Association of Midwives (*see* Useful Addresses, p. 436) can also put you in touch with a midwife in your province (*see* p. 91) who will follow you through with prenatal care and deliver your baby.

HOME BIRTH *You may want to consider having your baby at home in the heart of your family if you have had a previous labor and delivery that was straightforward.*

FINDING OUT MORE

Before you reach a final decision about the place of birth, ask other parents, midwives, and doctors about the reputation of the hospitals available to you. Then arrange a visit to one or two local units so that you can see for yourself and get a feel for whether you will be comfortable and relaxed there. Remember that feeling comfortable in labor is not just about physical issues such as the facilities and decoration of the rooms, it is also about the friendliness of the staff and the attitude they have toward birthing. I know that many women feel nervous about going into hospitals because they associate them with illness or possibly sad or unpleasant memories. But labor wards and prenatal clinics have a totally different atmosphere from any other hospital department. The patients are fit and healthy, in fact they are positively blooming, and all staff are participating in helping you have a happy and successful ending to your pregnancy.

QUESTIONS TO ASK ON A VISIT TO A MATERNITY UNIT

The best way to find out what your local maternity hospital can offer is to arrange a visit. The following questions should help you decide on your preferred type of maternity care and delivery.

GENERAL ISSUES

▶ Does the maternity department have particular interests or offer specialist services?

▶ What is the hospital's policy on different types of prenatal and delivery care? Does it, for example, offer midwifery care?

▶ Is there 24-hour anesthesia service available?

▶ Is there a special-care baby unit and neonatal intensive care unit (NICU)?

▶ Does it offer prenatal classes and tours of the labor ward and postnatal facilities?

▶ What is their view on birth plans?

LABOR AND DELIVERY ISSUES

▶ Are midwives flexible about special requests and different types of delivery; for example, are they willing to encourage women to give birth in any position that feels comfortable, be it lying, standing, or squatting?

▶ How long are the midwives' shifts? A 12-hour-shift system gives you a better chance of being cared for by the same midwife throughout your delivery.

▶ What is the hospital policy on induction, rupturing the membranes, pain relief, and routine electronic monitoring during labor?

▶ Would they be worried if labor was slower than normal or than expected?

▶ Are partners, friends, and family welcome in the delivery room? Are the numbers limited?

▶ Is there a 24-hour epidural service?

▶ Do they make use of breathing techniques to help relieve pain?

▶ Is there a birthing pool or can you bring a rented one with you?

▶ What are the forceps, vacuum, and cesarean section rates? Remember that a specialist or teaching hospital will have a higher number of these

than a small general hospital because they will be caring for women who are more likely to experience complications in labor.

▶ What is their rate of vaginal births after cesareans (VBACs)?

▶ Is there a hospital policy on episiotomy and repair of vaginal tears? Some units have trained their midwives to suture; others rely on on-call doctors.

AFTER THE BIRTH

▶ Are single rooms available? If so, how many and what do they cost? Do they have private bathrooms? Are they reserved for women who have had difficult births? What size are the general maternity units and how many beds per room?

▶ What is the usual length of stay after the birth? (This will probably be longer after a first baby than for subsequent births.)

▶ Will your baby be with you at all times or is there a separate nursery?

▶ Are specialist breastfeeding counselors available? This can be enormously helpful when trying to establish breastfeeding.

▶ What are the visiting hours?

▶ Are special diets, such as kosher or vegetarian, available?

▶ Will you need to bring items such as pillows, towels, and diapers?

THE WHO'S WHO OF MATERNITY CARE

You will meet a variety of health-care professionals during your pregnancy, labor, and birth and also during the postnatal period. The following is a brief description of the role each person plays.

Your Family Practitioner will usually arrange your booking into a maternity unit and meeting with the community midwives attached to the surgery and is likely to play an important role in the remainder of your pregnancy. Many FPs hold prenatal clinics and participate in shared prenatal care with the hospital clinics. Some may be involved in your delivery, either in the hospital or at home. All FPs contribute to postpartum care.

Midwives are nurses or other health-care workers who have undergone additional specialist training in childbirth, but their services are not available in all provinces or territories in Canada. Since the 1960s, regulated midwifery has become part of the health system in the provinces of British Columbia, Alberta, Manitoba, Ontario, and Quebec, and in the Northwest Territories and Nunavut. Alberta does not publically fund midwifery, and Saskatchewan has legislation but has not yet integrated midwifery. Midwifery is not yet legally recognized in the Atlantic provinces of New Brunswick, Nova Scotia, Prince Edward Island, or Newfoundland and Labrador.

Midwives are qualified to take responsibility for you and your baby before, during, and after normal birth. If complications arise in the pregnancy, your midwife will consult with other health-care professionals. Midwifery practice has now become largely standardized in all of the regulated provinces: midwives offer continuity of care within small group practises, choice of birthplace, and a focus on the woman as the primary decision-maker in her maternity care.

Obstetricians are doctors who are specialists in the care of pregnant women. If you do not already have your own obstetrician, you will be assigned at your first hospital visit to the care of a consultant obstetrician, whose name will appear on your prenatal notes. The consultant obstetrician heads a team of junior obstetricians and is usually linked to a team of midwives. You may meet him or her only occasionally if your pregnancy runs smoothly. If it is more complicated, you will see your consultant more often.

Pediatricians are doctors who are specially trained in the health of babies and young children. Every maternity unit works hand in hand with pediatricians to ensure that the babies they deliver are healthy and receive any medical help they need. A pediatrician is always present at the delivery of twins and higher multiple births, most instrumental deliveries (such as forceps), and cesarean sections. Every baby is checked by a pediatrician or a specialist midwife at birth and 5 minutes later, using the Apgar score, which assesses five key elements of a newborn baby's health: heartbeat, breathing, muscle tone, reflexes, and skin color.

Neonatologists are pediatricians with specialist skills in the care of newborn babies with problems. They run the neonatal intensive care unit (NICU). If your baby is born prematurely or is found to have a problem, a neonatologist will be involved in your baby's care.

WEEKS 6–10
THE DEVELOPING BABY

DURING THE NEXT FOUR WEEKS, YOUR DEVELOPING BABY WILL QUADRUPLE IN SIZE AND UNDERGO DRAMATIC CHANGES IN APPEARANCE. BY WEEK 10 THE EMBRYO HAS BECOME A FETUS AND IS STARTING TO RESEMBLE A HUMAN BEING.

Several facial features can now be recognized on ultrasound as the body is straightening and the limbs developing. The head continues to grow more rapidly than any other part of the body in order to accommodate the developing brain. The back of the head grows at a faster rate than the front; as a result the embryo is curled over the front of the body and appears to be nodding at its bulging heart. However, the body has started to lose its earlier commalike shape. A neck is appearing, the back is straighter, and the tail is disappearing.

The head now has a high forehead and, as the primitive facial bones develop and fuse together, eyes, nose, ears, and a mouth become recognizable. The primitive eyes and ears, which were mere swellings on the head at six weeks, are developing rapidly. By the end of the eighth week, the eyes have grown in size and already contain some pigment. By the 10th week, they are easily recognizable but will continue to be hidden behind sealed lids and cannot function until later in the second trimester, when the nervous system is fully formed. At each side of the head the depressions that will become ear canals have deepened and the inner ear starts to form. By the eighth week, the middle ear, which will become responsible for both balance and hearing, is formed and by 10 weeks, the external part of the ear (the pinna) has started to grow low down on the fetal head. The nostrils and upper lip can now be seen and inside the mouth there is a tiny tongue, which already has taste buds. Tooth buds for the future milk teeth are in place within the developing jawbones.

FUTURE LIMBS

Further miraculous changes are happening as your baby's limbs take shape. The folds of skin making up the limb buds condense and form cartilage, which will later develop into hard bones. These cartilaginous limb buds grow rapidly and wrists and paddle-shaped hands can soon be identified. The arms lengthen and by eight weeks, shoulders and elbows are present, making the upper limbs project forward. The webbed hands now develop separate fingers and by week 10, touch pads have appeared at the end of the stubby fingertips. The lower

2 x life size

	WEEKS
FIRST TRIMESTER	▶ 1
	▶ 2
	▶ 3
	▶ 4
	▶ 5
	▶ 6
	▶ 7
	▶ 8
	▶ 9
	▶ 10
	▶ 11
	▶ 12
SECOND TRIMESTER	▶ 13
	▶ 14
	▶ 15
	▶ 16
	▶ 17
	▶ 18
	▶ 19
	▶ 20
	▶ 21
	▶ 22
	▶ 23
	▶ 24
	▶ 25
	▶ 26
THIRD TRIMESTER	▶ 27
	▶ 28
	▶ 29
	▶ 30
	▶ 31
	▶ 32
	▶ 33
	▶ 34
	▶ 35
	▶ 36
	▶ 37
	▶ 38
	▶ 39
	▶ 40

◀ *A six-week-old embryo nested in the uterus.*

2 x life size

By the end of the 6th week, the embryo is 4mm in length and weighs less than 0.03oz (1g). By week 10, the fetus will measure 1¼in (30mm) from the top of its head to its bottom (crown to rump) and weigh 0.1oz (3–5g).

limb buds start to go through the same process, but the distinction between thighs, knees, calves, ankles, and toes progresses more slowly. Most of the muscles are now in place, and small, jerky movements can be seen on an ultrasound scan.

INSIDE THE BODY

Inside the body, the central neural tube is now differentiating into the brain and spinal cord. The nerve cells multiply rapidly, aided by support cells called glial cells, and migrate along pathways into the brain, where they connect with each other and become active. This is the beginning of the neural network that will later transmit messages from the brain to the body. The fetus has also developed some very basic sensory perceptions. It can respond to touch although it is still too early for you to be able to feel movements.

By week 10, the embryonic heart has developed into the definitive four-chambered heart. The two atria receive blood from the fetal circulation, while the ventricles pump blood out to the lungs and rest of the baby's body. Valves develop at the exit of all four chambers to ensure that the blood is always pumped in one direction and cannot leak back into the heart. The heart is beating at a rate of 180 beats per minute — twice the speed of your own heart.

Although the digestive system is developing rapidly, it will be some time before it is functioning properly. The stomach, liver, and spleen are all in place and the intestines grow so fast that loops are formed and for a time, some of these actually protrude through the baby's abdominal wall.

By the end of the embryonic period, the new fetus has all its major organs and body systems, although the brain and spinal cord will continue to develop

FETUS AT 10 WEEKS

The fetal intestines still protrude from the abdominal wall.

Shoulders and elbows develop and the arms project forward.

The webbed hands now develop fingers with touchpads.

THE AMNIOTIC SAC

The fetus continues to float within the amniotic sac, which is surrounded by an inner layer called the amnion and an outer layer called the chorion. These two layers are separated by a space (the extracoelomic cavity), which contains the yolk sac.

The small fingers of tissue called chorionic villi that sprout from the chorion are becoming concentrated in one circular area on the wall of the uterus; this will soon develop into the placenta. At this site, the villi are developing blood vessels and burrowing into the lining of the uterus, setting up their future access to your circulation.

Elsewhere, the chorionic villi are disappearing and the smooth chorion (known as the chorion laeve) is forming; this will fuse with the wall of the uterus in the second trimester, when the growing fetus has further distended the uterine cavity. The umbilical cord is now formed and blood is circulating through it, although the fetus is still receiving most nourishment from the yolk sac.

extracoelomic cavity

chorionic villi

umbilical cord

amnion

chorion

yolk sac

wall of uterus

throughout your pregnancy. During this critical period of structural development, the fetus is highly susceptible to the damaging effects of a variety of drugs, viruses, and environmental factors (*see* p.30). It is very rare for congenital fetal abnormalities to develop after this time.

YOUR CHANGING BODY

DURING THE NEXT FEW WEEKS, YOUR UTERUS WILL GROW SIGNIFICANTLY IN SIZE. BY EIGHT WEEKS IT IS THE SIZE OF A MEDIUM ORANGE AND BY 10 WEEKS THE SIZE OF A SMALL GRAPEFRUIT. HOWEVER, IT CANNOT BE FELT THROUGH YOUR ABDOMINAL WALL BECAUSE IT IS STILL BEHIND YOUR PUBIC BONE.

This growth in the uterus can only be achieved by increasing the blood flow to it. In the non-pregnant state the uterus receives about two percent of the total amount of blood that is pumped through the heart per minute (the cardiac output). Very early in pregnancy, this percentage increases dramatically and by the end of this trimester 25 percent of your cardiac output will be directed to the uterus to cope with the demands of the placenta and baby. This increase in cardiac output is mainly due to the volume of blood pumped with each heartbeat (the stroke volume) since your heart rate (the number of times the heart beats per minute) increases only slightly during pregnancy. The thick muscular walls of the heart are relaxed by pregnancy hormones and this allows the heart to increase the volume of blood it contains each time it fills (diastole) without having to increase the force with which it pumps the blood during contractions (systole). To ensure that your blood pressure does not become too high as a result of the rise in cardiac output and blood volume, the blood vessels throughout your body also develop an increased capacity to hold larger blood volumes — once again due to the increase in pregnancy hormones, especially progesterone. This is why your systolic blood pressure falls only slightly during pregnancy, but your diastolic blood pressure is markedly reduced, a change that occurs early in the first trimester and only returns to normal nonpregnant levels near to the time of delivery.

NOTICEABLE EFFECTS

As a result of these dramatic changes in your circulatory system, you will start to become aware of differences in the way your body is functioning. You will already have noticed that you need to urinate more frequently as a result of your kidneys working much harder to filter your blood more efficiently. If your breasts had not begun to change earlier, they will almost certainly be larger, heavier, and more tender now, because the milk ducts are already beginning to swell in preparation for lactation and the areola surrounding your nipples will be larger and darker in color. The sweat glands (called Montgomery's tubercles) in the areola, which look like little pimples around the nipples, have also enlarged and start to secrete a fluid to lubricate the nipples. This is one of the most reliable signs of a first pregnancy, but since they do not shrink completely after pregnancy this cannot be depended on as a diagnostic sign for subsequent pregnancies. An outer ring of lighter-colored tissue called the secondary areola starts to appear on the breasts, together with more visible veins, as a result of the increased blood flow.

DARKENING AREOLA *The area around the nipples becomes larger and darker in color.*

SPIDER NEVI *These tiny, spidery red lines on the skin are due to high levels of estrogen.*

CHANGES IN YOUR SKIN

One of the first things you may notice is that your skin is either more acne prone or drier than usual, due to your high progesterone levels. Many women also develop spidery red lines called spider nevi on their legs and across their upper chest. These are small blood vessels in the skin that have expanded due to the increased production of estrogen. They usually fade away after pregnancy and are nothing to be alarmed about. The blood supply to your skin has increased and because the veins are now much more dilated, you are better able to eliminate heat from your body surface. However annoying you may find your sudden intolerance of only moderately warm temperatures, this adaptation is essential because you need to be able to dispose of the rising heat that you generate from your increased metabolic rate and blood flow.

The skin of your genital area will start to darken and you will probably have noticed that your vaginal discharge has increased. This is due to the secretion of a watery substance which mixes with cells that are being shed from the vaginal walls. Normally this discharge is mucuslike and is usually clear or sometimes milky colored. It may stain your underwear but it should not be the source of any discomfort. If the discharge becomes yellow, develops an offensive odor, or causes you symptoms of itching or soreness, see your physician (*see* p.215).

HOW YOU MAY FEEL PHYSICALLY

SOME WOMEN SAIL THROUGH THE FIRST TRIMESTER FEELING NEITHER TIRED NOR SICK — INDEED SOME WILL NOT EVEN REALIZE THAT THEY ARE PREGNANT. FOR THE MAJORITY OF WOMEN, HOWEVER, THE FIRST THREE MONTHS ARE USUALLY DOMINATED BY UNPLEASANT SYMPTOMS — NAUSEA, VOMITING, AND EXHAUSTION.

No one can predict how you will feel during these early weeks of pregnancy because symptoms vary considerably from one woman to another and in each pregnancy that a woman has. Nor is there an accepted time for these common symptoms to start or finish. Some women feel exhausted from the time of the positive pregnancy test until they reach the second trimester, whereas others will only be troubled for a short time. Similarly, nausea may hit you hard and then disappear or be troublesome for many weeks.

MORNING SICKNESS

Morning sickness is, without doubt, the best known and most talked about side effect of early pregnancy — as many as 70 to 80 percent of all pregnant women will experience some degree of it. I have always thought it a poor description of the problem, since the reality is that many women are not physically sick, but they do feel nauseous. What is more, this feeling is rarely confined to the mornings — it can continue throughout the day or only be a problem in the evening. However, I do want to stress that it is also perfectly normal not to feel any nausea and if you happen to be one of these fortunate women, then count your lucky stars. Many women I meet in the early pregnancy clinic worry that

"...the reality is that many women are not physically sick, but they do feel very nauseous."

this is a warning sign that their pregnancy may be less robust or at greater risk of miscarriage. I promise you that you do not have to experience the misery of throwing up like clockwork every day in order to have a successful pregnancy.

No one has come up with the definitive answer as to why "morning sickness" or nausea occurs but there are several plausible theories. Like most baffling medical problems, nausea is probably the result of a combination of a number of different factors. One suggested cause is the high levels of the hormone human chorionic gonadotropin (HCG), which are present during the first trimester and then taper off at about 13 weeks. This would explain why nausea usually lifts between the 12th and 15th weeks of pregnancy, although some women continue to feel sick for much longer.

Another theory is that nausea is linked to low blood sugar levels, since it often occurs first thing in the morning after many hours without food, or at the end of the day when you may be tired and in need of rest and nourishment.

Another possible explanation is that the flood of progesterone in pregnancy relaxes the smooth muscles in the digestive tract and slows down the passage of food through it. As a result, the food you eat and the digestive acids that are produced to process it remain in your stomach for longer periods of time. This is why you may feel nauseous and may occasionally vomit as well.

Whatever the cause, I know from personal experience how distressing and uncomfortable, not to mention inconvenient, nausea can be while it lasts. Added to this, you may start to worry that your inability to keep any food or fluids down may be putting your baby at risk. I must reassure you that this is not

"...there is a wide spectrum of foods that women either crave or develop a violent aversion to in early pregnancy."

HOW TO RELIEVE MORNING SICKNESS

There is no magic cure, just a variety of remedies to try in different combinations to see which work for you. I often ask my patients about the individual remedies that helped them cope with their nausea and I have included some of their recommendations here, too.

▶ **Eat small, easily digestible meals** at regular intervals rather than just one or two large meals during the day. Dry toast, plain cookies, rice cakes, and savory crackers are

good standbys when you cannot stomach anything else. Cut down on the snacks when you start eating regular meals again or you will soon find that you are putting on unwanted pounds.

▶ **Stay clear of fatty food** because it can be particularly troublesome.

▶ **Bland foods** such as dry cornflakes and other cereals are a well-tolerated favorite and have the advantage that they are fortified with iron and vitamins. They are the case. However little you are eating or drinking, your baby will getting the best part, including everything it needs to develop normally. You may be feeling terrible, but your baby is fine.

MORE SERIOUS VOMITING

Occasionally, women vomit regularly and for such long periods of time (by which I mean weeks, not days) that they become dehydrated and weak because they cannot keep down fluids or food of any sort. This condition is called hyperemesis gravidarum and fortunately occurs only in about 1 in 200–500 pregnancies. However, if you do develop this problem, you will probably need to be admitted to the hospital briefly in order to have an intravenous drip give you the necessary fluids, glucose, and minerals to help you rehydrate and stop you feeling so weak and ill. If you do need to be hospitalized you will probably be advised to take some anti-vomiting medication (called antiemetics), either in pill form or via your IV drip. These drugs are known to be safe in early pregnancy and will not have any harmful effect on your baby. Ever since the thalidomide disaster during the 1950s and '60s, doctors are extremely careful about what they prescribe to pregnant women to combat nausea. The antiemetic drugs that are now used have an excellent safety record, so do take them if you are advised to, because they will help you through a difficult period.

PEPPERMINT TEA *The refreshing taste of peppermint tea seems to combat the metallic taste that often accompanies feelings of nausea.*

a good substitute for a meal when you can't cope with anything else.

▶ **If you feel particularly nauseous** when you wake up in the morning, try nibbling on plain crackers before you get out of bed.

▶ **Some women swear by acupressure wristbands** (normally used to prevent travel sickness). These work by pressing on the acupuncture point known as P6.

▶ **Try taking small amounts of ginger** either as ginger ale, ginger tea, ginger capsules, crystalized or root ginger, or gingersnaps and other ginger cookies.

▶ **Herbal teas** are also regularly recommended by my patients, especially peppermint tea, which has a refreshing taste that helps combat the horrible metallic taste in the mouth that frequently develops when you feel nauseous. For the same reason, brushing your teeth at regular intervals during the day can also be a source of relief.

CATNAPPING *No one knows why women feel incredibly tired in the early weeks of pregnancy, but while you feel this way, take a nap whenever the chance presents itself.*

FOOD AVERSIONS AND CRAVINGS

These often go hand in hand with morning sickness, although they can also occur on their own. Again, we don't know why they happen, nor why there is such a wide spectrum of foods that women either crave or develop a violent aversion to in early pregnancy. I remember how puzzled I felt when I was suddenly unable to drink my morning cup of coffee, and when orange juice seemed so heavy that I found it undrinkable. The smell of roasted meat of any color was repellent to me and, although a cheese lover since childhood, I could not look the smallest morsel in the eye without feeling seriously nauseous. I worried that the only sustenance I was offering my babies was grapefruit juice diluted with seltzer, together with the occasional piece of bread and butter accompanied by an apple or a tinned asparagus spear. Mind you, compared to some of the stories about I have heard about the food cravings of pregnant mothers, the oddities I've just described seem quite mild.

Cravings for salty food such as pickles at strange times of the day or night are also common. Perhaps this is our bodies' way of telling us that we need salt, but no one really knows. Similarly, we have all heard about pregnant women who develop a pica: a desire to eat an unusual substance such as chalk, coal, or grass or to smell substances such as mothballs. I have no practical experience of these, but I can reassure you that I know of no data to suggest that they have ever caused any harm to a pregnancy. There are only a few foods in pregnancy — such as liver and unpasteurized cheeses for example — that are potentially dangerous and you will find more information about these in the diet section of this book (*see* p.50).

FEELING TIRED

I suspect that the time-honored phrase "fatigue is the female condition" was first coined to describe a woman in early pregnancy. The feelings of exhaustion in the first few months can be quite overwhelming. I can remember finishing an ordinary day at work, reaching home, and being just about capable of putting my key in the lock before collapsing in a heap at the bottom of the stairs. There was nothing wrong; I simply couldn't overcome my exhaustion and climb to the top. No one has so far been able to give a good scientific explanation for this fatigue, although theories abound. Some doctors believe that it is caused by the soporific effects of the high levels of progesterone, while others attribute it to the huge physiological changes that are taking place — the raised cardiac output, blood volume and oxygen consumption. The speed at which the tiny embryo is growing is another explanation, but you may find it difficult to understand how a baby that is small enough to fit into the palm of your closed hand can bring about such a dramatic change in your energy levels.

Like every experience in pregnancy, fatigue passes, but I am giving it a special mention here because it often raises concerns in partners and other family members. They see a woman who is usually full of energy appearing limp and exhausted and, since fatigue is so often equated with illness, they may be worried. Rest assured that after a couple of months of needing extra sleep and catnaps, fatigue lifts, so for the time being just go along with what your body is telling you to do.

"The feelings of exhaustion that many women experience in the first few months can be quite overwhelming."

YOUR EMOTIONAL RESPONSE

IF YOU ARE SUFFERING FROM WILD FLUCTUATIONS IN MOOD, THESE ARE UNDOUBTEDLY THE RESULT OF MAJOR HORMONAL CHANGES OCCURRING IN EARLY PREGNANCY. ONE MINUTE YOU MAY BE TALKING EXCITEDLY ABOUT THE FUTURE, AND A FEW MINUTES LATER YOU FIND YOURSELF WEEPING LIKE AN OVERFLOWING BATHTUB ABOUT SOME TRIVIAL ISSUE.

You may also find yourself verbally lashing out at a harmless comment your partner makes and accusing him of not understanding how you are feeling. Since you yourself may not know how you are feeling, or why you are so emotionally fragile, you can recognize how difficult it is for him at this time. The only practical thing to do is talk to him about how confused you feel and reassure him (and yourself) that you have not undergone a permanent character change. Although your mood swings can be very intense, leaving you feeling helpless and out of control, keep in mind that they are temporary and just one of the many side effects of a completely normal pregnancy.

You may also be feeling anxious about the future, the birth and your ability to be a good parent. However well you are adjusting to the important changes that this new baby will bring to your life, when you are feeling tired and nauseous you may still be daunted by the prospect of it.

COMMON CONCERNS

THE MOST COMMON CONCERN AT THIS STAGE OF PREGNANCY IS ABOUT MISCARRIAGE, THE MAJORITY OF WHICH OCCUR IN THE EARLY WEEKS. BUT NOT EVERY WORRYING SYMPTOM MEANS MISCARRIAGE IS INEVITABLE AND WITH EACH WEEK THAT PASSES YOUR PREGNANCY IS BECOMING MORE SECURE.

As many as one in three women have some sort of bleeding during the first trimester ranging from brown to bright red spotting to large blood clots. In the majority of cases, it settles down and does not mean that there is any serious problem, since most women go on to have healthy babies. Having said that, I do understand how alarming bleeding can be.

As a safety measure you may be offered an early ultrasound scan, during which it may be possible to identify the pregnancy sac in the uterine cavity and the fetal pole and yolk sac developing. This will be very reassuring. Some women are frightened that a scan may increase the bleeding (it will not) or confirm their fears that the pregnancy has been lost. These feelings are understandable, but it is always the best plan to establish what is happening at the earliest opportunity.

I will never forget how distressed I felt when I experienced a heavy bleed at eight weeks into my pregnancy. I was sitting quietly in a meeting of a large number of medical colleagues and suddenly, without warning, I realized that my seat was warm and wet and that I was bleeding. There was no pain and no forewarning — it just happened. I immediately assumed that I was miscarrying

DECLINING RISK OF MISCARRIAGE

▶ **Miscarriage is the most common complication** of pregnancy and by definition can occur at any gestational age up until 20 weeks (see p.430). However, the vast majority of miscarriages occur very early on, even before the pregnancy can be recognized on an ultrasound scan.
▶ **If you are six weeks from your last menstrual period**, the risk of miscarriage has fallen to about 15 percent or 1 in 6 pregnancies. At this stage it is usually possible to see the yolk sac in your uterus and the fetal pole inside it on an ultrasound scan.
▶ **By eight weeks, the risk is much smaller** and, if a fetal heartbeat can be seen on the scan at this stage, your risk of miscarriage has fallen to five percent. Looked at more positively, this means that 95 percent of pregnant women with a fetal heartbeat at eight weeks can expect their pregnancy to continue and to take home a baby at the end of it.
▶ **After 12 weeks**, the risk of miscarriage is no more than one percent. So the message here is that, as pregnancy progresses, the risk of miscarriage falls dramatically and, by the time you reach the end of this trimester you are very unlikely to experience this distressing event.

"Bleeding in early pregnancy is always worth investigating and, even if it is heavy, does not necessarily mean that the pregnancy is over."

and after leaving the meeting as discreetly as possible for a woman with blood all over her clothes, I went home and cried. I nearly cancelled my scan the next day but my husband (who is always practical and optimistic) persuaded me to go and find out exactly what the situation was. Happily, the scan showed two little embryos who appeared quite unruffled by the bleeding of the day before. Bleeding in early pregnancy is always worth investigating and, even if it is heavy, does not necessarily mean that the pregnancy is over.

ABDOMINAL PAIN

Most pregnant women experience some abdominal aches and pains in early pregnancy. They are always a source of worry but do try to remember that most of the time they simply reflect that enormous changes are occurring in your pelvic organs, particularly your growing uterus. All this growth occurs at the end of the same ligaments and muscles that were attached to your uterus in its non-pregnant state. So it is hardly surprising that the inevitable stretching of these ligaments results in some twinges and discomfort.

On the other hand, if your abdominal pains become constant or very severe, tell your doctor immediately, because they may be a sign that you have an ectopic pregnancy, which needs to be investigated and treated as a matter of urgency. Most ectopic pregnancies declare themselves during this stage of pregnancy and if you develop severe abdominal pain, your doctor will arrange for you to have an ultrasound scan to see if the pregnancy sac is in the uterine cavity. If there is no sac in the uterus, you will need further investigative tests, which may include a laparoscopic examination under general anesthetic.

FEELING DIZZY

Dizziness and feeling faint or light-headed are also very common symptoms in early pregnancy. Most of the time these symptoms are harmless, but if they keep occurring they can become a cause for concern. If you feel faint or light-headed while sitting down, one of the most likely explanations is that your blood sugar levels are low. This is quite common in the first trimester when many women find it very difficult to eat properly; you can solve it by making sure that you keep a supply of small carbohydrate snacks with you and eating them regularly.

If you find yourself feeling faint or dizzy when you stand up suddenly or have been standing up for a long period, this is because there is insufficient blood reaching your brain at that moment. Your blood supply has increased, but when you are upright, it pools in your legs and feet. When you stand up suddenly, the blood rushes into your legs and the supply to your brain is reduced.

THINGS TO CONSIDER

AT THIS STAGE OF PREGNANCY THERE ARE RARELY ANY PRESSING CONCERNS — JUST A PERIOD OF GENTLE ADJUSTMENT TO THE IDEA THAT YOU ARE CARRYING A NEW LIFE AND A FEW STRATEGIES THAT WILL HELP LAY A GOOD FOUNDATION FOR THE MONTHS AHEAD.

VISITING THE DENTIST

There are several good reasons why you should visit a dentist regularly over the next 40 weeks. In pregnancy your gums become softened by pregnancy hormones and are more likely to bleed and become infected. Thorough toothbrushing and flossing, together with cleaning and plaque removal by your dentist, will help you limit your chances of tooth decay and gum disease during your pregnancy.

Your dentist will always try to avoid performing any tooth or jaw X-rays when you are pregnant, but if your dental problems are serious and causing you pain, let me reassure you that your mouth is a long way (in X-ray terms) from your tiny embryo, and that there are lots of gadgets to help ensure that the rays do not spread anywhere else. Local anesthetics are also perfectly safe, so you do not have to endure dental procedures without pain relief.

A PREGNANCY BRA

"You will love this new baby every bit as passionately as you do your other child."

Your breasts will have begun to increase in size and, for some women, may have become very uncomfortable, even painful. Now is the time to invest in a couple of good pregnancy bras because sagging breasts will be the source of physical discomfort and backache, not to mention distress at your own appearance. I remember thinking that there was no point in buying a new set of bras at this stage, because I wrongly assumed that I would grow out of them in a month or so and then need to invest in another set. The reality is that your breasts enlarge during the first three months of pregnancy and then do not change much until after the birth when you start breastfeeding at which point you need a completely different type of breast support. The best way to be sure that you buy the right type of bra is to find a department store that has salespeople with particular expertise in fitting a pregnany bra. A pregnancy bra has good support all the way around, including the underarm and back sections. Underwired bras are not a good option; the wiring will dig into your breasts and may harm the later development of breast milk ducts. If your breasts were full before you became pregnant, you may want to wear a bra to bed at night.

Women who have had cosmetic breast implants may be feeling especially tender now that their own breast tissue is growing. The skin over the breasts may feel taut and uncomfortable, too. You may be wondering if you will be able to breastfeed, and this largely depends on where the incisions were made to insert your implants. If cuts were made around the areola of your nipples, milk ducts and nerves that are essential to breastfeeding may have been severed. If incisions were made under your breasts, there is a good chance these are unaffected.

MATERNITY BRA *It is never too early to be fitted for a good supportive bra since your breast size increases right from the start but then will not change much more during the pregnancy.*

TELLING THE REST OF THE FAMILY

If you have other children, you may well be anxious about how this new pregnancy will affect them and how they will react to their new sibling. There is no doubt that, while many older children are thrilled to learn that there will be a new baby arriving in the family, some younger children will not be so delighted. At this early stage I think it is probably best to wait a little while before telling your existing children that you are pregnant.

However, if you have experienced early pregnancy problems and needed to go into the hospital to resolve them, young toddlers may be extremely upset by your sudden disappearance and "illness." In the world of a young child, mommies are meant to be reliably available, rock-solid figures and disappearing at short notice can be disturbing. If you find yourself in this situation, my advice is to explain that you have been unwell and be as honest as possible. The details you share with your children will depend on their ability to comprehend, but whatever you say to them, emphasize that you are going to get better quickly.

HOW CAN I LOVE ANOTHER CHILD?

Some women worry that they will not love their new baby as much as their existing children and they can't imagine how this new addition will fit into their family set-up. I can assure you that such thoughts will seem ridiculous in a year's time. You will look back and not be able to imagine what life was like before this birth and love this baby every bit as passionately as you do your other child.

WEEKS 10–13
THE DEVELOPING BABY

THE FETAL STAGE HAS BEGUN AND ALL OF YOUR BABY'S VITAL BODY ORGANS ARE NOW IN PLACE. FROM THIS TIME ONWARD, YOUR BABY'S DEVELOPMENT WILL BE CONCERNED ENTIRELY WITH THE GROWTH AND MATURATION OF THESE MAJOR BODY SYSTEMS.

During the next few weeks the fetus will grow rapidly and steadily, at a rate of about ½in (10mm) per week and its weight will increase five-fold. If you have an ultrasound scan at this stage, you will be amazed by how easy it is to recognize the various parts of your baby's body and that it is already starting to look more and more like a tiny human.

The fetal head is still relatively large, accounting for approximately one-third of its length from the crown of its head to its bottom (the crown rump length or CRL), but the growth of the rest of the body is starting to catch up. The head is now supported by a recognizable neck and the features on the face are better defined, since all of the facial bones are completely formed. The forehead is still high, but there is now an obvious jaw line and chin and the nose is more pronounced; 32 tooth buds are in place. The eyes are fully developed and although still quite widely spaced, now appear closer to the front of the face. The eyelids are still developing and remain tightly closed. The external ears (pinna) become more clearly visible as they enlarge and assume their adult shape. They have now moved from the base of the skull to a higher position on the sides of the fetal head. The inner ear and middle ear are completely developed. The fetal skin is still thin, transparent and permeable to the amniotic fluid and a layer of fine hairs now covers most of the body.

YOUR BABY'S LIMBS

The fetal body appears much straighter than it was just a few weeks ago. The limbs are growing rapidly, and shoulders, elbows, wrists, and fingers can be clearly seen. The lower limbs are developing too, but their growth will be at a slower pace for some time. The fingers and toes are separating into individual digits and tiny nails are now present. At about 12 weeks, hard bone centers develop in the cartilage of the fetal bones, a process called ossification. As calcium continues to be deposited in these centers, the skeleton will gradually calcify and harden. This formation of hard bone continues long after your baby

◀ *By 10 weeks, the fetus is already a recognizable human being.*

WEEKS

FIRST TRIMESTER ▶ 1
▶ 2
▶ 3
▶ 4
▶ 5
▶ 6
▶ 7
▶ 8
▶ 9
▶ 10
▶ 11
life size ▶ 12
▶ 13
SECOND TRIMESTER ▶ 14
▶ 15
▶ 16
▶ 17
▶ 18
▶ 19
▶ 20
▶ 21
▶ 22
▶ 23
▶ 24
▶ 25
▶ 26
THIRD TRIMESTER ▶ 27
▶ 28
▶ 29
▶ 30
▶ 31
▶ 32
▶ 33
▶ 34
▶ 35
▶ 36
▶ 37
▶ 38
▶ 39
▶ 40

"The fetus is now moving around quite vigorously inside the amniotic sac, producing small jerky movements ..."

FETUS AT 10 WEEKS

A 2-D ultrasound reveals the fetus free-floating in the black circle of the amniotic sac. The faint white line is the sac's outer layer, called the chorion, which is still separate from the uterine wall.

is born and will not be complete until adolescence. The fetus is now moving around quite vigorously inside the amniotic sac, producing small jerky movements of its body and upper limbs rather than simply free-floating. However, you are still quite unaware of its movements. The muscles of the chest wall are starting to develop and practice breathing movements along with the occasional hiccup and swallowing movements can be seen on the ultrasound. Even more excitingly, your baby is starting to make reflex responses to external stimuli. For example, if your abdomen is prodded, the baby will try to wriggle away from the intruding finger. If a hand or foot happens to brush against the baby's mouth, the lips purse and the forehead may wrinkle — this is the very first sign of the future sucking reflex. Similarly, if the eyelids are touched, an early blinking reflex can be seen. However, these are only reflex movements and it is generally accepted that the fetus does not have the ability to feel pain until about 24 weeks of gestation.

INSIDE YOUR BABY'S BODY

Inside your baby's body, the ovaries or testes have fully formed, and the external genitalia are developing from a small swelling between the fetal legs into a recognizable penis or clitoris. In theory, an experienced ultrasound scanner may be able to determine the sex of your baby at this early stage, but if you rely on the diagnosis now you might be in for a surprise at the birth.

The heart is now fully functional and pumping blood to all parts of the fetal body at a rate of 110–160 beats per minute. This is slower than it was a few weeks ago and will continue to slow down as the fetus becomes more mature. It may be possible to hear the heartbeat with a sonicaid machine placed over your lower abdomen, just above the pubic bone. This device uses Doppler ultrasound waves and is completely harmless to your baby. During the early weeks of pregnancy the embryo's blood cells were manufactured in the yolk sac, but by 12 to 13 weeks the sac is fast disappearing, and this essential task is taken over by the fetal liver. Later in the second trimester, the fetal bone marrow and spleen will make important contributions to the production of blood.

The chest and abdomen are gradually straightening out, and the intestines, which a few weeks ago were coiled around the umbilical cord in the amniotic cavity, are now firmly behind a closed abdominal wall. The fetal stomach is now linked to the mouth and the intestines — an important development because the fetus now begins to swallow small amounts of amniotic fluid. This will later be excreted as urine when the fetal kidneys start to function.

The volume of amniotic fluid at 12 weeks is about 30ml — less than 6 teaspoons. The amniotic fluid has many protective functions not the least of which is to provide a sterile swimming pool maintained at a constant temperature (slightly higher than your own) in which the baby moves freely. Later on, waste products excreted in the fetal urine will be absorbed from the amniotic fluid back into the maternal blood by passing through the placental membranes.

life size

At 10 weeks, the fetus measures 1¼in (30mm) and weighs 0.1oz (3–5g). By the 13th week, it is 3in (80mm) long and weighs about 1oz (25g).

FETUS AT 13 WEEKS *The fetal arms have developed rapidly — elbows, wrists and hands with fingers are clearly visible on this three-dimensional ultrasound. The fetus makes reflex responses when its hand brushes its face.*

THE PLACENTA

YOUR FULLY-FORMED PLACENTA IS NOW YOUR BABY'S LIFE SUPPORT SYSTEM. IT IS A COMPLEX
PIECE OF BIOLOGICAL ENGINEERING THAT SUPPLIES ALL YOUR BABY'S NEEDS VIA YOUR
BLOODSTREAM, YET ALSO ACTS AS A BARRIER AGAINST INFECTIONS AND HARMFUL SUBSTANCES.

The placenta has been developing rapidly and by 12-13 weeks its structure is complete, although it will continue to grow in size throughout the remainder of pregnancy. By the end of the first trimester, it is fully established and performs a variety of essential functions for the rest of the pregnancy. In essence, the placenta is a sophisticated filtering system that allows your baby to breathe, eat and excrete. It also acts as a protective barrier that shields your baby from most infections and potentially harmful substances. In addition, the placenta is responsible for producing increasing quantities of hormones that help to maintain the pregnancy and prepare your body for birth and breastfeeding.

All of this placental activity uses up a considerable amount of energy, and the metabolic rate of the placenta is similar to that of the adult liver or kidney. Furthermore, the successful functioning of the placenta depends upon a good maternal blood supply to the spiral arteries in the uterine wall. This is why smoking and disorders such as high blood pressure and preeclampsia (see p.425) that reduce the blood flow to the placenta, have a dramatic effect on its function and on the growth of the fetus.

A NETWORK OF TREES
The placenta is best understood by imagining a network of branching trees made up of about 200 trunks. These divide into limbs, branches, and twigs, which are covered with an extensive network of chorionic villi, the majority of which float in a lake of maternal blood called the intervillous space. Some of the longest branches grow down into the decidual lining of the uterus. A few travel even further, penetrating the deeper layers of the uterine wall to access the maternal blood vessels. These anchoring villi help to form the lower boundary of the intervillous space.

THE UMBILICAL CORD
The umbilical cord is now fully formed and consists of three blood vessels: a single large vein, which carries oxygen-rich blood and nutrients from the uterus to the fetus, via the placenta; and two small arteries, which transport waste products and oxygen-depleted blood from the fetus back to the mother for recharging. The three vessels are coiled like a spring to ensure that the growing baby can move around easily within the amniotic sac and are covered by a thick protective coating called Wharton's jelly.

Doppler scan of the umbilical cord shows blood flow via a single large vein (blue) and two arteries (red).

THE LIFE SUPPORT SYSTEM

The extensive network of chorionic villi are bathed in maternal blood inside the intervillous space. Although nutrients and waste products can pass freely through the chorion (a thin membrane that surrounds the villi), the chorion acts as a barrier, too, protecting the fetus from infections and environmental poisons.

Magnified images of the placental surface reveal a forest of chorionic villi.

BABY

umbilical cord connecting the fetus to the placenta

chorionic plate — blood hits this upper boundary and flows downwards

chorionic villi containing placental blood vessels, which are bathed in maternal blood

intervillous space containing a pool of maternal blood

chorion — this protective membrane surrounds the villi

maternal vein carries away deoxygenated blood and waste products

decidual plate — the lower boundary of the intervillous space

maternal spiral artery — oxygenated blood spurts into the intervillous space

uterine muscle

MOTHER

TRANSFER OF OXYGEN AND NUTRIENTS

With every beat of your heart, blood from your arteries in the lower boundary of the intervillous space (the decidual plate) spurts into the intervillous space like a fountain. The blood hits the upper boundary (the chorionic plate) and then flows downwards bathing the chorionic villi before seeping away through the veins in the decidual plate. The large number of blood vessels in the chorionic villi and the relatively sluggish flow of your blood through the intervillous space gives ample opportunity for oxygen and nutrients to pass to the fetal circulation. At the same time, carbon dioxide and other waste products from the fetus are transferred into the intervillous space and carried away in your blood.

SEPARATE CIRCULATIONS

Despite their very close proximity in the intervillous space, the maternal and fetal circulations remain entirely separate and never mix. They are separated by a thin membrane, in places as little as one cell thick. This protects the developing fetus from infections and other damaging substances such as pesticides, alcohol, and some drugs. Furthermore, any bleeding in pregnancy usually originates from the pool of maternal blood, not from the fetus. The fetal circulation is protected, even if the placenta is damaged.

YOUR CHANGING BODY

BY THE END OF THIS TRIMESTER YOUR WAIST WILL PROBABLY HAVE THICKENED SLIGHTLY AND YOU WILL HAVE PUT ON A LITTLE WEIGHT. YOUR TUMMY MAY BE STARTING TO SWELL TOO, BUT THIS IS MORE LIKELY TO BE DUE TO MILD BLOATING AND SLUGGISH BOWELS THAN TO YOUR GROWING BABY.

"By 12 weeks your uterus will be the size of a large grapefruit... by 14 weeks it will be the size of a small melon."

At 10 weeks the size of your uterus will be equivalent to a large orange. By 12 weeks it will have reached the size of a large grapefruit and by 14 weeks it will be the size of a small melon. Sometime between 11 and 14 weeks, depending on your body weight and the size of your pelvis, your doctor will be able to feel the enlarging uterus through your abdominal wall just above the pubic bone. Of course, if you are expecting twins or triplets, the enlarging uterus rises above the pelvic brim at an earlier stage. Indeed, before the days of ultrasound scans, this was one of the first signs of a multiple pregnancy.

Your breasts will have continued to develop under the influence of progesterone and several other hormones, the production of which has been steadily increasing during this first trimester. Some previously small-chested women are alarmed to find themselves going up three or four bra cup sizes in the first 12 weeks of pregnancy. If this is the case with you, don't panic, you will probably find that your breasts stop filling out fairly soon and then will only increase a little more in the last month or so before the birth. If your breasts were full before you became pregnant, you may want to wear a bra to bed at night now for support. If they feel very tender, try using a soothing massage cream on the breast tissue and nipples.

INCREASING YOUR OXYGEN SUPPLY

Many women notice that they occasionally feel breathless by the end of the first trimester; a symptom that sometimes continues throughout pregnancy. The major changes that have occurred in your heart and blood vessels mean that almost every organ in your body is now working much harder, demanding a dramatic increase in your oxygen supplies. Your oxygen requirements rise by 15–20 percent during pregnancy, and half of this is used by the growing uterus, placenta, and baby. The other half is needed to fuel the work of the heart and kidneys, although some is directed to the respiratory muscles, breasts, and skin.

To achieve this extra supply, your lungs need to make a special adaptation to take in an increased volume of oxygen and expel an increased amount of waste carbon dioxide with every breath that you take. This is called the tidal volume of air and it increases by 40 percent during pregnancy. When you exercise or exert yourself, your tidal volume and oxygen consumption increase way above their pre-pregnancy levels. Although the exact mechanisms for achieving this are not understood, we do know that progesterone makes an important contribution. It effectively allows your lungs to hyperventilate or overbreathe and that is why you experience feelings of breathlessness.

HOW YOU MAY FEEL PHYSICALLY

BY THE END OF THE FIRST TRIMESTER, YOU ARE LIKELY TO BE GETTING BACK INTO YOUR STRIDE AND FEELING MORE LIKE YOUR OLD SELF. HOWEVER, EVERY PREGNANCY IS DIFFERENT — THERE ARE NO HARD AND FAST RULES GOVERNING HOW YOU SHOULD OR SHOULD NOT FEEL.

For many women, the nausea and vomiting that often dominate the first 10 weeks of pregnancy has started to settle down, but for the less fortunate it may persist for longer. No one can predict a pregnancy experience exactly. However, as the nausea improves, you will be able to start eating normally once again, and if you have been worrying about how little nourishment you and your baby have been receiving, this is a welcome change.

Your uterus has already enlarged considerably, and as the ligaments attaching it to the sides of your pelvis have been stretched, it is quite normal to experience the odd twinge or muscular ache. Of course, if the pain continues or becomes severe, seek advice from your doctor as soon as possible. Now that the uterus is moving up into the abdominal cavity, there should be less pressure on your bladder, giving you some respite from the constant calls to urinate.

You may still be experiencing bouts of severe tiredness, but in general, the complete exhaustion characteristic of the first 10 weeks of pregnancy is beginning to lift and you should be feeling more energetic. Doubtless there will still be days when you feel dreadful but these are becoming less frequent now, and after a bad day you will be pleasantly surprised at how quickly you are able to bounce back. Indeed, some women feel physically exhilarated at this stage in pregnancy. Whatever is the case for you, take this period of transition at your own pace and aim to deal with life one day at a time.

"...after a bad day you will be pleasantly surprised at how quickly you are able to bounce back."

YOUR EMOTIONAL RESPONSE

IF YOU HAVE BEEN TROUBLED BY MOOD SWINGS, THESE ARE LIKELY TO BE SETTLING DOWN NOW THAT YOU HAVE HAD TIME TO MAKE SOME PHYSICAL AND MENTAL ADJUSTMENTS TO BEING PREGNANT. THAT SAID, THERE MAY STILL BE TIMES WHEN YOU FEEL INEXPLICABLY ANXIOUS OR IRRITABLE.

Just getting to the end of the first trimester eliminates an important source of worry because from now onwards you are extremely unlikely to suffer a miscarriage or later pregnancy loss. The reality is that the vast majority of miscarriages have occurred well before 10 weeks of gestation. After 12 weeks, the risk of losing a pregnancy is no more than one percent.

Many women tell me this was the point in their pregnancy when their partner first started to come to terms with the idea that he was going to become a father, and that there was going to be a baby in the house in the not too distant future. Even if his reaction is not exactly what you had hoped for, it is a relief that someone else is at least sharing the realization of what being pregnant is all about. Up until now, there have probably been days when it has been difficult to believe that you are pregnant but from now on, there will be no doubt in your mind, particularly after your prenatal visit and having enjoyed the excitement of seeing your tiny baby on an ultrasound scan for the first time (*see* p.124). Like many other important things in life, dealing with certainty is much easier than dealing with uncertainty.

Some women are able to relate to their unborn baby from a very early stage in the pregnancy, whereas others find it virtually impossible until much later in pregnancy, particularly when it is a first pregnancy. I want to say here that there is nothing odd about talking to your baby and generally including this new person in your everyday life, if that feels right for you. Nor is it odd if you cannot begin to imagine that the tiny fetus growing inside you is going to develop into a real human being. What you do and how you feel is in no way an indication of how good or bad a mother you will turn out to be; it is just another example of how individual we human beings are.

"...this may be the point when your partner first starts to come to terms with the idea that he is going to be a father."

TELLING PEOPLE YOUR NEWS

Now that you feel more secure about your pregnancy and no doubt convinced that everyone around you must have noticed that you are beginning to change shape, you will probably decide to tell people that you are pregnant. Sharing your news with friends and family is usually a cause for celebration although inevitably there will be at least one person for whom the subject of pregnancy is difficult. Only you can know who to tell and how to handle the situation but it is worth remembering that, a bit like deciding on a guest list for a wedding, there may always be someone who feels left out or upset by your news.

This is a good point to refer back to the section on work and maternity rights (*see* pp.58–63) because this is a subject that you should start thinking about sooner rather than later. You need to be clearly aware of your employment rights before you share your news with your boss or head of personnel.

EXCITING NEWS *Most women begin to feel more secure about their pregnancy as they come to the end of the first trimester — and are ready to share their news.*

YOUR PRENATAL CARE

YOUR FIRST PROPER PRENATAL VISIT WILL PROBABLY TAKE PLACE DURING THESE WEEKS. THE PURPOSE OF THIS VISIT IS TO IDENTIFY POTENTIAL PROBLEMS AND CREATE A SET OF INDIVIDUAL PRENATAL MEDICAL CASE NOTES THAT DETAIL ALL YOUR CURRENT AND PAST MEDICAL HISTORY.

For your first prenatal visit, you will need to set aside a couple of hours during which you will be asked a large number of detailed questions about your general health and your previous medical and gynecological history. Your responses will form the basis of your medical notes. This visit provides an opportunity to discuss your prenatal care with midwives and doctors and make arrangements for any tests that you may wish to have performed (*see* pp.134–43). Some maternity care providers suggest that you carry your own notes for the duration of your pregnancy so that you always have them to hand wherever and whenever you may need medical or midwifery assistance. For the majority of pregnant women, these notes will record the fact that you are at low risk of any complications and can be reassured of a trouble-free pregnancy.

During your visit, it is very important that you discuss every aspect of your medical history and social circumstances with your maternity caregivers, so do try to answer these questions as openly and fully as possible.

YOUR PREVIOUS PREGNANCIES

Your past obstetric history (if any) is important because the outcome of previous pregnancies and any problems that you may have had will help your caregivers assess whether you can be classified as low risk or high risk in your current pregnancy. This will help determine the type of prenatal care you receive. For every past pregnancy you will be asked about the gestation in weeks at the time of delivery, the weight of your baby, whether the labor was spontaneous or induced, the method of delivery and any complications that arose prenatally, during the delivery, and postnatally. If your previous pregnancy was complicated and you were cared for at another hospital, your midwife and doctor may ask that hospital for a detailed summary of your notes.

Some women feel sensitive about a previous termination of pregnancy and would prefer not to have this information recorded in their hand-held notes,

QUESTIONS AT YOUR FIRST PRENATAL VISIT

The following list is not exhaustive but should give you a feel for the sort of information that your maternity caregivers need to know.

▶ **What is the date of your last period?** Your Estimated Date of Delivery (EDD) will be calculated according to this date (see p.79) so try to work it out before your visit.

▶ **Have you had problems becoming pregnant and if so, how was this pregnancy achieved?** Assisted fertility treatments such as IVF increase the chances of a multiple pregnancy, which needs specialist care.

▶ **Have you had any problems in this pregnancy so far?** This includes major concerns such as bleeding and abdominal pain, but you should also mention minor problems such as vaginal discharge. Your caregiver can then arrange for you to have appropriate investigations and treatment.

▶ **Do you smoke cigarettes or use recreational drugs?** If you haven't managed to give these up yet, this is an opportunity to ask for help to do so.

▶ **Do you have a medical illness?** If you have an illness such as diabetes, asthma, high blood pressure, thrombosis (blood clots), kidney or heart disease, you may need to see a specialist doctor during your pregnancy and the type and dosage of drugs that you are taking may need to be altered.

▶ **Are you taking any medications?** Do make sure that you mention any medicines and preparations that you are taking whether they are prescription drugs, over-the-counter medicines or complementary remedies.

▶ **Do you suffer from any allergies?** It is important to record any allergies such as hay fever, asthma as well as any allergic response you may have to medications, foods, adhesive bandages, and iodine.

▶ **Have you ever suffered from a psychiatric illness?** You may feel that this is an intrusive question, but pregnancy can have a profound effect on some psychiatric disorders. It is important that you discuss any problems that you may have had in the past, so that your caregivers can help you minimize future problems. Postpartum depression, for example, is very likely to recur but it can be treated effectively if it is recognized which theoretically could be picked up and read by anyone. You may have similar concerns if you had assisted fertility treatment to achieve this pregnancy (believing this to be a private matter between you and your partner). I can understand these feelings, but you do need to discuss every part of your history at the prenatal visit to ensure that potential future complications can be identified and prevented. However, you can ask that this information is not recorded in your hand-held notes, and your caregiver will honor this request.

YOUR FIRST PHYSICAL EXAMINATION

How detailed a physical examination you undergo at your prenatal visit varies between hospitals and local doctor's offices. When I was a junior trainee in obstetrics, a thorough physical examination of the heart, lungs, abdomen, legs, skin, and breasts, together with a routine pelvic and vaginal examination and

quickly. The best way to do this is to identify those women who are at risk before it develops.

▶ **Have you undergone abdominal or pelvic surgery?** Previous surgical procedures may determine how you should deliver your baby. An elective Caesarean section is sometimes the preferred option if you have had, for example, surgery to remove a fibroid from your uterus. On the other hand, a vaginal delivery may be a better option if you have lesions or scar tissue as a result of a gastrointestinal or bladder operation. Always mention previous surgery, however minor you think it may have been.

▶ **Have you ever had a blood transfusion?** A previous blood transfusion will alert your caregivers to the possibility that you may have developed atypical antibodies in your blood or be at risk of a blood-borne infection such as hepatitis or HIV. These are extremely unlikely complications nowadays because transfusion services here are carefully monitored and are now considered among the safest in the world. However, this may not be the case if you have had a transfusion in some other countries.

▶ **Do you have a history of infection, particularly a sexually transmitted disease?** All maternity caregivers will screen you for immunity to rubella and possible infection with syphilis. You may also be offered screening for Hepatitis B, Hepatitis C, and HIV infection. I strongly advise you to give full information about your possible exposure to infections and to undergo any screening tests that you are offered. The implications of these tests are discussed later in this section. Ignorance is not bliss for pregnant women. Knowledge will provide you and your unborn baby with an opportunity to reduce the damage the infection can cause.

▶ **Do you have a family history of twins, diabetes, high blood pressure, thrombosis, tuberculosis, congenital abnormalities or blood disorders?** If there is one or more of these in your family history, this does not necessarily mean that you will suffer from them during your pregnancy but it does alert your caregivers to watch for signs that a potential problem is developing.

pap smear test were performed routinely by a doctor, either at the time the midwife took down the details or a week or so later. Now, the physical examination tends to be much less intrusive, partly because most pregnant women are generally fit and well, but also because we are conscious that prenatal care providers are not general physicians and specific medical problems are best dealt with by a referral to a specialist. Some clinics include a routine examination of your heart and lungs, but these are not usually very informative when carried out by doctors who are not specialists.

If you have never had a medical problem and this is your first pregnancy, the physical examination at your first prenatal visit may be confined to measuring your height, weight, and blood pressure, and examining your hands, legs, and abdomen.

PRENATAL VISIT *Being candid about any previous pregnancies and your past medical history will help your caregivers tailor your prenatal care.*

Height

If you are less than 5ft (1.5m) tall, your caregiver may be concerned that your pelvis is also smaller than average and that this may lead to problems at the time of delivery. For the same reason, your shoe size used to be recorded in your notes. However, the reality is that your height and shoe size are not reliable measures of the capacity of your pelvis; your ability to deliver a baby cannot be accurately assessed until you are in full-blown labor. So I think that worrying about your height at this stage in pregnancy is not helpful. I have seen plenty of very short women deliver big babies and, conversely, I have seen some small babies experience problems negotiating an ample pelvis in a tall woman.

Weight

Your weight at the first prenatal visit is a more useful measurement than either your height or your shoe size, because you are more likely to experience problems during pregnancy and at the time of delivery if you are either significantly underweight or overweight (*see* p.41). Pregnant women are weighed at every prenatal visit. If you are significantly overweight at the beginning of your pregnancy, or if you have diabetes or you develop gestational diabetes, your caregivers will monitor your weight throughout your pregnancy and may recommend that you follow a calorie-controlled eating program.

WHY YOU MAY NEED SPECIAL CARE

The following factors may mean that you need specialist prenatal care:	These risk factors may mean that you need extra care during delivery:
▶ Previous preterm delivery (before 37 weeks)	▶ Previous Cesarean section
▶ Recurrent miscarriages	▶ Previous long labor and instrumental delivery (forceps or ventouse)
▶ Baby with a congenital abnormality	▶ Previous failed induction of labor
▶ Preeclampsia or high blood pressure in previous pregnancy	▶ Previous birth of baby weighing more than 9lb (4kg) or less than 5½lb (2.5kg)
▶ Diabetes or gestational diabetes	▶ Excessive bleeding after a birth (postpartum hemorrhage)
▶ Previous thrombosis (blood clot)	
▶ Previous birth of baby weighing more than 9lb (4kg) or less than 5½lb (2.5kg)	▶ Problems with an anesthestic
▶ Pregnancy with identical twins (see p.123)	▶ Urinary or bowel problems after a delivery
	▶ Current twin pregnancy

"...the reality is that your height and shoe size are not reliable measures of the capacity of your pelvis..."

Legs and hands

The appearance of your legs and hands is another useful baseline measurement at your appointment and some midwives and doctors keep a regular check on this during pregnancy. The colour and state of your fingernails is a useful factor when assessing your general health since they can reflect your diet and whether you are anemic. Spider nevi (small broken veins with a spiderlike appearance) and reddening of the palms and soles are to be expected in pregnant women, but the sudden appearance of lots of broken veins or areas of bruising suggests that you need investigations, including blood clotting tests.

The other sign that will be looked for is swelling or puffiness of your fingers, feet, ankles and lower legs, which may indicate problems with fluid retention. In later pregnancy, a degree of swelling in these areas is quite common, especially at the end of a busy day, but any sudden swelling or progressive increase in swelling needs to be taken seriously since it suggests that you are at risk of developing preeclampsia (*see* p.425).

Abdomen

Your midwife or doctor will examine the size of your expanding uterus at the prenatal visit and will also want to see whether you have any scars from previous operations and exactly where these are positioned. Provide as much detail as you can about previous abdominal or pelvic surgery, because this can influence

"Your blood pressure will be checked at every prenatal visit."

decisions about how your baby would be best delivered. For example, having your appendix out could have been a simple uncomplicated operation leaving you with a small scar on your right side. But if your appendix burst and you developed peritonitis, you may well have undergone a major abdominal operation as an emergency and have been left with a scar that extends all the way down your abdomen and dense adhesions inside your abdominal cavity. For similar reasons, whether the scar is smooth, puckered or tethered to underlying tissues is also useful information to note. So, too, are details about any post-operative complications, such as a wound infection.

Later in pregnancy, it is perfectly normal to notice stretch marks or stria appearing on your abdomen. However, if you suddenly develop livid stretch marks at this early stage in pregnancy it can be a sign that you are on steroid medication or have an underlying hormonal problem. Your midwife or doctor will arrange for you to see a specialist promptly.

Vaginal and pelvic examinations

Routine vaginal examinations in the clinic and at later prenatal visits are no longer considered necessary but if you have a discharge or have experienced some bleeding, your midwife may examine your cervix, take a swab to identify any infection and, sometimes, take a cervical smear for testing.

We now recognize that trying to judge the capacity of your pelvis at this early stage does not really contribute very much to the planning of your prenatal care. However, there are situations when it may be helpful for you to be examined internally at this visit — for example, if you have had a previous cesarean section because you failed to progress in labor and the cause was attributed to the ischial spines of your pelvis being too prominent or your pubic arch being too narrow to let the baby through.

Breasts

Breast examination is not performed routinely at all visits but my personal opinion is that it should be. Fortunately, breast cancer is uncommon in women under the age of 40 years, but when it does develop in younger women, the tumor is usually estrogen dependent, which means that pregnancy can greatly accelerate both the local growth and distant spread of the abnormal cells. Midwives and obstetricians may not be the best clinicians to identify every suspicious breast lump, but it is probably better that they identify some rather than none at all, since early diagnosis and treatment for these women may greatly improve their future prognosis.

URINE TESTS

You will be asked to produce a sample of urine at your first and all subsequent prenatal visits, which will be tested immediately with dipsticks specially treated to identify sugar, protein, and ketones (chemicals produced when fat is metabolized) in your urine. Normally, our kidneys filter out all of the sugar and protein from our urine. However, during pregnancy the increase in blood flow places a further load on a woman's kidneys, and as a result, the urine of pregnant women sometimes contains a small amount of sugar or protein. This always needs to be investigated further. Ketones are typically found in the urine of diabetic people, but in healthy pregnant women they are sometimes present if your metabolism is upset, such as when you have not been eating enough or have been vomiting.

Glycosuria — sugar in the urine

Although as many as half of all pregnant women have sugar in their urine on a single occasion during the second or third trimester, sugar in the urine at your visit or persistent levels at later prenatal visits are a source of concern, since they suggest that you may be developing gestational diabetes, a condition that affects

MONITORING BLOOD PRESSURE

Checking and recording your blood pressure at the first visit is important because this measurement will be used as the baseline reading against which all subsequent readings are compared during your pregnancy. Your blood pressure will then be measured at every prenatal visit regardless of where it takes place.

▶ **A reading of around 120/70mm Hg** is usual for most women. The first figure (120) refers to your systolic blood pressure, which means the pressure in the main blood vessels as your heart pumps blood around your body. The second figure (70) is the diastolic blood pressure – the pressure in your arteries when the heart is at rest. Both the systolic and diastolic readings are important, but if you have a diastolic blood pressure reading of 90 or greater, this will prompt your caregivers to suggest that you be seen by a specialist team for advice.

▶ **A persistent increase of 20** to either or both of your baseline figures is usually a cause of concern since it suggests that you may be at risk of developing problems such as preeclampsia (see p.425). Of course, blood pressures vary a great deal between different women during

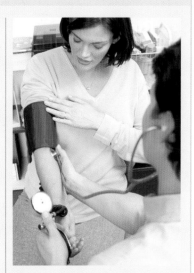

pregnancy, so this figure should be regarded simply as a useful rule of thumb.

URINE TEST *A dipstick is used to detect sugar in the urine. The chemically treated tip changes color according to the amount of glucose that is present.*

about five percent of pregnant women (*see* p.426). If you have glycosuria at the first prenatal visit, the first advice you will be given is to limit your intake of sweet foods (particularly cakes, candy, and chocolates, fruit juices, and fruit such as bananas, pineapple, and melons). If your urine contains sugar at your next prenatal visit, you will probably be advised to have an early glucose tolerance test to establish whether the cause is gestational diabetes or whether you have simply eaten too much sugar-rich food just before your urine test.

Proteinuria — protein in the urine

There are several important causes of proteinuria in pregnancy so your doctor or midwife will want to investigate you thoroughly on any occasion that it is found. If you are found to have protein in your urine at your initial visit, you will be asked to produce a clean midstream sample of urine. To do this you will be given a special pack that contains a cleansing pad to wipe away organisms from your vulva and a sterile collection cup. After cleaning your vulva, you need to pass the first few drops of urine into the toilet and then collect a midstream sample of your urine into the cup to be sent off to the laboratory for testing.

The most common cause of proteinuria is an infection in your kidneys or urinary tract. You are more prone to these infections in pregnancy because the tubes that connect your kidneys to your bladder and your bladder to your urethra are relaxed under the influence of pregnancy hormones. This makes it much easier for infective organisms to gain access to your bladder and kidneys. Most importantly, the usual early sign of a urine infection — pain or discomfort when urinating, called cystitis — is often missing in pregnancy, which means that you can develop a full-blown infection of your kidneys (pyelonephritis) with very little warning. This is a potentially serious problem, because urine infections can cause the uterus to become irritable. If they are left untreated, they may lead to miscarriage or premature labor. Furthermore, repeated urine infections can cause permanent scarring of the kidneys. If an infection is diagnosed, you will be given appropriate antibiotic treatment and a further test will be performed approximately one week after completing the course of tablets to ensure that the infection has cleared. Some prenatal clinics suggest that you have a midstream sample test as a routine part of your initial visit to avoid missing a silent urine infection that has not produced symptoms.

More rarely, protein in the urine at your initial visit can be a sign that you have underlying kidney disease, in which case you will probably be under the care of a specialist kidney (renal) doctor already. Occasionally, however, underlying renal disease is identified for the first time during regular urine tests in pregnancy. In later pregnancy, proteinuria is one of the important signs of preeclampsia (*see* p.425). If at this early stage you have protein in your urine that is not caused by an infection or a previous history of renal problems, this will alert your midwife and doctors to the fact that you are a high-risk pregnancy and may develop preeclampsia or other complications at a later stage.

YOUR FIRST ULTRASOUND SCAN

Some maternity units now offer pregnant women a dating ultrasound scan between eight and 12 weeks (*see* next page) to measure the baby's size and establish the due date. You may also be offered a nuchal fold translucency scan (*see* p.136) between 11 and 14 weeks for the early detection of Down syndrome, although this scan is not yet routinely available.

If you are carrying twins, a scan at 12 weeks or earlier will identify which type of twins you are carrying (*see* p.125). This is an important detail to establish early on because it has implications for your prenatal care: identical twins are at greater risk of congenital abnormalities and complications such as intrauterine growth restriction (IUGR) and will therefore need specialist care. In fact, 70 percent have serious problems and only 30 percent are uncomplicated. If you are pregnant with non-identical twins, normal prenatal care is often all that is needed, although you are more likely to deliver early because of the extra size and weight of the babies inside your uterus.

All women are offered a scan at 18–20 weeks, which is usually referred to as the fetal anatomy scan (*see* pp.173–76). By this stage, it is possible to get a clear picture of the development of your baby's organs and body systems, and the majority of structural abnormalities can be detected during this scan. If a problem is found you will probably have further specialist scans but the majority of women will not need further scans.

ULTRASOUND SCANNING *An early scan is a valuable baseline because it can be used to establish the exact stage of your pregnancy.*

DATING ULTRASOUND SCAN

THE DATING ULTRASOUND SCAN AT 12 WEEKS MEASURES THE SIZE OF THE FETUS SO THAT FUTURE PRENATAL CARE CAN BE ORGANIZED AROUND YOUR BABY'S GESTATIONAL AGE — THE EARLIER THE SCAN, THE MORE ACCURATE THE DATING MEASUREMENTS WILL BE.

HOW SCANS ARE USED

▶ **5–8 weeks** Pregnancy viability scan shows sac in uterus; after 6 weeks fetal pole and heartbeat detectable; dating using CRL measurement

▶ **11–14 weeks** Nuchal fold translucency scan screens for Down's syndrome; dates pregnancy

▶ **12–14 weeks** Dating of pregnancy using CRL and BPD. Scan confirms growth, heartbeat and brain formation

▶ **20 weeks** Detailed anatomy scan examines baby for heart, kidney, bladder, spine, brain, and limb abnormalities; checks growth of head, body, and limbs; checks the position of the placenta

▶ **30 weeks plus** Detailed scans to detect placental problems, intra-uterine growth retardation and volume of amniotic fluid

SCAN AT 10 WEEKS *The fetal arms and hands are developing. A yolk sac is visible below the baby's head.*

▶ **Ultrasound scans,** as their name implies, work by emitting high-frequency sound waves, which are sent through a pregnant woman's body using a handpiece called a transducer. These soundwaves are reflected back from the solid tissues of the developing baby and translated into images on a computer screen. There is no radiation involved in ultrasound, only sound waves.

▶ **During the hour before an abdominal ultrasound scan,** you will be asked to drink several glasses of water and to avoid emptying your bladder. You may find this a little uncomfortable but there is a good reason for it. When your bladder is full, the ultrasound waves are

reflected through this water-filled window lying immediately over the uterus and tiny baby, producing much clearer images.

You will be asked to lie down and lubricating gel is smeared onto the lower part of your abdomen to ensure good contact with the transducer. The sonographer, usually a doctor or technician, then moves the transducer smoothly forwards and backwards to produce ultrasound images on a computer screen.

▶ **For a vaginal scan** a tubular probe is introduced into your vagina. There is usually no need to fill your bladder because the probe is close enough to your uterus to produce clear pictures. Many women worry that a vaginal scan may be painful or will damage their pregnancy, but this is not the case. If you do have any vaginal bleeding afterwards, it was going to happen anyway and was not caused by the vaginal probe.

▶ **The key measurements** taken at the 12-week dating scan are the crown rump length (CRL) — the distance between the top of your baby's head (crown) and bottom (rump) — and the biparietal diameter (BPD), which is the distance between the two parietal bones on each side of the baby's head. The size of the limbs cannot be measured accurately while the baby is still in a curled position, so the length of the thigh bone or femur (FL) will not be used to assess fetal size until the middle of the second trimester.

Your baby's heartbeat will also be monitored — an extraordinary sight, as it beats fast and furiously.

If your dates don't tally with the measurements, it may be because your dates are wrong or there is a problem with the pregnancy. You will probably be asked to come back for another scan at a later date to ensure that all is progressing well.

▶ **Twin pregnancies** are often diagnosed during the 12-week scan, although they can be detected as early as a six-week scan when two pregnancy sacs are usually clearly visible in the uterus. At 12 weeks the

sonographer will be able to detect whether you are carrying identical (monochorionic) or nonidentical (dichorionic) twins by examining the thickness of the membranes that separate the two amniotic sacs in the uterus. If only two thin layers of amnion (the sac's inner layer) separate the cavities, the twins are identical. If a thicker membrane made up of two layers of amnion and two layers of chorion (the sac's outer layer) separates the twins, they are nonidentical.

DATING SCAN AT 12 WEEKS

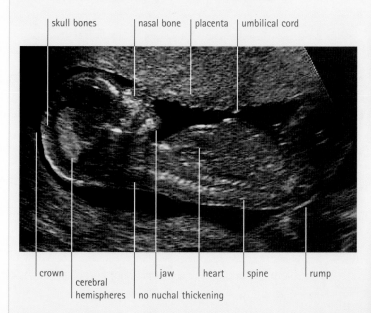

skull bones | nasal bone | placenta | umbilical cord

crown | cerebral hemispheres | no nuchal thickening | jaw | heart | spine | rump

INTERPRETING A SCAN *Dense tissues such as bone appear white, while fluid-filled areas are dark. At 12 weeks this fetus has well-formed skull bones and a clearly defined spine. The heart is visible as a small dense area mid-chest that pulsates on screen. The placenta is visualized as a spongy mass connected to the blood-filled umbilical cord, which appears white because blood cells reflect sound waves.*

IN PROFILE *The cerebral hemispheres are clearly visualized. The sharp profile shows that the nasal bone has formed.*

BPD

BIPARIETAL HEAD DIAMETER *This is one of the baseline measurements plotted on a graph to monitor fetal growth.*

BLOOD TESTING *You are usually asked to provide blood samples for several blood tests at your first prenatal visit.*

BLOOD TESTS

A variety of blood tests will be performed at your first prenatal visit. Some are routine for all pregnant women, but you may be offered additional tests depending on your medical and obstetric history.

Your blood group

This will be one of the four types found in humans: A, B, AB, or O. The most common is O, followed by A and B, and then the rarer AB. For each of these combinations, the individual is either Rhesus positive or negative, the most common type being Rhesus positive. So your blood type card reads: O Rhesus positive or negative, A Rhesus positive or negative, and so on for each blood group. Rhesus status is especially significant in pregnancy because an Rh-negative mother who carries an Rh-positive baby can develop damaging antibodies to her baby's blood (*see* p.128 and p.424).

Establishing your blood group early in pregnancy is very important. The journey through pregnancy is one of the few times in your life when you are at increased of risk of catastrophic bleeding requiring a blood transfusion, so it is essential that your exact blood group is known, included in your maternity records, and available at any time of the day or night. Until very recently, the most important cause of maternal death in the Western world was hemorrhage or blood loss, and in countries that do not have access to blood transfusion services, it remains so. We should never forget these facts or take them for granted. Of course, most women do not experience any bleeding in pregnancy and have no need of a blood transfusion. But for the few that do, knowledge of their blood type can save valuable time for the laboratory staff who are trying to cross-match stored samples of blood with the exact group of the pregnant woman. This is why you will have a blood sample taken if ever you are admitted to a maternity hospital with a problem that could result in a blood transfusion.

Hemoglobin level and blood count

The hemoglobin level in your blood is a measure of the oxygen-carrying pigment in your red blood cells. The normal range for women is 105 to 150 grams per liter of blood in your body. If the level is low, this means that you are anemic and you will be advised to eat foods with a high iron content (*see* p.47) and may be prescribed iron tablets as well. Anemia (*see* p.423) can cause you to feel very tired and may also lead to problems if you have excessive bleeding at the time of delivery.

The full blood count also analyzes numbers of red blood cells, white blood cells, and platelets to provide further information about your general health. For example, it may suggest that your anemia is not due to a lack of iron alone but other factors, such as vitamin deficiencies, which can be identified and treated.

Immunity to rubella

In Canada, every pregnant woman is tested to see whether she is immune to rubella. The fetal damage that a first infection with rubella can cause during early pregnancy has already been discussed (*see* p.32 and p.411). If you are found to be non-immune at your prenatal visit, you will be given advice as to how you can best avoid exposure to infection during your pregnancy and offered immunization as soon as your baby has been delivered. Some women may also need screening for toxoplasmosis (*see* p.412), recent chickenpox exposure (*see* p.411), and other less common infections such as hepatitis (*see* p.129 and p.117) and human immunodeficiency virus (HIV *see* p.130 and p.414).

Sexually transmitted diseases

Pregnant women are routinely screened for syphilis infection (*see* p.413) and offered prompt treatment with penicillin if they are found to be infected. Because syphilis is relatively uncommon today, some clinicians have suggested that screening should be discontinued and the resources used to search for other infections. However, it is important to remember that undetected infection with syphilis during pregnancy can be the cause of severe congenital and developmental problems in the baby. Since syphilis can be treated so swiftly and easily, I believe that we should continue to screen for it routinely during pregnancy. Sadly, the incidence of syphilis is increasing in Eastern Europe, Russia, and Africa. If you have lived in any of these countries and are now receiving prenatal care in Canada, it is especially important that you are screened to prevent damage to yourself and your baby.

Infection with chlamydia and gonorrhea (*see* p.413), two other sexually transmitted diseases, is more likely to cause problems with infertility. However, chlamydia infections are also the cause of serious eye infections in newborns, so if you think you may be at risk, do tell your midwife and doctor so that they can help you prevent problems from developing.

RHESUS NEGATIVE PREGNANCIES

▶ **If your blood group is Rhesus negative**, problems can arise in pregnancy if your baby inherits Rh-positive status from your partner. If this occurs there is a risk that your immune system will produce antibodies to your baby's red blood cells that cause anemia and distress for the baby in the uterus and anemia (see p.433) and jaundice (see p.434) after the birth.

▶ **Rhesus status is rarely a problem** in a first pregnancy but if you are exposed to some of your baby's blood during childbirth you may develop antibodies that could cause problems in a subsequent pregnancy. For this reason all Rh-negative mothers are checked for anti-D antibodies during their prenatal-visit blood tests.

▶ **If you have developed antibodies**, you will be offered further blood tests every four weeks, and your baby will be carefully monitored for signs of anemia or heart failure.

▶ **Even if you have not developed antibodies**, maternity units now offer routine preventative RhIg (Rh immune globulin) injections, which mop up Rh-positive fetal blood cells and prevent the development of destructive maternal antibodies. These are offered at 28 weeks in the first pregnancy, unless the father is also Rh-negative, in which case there is no risk that the baby's blood will be incompatible. This anti-D program has made rhesus hemolytic disease of the newborn relatively rare.

▶ **All Rh-negative mothers** who give birth to a Rh-positive baby are given an RhIg injection within 72 hours of delivery. A blood test establishes the level of fetal cells present in her circulation, and if the concentration is high, another dose of RhIg may be needed.

▶ **Rh-negative women** who have amniocentesis (see pp.140–43), chorionic villus sampling (see p.140), external cephalic version (see p.271), or those who have vaginal bleeding or abdominal trauma during pregnancy are given an injection of RhIg within 72 hours. Those who miscarry and require surgical evacuation of the uterus or who undergo termination of pregnancy or who have an ectopic pregnancy are also treated with RhIg.

KEY

— mother's blood

+ baby's blood

▲ antibodies

FIRST PREGNANCY *Maternal and fetal circulations do not usually mix during pregnancy but during birth the mother may be exposed to her baby's blood.*

SUBSEQUENT PREGNANCY
If the mother has developed antibodies to her baby's red blood cells they may cause problems in a future pregnancy.

Autosomal recessive disorders

Some genetic disorders are passed on only if both parents have copies of the faulty gene, and you may not know if you are only a carrier (in other words, if you have just one copy of the mutation). Among white people of North American and European origin, the most common of these disorders is cystic fibrosis, which affects all the fluid- and mucus-producing glands in the body, leading to thick, abnormal secretions. Among the Ashkenazi Jewish population, Tay-Sachs disease, in which harmful chemicals accumulate in the brain, is most common. If you are of African or Mediterranean origin, sickle-cell anemia and thalassemia, both abnormalities of the oxygen-carrying hemoglobin, are most common, and you will be offered a special electrophoresis test of your hemoglobin to determine whether you have sickle-cell or thalassemia trait.

If you carry the sickle-cell trait, it is important that your partner's sickle cell status is established early on, since there is a chance that your baby could inherit a double dose of the trait and develop the full-blown sickle-cell disease (*see* p.417 and p.424). Similarly, if you carry the A or B thalassemia trait, you will need to arrange for your partner to be tested too. A baby with full-blown thalassemia (*see* p.424) suffers from very severe anemia and iron overload, which eventually leads to multiple organ failure.

Hepatitis B and C

These viral infections cause liver disease but it is unusual for women to be infected for the first time during pregnancy. Both are more common if you have used intravenous drugs, had multiple sexual partners, or have been exposed to infected blood. If you have received a blood transfusion in a country where the screening of blood products is not rigorous, you may be at risk. The hepatitis B virus does not cross the placenta during pregnancy, but if you carry the virus, your baby will be at risk of infection at the time of delivery. The virus is not transmitted in breast milk, but babies are occasionally infected by blood if the mother's nipples are cracked and bleeding. As many as half of all babies infected with hepatitis B will develop cirrhosis or cancer of the liver in later life. This is why it is so important to know whether you are hepatitis B positive during pregnancy; if you are, your baby can be protected by IgG immunoglobulin treatment at delivery and immunized with hepatitis B vaccine soon afterward.

Hepatitis C infection is an important cause of liver disease worldwide, but it is only rarely transmitted to the baby during pregnancy or delivery. However, the risk is greatly increased if you are HIV positive (*see* p.130 and p.414). Screening for hepatitis C is not routine but may be offered to you.

"...it is essential that your exact blood group is known, included in your maternity records, and available at any time of the day or night."

HUMAN IMMUNODEFICIENCY VIRUS (HIV)

MY VIEW IS THAT EVERY PREGNANT WOMAN SHOULD BE SCREENED FOR HIV INFECTION. IF YOU

ARE FOUND TO BE POSITIVE, YOU WILL BE OFFERED THE BEST ADVICE AND TREATMENT FOR

YOU AND YOUR BABY; IF FOUND TO BE NEGATIVE, YOU WILL BE GREATLY REASSURED.

HIV is a retrovirus capable of incorporating itself into the genetic code, especially of white blood cells, which are responsible for fighting infection. HIV infection (see p.414) has now become an epidemic worldwide and until very recently, being HIV positive invariably led to the development of full-blown autoimmune deficiency syndrome (AIDS). Today the situation has changed dramatically: people who are HIV positive can now receive antiretroviral drugs, which can protect them from the onset of AIDS.

HIV IN PREGNANCY

For pregnant women, knowing that they are HIV positive can improve their personal survival, thanks to the new drugs available. It will also significantly reduce the risk of their babies becoming infected. Delivery by cesarean section and avoiding breastfeeding reduce the risk. These measures coupled with maternal antiretroviral drug treatment at and around the time of delivery cut the chance of a baby being infected with HIV from 20 percent to less than two percent. However, none of these medical advances can be offered if your prenatal caregivers do not know that you are HIV positive.

OPPOSITION TO SCREENING

Some years ago I was involved in trying to introduce routine screening for HIV in our prenatal clinic at St. Mary's Hospital, London. We met considerable opposition from patients, midwives, and doctors, who were all concerned that the implications of being found to be HIV positive were so devastating that they should not be revealed as part of prenatal screening. The Royal College of Midwives actually advised members that routine screening was an invasion of a pregnant woman's privacy.

A CHANGE IN ATTITUDE

Several events had to occur before this attitude changed. First was the publication of European studies showing that the measures described above could reduce the transmission of HIV from mother to baby.

Next came the introduction of the antiretroviral drugs used singly and in combination, which appeared to offer a greatly improved chance of halting the progression of HIV to full-blown AIDS.

The tragedy in our hospital was that it was only after two six-month-old babies were admitted with life-threatening infection caused by AIDS that the real importance of prenatal screening for this disease began to be fully understood by all parties concerned.

The mothers of these two babies had not been offered testing for HIV during pregnancy by their local hospital. Having witnessed the horror of their children's suffering they wanted to support the introduction of routine screening.

POSITIVE APPROACH

During the months that followed, the uptake of HIV screening in our prenatal clinic rose from 30 percent to over 95 percent.

Much of the credit for this change in practice must go to the two specialist midwives who introduced the service. Their positive and supportive approach toward HIV screening was crucial in changing the attitudes of patients and their medical and midwifery colleagues.

Your blood test results

The results of your blood tests will be available in about two weeks and are usually filed in your maternity records. At your next visit, these notes will be given to you to keep for the remainder of the pregnancy. The exact date of your next visit will depend on the type of prenatal care you have chosen; if this is hospital based, it may vary between different hospitals. In my own unit we usually see women at about 17 weeks — after their serum screening blood test result is available — in order to discuss the results of these tests and ensure that any necessary action is taken. The booking notes then become "hand-held" by the pregnant woman. Any important abnormal test results may be duplicated and filed in a separate set of hospital-based records for the few women who have been identified as having high-risk pregnancies.

COMMON CONCERNS

YOU MAY NOT HAVE MANY CONCERNS AT THIS POINT. THE RISK OF MISCARRIAGE IS DIMINISHING; YOU HAVE SURVIVED THE EARLY PREGNANCY COMPLAINTS; AND YOU ARE NOT YET PREGNANT ENOUGH FOR THE LATER ONES.

Although your risk of miscarriage is now considerably reduced, any bleeding in early pregnancy invariably raises the fear of miscarriage occurring, especially if you have suffered one in the past, or experienced problems earlier in this pregnancy. So if you do experience some vaginal bleeding, see your doctor and have an ultrasound scan at the earliest possibility — in the majority of cases it will reassure you that nothing is wrong and that the bleeding is insignificant. If this is the case, it is a good idea to make sure that your doctor examines you internally and looks carefully at your cervix. In early pregnancy the flood of hormones can make its surface very fragile and prone to bleeding, particularly if you develop a mild infection, such as yeast. If there is any concern about the appearance of your cervix, your doctor will probably take a pap smear.

VARICOSE VEINS

Although varicose veins tend to be much more common in later pregnancy (*see* p.235) some women, particularly those who had varicose veins in a previous pregnancy, will have symptoms of aching and discomfort much earlier. If this applies to you, do make sure that you start wearing good support hose every day. Prompt attention to varicose veins in pregnancy can greatly reduce the problems that tend to develop at a later stage.

"In early pregnancy the flood of hormones can make the surface of your cervix very fragile and prone to bleeding..."

YOUR SEX LIFE

Some women find pregnancy brings added sexual fulfillment. The marked increase in vaginal secretions, together with the greater blood flow to all of the genital organs may mean that sex is more pleasurable than before. For many couples, there is the added thrill of being able to have unprotected sex, which can be a highly erotic sensation after years of using contraception. Added to this is the wonderful closeness that arises from the knowledge that you and your partner have created a life together. For many couples, this is a very powerful emotion, which enhances their lovemaking.

However, for many women, sex suffers. In spite of the many "sexy" images of famous women in late pregnancy that we are subjected to in newspapers and magazines, the fact remains that many mothers-to-be do not consider themselves to be very sexually appealing during their pregnancy and may start to feel this way as early as the third month when their shape starts to change. Being pregnant may change your perception of yourself and your partner's perception of you as a sexual partner and there are also physical and emotional reasons why your sex life may be different or diminished during pregnancy. During the first three months a woman may experience a lower libido because she feels nauseous or exhausted; her breasts might be too tender to touch; she might have had some bleeding or have reason to worry about the risk of miscarriage; or she might simply not feel like having sex. Later on, heartburn, indigestion, tiredness, sheer size and inability to get comfortable mean that women may have sex less often and find it less enjoyable. Even though loss of libido is extremely common, it can still come as a shock to both partners.

If you are feeling insecure about these issues, it is vital that you talk to your partner. You need to reassure each other that your feelings for each other have not changed just because one or both of you is not very interested in making love.

CLOTHES AND HAIR

Most likely your clothes are starting to feel tighter round the waist now, but it is sensible to resist the temptation to rush out and buy a completely new wardrobe of clothes at this early stage. If this is your first pregnancy you can usually get by with some looser tops from your existing wardrobe perhaps with one or two

"In spite of the many 'sexy' images of famous women in late pregnancy, the fact remains that many mothers-to-be do not consider themselves to be sexually appealing..."

ENROLLING FOR PRENATAL CLASSES

▶ **You will not start your prenatal classes** until your sixth or seventh month, but many of these classes get booked up months in advance, so you should start researching now to find out what is available in your area.

A good prenatal class should explain the physiology of pregnancy; describe the best breathing techniques for labor; help you prepare yourself for an active birth; and provide exercises that will make you stronger for the day itself. Your instructor should discuss labor fully and honestly, giving a full description of pain-relief options. She should also give advice on basic baby care for the days and weeks following the birth. Some classes have followup groups after the birth.

▶ **All prenatal classes encourage fathers-to-be to attend,** although your partner should not feel pressured to attend every session. Many courses arrange classes for men so that they can discuss their feelings in a more open way and learn how they can be of most help during labor.

▶ **Prenatal courses are run by hospitals and public health units,** as well as privately. These can be very useful if you are planning a hospital birth. You will have an opportunity to put questions to the midwives and other obstetric personnel, and this will make you all the more familiar with the way the labor ward works. By the time you arrive for the birth, you will be even more relaxed about your surroundings.

▶ **Questions to ask** before you enroll include who sponsors the classes; is the instructor certified by any organizations; can the instructor provide references; how many classes are in the series; and what topics are covered (see pp.436–38).

▶ **Even if this is not your first baby,** enrolling in an prenatal class is still a good idea. You may be a little rusty when it comes to remembering the details of labor or the correct breathing techniques.

▶ **One of the best spin-offs from attending an prenatal class** is the chance to meet women who are having babies at around the same time as you and who live in your area. Many women find that they make wonderful, enduring friendships in their prenatal classes.

pairs of pants or skirts with an elasticated waist. Wearing your partner's jeans for a few weeks may be an option. If you have been pregnant before, you may well find that you need to change into roomier garments earlier than you did in your first pregnancy. Once the muscles of the abdominal wall have been stretched by pregnancy, they are never quite as tight as they used to be.

Trips to the hairdresser are a good way to boost morale but many women tell me they are concerned that the chemicals in hair dyes might be potentially dangerous. There is no evidence that this is so; most permanent and nonpermanent dyes contain chemicals that have been in use for many years and are unlikely to be toxic in the kind of doses used to color hair every few months. However if you are worried, you could stick to highlights, which only color the hair shaft rather than expose the whole scalp to dye, and if you color your own hair, wear gloves and do it in a well-ventilated space.

PRENATAL TESTS

Screening and diagnostic tests for fetal abnormalities make up one of the most complex areas of prenatal care. I can appreciate that if you have been sailing through pregnancy so far, these may be topics you feel reluctant to consider — but I would urge you to read on. I hope the information here will help steer you through the options available and enable you to base your choices on the most up-to-date evidence and information. This will give you confidence in any decisions that you may need to make.

All screening tests are optional and you and your partner have the choice of whether or not you wish to have them. There is no right or wrong answer; each couple will have to decide what is right for them after considering all the available information. Although the vast majority of babies are born healthy, when problems do occur they tend to do so during fetal development because of an inherited genetic condition, an acquired problem due to, for example, an infection or a medication, or for no known reason. If an abnormality is detected through screening, it gives you and your partner the chance to prepare yourselves emotionally and practically for the prospect of caring for a child with a disability or for the possibility of terminating the pregnancy, depending on the extent of the problem. (For a fuller discussion on congenital abnormalities *see* pp. 144–47.)

DO I NEED TO HAVE TESTS?

All women have a chance of delivering a baby with an abnormality but a number of factors increase the risk and these should be taken into account when you decide which, if any, tests to have. You are at increased risk if:

• you have had a previous pregnancy that was affected by an abnormality
• you or your partner has a family history of genetic disorders or abnormalities
• you are over 35 years of age
• you take or have taken medications that are known to harm a developing baby.

WHAT IS AVAILABLE?

First trimester screening is expensive because it requires counseling and scanning expertise to achieve high detection rates and ensure good follow-up care. Although provisions vary from one municipality to the next, many more hospitals are now exploring the possibility of introducing first trimester screening to high-risk groups of women even if they are unable to provide this facility for everyone. The two main categories of first trimester tests are screening tests and diagnostic tests and the difference between them is important.

Screening tests are usually offered initially and these will identify most, but not all, of those at risk of carrying a baby with an abnormality. They cannot diagnose a problem; they simply establish a risk figure on which women then have to base their decision whether to go on to have further investigations. Screening tests include a variety of serum (blood) tests and ultrasound scans (*see* p.124 and p.174), which include a specialized ultrasound scan that measures the Nuchal Translucency (NT). With every test you need to consider the detection rate and the false positive rate (*see* chart below).

A false positive means that a test result that is positive is later shown to be negative. A positive screening test prompts prenatal caregivers to offer an invasive test to confirm the diagnosis, so if the false positive rate is high, many women with pregnancies that are actually free of problems are exposed to further tests that they do not need.

Diagnostic tests give a clear answer as to whether or not a fetus has an abnormality but these invasive tests are not routine, since they all require samples of the amniotic fluid, placenta, or fetal blood to be taken from inside the uterus

and these procedures carry a small but significant risk of miscarriage. The only definitive tests for Down syndrome (*see* p.147) are chorionic villus sampling (CVS), amniocentesis, and cordocentesis. Whether or not you choose to have one of these tests will depend on your views on abnormalities and how you would want to act if you knew for sure that your baby was affected by one.

HOW ACCURATE ARE THE TESTS?

The detection rate of Down syndrome has effectively tripled over the last 15–20 years in specialist centers thanks to the work of committed obstetricians and scientists specializing in the field of first trimester screening.

The most important practical problem in prenatal screening is that it is difficult to achieve a high detection rate of affected babies and at the same time maintain a low false positive rate. In the past, we had only maternal age of 35 years or

SCREENING TEST COMPARISONS

The development of new tests over time has raised detection rates for abnormalities such as Down syndrome from 30 percent to 85 percent. The most recent advance in screening – the integrated test – has the lowest false positive rate at just one percent, resulting in fewer invasive tests.

Method of screening	Timing (weeks)	False positive rate	Detection rate	Number of babies found to be affected after test result is positive
Maternal age		5%	30%	1:130
Triple test (p.137)	14–22	5%	69%	1:56
Quadruple test (p.137)	14–22	5%	76%	1:50
NT measurement (p.137)	11–14	5%	80%	1:47
Combined NT and serum test (p.137)	11–14	5%	85%	1:45
Integrated test (p.138)	11–14/15–22	1%	85%	1:9

TIMING OF TESTS

DATE	TEST
11–14 weeks	Nuchal Translucency (NT) (screening)
15–20 weeks	Triple or quadruple (Bart's serum test) screening
19–20 weeks	Fetal anomaly scan (see p.174) (diagnostic)
11–14 weeks	Combined NT and serum test (screening)
11–14 weeks and 15–22 weeks	Integrated test (screening)
11–14 weeks	Chorionic villus sampling (CVS) (diagnostic)
14–16 weeks	Amniocentesis (diagnostic)
20–40 weeks	Cordocentesis (diagnostic)

more to identify those women who are at greater risk and most maternity units routinely offer these women amniocentesis. However, if the mother's age alone is used to decide whether an invasive test such as amniocentesis or CVS is performed, only 30 percent of babies affected by Down syndrome will be identified. If maternal age is combined with serum screening, the detection rate rises to 65 percent, but that is still only two-thirds of affected babies. However, when Nuchal Translucency (NT) is measured at 11–14 weeks the detection rate rises to 80 percent, and when the NT measurement is combined with a blood test that measures free beta-hCG and PAPP-A hormone levels, the detection rate is as high as 85 percent.

A further advance in screening is the integrated test (see p.138), with a detection rate of 85 percent and a false positive rate of just one percent. In effect, this means that almost 9 out of 10 babies with Down syndrome can be detected, and only 1 in 100 women will be wrongly identified as at risk and offered further tests that prove to be unnecessary.

NUCHAL TRANSLUCENCY (NT)

This screening test was developed at King's College Hospital, London in the 1990s to improve the detection of Down syndrome as early as possible in pregnancy. The scan is performed between 11 and 14 weeks by hospital-based specialists and is based on an ultrasound measurement of the depth of fluid present under the skin behind the neck of the fetus (see box right). Although an NT is not offered to every pregnant woman, it is usually available on request, and you may have to pay for the test.

An increasing number of physical markers for Down syndrome are being identified. For example, a recent finding by Professor Kypros Nicolaides at King's College Hospital, London is that babies with Down syndrome lack a nasal bone. By examining the baby's profile during the NT scan, he believes that the detection of Down syndrome can increase to over 90 percent, and the false positive rate be reduced to as low as one percent.

SERUM SCREENING TESTS

The various different serum screening tests that are currently available measure three or more substances in your blood to predict whether your baby is at risk of Down syndrome, certain other chromosomal (genetic) abnormalities. or an open neural tube defect such as spina bifida (see p.146 and p.418). Serum screening tests are probabilities, or estimates of risk; they do not provide a definite answer. When you undergo a test, it is important to remember the following:

• An abnormal serum screening test (screen positive) does not mean that your baby has one of these abnormalities, but it does mean you are at greater risk, and may want further tests.

• If the baby is found to have a chromosomal disorder, you will be faced with the choice of whether or not to continue with your pregnancy.

Carrying out the test

Serum tests are usually performed at about 15 to 16 weeks at your maternity unit or obstetrician's office. The best known test, often called the triple-screen test, measures three substances in the blood: alpha-fetoprotein, beta-hCG, and estriol. In babies with Down syndrome, the aFP and estriol levels tend to be lower and the hCG higher. The quadruple or Bart's test, developed at St. Bartholomew's Hospital, London, combines the Multiple Marker Screening Test with screening for a substance called inhibin A.

The blood sample is sent to a specialist laboratory and analyzed for the different

MEASUREMENT OF NT

During an ultrasound scan at 11–14 weeks, the technician measures the fetus and the depth of the fluid under the skin behind the neck of the fetus (the nuchal translucency).

This screening test can only give you an indication of risk and is not a conclusive answer as to whether or not your baby has Down syndrome.

▶ **If the fluid measurement is below 3mm**, your baby is unlikely to have a problem. This will be the result for 95 percent of women.

▶ **If the measurement is between 4 and 7mm**, there is a probability that your baby has Down syndrome – the higher the measurement, the higher the chance. A measurement between 3 and 4mm is borderline.

▶ **If your NT measurements are high or borderline**, you will be counseled about the implications and offered the option of undergoing

LOW RISK *This fetus has only a small depth of fluid behind its neck and is at low risk of Down syndrome.*

HIGH RISK *The larger depth of fluid marked here puts this fetus at a higher risk of Down syndrome.*

an invasive prenatal test, such as a chorionic villus sampling or amniocentesis. Only five percent of pregnant women will find themselves in this situation.

▶ **If you decide not to have an invasive test** following an NT measurement that was high or borderline, I strongly advise you to ensure that you have a detailed anomaly scan at 20 weeks. This is

because babies with a thicker nuchal translucency have an increased chance of heart, gut, and other structural abnormalities that will be visible on an ultrasound scan. If some or any of these are identified, your prenatal caregivers will be able to arrange for appropriate paediatric help and advice before, during, and after the delivery if you decide to continue with the pregnancy.

"There are no right or wrong answers to these dilemmas, which is why you need to discuss openly and honestly how you would want to act upon an abnormal test result."

substances. The results are then fed into a computer program together with your age and the exact gestational age of your baby. The risk assessment is usually available within five working days and, depending on the type of prenatal care you have chosen, you either have to phone for the result or you will be contacted by your obstetrician or midwife. In the vast majority of cases, the test results will be low risk, but for the few results that show a high risk, it is very important that you receive the news as early as possible in order to provide you with the maximum amount of time to arrange further investigations if you wish to have them.

Your risk assessment
Out of the computer comes a risk assessment, such as 1 in 45 or 1 in 450. Translated into simple terms these numbers mean that for every 45 or 450 pregnancies, one baby is likely to be affected by the abnormality and either 44 or 449 babies are unlikely to be at risk of the abnormality. Hence, large numbers are good news, while lower numbers will raise the alarm that a baby may have a problem.

It sounds simple, but the reality is quite complicated. Some couples will consider that a risk of 1 in 45 is worrying, while others will interpret that 1 in 45 as a risk that they are prepared to accept. At the other end of the scale, most couples and their obstetricians will consider a serum screening result of 1 in 450 as very reassuring while for others, the possibility that

their baby may be affected by a small but finite chance of an abnormality prompts them to undergo further tests. Of course, what the numbers cannot possibly take into account is your past experience and your personal views about having a baby affected by an abnormality, or alternatively, electing to terminate a pregnancy with a proven abnormality. There are no right or wrong answers to these dilemmas, which is why you need to discuss openly and honestly with your partner, obstetrician, and genetic counselor how you would want to act upon an abnormal test result.

INTEGRATED SCREENING
The most recent advance in prenatal screening has been the development of the integrated test. This combination of tests provides a high detection rate for Down syndrome, Edward syndrome (see p.415), and neural tube defects such as spina bifida. It also has a much lower false positive rate when compared to other screening tests. The integrated test is performed in two stages:

• **Stage 1** The first part of the test is best performed in the first trimester at 12 weeks, but it can be undertaken at 11–14 completed weeks. The date on which you should have stage 1 of the integrated test is decided by menstrual dating, or by the results of ultrasound scan, if one has been performed earlier. A detailed ultrasound scan is performed to confirm the exact gestational age of the pregnancy and measure the nuchal translucency. A blood sample is taken at the same time to measure the levels of pregnancy-associated plasma protein A (PAPP-A), and the woman is then advised when to have the second blood sample taken.

• **Stage 2** The second stage of the integrated screening test ideally takes place in the second trimester at 15–16 completed weeks of pregnancy, but can be undertaken up to 22 weeks. Your obstetrician, midwife, or hospital doctor will take a second blood sample, which is sent off to the laboratory for analysis. Four serum levels are measured at this time: alpha-fetoprotein (AFP); unconjugated estriol (uE3); free beta human chorionic gonadotropin (free beta-hCG); and inhibin-A (inhibin).

Calculating the risk

The measurements of the five blood tests and the NT result are fed into the computer, together with the mother's age, to estimate her risk of having a baby with Down syndrome or an open neural tube defect. The results of the integrated

NEW DEVELOPMENTS

For a risk faster assessment, the blood tests can be done a few days earlier (either in the doctor's office, or with a take-home card that a woman mails in herself). Then, at 10 weeks, she comes in for the NT scan. The blood test results and the NT measurement are fed into the computerized risk assessment program, and the genetic counselors can give her a risk estimate at once. If the risk is high, she may choose to have chorionic villus sampling that day. CVS specimens can be analyzed using FISH (fluorescent in-situ hybridization), usually getting a preliminary report within 24 hours.

test are usually ready within 3–5 working days of the second blood sample being taken, because the integrated test result depends on analysis of both blood samples. The results are sent to your obstetrician or prenatal clinic. Although your risk of having a baby with Down syndrome can be estimated on the basis of the first stage information alone, this is not nearly as accurate as the combined results from the two-stage integrated screening test.

Test results

If the risk calculated from the test is 1 in 150 or greater (which means 1 in a number lower than 150), the integrated test result is reported as screen positive for Down syndrome and the woman will be offered a diagnostic test, usually an amniocentesis. Approximately 1 in 100 of all women who are screened will be in the screen-positive group and after amniocentesis about 1 in 10 of these women will be shown to have a baby with Down syndrome. This means that 10 invasive procedures will be performed to identify one baby affected by Down syndrome. These figures are a great improvement when compared to the testing process when based on the triple serum screening test alone, in which over 50 invasive tests are performed to detect a single case of Down syndrome (*see* table p.135). The integrated test also identifies 6 out of 10 women carrying a baby with Edward syndrome (*see* p.415) — a detection rate of 60 percent.

Neural tube detection

The level of AFP alone is used to determine whether there is an increased risk of having a pregnancy with an open neural tube defect, such as spina bifida. Women with a raised AFP level

(2.5 times the normal average or greater) are reported as screen positive and are then offered further tests such as a detailed ultrasound scan. Most babies with anencephaly (*see* p.418) and some 86 percent of babies with an open spina bifida can be detected in this way. Approximately 1 in 100 of all women screened will fall into the screen positive group for an open neural tube defect, and about 1 in 20 women with screen positive results have an affected pregnancy.

Factors that alter results

A variety of factors that can affect the various blood levels may need to be taken into account when calculating your integrated test result:

• Blood levels for some markers tend to be lower in overweight women and those with insulin-dependent diabetes.

• Levels for some markers may be higher in slender women as well as those of African-American origin.

• Levels may differ in women who are pregnant following IVF treatment.

• All blood markers are raised in twin pregnancies and are therefore unreliable.

• Vaginal bleeding just before the second blood test can raise AFP levels, as can amniocentesis testing.

If you have had a previous pregnancy affected by fetal abnormality, the result will always be reported as screen positive. Amniocentesis is usually offered, even if the integrated test result records a risk that is smaller than 1 in 150.

CHORIONIC VILLUS SAMPLING (CVS)

This prenatal diagnostic test is usually performed at 11–14 weeks (although it can also be performed later in pregnancy) and involves obtaining a small tissue sample (a biopsy) from the placenta (*see* box). Since the baby and the placenta develop from the same cells, the chromosomes in placental cells are the same as in the cells from the baby. The majority of women who undergo a CVS test, do so to exclude Down syndrome. However, it is also used if a specific gene disorder is suspected, such as sickle-cell anemia or thalassemia major (*see* p.417). Fresh tissue can be collected and tested before 12 weeks, so a pregnancy with a severe chromosomal abnormality can be diagnosed in time for a suction termination of pregnancy to be performed, if this is what the parents choose.

Disadvantages of CVS

No invasive prenatal test is completely problem-free and before you decide to undergo CVS, you should consider the following:

• The risk of miscarriage after CVS appears to be slightly higher than for amniocentesis, affecting approximately one percent of women who undergo CVS. This higher risk may be because the test is performed earlier in pregnancy, and the pregnancy may have been going to miscarry anyway, but it is still a cause for concern.

• There is also evidence that when the CVS is done very early, the baby may develop an abnormality in the growth of its limbs.

• Occasionally, the placental tissues contain mosaic cells (abnormal cells that suggest that the baby has a chromosomal abnormality) when no significant abnormality is present. In this situation you will probably be advised to undergo an amniocentesis at a later date to check the results.

AMNIOCENTESIS

Amniocentesis is the most commonly performed invasive test. It involves taking a sample of the amniotic fluid around the baby, which is then sent

HAVING A CVS TEST

If you undergo a chorionic villus sampling test, you will first be given an ultrasound scan to identify exactly where the placenta is lying. The test requires a small sample of tissue from the placenta, and the amniotic sac has to be avoided during the procedure.

▶ A local anesthetic is injected into your abdominal wall to numb the area before a fine double-barreled needle is introduced into your uterus at the correct site to access some chorionic villi – the frondlike projections in the placenta.

▶ A syringe containing some special culture fluid is attached to the end of the needle and the placental cells are sucked up into the syringe.

▶ The tissue obtained is fresh living placenta, which means that when it reaches the cytogenetics laboratory culture and analysis is much quicker than from fetal skin cells cultured from an amniocentesis sample. You will probably receive a provisional test result within 72 hours and a conclusive result in about 10 days.

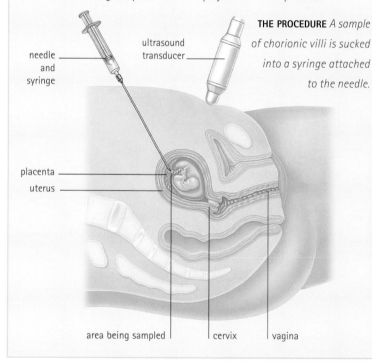

THE PROCEDURE *A sample of chorionic villi is sucked into a syringe attached to the needle.*

needle and syringe

ultrasound transducer

placenta

uterus

area being sampled | cervix | vagina

CVS SAMPLE *A magnified image shows a tissue sample taken from the budding chorionic villi.*

to the laboratory for analysis. The test is usually performed at 14–16 weeks of pregnancy, but can be performed up to 26 weeks. You will be offered an amniocentesis test if:
• you are more than 35 years of age
• you have a personal or family history of a baby with Down or another chromosomal abnormality
• you have had an abnormal nuchal translucency scan result or a high-risk serum screening result in your current pregnancy.

When the amniocentesis sample reaches the cytogenetics laboratory, the fluid is spun hard to collect cells from the baby's skin together in a pellet. These cells have floated off the surface of the skin into the amniotic fluid in much the same way that our skin cells float off into bathwater. These fetal skin cells then have to be encouraged to grow in tissue culture, which takes time (usually three to four weeks) and much expertise. They then have to be brought to a stage where they are actively dividing (called the metaphase stage) to perform the chromosomal analysis. Sometimes the cells cannot be encouraged to grow or are very slow in growing, which can delay your result. Rarely, the cells that are cultured are found to be your own and not your baby's; in these circumstances you would need to undergo a further amniocentesis.

Occasionally, the placental tissues contain mosaic cells (abnormal cells that are not representative of the baby's general chromosmal makeup). In this situation you will probably be advised to undergo a second amniocentesis at a later date to check the results of the first test. Amniocentesis is not usually performed until 14–16 weeks of pregnancy because before this time, the number of fetal skin cells may be insufficient to set up a culture and obtain a result. Removing fluid from the amniotic pool at too early a stage may also cause problems with the development of the baby's lungs.

Pros and cons of amniocentesis

A positive aspect of amniocentesis is that it is extremely rare for the results to be wrong and the

HAVING AMNIOCENTESIS

This procedure takes about 20 minutes and is performed using ultrasound guidance to find the best point to insert the amniocentesis needle. The optimal spot is where the needle can enter through the uterine wall and reach a pool of amniotic fluid, without touching either the placenta or the baby.

▶ The operator will probably put some local anesthetic into your skin at this spot to reduce any discomfort, but the amnio needle is so thin that you will find this procedure is even less painful than a blood sample being taken from your arm.

▶ Once positioned in the right place, a syringe is attached to the outer sheath of the needle and the sample of amniotic fluid (about 10–20ml, the equivalent of 4 teaspoonfuls) is sucked into the syringe.

needle and syringe

ultrasound transducer

REMOVING A SAMPLE
Care is taken to find a place where fluid can be removed without touching the fetus or the placenta.

placenta

amniotic fluid

uterus

cervix

▶ The needle is then removed and the baby is scanned carefully to ensure that all is well.

▶ You will be advised to rest and avoid strenuous activity for 24 hours.

Some women feel slightly sore for an hour or two afterward. A few have spotting of blood or leaking of amniotic fluid from the vagina. This usually stops within a short time.

risk of miscarriage is low. Although generally quoted as one percent, in units that are performing many of these procedures the risk is much lower — on the order of 1 in 300 or 0.3 percent. The risk of miscarriage is highest within two weeks of having the amniocentesis performed. It is relevant that only pregnancies with potential problems are going to undergo this test, so later complications may not be directly related to the procedure and may have been going to happen anyway.

The downside to amniocentesis is that you will not have the results before about 17–18 weeks of pregnancy. This means that if the result shows an abnormality and you choose to terminate the pregnancy, you will have to undergo an induced labor to deliver the baby vaginally (*see* pp. 294–97).

NEW DEVELOPMENTS IN CHROMOSOMAL ANALYSIS

If you are particularly distressed by the thought of a three-week wait for your results, you should ask about a new technique that has become available in some specialist centers called amnio-PCR. Using a powerful molecular biology technique — the polymerase chain reaction (PCR) — the DNA in the fetal skin cells can be multiplied massively to provide sufficient quantities to allow the diagnosis to be made within a couple of days.

FISH or fluorescent in-situ hybridization is another new form of sample testing that is becoming more widely available. This method tags pieces of DNA from a specific chromosome with fluorescent colored markers. These are then placed on the cells that are being tested where they glow (fluoresce) with a specific color that is easily seen under the laboratory microscope. The beauty of this technique is that the cells being examined do not have to be nurtured to the point where they are actively dividing to see whether or not the correct number of chromosomes are present.

CORDOCENTESIS

This procedure involves taking a sample of the baby's blood from the umbilical cord and is only performed after 18 weeks, when the blood vessels in the umbilical cord are large enough to be clearly visualized. Under ultrasound control, a needle is inserted through the mother's abdominal wall into the uterus and guided into a blood vessel in the cord close to where it emerges from the placenta. The risk of miscarriage is between one and two percent and the test is undertaken only by experienced technicians in specialized units.

Cordocentesis is the quickest way to diagnose a chromosomal abnormality because the fetal blood can be directly and rapidly analyzed. Less commonly, cordocentesis may be used to measure the fetal hemoglobin in a pregnancy affected by rhesus incompatibility (*see* p.128 and p.424). Fetal blood transfusions are also performed by cordocentesis.

Occasionally, the possibility that a fetus has been infected with rubella or toxoplasmosis needs to be confirmed in later pregnancy with a blood sample taken from the umbilical cord.

FETOSCOPY

In this procedure a thin, illuminated telescope is inserted through the cervix and into the uterus to look at the baby, particularly the limbs, genitals, spine, and skin, together with the color of the amniotic fluid. Some rare liver and skin disorders in the fetus can be diagnosed by fetoscopy and tissue samples obtained for laboratory confirmation. It is a high-risk intervention, which may lead to late miscarriage or preterm delivery and is only performed in exceptional circumstances.

CONGENITAL DISORDERS

Congenital means "born with." The term includes all genetic disorders and any physical or structural abnormality that may be present in a baby. This section will help you understand how and why many congenital disorders arise and give a context to many of the prenatal tests that have been described already. An increasing number of abnormalities can now be diagnosed prenatally, enabling parents and caregivers to plan treatment, although some abnormalities become apparent only after a baby is born.

Genetic disorders are caused by abnormalities in our genetic material that are either inherited or arise when a previously normal gene mutates (undergoes a change that makes it function abnormally). Some genetic disorders in the fetus are known to be due to the presence of a single or several abnormal genes. Others result because the number, shape, or arrangement of one of the chromosomes is abnormal. Still more are due to a complex interaction between environmental factors and genes, which is not fully understood. Spina bifida and cleft lip/palate are two examples. Only a few, mainly Down syndrome and spina bifida, are screened for regularly in pregnancy, although diagnostic tests and genetic counseling are available to couples who have particular risk factors or a family history of genetic diseases or other congenital abnormalities.

CHROMOSOME ABNORMALITIES

Before, during, and after fertilization the two sets of chromosomes (one from your egg and one from your partner's sperm) that make up your baby's complement of 23 pairs undergo a complex series of divisions and rearrangements. If one of the chromosomes is abnormal, or too many or too few chromosomes are left in the fertilized egg, an abnormal embryo or fetus may develop. Most are miscarried early, but sometimes the pregnancy continues and an abnormal baby is born.

About 6 babies in every 1,000 are born with a chromosomal abnormality. In stillborn babies the figure rises to 6 in every 100. The most common abnormalities are disorders in the number of chromosomes (either too many or too few), and the names reflect the number of the pair of chromosomes they affect.

Trisomies occur when three copies of one chromosome are present. Most trisomies are due to abnormal cell division (meiosis) in the egg, which occurs before fertilization. They are much more common in older women, because older eggs are more likely to be abnormal. The most common trisomies are Down syndrome/Trisomy 21 (*see* p.147); Patau syndrome/Trisomy 13 (*see* p.415); and Edward syndrome/Trisomy 18 (*see* p.415).

Monosomies arise when one chromosome is completely missing. The most common type of monosomy, Turner syndrome (*see* p.416), is the loss of an X chromosome in girls.

Triploidy is when the embryo has an extra set of 23 chromosomes (*see* p.415).

Extra sex chromosomes occur in disorders such as Klinefelter syndrome (*see* p.416), in which boys have an extra X chromosome.

Translocations (*see* p.415) are abnormal arrangements of the correct number of chromosomes. When the transfer of genetic material occurs between two chromosomes, genetic material can be lost, augmented, or simply exchanged.

DOMINANT GENETIC DISEASES

In these inherited diseases, only one abnormal gene is necessary for the disease to develop. Males and females are equally affected and have a 50 percent chance of passing the gene and the disease on to their children. Unaffected individuals cannot pass on the gene or the disease. Dominant diseases are rarely fatal in early life because affected individuals would die before passing on the genes.

There is invariably a family history of the disease, but because dominant diseases are expressed to a greater or lesser degree in different individuals this may be difficult to establish without the help of a geneticist. In familial hypercholesterolemia (*see* p.416), for example, babies of affected parents can be tested at or after birth for high blood levels of cholesterol. Some of the dominant neurological disorders, such as Huntington's Disease (*see* p.416) and myotonic dystrophy, can now be diagnosed prenatally, thanks to advances in gene mapping technology, which can pinpoint the abnormality in DNA samples obtained by amniocentesis or CVS.

INCIDENCE AND CAUSES

▶ Major congenital abnormalities (such as heart or neural tube defects) are present in 4% of newborn babies and cause 1 in 4 perinatal deaths.

▶ Minor congenital abnormalities, such as an extra finger or toe, are present in at least 6% of newborns.

▶ About 40% of congenital problems are inherited as a result of genetic factors.

▶ Around 7% are acquired due to damage during development by infection (5%), exposure to drugs (2%), chemicals, X-rays, or metabolic disorders, such as uncontrolled diabetes.

▶ About 50% of congenital disorders are unexplained, although it is likely that the majority of these will be found to have a genetic origin or result from a mixture of environmental and genetic factors.

RECESSIVE GENETIC DISEASES

In these diseases two copies of the abnormal gene (one from each parent) are needed for the disease to develop. The recessive gene is usually masked by a normal dominant gene, and hence there may be no family history of affected individuals. However, when both parents are carriers, all of their male and female children have a 1 in 4 chance of inheriting two recessive genes and developing the disease, and a 2 in 4 chance of becoming a symptomless carrier of the disease.

Many recessive disorders can be diagnosed prenatally. Cystic fibrosis, sickle-cell anemia, and thalassemia (*see* p.417) are detected by DNA

"The most common congenital abnormalities are caused by disorders in the number of chromosomes — there can be either too many present or too few."

analysis from amniocentesis or CVS samples, whereas biochemical disorders such as Tay-Sachs disease (*see* p.416) and phenylketonuria (*see* p.417) are diagnosed from blood samples.

SEX-LINKED GENETIC DISEASES

Diseases such as hemophilia, Duchenne's muscular dystrophy (*see* p.417), and Fragile X syndrome (*see* p.418) are caused by a recessive gene located on the X (female sex) chromosome. The disease only affects men, because women have a second X chromosome to mask the effect of the recessive gene. Women are carriers of the disease, which means that their children have a 50 percent chance of inheriting the abnormal gene. A daughter may not inherit the gene at all, or she may become a symptomless carrier because the second X chromosome will prevent her from developing the disease. A son has a 50 percent

chance of developing the disease, because the Y chromosome inherited from his father will be unable to mask the disease. There is no male-to-male transmission of X-linked disorders, but occasionally an X-linked disorder may arise from a new random gene mutation.

NEURAL TUBE DEFECTS

Neural tube defects (*see also* p.418) are one of the most common serious congenital abnormalities. In the absence of prenatal screening, about 1 in every 400 babies is affected. Although the exact gene or genes have not been identified, these disorders tend to run in families. Incidence varies widely from one region to the next and has a strong connection with diet. Babies born with neural tube defects such as spina bifida are often severely handicapped and require frequent surgical procedures and hospitalization. Disability typically consists of weakness or paralysis of the legs and urinary and fecal incontinence.

GENETIC COUNSELING

Couples who know they have a family history of genetic disease or have already had a child with an inherited disorder are strongly encouraged to undergo genetic counseling when they are planning to get pregnant. They may wish to undergo prenatal diagnostic procedures such as chorionic villus sampling, amniocentesis, or specialist ultrasound scans during pregnancy. Furthermore, for certain conditions it is now possible to offer them preimplantation genetic diagnosis (PGD). PGD is a technique in which eggs are fertilized in vitro and one of the cells of the tiny embryos are analyzed to ensure that it is free of the genetic disorder before being implanted into the mother's uterus.

PRENATAL DIAGNOSIS

You may need genetic counseling and/or prenatal diagnosis if you have or have had:

▶ A child with a birth defect, chromosome abnormality, or genetic disorder

▶ A family history of either of the above

▶ A child with undiagnosed mental retardation

▶ An abnormal prenatal serum screen result

▶ A fetus with suspected abnormal ultrasound findings

▶ A maternal medical disorder that predisposes your baby to congenital abnormalities

▶ Exposure to an environmental hazard (teratogen) in your current pregnancy

▶ A parent known to be a carrier of a genetic disorder

▶ A history of recurrent miscarriage or fetal loss

▶ A previous neonatal death

DOWN SYNDROME

ALTHOUGH DOWN SYNDROME (TRISOMY 21) IS THE MOST COMMON CHROMOSOMAL
ABNORMALITY SEEN IN LIVE-BORN BABIES, NUMBERS HAVE FALLEN FROM 1 IN EVERY 600 BIRTHS TO
1 IN 1,000 IN RECENT YEARS, THANKS TO IMPROVED ACCURACY IN PRENATAL TESTING.

In 95 percent of cases of Down syndrome there is no family history. In three percent of cases, the extra chromosome 21 is attached to another chromosome (a translocation) and is inherited from one parent, who usually shows no signs of the problem. In the remaining two percent, mosaicism is present, which means that some cells in the body contain a third chromosome 21, whereas others have the normal two.

The risk of Down syndrome increases sharply with age (see below), but since older pregnant mothers are routinely offered screening, most Down babies are now born to women under 35. As a result, screening for all pregnant women is now being introduced.

Although about 50 percent of Down syndrome babies miscarry, 9 out of 10 full-term Down babies survive the first year of life. These babies are, however, at high risk of abnormalities of the heart or intestine and problems with hearing and eyesight, and usually have reduced muscular tone and are floppy. Physical features include slanting eyes, a single skin crease on the hands and feet, and a protruding tongue. The bridge of the nose is shallow or absent, which often means that the child is snuffly and susceptible to colds and chest infections.

All Down children are mentally handicapped, but the severity of the handicap is variable and difficult to predict before birth. Recent advances in the way Down children are educated has led to many leading relatively independent lives as adults. The average life expectancy is about 60 years of age, although leukemia is common in childhood and thyroid disease and a form of Alzheimer's disease are common in adults.

The Nuchal Translucency scan is an early screening test for Down syndrome (see p.137). Routine ultrasound scans may detect other markers, such as the absence of a nasal bone, or heart, kidney, and gut abnormalities. Skin creases on the hands and eyelids are also indications that a baby may be affected. However, some babies with Down syndrome have no obvious structural signs, and are not detected until after birth.

RISK OF DOWN SYNDROME

Maternal age at EDD	Under 25	25	26	27	28	29	30	31	32
Risk of Down syndrome	1:1500	1:1350	1:1300	1:1300	1:1100	1:1000	1:900	1:800	1:680
Maternal age at EDD	33	34	35	36	37	38	39	40	41
Risk of Down syndrome	1:570	1:470	1:380	1:310	1:240	1:190	1:150	1:110	1:85
Maternal age at EDD	42	43	44	45	46	47	48	49	50
Risk of Down syndrome	1:65	1:50	1:35	1:30	1:20	1:15	1:11	1:8	1:6

*EDD= expected delivery date

WEEKS 13–26
THE SECOND TRIMESTER

In the second trimester, your baby will grow steadily and the basic structures and organ systems that were formed in the first trimester will be further developed and consolidated. The size overall of the fetus will increase three- to four-fold, and its weight a dramatic 30–fold. Although over the coming weeks you will start to look noticeably pregnant, this is often a time of renewed energy, good health, and a sense of well-being.

CONTENTS

WEEKS 13–17

152 The developing baby

156 Your changing body

157 How you may feel physically

160 Your prenatal care

162 Things to consider

164 Diet and exercise

WEEKS 17–21

166 The developing baby

170 Your changing body

172 How you may feel physically

173 Your prenatal care

174 Your 20-week scan

177 Common concerns

178 Things to consider

WEEKS 21–26

180 The developing baby

184 Your changing body

186 How you may feel physically

188 Your prenatal care

189 Common concerns

194 Things to consider

YOUR BABY
IN THE SECOND TRIMESTER

WEEK 14 THE EYES
ARE NOW POSITIONED
AT THE FRONT OF THE
FACE WITH THE EYELIDS
TIGHTLY CLOSED.

"Your fully formed baby grows rapidly
during the second trimester and can soon
be felt kicking in the uterus."

WEEK 16 THE DIFFERENCE BETWEEN THE
MALE AND FEMALE GENITALIA IS INCREASINGLY
OBVIOUS. THIS MALE FETUS NOW HAS A SOLID
SCROTUM AND A RUDIMENTARY PENIS.

WEEK 20 THE EXTERNAL EARS ARE PERFECTLY FORMED, AND THE FETUS CAN HEAR BODY SOUNDS INSIDE THE UTERUS AND LOUD NOISES FROM THE WORLD OUTSIDE.

WEEK 21 A GLIMPSE OF THE FETAL FACE SHOWS A RECOGNIZABLE PERSON WITH A CLEARLY DEFINED NOSE AND FULLY DEVELOPED LIPS AND TONGUE.

WEEKS 13–17

THE DEVELOPING BABY

YOUR BABY IS LOOKING MORE AND MORE LIKE A HUMAN BEING. ALTHOUGH THE HEAD IS STILL RELATIVELY LARGE, THE LENGTH OF THE BODY IS INCREASING RAPIDLY. THE DEVELOPMENT OF THE LEGS IS CATCHING UP WITH THE ARMS AND VERY QUICKLY OVERTAKES THEM IN LENGTH. THE LIMBS NOW APPEAR TO BE IN BETTER PROPORTION WITH THE REST OF THE BODY.

Fingernails can be seen and toenails will start to develop in a few weeks. The trunk has straightened out, but the body still looks thin and is only covered by a layer of fine translucent skin through which the underlying blood vessels and bones can be seen clearly. Very soon, a protective layer of brown fat will start to form, which will help keep the baby warm.

The facial bones are complete, and the facial features are more delicate and much easier to recognize. The nose appears more pronounced and the external ears now stand clear of the sides of the head. The tiny bones in the inner ear have hardened, which allows the fetus to hear sounds for the first time. The eyes are looking forward, although they are still quite widely spaced, and the retina at the back of the eye has become sensitive to light. Although the eyelids are fully formed, they will continue to remain closed for most of the second trimester. However, your baby has already started to be aware of bright light beyond your abdominal wall. The recent development of facial muscles means that your baby can now make — but not yet control — facial expressions. If you happen to have an ultrasound scan at this stage, you may see your baby frowning, grimacing, or even squinting at you. Eyebrows and eyelashes start to develop, and the downy hair on the head becomes coarser and now contains some pigment. Inside the mouth, taste buds are appearing on the tongue.

INTRICATE MOVEMENTS

Perhaps the most important step forward in your baby's development is that all the connections between the brain, nerves, and muscles have been made. The nerves linking the muscles to the brain begin to develop a fatty coating of a substance called myelin, which helps transfer messages to and from the brain. As a result, the fetus is now capable of a wide range of quite intricate movements. The limbs can now move around their joints because the muscles that control this movement are now able to contract and relax. The arms are

◄ *At 14 weeks, the fetal eyelids are fused, but the eyes are sensitive to light.*

	WEEKS
FIRST TRIMESTER	▸ 1
	▸ 2
	▸ 3
	▸ 4
	▸ 5
	▸ 6
	▸ 7
	▸ 8
	▸ 9
	▸ 10
	▸ 11
	▸ 12
	▸ 13
SECOND TRIMESTER	▸ 14
	▸ 15
	▸ 16
	▸ 17
	▸ 18
	▸ 19
	▸ 20
	▸ 21
	▸ 22
	▸ 23
	▸ 24
	▸ 25
	▸ 26
THIRD TRIMESTER	▸ 27
	▸ 28
	▸ 29
	▸ 30
	▸ 31
	▸ 32
	▸ 33
	▸ 34
	▸ 35
	▸ 36
	▸ 37
	▸ 38
	▸ 39
	▸ 40

life size

NERVE FIBERS *Signals pass quickly from the fetal brain to the muscles and limbs now that the nerve fibers are coated with fatty myelin sheaths.*

CHORIONIC VILLI *The frondlike villi (colored green) in the placenta allow the exchange of gases and nutrients with the mother's blood.*

now long enough for the hands to meet together over the fetal body. When the hands touch they grasp each other and anything else they encounter — such as the umbilical cord. The fingers now curl and the arms and legs flex and extend. The fetus can make a fist or suck its thumb.

Despite all this activity, most first-time mothers are not aware of the fetal movements because the amniotic fluid acts as a cushion and the baby is still not large enough to directly stimulate the nerve endings in the wall of the uterus. Some second-time mothers who know what to expect report that they can feel "quickening" — fluttering sensations in their abdomen — but definite fetal movements are not usually recognized until about 18 or 20 weeks.

THE PLACENTA

The placenta continues to grow in size and produce essential hormones (*see* pp.158–59), which are needed throughout pregnancy to ensure that the baby's growth is on target and the mother's uterus and breasts continue their growth and development. In addition to providing the oxygen and nutrients that your baby needs until the time of delivery, the placenta has now formed a very sophisticated barrier that will help combat the risk of many infections for the rest of your pregnancy. In addition, the placenta will dilute the effect of any medical drugs on the baby, as well as nicotine and alcohol taken by the mother. By the end of the 16th week of pregnancy, the placenta has thickened to a depth less than ½ inch (1cm) and now spans around 3in (7–8 cm).

THE AMNIOTIC FLUID

The amniotic fluid, which fills the sac surrounding the fetus, plays a very important role in fetal development at this stage. It allows freedom of movement and the development of essential muscular tone, while protecting your baby from knocks and bumps. During the first trimester, the amniotic fluid was absorbed through the fetal skin, but in the early weeks of the second trimester the fetal kidneys start to function. From now on your baby will swallow amniotic fluid and excrete the fluid back into the amniotic cavity. Although the amount of amniotic fluid remains relatively constant, it is being absorbed and replaced continuously. The presence of the right amount of amniotic fluid is particularly important for the development of the fetal lungs. Although your baby will continue to obtain all its oxygen and nutrient supplies from the placenta until birth, the lungs must be able to float in a full bath of amniotic fluid in order to expand and develop optimally in preparation for breathing in the outside world. At this stage the bath contains about 180–200ml of amniotic fluid, which is equivalent to the contents of an average paper cup. During this period, the fetus starts to shed some of its own skin cells into the amniotic fluid. This is an important milestone because these cells can be used to determine the chromosomal status of your baby if you decide or are advised to have an amniocentesis test (*see* pp.140–42). Until now the skin cells available were too few to be a reliable source of information about your baby, which is why amniocentesis is usually not recommended until 15–16 weeks of gestation.

life size

At 13 weeks, the fetus is about 3in (8cm) long and weighs about 1oz (25g). By the start of the 17th week, its size has increased dramatically to about 5in (13cm). Its weight is now about 5oz (150g).

17 WEEKS OLD *On a 3-D ultrasound the fetus is seen wriggling and floating, but its movements are cushioned by the amniotic fluid and may not yet be felt.*

YOUR CHANGING BODY

YOU WILL PROBABLY HAVE NOTICED THAT YOUR WAIST HAS BECOME A LITTLE THICKER BY NOW AND YOUR TUMMY HAS BECOME ROUNDER BUT THE EXACT TIME IN WEEKS AT WHICH YOU BECOME NOTICEABLY PREGNANT TO OTHER PEOPLE DEPENDS VERY MUCH ON YOUR PREPREGNANCY WEIGHT AND SHAPE.

"Work colleagues and friends who are not in the know may now be looking quizzically at your abdomen."

Nevertheless, during the next few weeks you will be conscious of the fact that you are starting to "show" and that work colleagues and friends who are not in the know are starting to look quizzically at your abdomen. At the beginning of the second trimester, your uterus has grown to the size of a small melon and as a result can now be felt rising out of your pelvic cavity. From now on, its size can be easily assessed by gentle abdominal palpation.

SKIN PIGMENTATION

Increased skin pigmentation is very common in pregnancy and usually starts to be noticeable at the end of the first or the beginning of the second trimester. The extra estrogen secreted by your body stimulates cells in your skin called melanocytes to produce pigment that darkens the skin. The areola around your nipples may be the first noticeable change; in addition to becoming darker, the areola usually increases in size as well. Moles, birthmarks, and freckles are also likely to enlarge and darken, as will any areas of scar tissue. Most women develop a linea nigra or "black line" of pigmentation, which stretches down the center of their enlarging abdomen. The linea nigra can be prominent in some women from early in the second trimester, whereas in others it does not appear until a little later in the pregnancy. All these changes in color are entirely normal and usually fade away after the baby is born.

INCREASED BLOOD FLOW

None of these changes to your body would be possible without an increase in your circulating blood volume and important adaptations in the way that your heart and blood vessels work. The water content of your blood increased early in your pregnancy, but now the volume of red blood cells is becoming measurably larger. Your cardiac output (the amount of blood that is pumped through your heart per minute) continues to increase. Your stroke volume (the volume of blood pumped by your heart at every beat) and heart rate will also increase but thanks to the action of progesterone, your blood vessels will cope with these dynamic changes by becoming more dilated and relaxed.

At the beginning of the second trimester, 25 percent of your blood is being directed to the uterus in order to support your growing baby and placenta, which is an enormous increase compared to the two percent that your uterus used to receive before you became pregnant.

The blood flow to your kidneys will continue to rise until the 16th week, after which it levels off. The filtering capacity of your kidneys, which started to increase in the first trimester, is now 60 percent higher than it was before you were pregnant and will stay at this level until the last four weeks of your pregnancy, when it will fall again. However, the tiny tubules in your kidneys, responsible for reabsorbing the substances that pass through them, are now working overtime. Hence, it is not uncommon for your urine to contain small amounts of sugar and protein.

HOW YOU MAY FEEL PHYSICALLY

NOW THAT YOUR PREGNANCY HAS ENTERED ITS SECOND TRIMESTER, YOU WILL BE MUCH MORE CONFIDENT THAT THIS BABY IS GOING TO BECOME A REALITY. ON A PHYSICAL LEVEL, YOU WILL MOST PROBABLY BE FEELING LESS NAUSEOUS AND BE REGAINING SOME OF YOUR USUAL VITALITY.

You have probably started to tell friends, family, and colleagues that you are pregnant and find you have become the focus of much attention, congratulations, and advice about what you should and should not be doing as a pregnant woman. Advice is usually offered freely, not just by close family members and friends, but also by people you hardly know, and although it is almost always well meaning, there are times when it may be confusing and even distressing, not to mention entirely irrelevant to your pregnancy. There is absolutely no need for you to be elated one moment and desperately worried the next by such potentially erroneus information, so be careful who you discuss your pregnancy with at this stage. Remember to treat unsolicited advice and cautionary tales with a large grain of salt.

MINOR IRRITATIONS

There are some minor problems that may become noticeable in the early weeks of the second trimester. For example, some of you will notice that your nose is permanently stuffy, although you are not suffering from a cold. You might even be experiencing nosebleeds, blocked ears, and bleeding gums. These symptoms are nothing to worry about, but because they are due to the increased blood

"remember to treat unsolicited advice and cautionary tales with a large grain of salt."

THE MAJOR PREGNANCY HORMONES

From the first day of your pregnancy most of the subtle and more dramatic changes in your body and the way it is functioning are under the control of key hormones. These are produced from existing sources and glands within your body but also, increasingly as the pregnancy progresses, by the placenta and the developing baby.

HORMONE	WHAT IT DOES	WHERE PRODUCED
Human Chorionic Gonadotropin (HCG)	Maintains secretion of pregnancy hormones estrogen and progesterone by the corpus luteum in the ovary until the placenta takes over.	Produced in large quantities by the young placenta peaking at 10–12 weeks, then declining rapidly.
Estrogen	Increasingly high levels in pregnancy boost the blood flow to body organs and promote the dramatic growth and development of the uterus and breasts. Softens collagen fibers in connective tissue to allow ligaments to become more flexible.	Over 90 percent is a type called estriol, which is produced by the placenta; fetus is also involved in the estrogen production process.
Progesterone	Relaxes blood vessels to cope with increased blood flow. Has similar relaxing effects on digestive and urinary tracts. Hypnotic effect may induce placid feelings in pregnancy. Relaxes muscles and helps ligaments and tendons loosen to accommodate the growing uterus and prepare the birth canal for delivery. Prevents contractions until birth is due. Prepares the breasts for lactation.	Until week 6–8, corpus luteum produces progesterone to maintain the pregnancy. By the end of the first trimester, progesterone is produced entirely by the placenta.
Human Placental Lactogen (HPL)	Similar to growth hormone, HPL accounts for 10 percent of the placenta's protein production. Diverts mother's glucose stores to the fetus; also has effects on maternal insulin production and uptake to help the transfer of nutrients to the fetus. Has a role in breast development and in milk secretion after delivery.	Produced by the placenta from five weeks onward; levels rise throughout pregnancy.

HORMONE FACTORIES *The key site of hormone production in early pregnancy is the maternal ovary (far left), but by 12 weeks the placenta and fetus take control. The placenta both produces hormones and martials the fetal and maternal resources to produce estrogen.*

Increasing hormone concentration

0 5 10 15 20 25 30 35 40
Weeks

KEY

— Human chorionic gonadotropin
— Estrogen
— Progesterone
— Human Placental Lactogen

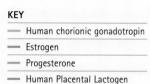

KEY HORMONES *A graph illustrates the surge in HCG hormone early in pregnancy and the steady rise in levels of estrogen, progesterone, and HPL throughout pregnancy.*

HORMONE	WHAT IT DOES	WHERE PRODUCED
Prolactin	Stimulates breasts to produce milk. Prolactin levels increase during pregnancy, but their effect is blocked until after the birth.	Produced in the anterior lobe of the pituitary gland in the brain.
Relaxin	An insulin-like substance in the blood that helps soften the pelvic ligaments for delivery and also aids cervical ripening (softening and thinning) ready for dilatation and childbirth.	The ovaries produce relaxin.
Oxytocin	Causes the muscles of the uterus to contract. Levels rise in the first stage of labor and are further stimulated by the widening of the birth canal. Oxytocin helps the uterus contract after childbirth and is stimulated by the baby sucking on the nipple during breastfeeding.	Produced by the posterior lobe of the pituitary gland. Receptors in the uterus increase in late pregnancy, enabling oxytocic drugs to be used to induce and augment labor.
Cortisol and Adrenocortico-tropic hormone (ACTH)	Production increases from the end of the first trimester onward. Effects contribute to stretch marks and high blood glucose levels. Cortisol has an important role in helping mature the fetal lungs.	Cortisol secreted by the maternal adrenal glands and the placenta. ACTH from the pituitary gland prompts release of cortisol.
Androgens (testosterone and similar hormones)	Vital building blocks for the production of estrogen during pregnancy. Some testosterone is needed for the development of the male external genitalia.	Produced largely by the fetal adrenal gland. Fetal testes also produce testosterone.

HORMONE EFFECTS *The expansion of your uterus is made possible by a boost in blood flow due to estrogen and the softening effect of progesterone on your ligaments and muscles. After birth, prolactin and oxytocin stimulate your breasts to produce milk.*

"You may find that you are increasingly forgetful — a symptom that is jokingly referred to as maternal amnesia."

flow to the mucous membranes of your nose, mouth, ears, and sinuses, they are likely to remain with you for the rest of the pregnancy. So it makes sense to think about ways to alleviate these symptoms, even though it is unlikely that you will be able to get rid of them altogether until the baby is born.

Try to avoid spending too much time in hot, dry environments at work and home, especially those with central heating and air conditioning, both of which dry out the air. You can improve the atmosphere by using inexpensive, portable humidifiers in the rooms you use most frequently. If you experience repeated nosebleeds, then you should discuss this with your doctor, who may suggest that you visit a specialist.

You may find that you are increasingly forgetful — a symptom that is often jokingly referred to as maternal amnesia. I think it is simply a reflection of the the fact that women are so preoccupied with the excitement of pregnancy during this period that other things seem less important and fail to register. Even if you find yourself forgetting things and unable to multi-task in your usual way, rest assured that this vagueness often abates later in pregnancy and you will almost certainly be back to your normal self after the birth.

YOUR PRENATAL CARE

EVEN THOUGH MOST WOMEN REMAIN PHYSICALLY FIT AND WELL THROUGHOUT PREGNANCY, IT IS USUAL TO SEE YOUR PRENATAL CAREGIVERS ABOUT EVERY FOUR WEEKS DURING THE SECOND TRIMESTER.

The exact timing of your visits depends upon when you began prenatal care, the results of your blood and urine tests, the type of care you have chosen, and whether you have any particular problems that need attention, but the procedure at each routine checkup is usually much the same.

• Your urine will be tested for protein and glucose. It is not unusual to find small amounts of these in your urine on isolated occasions, but if either substance is found at several visits, an early glucose tolerance test to check for gestational diabetes may be advisable (see p.212).

• Your blood pressure will be measured to make sure that you are not at risk from some of the common complications of pregnancy.

• Your doctor or midwife will most likely examine your hands and feet to ensure that you have no swelling or edema.

• Your abdomen will be examined and the distance between the fundus (the dome-shaped top of your uterus) and your symphysis pubis (pubic bone) will be measured to ensure that the uterus is growing steadily by about 1cm per week. This measurement, which is always expressed in centimeters, is known as the symphyseal-fundal height (SFH). At 14 weeks it will be about 14cm and by 16 weeks it will be about 16cm. Of course, measurements vary depending on a woman's height and build, together with the number of babies she is carrying and the quantity of amniotic fluid. If you are carrying twins or more, your fundal height will be much higher than would normally be expected for the number of weeks of your pregnancy.

• Your caregivers will also listen to your baby's heartbeat by placing a special monitor called a Doppler ultrasound over your uterus. This uses Doppler sound waves (which are completely safe for use in pregnancy) to record your baby's heart rate, which at this stage in pregnancy will be about 140 beats per minute — approximately double your own.

• Most prenatal caregivers weigh pregnant women at every clinic visit (see p.408).

YOUR PRENATAL VISITS

Whether you receive your prenatal care from a single doctor or midwife or your caregivers are part of a larger practice, your prenatal care is likely to follow a similar pattern. Your appointments may not correspond exactly to this chart, but they will follow the same general pattern.

8–12 weeks	First prenatal visit	34 weeks	Blood test for anemia; discuss birth plan, vitamin K injections for newborn baby, and infant feeding
16–18 weeks	First trimester serum screening tests, NT (nuchal translucency ultrasound)		
16–20 weeks	Results of blood tests	36–41 weeks	Weekly visits to doctor/midwife
18–20 weeks	Detailed fetal ultrasound scan	35–37 weeks	Group B Streptococci (GBS) screening
24 weeks	See midwife/doctor	41 weeks	Visit with doctor. Discuss possible induction of labor
28 weeks	Blood tests for anemia, glucose screening, receive Rhogam injection if blood group is Rhesus negative		
30 weeks	See midwife/doctor	41 weeks and 3 days	Attend the labor and delivery unit at the hospital for non stress test (NST), which is a tracing of the baby's heart rate, and an ultrasound scan to assess fluid volume and fetal well-being
32 weeks	See midwife/doctor		

PRENATAL RECORDS

It is a good idea to request a copy of your prenatal records sometime between the initial visit and the 18–20-week scan. This provides you with clear documentation of what has happened in the past and during your current pregnancy, which you can immediately share with any doctor or midwife that you may need to consult. Having your records available also makes it possible for you to review your progress in the journey through pregnancy anytime you want to. Most pregnant women are very good at remembering to bring their notes to prenatal appointments; consequently, lost records are rarely a problem.

THINGS TO CONSIDER

AT THIS STAGE OF PREGNANCY YOUR IMMEDIATE CONCERN IS PROBABLY FINDING SOMETHING SUITABLE TO WEAR TO WORK. YOU MAY ALSO BE WONDERING IF SOME OF THE SIDE EFFECTS OF PREGNANCY CAN BE PREVENTED — FOR EXAMPLE, BY TAKING EXTRA CARE OF YOUR SKIN.

STRETCH MARKS

The vast majority of pregnant women will develop some stretch marks during pregnancy. These are caused by the collagen beneath the skin tearing as it stretches to accommodate your enlarging body. Stretch marks can make an appearance at an early stage in pregnancy, and they tend to occur initially on the breasts, because these are the first parts of the body to start expanding, and then on the abdomen, hips, and thighs. The number and extent of stretch marks varies greatly from one woman to the next and is determined mainly by your genes and your age. As you get older your skin loses its elasticity, making stretch marks more likely. There is some evidence that if you are physically fit and well toned before pregnancy and ensure that your weight gain during pregnancy is gradual, you can limit their appearance.

STRETCH MARKS *If you are prone to stretch marks there is nothing you can do to prevent them. However, their dark appearance will fade with time and they will be much less noticeable.*

If you do develop stretch marks — and remember, few women do not — rest assured that, with time, their pink appearance (together with any itching) will fade. They will not disappear altogether but will become a lighter silvery shade that makes them less visible. There are numerous anti stretch mark creams on the market, but despite what the manufacturers would like us to believe, I'm afraid that no cream applied to your skin can have much effect on what is happening to the deeper layers of collagen that lie well below the surface. That said, massaging creams into your skin to keep it smooth and supple is very pleasurable — and any good moisturizing cream will do.

WHAT TO WEAR

You will find that some of your favorite clothes no longer fit, but try to resist the temptation to go out and buy a whole new wardrobe. You are well advised to wait and buy clothes for the last trimester, by which time there will be very little in your current wardrobe that you will be able to wear. You also need to consider the change in seasons between now and the final months of pregnancy. So look carefully at your current wardrobe, put away anything that has become out of the question or feels even slightly uncomfortable, and concentrate on what still fits and can be worn for the next few weeks.

It is very tedious to have only a limited selection of clothes, so this is a good time to review some of your partner's T-shirts, sweatshirts, and jeans to see if any are suitable. Borrowing larger sizes from your partner or friends is a great way to get through this transition period. You will then be able to save your clothes budget for the later stages of pregnancy, when you are likely to be desperate for a few new things to wear.

COSMETIC EFFECTS

If you feel that having tanned legs and arms and a brown belly are essential to your self-esteem, be aware that, in general, you will tan more quickly during pregnancy because the amount of pigment in your skin has increased. It is a good idea to avoid long periods in the sun to minimize the risk of burning, and prematurely aging your skin. Tanning beds should be avoided for much the same reason. When you are in the sun, make sure that you use a high-SPF sunblock on your face, neck, and shoulders. Alternatively, try self-tanning products, all of which are safe to use in pregnancy.

If you want to get rid of unwanted hair, depilatories are safe to use but shaving or waxing may be your preferred option if you want to minimize contact with chemicals. Avoid waxing over any heavily pigmented moles or varicose veins.

Those of you with tattoos and piercings may have a few questions now that you are pregnant. A belly ring or bar will become uncomfortable as your abdomen grows and is unlikely to stay in place when your navel begins to protrude in late pregnancy, so have it removed sooner rather than later. Nipple rings can be left in place for now but will need to be taken out if you want to breastfeed. Tattoos on any area of your body that expands may change beyond recognition. You should not have any new piercings or tattoos during pregnancy because of the risk of infections such as hepatitis B and C (*see* p.129), and HIV (*see* p.414).

TIGHT FIT *Put away anything that no longer fits and see if you can borrow a bigger size.*

WEEKS 17–21
THE DEVELOPING BABY

THE GROWTH OF YOUR BABY'S BODY AND LIMBS CONTINUES VERY RAPIDLY DURING THIS TIME AND, AS A RESULT, THE HEAD NOW APPEARS IN BETTER PROPORTION TO THE REST OF THE BODY. BY THE END OF WEEK 20 THE HEAD MAKES UP LESS THAN ONE-THIRD OF THE TOTAL LENGTH OF THE FETUS.

Your baby's legs in particular have undergone an amazing growth spurt and are now longer than the arms. From this point onward, the rate of growth of the body and limbs will start to slow down, although the fetus will continue to gain weight at a steady pace until the time of delivery. This relative slowing in physical size is an important milestone because it marks the fact that the baby is now developing in different ways. The lungs, digestive tract, and nervous and immune systems are all starting to mature in preparation for life in the outside world. The skeleton can now be seen clearly on an X-ray because further calcium has been deposited in the bones to harden them.

Your baby's sexual organs are now well developed and the difference between the male and female external genitalia is increasingly obvious. Inside the body of a baby girl, the ovaries contain the three million eggs that she will be born with; the uterus is fully formed and the vagina is starting to become hollow. A baby boy's testes have not descended from the abdominal cavity into the scrotum, but a solid scrotal swelling alongside a rudimentary penis can often be seen between the boy's legs on an ultrasound scan. An ultrasound scan at 20 weeks should be able to determine the sex of your baby, provided she or he is facing the right way. On the chest wall of both boys and girls, early breast tissue (mammary glands) has developed and nipples can be seen on the skin surface.

IMPROVING SENSES
Although your baby's eyelids are still generally closed, the eyeballs can roll from side to side, and at the back of the eye, the retina is light-sensitive because nerve connections to the brain have been established. Your baby's taste buds are so well developed that they can now distinguish between sweet and bitter flavors (although these are unavailable in utero) and many of the first "milk" teeth have developed inside the gums. The mouth opens and closes regularly, and an ultrasound scan may capture your baby sticking its tongue out. Although it still has no conscious thoughts, it now hears sounds very clearly such as those of

◀ *At 19 weeks, the facial features are already remarkably refined.*

life size

WEEKS
FIRST TRIMESTER 1 2 3 4 5 6 7 8 9 10 11 12 13
SECOND TRIMESTER 14 15 16 ▶17 ▶18 ▶19 ▶20 ▶21 22 23 24 25 26
THIRD TRIMESTER 27 28 29 30 31 32 33 34 35 36 37 38 39 40

"The fetus may move around vigorously if exposed to loud noises such as music at a rock concert."

your heart beating, blood pulsing through the vessels in your lower body, and your digestive system churning around. It is often suggested that one reason why newborn babies usually stop crying when they are placed over their mother's left shoulder is that they recognize the comforting memory of her heartbeat.

The fetus can also hear sounds from outside your body and may jump or move around vigorously if exposed to loud noises such as music at a rock concert. The pattern of the fetal heartbeat, now clearly audible if an electronic monitor or Doppler ultrasound is placed on your abdomen wall in the correct place, also changes in response to loud external sound. The skin has also become responsive to touch and, when firm pressure is placed on your tummy, your baby will move away from the intruding stimulus.

NEW NERVE NETWORKS

All of these sophisticated developments in your baby's senses are due to the fact that the nervous system is developing rapidly and maturing steadily. New nerve networks are being formed continuously and acquiring fatty, insulating myelin sheaths, which enables them to transmit messages to and from the brain at great speed. A fibrous sheath starts to grow around the nerve bundles in the spinal cord to help protect them from mechanical damage. These adjustments to the nervous system help your baby become much more active. Even though you may not be able to feel the movements yet, your baby is constantly moving,

FETUS AT 19 WEEKS

A fine covering of downy hair forms on the eyebrows and upper lip.

Your baby now hears sounds very clearly — your heart beating and the rumblings of your stomach.

twisting, turning, stretching, grasping, and doing somersaults. This increase in muscular activity allows movements to become more refined and purposeful, improving motor skills and coordination and helping develop stronger bones.

SKIN AND HAIR

The fetus starts to look a little plumper and less wrinkly during this stage of pregnancy as thin layers of body fat begin to form. Some of this fat is insulating brown fat, which starts to be deposited in pockets at the nape of the neck, behind the breastbone, around the kidneys, and in the groin areas. Babies that are born prematurely or are underweight have very little brown fat, which is why they have such difficulties trying to maintain their body temperature and become cold very quickly.

There is still very little fat beneath the skin, so the blood vessels, particularly those around the head, are clearly visible and the skin continues to look red and translucent. However, your baby's entire body is now covered with a fine downy layer of lanugo hair, which was first seen around the fetal eyebrows and upper lip at about 14 weeks. Lanugo hair is thought to be one of the mechanisms that help the fetus keep warm until it has sufficient fat stores. This is probably why babies born before 36 weeks are usually still covered in lanugo, while those born at full term have shed most of the hair during the last few weeks in the uterus. This fine covering of skin hair also helps ensure that the baby remains covered in the thick white waxy coating, called vernix, that starts to be secreted from the sebaceous glands in the skin during this second trimester. The vernix protects the fetal skin from fingernail scratches and prevents it from becoming waterlogged during the many weeks that it is immersed in amniotic fluid.

SUPPORT SYSTEMS

The placenta continues to be the fetal life support system and is now fully developed functionally. However, it will continue to grow, tripling in size by the end of a normal pregnancy. Up until now, it weighed more than the fetus, but from this point onward the fetal weight overtakes that of the placenta.

It is quite common to find the placenta lying low in the uterus during the 20-week ultrasound scan, but this is not a cause for concern at this stage. Although the placenta is firmly attached to the uterine wall, the uterus surrounding it will grow considerably both upward and downward during pregnancy. The lower segment of the uterus starts to form in preparation for delivery at around 32 weeks, with the effect that the majority of placentas are no longer low lying when visualized on an ultrasound scan. Of course, the placenta

life size

At 19 weeks the fetus now measures about 6in (15cm) from crown to rump. Its weight is now about 8oz (225g). By the end of 21 weeks, its length is around 7in (17cm) and it weighs about 12oz (350g).

does not change its position; instead, the uterus grows around the placenta at a different rate and at different times in the pregnancy. In fact, the uterus continues to grow until about 37 weeks and, at term, less than one percent of women have a low-lying placenta (*see* p.240 and p.427).

The pool of amniotic fluid around the fetus continues to increase: by the end of the 20th week it contains about 11fl oz (320ml). This is a dramatic increase when compared to the 1fl oz (30ml) of amniotic fluid that was present in the uterus at 12 weeks. The temperature of the fluid remains at 99.5°F (37.5°C), which is slightly higher than the mother's body temperature. This is another factor that keeps the fetus warm.

YOUR CHANGING BODY

FOR SOME WOMEN, WEIGHT INCREASES GRADUALLY, WHILE OTHERS NOTICE A BIG SPURT ONE WEEK AND NO APPARENT INCREASE DURING THE NEXT. OVERALL, YOU WILL GAIN, ON AVERAGE, 1–2LB (0.5–1KG) PER WEEK DURING THIS PERIOD, AND BY WEEK 21 YOU WILL DEFINITELY LOOK PREGNANT.

At 18 weeks the fundus of your uterus can be felt midway between your pubic bone and navel (umbilicus) when your midwife or doctor gently palpates your tummy; by week 21 it will probably be at or just below your navel. The symphyseal fundal height (the distance between the top of your uterus and your pubic bone) will be 21cm. Although this measurement is not as accurate as a scan, it is a quick way to establish that your baby is growing satisfactorily.

"...your blood pressure has not shot through the roof because most of your blood vessels have become more dilated and flexible..."

FEELING THE HEAT

The volume of blood in your circulation continues to increase steadily and by 21 weeks it will measure nearly 11 pints (5 liters). This increase is needed to supply the many organs in your body that are now working much harder than usual. The uterus is receiving the biggest share of this extra blood flow, which is vital to perfuse the placenta and provide sufficient oxygen and nutrients for your baby; an extra 17 fl oz (0.5 liters) of blood will continue to be pumped to your kidneys every minute for the rest of your pregnancy. A higher than normal proportion of your blood flow is also going to your skin and mucous membranes and their blood vessels have become dilated to accommodate it. This is one of the reasons why pregnant women have blocked and stuffy noses, feel the heat, sweat more profusely, and feel faint during pregnancy.

EXTRA BLOOD VOLUME

To deliver this extra blood to your organs, your cardiac output must continue to increase gradually and by 20 weeks, your heart is pumping about 15 pints (7 liters) of blood per minute. However, your heart rate (the number of times your heart beats every minute) cannot be allowed to rise too much or you would start to experience palpitations. The extra blood volume and the stronger pumping activity of your heart should logically result in your blood pressure rising dramatically, but important changes that are taking place in the blood vessels, which usually prevent these problems from developing.

One of the major reasons why your blood pressure has not shot through the roof is because most of the blood vessels in your body have become more dilated and flexible (known medically as a fall in their peripheral resistance). They contain much more blood than they used to, thanks to the action of progesterone and other hormones, and this extra blood volume and your dilated blood vessels can lead to unwelcome physical symptoms such as varicose veins (*see* p.235) and hemorrhoids (*see* p.217). This fall in peripheral resistance ensures that, in most cases, blood pressure alters very minimally during the first 30 weeks of pregnancy, unless complications such as pregnancy induced hypertension develop (*see* p.425). After 30 weeks there is a normal tendency for the blood pressure to rise, but this increase should never be fast or excessive.

LINEA NIGRA *This line of pigmentation down the abdomen is usually more noticeable in women with dark or olive skin.*

CHANGES TO YOUR SKIN

As a result of the dilated blood vessels in your skin and the high levels of estrogen in your body, you are likely to notice tiny red marks called spider nevi appearing on your face, neck, shoulders, and chest.

The pigmentation in the skin around your nipples, genitalia, and the linea nigra down your tummy will continue to be more noticeable. This line, which is more prominent in some women than in others, marks the point where the right and left abdominal muscles meet in the midline. These strap muscles will start to separate from now on to accommodate your growing uterus, but why this should be accompanied by increasing pigmentation on the surface of your abdominal skin is a bit of a mystery.

Some women develop chloasma — also called the mask of pregnancy — on their face. In fair-skinned women the chloasma appears as darker, brownish patches mainly on the bridge of the nose and cheekbones and sometimes around the mouth. On darker skin, the patches appear lighter than the normal skin tone. Since all of these skin pigmentation changes are due to pregnancy hormones, they usually disappear or fade quite quickly after the baby is born.

CHLOASMA *This brown pigmentation usually develops symmetrically on the cheeks and other areas of the face.*

HOW YOU MAY FEEL PHYSICALLY

BY NOW, YOU ARE PROBABLY REDISCOVERING YOUR PREPREGNANCY ENERGY LEVELS. INDEED, MANY WOMEN FIND THAT, ALTHOUGH THEY NOW LOOK PREGNANT, THEY DON'T FEEL VERY DIFFERENT PHYSICALLY FROM THE WAY THEY DID BEFORE THEIR PREGNANCY BEGAN.

Your appetite will return — indeed it may increase — and you will find that you can once again enjoy normal meals. Make the best of this time in pregnancy and make sure that you follow a well-balanced nutritious diet (*see* pp.43–49). It will not be very long before your appetite is upset again, this time because of heartburn, indigestion, reduced stomach capacity, constipation, and all of the other gastrointestinal problems that develop in later pregnancy as the baby grows inside your abdominal cavity and your digestive system becomes sluggish.

Your sex drive may also have returned and for many couples this is a reassuring sign that pregnancy has not permanently changed their physical relationship. Indeed, some find that their sex life becomes particularly enjoyable during this trimester. A variety of factors contribute to this. Physically you are generally feeling better, which is important since nausea and fatigue are real passion killers, and your hormone levels are less likely to be swinging all over the place. In addition, both you and your partner may be feeling more relaxed in this trimester, having had time to get used to the idea of you being pregnant.

The first time you become aware of your baby's movements is a physical experience that is almost inseparable from the emotional response that follows it. If you have not had a baby before, you may dismiss these first fluttery sensations as gas, but after a while you realize they are unrelated to your digestion; they feel quite different. No one can predict the exact date when you will feel your baby moving around, but it is likely to happen now or very soon.

FIRST FLUTTERS *It may take a while before you are certain that you are feeling your baby move.*

YOUR EMOTIONS

By now you have probably told most of the people with whom you have regular contact that you are expecting a baby but, even if you have been keeping the news to yourself, your changing shape will have given other hints that you are pregnant. Whether you are at home or at work, you are likely to find that everyone around you wants to talk about your pregnancy. Like many women, you may enjoy this new-found closeness with relative strangers and welcome the chance to share your excitement about the pregnancy. There are very few occasions in life when we embark on a deeply personal conversation with a complete stranger and then allow them to pat our tummy or place a paternalistic arm around our shoulders. This happened all the time when I was pregnant and I confess that, after some initial feelings of surprise, this generous display of warmth and goodwill confirmed for me that I was going through a very special time, and that everyone around me recognized this fact. Having said that, I do appreciate that some women view this outside interest in their pregnant state as an unwanted invasion of their privacy. If you find yourself in the latter group you may need to find ways to protect yourself from becoming resentful and angry.

Overall, this is one of the most enjoyable stages in pregnancy and you are probably feeling more serene and calm than usual. Try to enjoy the relative peace of the second trimester because the third trimester will probably bring with it some emotional highs and lows, not to mention some physical discomfort.

"...you may enjoy this new-found closeness with relative strangers and welcome the chance to share your excitement about the pregnancy."

YOUR PRENATAL CARE

YOU WILL SEE YOUR PRENATAL CAREGIVERS EVERY FOUR WEEKS DURING THE SECOND TRIMESTER FOR CHECKS ON YOUR URINE, BLOOD PRESSURE, AND THE HEIGHT OF YOUR FUNDUS. YOUR BABY'S HEARTBEAT WILL BE LISTENED TO USING A DOPPLER ULTRASOUND MONITOR OR A FETOSCOPE.

If you have not already been given the results of your early blood tests and serum screening tests, this will be done at one of your prenatal appointments during this stage of pregnancy.

THE FETAL ANATOMY SCAN

Most maternity units in Canada offer women an ultrasound scan at about 20 weeks (*see* pp.174–75), although the exact timing varies from one unit to another to complement additional prenatal tests such as serum screening blood tests. However, it is usually performed between 18 and 22 weeks and is frequently referred to as the fetal anatomy scan because at this stage of pregnancy, your baby's organs and major body systems are sufficiently developed for it to be possible to detect the vast majority of potential structural abnormalities. The majority of anatomy scans will demonstrate that your baby

YOUR 20-WEEK SCAN

BY AROUND 20 WEEKS YOUR BABY IS SUFFICIENTLY DEVELOPED FOR MOST OF THE MAJOR ORGANS AND BODY SYSTEMS TO BE VIEWED ON ULTRASOUND AND CHECKED FOR SIGNS OF A PROBLEM. FOR MOST WOMEN, THIS SCAN WILL REASSURE THEM THAT ALL IS PROGRESSING WELL.

Below is a summary of the most common checks during this scan but they will not necessarily occur in this order, because your baby will be moving around constantly and may not always be in the right position. Measurements and observations of your baby will be taken as the opportunity allows. The sonographer will only check off the boxes on the checklist when everything has been seen clearly. So if the position of

your baby makes this impossible at first, you may be asked to walk around and then return for further measurements or even come back in a week or so for a further attempt.

▶ **The fetal heartbeat** is usually the first item to be checked. The sonographer will also look for the four chambers of the heart. If a specialized heart scan is needed, this usually takes place at 22–24 weeks.

▶ **In the abdominal cavity,** the shape and size of the stomach, intestines, liver, kidneys, and bladder will be examined and the sonographer will check that your baby's intestines are now completely enclosed behind the abdominal wall. The diaphragm, the muscular shelf that separates the chest from the abdominal cavity, should be complete and the baby's lungs should be developing. Although abnormalities in any of these organs are uncommon, you will find information about some of the problems that may be identified on pages 415–21.

▶ **Your baby's head and the spine** will be examined, starting with the covering bones of the skull, to check that they are complete. The fetal spine has straightened, which means that the sonographer can move the scanning probe up and down, checking each bone, or vertebra to make sure that there is no evidence of spina bifida (*see* p.418).

▶ **The brain** contains two ventricles or fluid-filled cavities, positioned on the left and right side of the midline,

HOW YOUR BABY MEASURES UP

The measurements taken during the scan help establish whether your baby is the right size for your dates. They are recorded as abbreviations in your notes, with measurements in millimeters, which are checked against charts of normal values. This provides an estimate of the size of your baby in terms of weeks out of 40.

BPD	Biparietal diameter (the distance between the side bones of your baby's head)	45mm = 19+/40
HC	Head circumference	171mm = 19+/40
AC	Abdominal circumference	140mm = 19+/40
FL	Femoral length (length of the thigh bone)	290mm = 19+/40

These measurements suggest that this fetus is appropriately grown for 19 plus weeks of gestation. Assuming that the scan was performed at 19–20 weeks, the baby is the right size for dates.

DETAILS FROM A 20-WEEK SCAN

chin | lung | liver | bowel

neck | spine | diaphragm | blood vessels

UNDERSTANDING YOUR BABY'S SCAN

This right-side image of the fetus shows the chin and neck (far left in image) and the lung is visible as a pale area above the diaphragm, the dome-shaped sheet of muscle that separates the chest from the abdomen. The liver appears as a large shadow below the diaphragm, punctuated by two blood vessels, which appear as black circles. The dark M shape (top right in image) is the fetal bowel.

FETAL HEART *The four chambers of the heart are clearly shown.*

LEG AND FOOT *The length of the femur (thigh bone) is a good growth indicator.*

SPINE *Each individual vertebra in the spine is counted and checked.*

which are lined with a special system of blood vessels called the choroid plexus. Rarely, the ventricles are enlarged (*see* cardiac abnormalities, p.420) or the choroid plexus contains cysts (*see* p.419). In the unlikely event that these problems are identified, you will be offered further scans.

▶ **The position of the placenta** will be recorded as lying on the anterior or posterior wall, or at the fundus (top) of the uterus. It is quite common for the placenta to be low-lying at this stage and you may be advised to have another scan at about 32 weeks to check that it is positioned higher.

The umbilical cord will be checked and the place where it inserts into the placenta may be noted. Most of the time it is in the center, but if it is at the very edge of the placenta (known as velamentous cord insertion, *see* p.429), there may be problem.

▶ **The volume of amniotic fluid** will be assessed, to ensure that there is neither too much, a condition known as polyhydramnios (*see* p.426), nor too little (oligohydramnios, *see* p.426). In either case you will need to have further investigations that include a scan in a few weeks' time.

▶ **The sex of your baby** can sometimes be determined if the scan reveals a penis between the fetal legs. But it is not always possible to conclude that you are carrying a girl because the penis can be hidden. For this reason, some hospitals are unwilling to disclose these findings.

UNDERSTANDING
YOUR SCAN *Your doctor*
will be able to help
interpret exactly what
you are seeing.

appears to be developing normally. Far from being a cause for concern, it will offer you and your partner great reassurance, not to mention the thrill of seeing your baby in great detail. For many couples, this is the magical moment when they realize that their pregnancy is going to result in a real human being. Most maternity units will offer you a printed picture for your family album; my twin girls are still entranced by the photo of themselves at the 20-week scan.

CONFIRMING RESULTS

For some women the scan result may show one or more causes for concern. Many abnormalities are accompanied by physical signs which are described as markers for a disorder or syndrome. For example, about 70 percent of babies with Down syndrome have structural abnormalities in their heart or gut, a single skin crease in the palm of their hands, and slanting eyes with epicanthic folds that can often be seen on an ultrasound scan. When a scan picks up a physical sign that suggests Down syndrome, I almost always advise the parents to have an amniocentesis test (*see* pp.140–43). They then have a diagnosis they can be certain of and can be given full counseling and advice on their next step.

Although the 20-week scan provides vital information, I should make it clear that a normal scan cannot guarantee that a baby does not suffer from an abnormality. About 30 percent of babies with Down do not have an obvious structural marker. It is also impossible to prenatally diagnose problems such as mental retardation, autism, or cerebral palsy. Scans do have limitations, even when the sonographer is expert and the machinery is state-of-the-art.

COMMON CONCERNS

MOST OF THE COMPLAINTS THAT CROP UP IN THE SECOND TRIMESTER ARE MINOR, AND MANY OF THEM ARE DUE TO YOUR BLOOD VESSELS DILATING TO COPE WITH THE EXTRA VOLUME OF BLOOD CIRCULATING IN YOUR BODY.

Feeling dizzy or faint is a very common symptom during the second and third trimesters of pregnancy, and is rarely a serious problem. As I explained earlier, the blood vessels around your body, and particularly in the veins of your pelvis and legs, now contain a much larger volume of blood. When you stand up quickly, you may feel momentarily dizzy because all that extra blood in your leg veins needs a bit of extra time to be redistributed to your head and other organs. Headaches are another common complaint. Most of the time they are due to tension and anxiety or to your nasal congestion. However, always seek prompt advice if you find that you are suffering repeated headaches because they can be the first sign that you are developing high blood pressure (*see* blood pressure problems, p.425).

APPLYING CREAM *Using moisturizing cream will help improve itchy, flaky skin on your legs, arms, and abdomen.*

SKIN RASHES

Pregnant women are very susceptible to a wide range of skin rashes, which are usually due to the massive hormonal changes occurring in your body. However, always check with your doctor or midwife if you experience persistent problems.

It is not unusual to develop dry patches of flaky and highly itchy skin, most commonly on your legs, arms, and abdomen. Applying simple moisturizing creams usually helps, but occasionally an antihistamine or even a low-dose steroid cream may be needed to relieve the irritation. The dilated blood vessels in your skin may make it look pinker, or even blotchy, which can sometimes be mistaken for a rash.

Since your skin needs to get rid of the extra heat from these dilated blood vessels, it is normal for you to sweat more. As a result, you may develop a sweat rash under your arms or breasts and in the groin areas, where sweat accumulates and does not have much chance to evaporate quickly. Wearing looser clothes, preferably cotton, and avoiding synthetic fabrics close to your skin will reduce the problem, as will careful hygiene and using unscented soaps and deodorants. Occasionally, a sweat rash can become infected with a fungal organism (for example, yeast *see* p.216). These are not serious, but can make you itchy and uncomfortable and you may need a prescription topical antifungal cream to help clear the infection.

THINGS TO CONSIDER

THE CHANCES ARE THAT THE CLOTHES YOU NEED TO WEAR NOW ARE QUITE DIFFERENT FROM THOSE THAT YOU IMAGINED YOU WOULD BE WEARING AT THIS STAGE. FEEL PLEASED IF YOU RESISTED THE TEMPTATION TO BUY NEW OUTFITS AT THE FIRST SIGN OF YOUR GROWING BELLY.

"... many women feel the urge to go on vacation — a sort of 'make hay while the sun shines' type of break."

Now is the time to give some thought to what clothes you really need to be comfortable at work and at home. Think of this exercise as being similar to packing for a vacation when your baggage allowance is restricted. There is no shortage of sources for maternity clothes — they can be found in the big department stores, in certain mall chains, and in maternity stores and mail order catalogs — but careful selection is the key.

Mix-and-match separates are usually the best solution, since they offer the greatest flexibility and you can accommodate repeated changes in your size relatively easily. The main difference between special pregnancy tops and normal jackets or shirts is that the front is longer than the back so that, once your belly has been taken into account, both are the same length. However, the back of some jackets have a way of expanding to fit your enlarging shape, so if you need to wear suits or jackets to work, you could well find that buying yourself one good jacket and changing the skirt or pants as and when your growing abdomen demands it, is the best way to deal with your changing size.

When it comes to skirts and pants, the priority is to find clothes with a comfortable, expanding waistline. In the short term, buying pants a couple sizes larger than usual works well, but you will soon find that this is not the long-term answer, since the elastic waist starts to dig into you as the weeks go on. Proper maternity skirts and pants have clever button elastics or panelling at the top, both of which allow for your expanding waist and provide comfort for the later stages of your pregnancy. You might also want to invest in some drawstring pants or a dress with no waist to see you through a good part, if not all, of the remaining months.

Maternity pantyhose provide more support than ordinary pantyhose and even though you will probably have to buy different sizes as your pregnancy continues they are a good investment. I can remember how much more comfortable I felt when I was wearing them and how conscious I was of my tired and aching legs when I did not. Avoid knee socks, which can block circulation at the top of your calf and encourage the formation of varicose veins. Cotton-rich ankle socks allow your skin to breathe and do not impede circulation.

If swimming is part of your exercise routine, buy a swimsuit that will see you through the whole nine months. You will feel a lot more comfortable in a special maternity bathing suit, many of which can be bought for around the same price as an average swimsuit.

A 40-week pregnancy spans several seasons and most of your major clothing purchases need to be for the season when your body shape has altered most significantly. If your first and second trimesters fall in the summer months, you may have several items of loose clothing in your wardrobe to tide you over until your shape demands a formal shopping expedition. If your third trimester is in the winter months, resist the temptation to buy an expensive winter coat in a larger size, since you are unlikely to want to wear it next winter after your baby has been delivered. In the meantime you could borrow a coat from a friend, or buy an A-line design with no front fastenings, which can be used indefinitely.

A CHANGE OF SCENERY

During the second trimester many women feel the urge to go on vacation or a weekend away — a sort of "make hay while the sun shines" type of break. Now that cheap flights are available to all corners of the globe, I find the question of traveling in pregnancy and how safe it is crops up continually. Most of the answers are to be found in the Staying Safe in Pregnancy section, which includes a full discussion about travel in pregnancy, safety of immunizations, and the various precautions you should take (*see* pp.36–37).

As far as advice specific to this stage of pregnancy goes, if you have had previous pregnancy complications, think carefully about traveling abroad at this time; the last thing you need is to find yourself a long way from home, should something unpredictable happen. Coping with an unforeseen problem is distressing enough without having to deal with a foreign language, a different healthcare system, and the uncertainty of knowing whether your health insurance will cover the situation. However, if you have no history of problems and your doctor has said that you are fit to travel, then it is highly unlikely that you will encounter any pregnancy-related problems during your vacation.

TAKING A BREAK *This stage of pregnancy can be a good time for travel as long as you have no pregnancy problems.*

WEEKS 21–26

THE DEVELOPING BABY

YOUR BABY IS CONTINUING TO GROW IN LENGTH AND TO PUT ON WEIGHT STEADILY, ALTHOUGH IT WILL BE SOME TIME BEFORE IT DEVELOPS A PLUMP, CHUBBY APPEARANCE. THE FACIAL FEATURES ARE NOW VERY WELL DEVELOPED AND EYEBROWS, EYELASHES, AND HEAD HAIR ARE CLEARLY VISIBLE.

The skin still looks pink and wrinkly, but no longer appears completely translucent, because some subcutaneous fat is being laid down. Two distinct layers of skin have developed: the surface layer or epidermis and a deeper layer called the dermis. The epidermal skin layer now carries a surface pattern on the fingertips, palms, toes, and soles of the feet, which is genetically determined and gives rise to a unique set of finger- and toe prints for this future human being. The underlying dermis grows little projections containing blood vessels and nerves. The surface of the skin remains covered with a fine layer of lanugo hair and a thick coating of white vernix. This waxy protective coat will remain until just before birth: babies that are born prematurely are often still covered with a thick layer of vernix, whereas babies born late or post mature, have lost all their vernix and, as a result, their skin is dry and flaky.

INSIDE THE BODY

Several important developments are occurring inside your baby's body. The nervous and skeletal systems continue to mature, so that, instead of just wriggling or floating, movements become more deliberate and sophisticated, including kicks and somersaults. The fetus practices thumb-sucking and starts to hiccup. Any object that the hands encounter is firmly grasped and, amazingly, this grip is strong enough to support the baby's entire body weight.

The brain is developing and its activity can be monitored electronically on an electroencephalogram (EEG). By 24 weeks, the fetal brainwave patterns are similar to those of a newborn infant. The brain cells that have been programmed to control conscious thought are beginning to mature and research suggests that from this time onward, the fetus starts to develop a primitive memory. Certainly, your baby can now respond to noises in your body and also to loud outside sounds and your physical movements. It is thought that a baby can distinguish between his mother's and father's voices at this stage, and is able to recognize them after birth. Studies have shown that babies are able to recognize a

◄ *A fetoscope of a 21-week-old fetus in the uterus.*

WEEKS

FIRST TRIMESTER

▶ 1
▶ 2
▶ 3
▶ 4
▶ 5
▶ 6
▶ 7
▶ 8
▶ 9
▶ 10
▶ 11
▶ 12
▶ 13

SECOND TRIMESTER

▶ 14
▶ 15
▶ 16
▶ 17
▶ 18
▶ 19
▶ 20
▶ **21**
▶ **22**
▶ **23**
▶ **24**

life size

▶ **25**
▶ **26**

THIRD TRIMESTER

▶ 27
▶ 28
▶ 29
▶ 30
▶ 31
▶ 32
▶ 33
▶ 34
▶ 35
▶ 36
▶ 37
▶ 38
▶ 39
▶ 40

life size

The 21 week-old fetus measures around 7in (17cm) and weighs about 12oz (350g). By the end of the second trimester, it will have increased in size to about 10in (25cm) from crown to rump and weighs just about 2lb (1kg).

particular piece of music that they have "heard" repeatedly in utero. This theory might explain why my young daughters always seem to feel comfortable and relaxed when they hear Italian opera or Nina Simone — both are acquired tastes, but the twins were exposed to them repeatedly while I was pregnant.

The eyelids will be open toward the end of this period. Although most babies have blue eyes at birth, the final color of their eyes is not known until many weeks after delivery.

A cycle of sleeping and waking has started to develop. Unfortunately, this is not always synchronized with your daily pattern and you may find yourself worrying about the lack of movements during the day, only to find that you are kept awake for most of the night because the baby is buzzing around.

The fetal heart rate has slowed considerably from 180 to 140–150 beats per minute by the end of the second trimester. From this point onward, monitoring the heart rate pattern on an electronic fetal monitor becomes one of the most useful methods of assessing your baby's well-being.

The fetus is opening and closing its mouth regularly as large quantities of amniotic fluid are ingested. The fluid is digested and waste products from the metabolic processes in the fetal body are passed across the placenta, via the umbilical cord, to be disposed of in the mother's blood. The remainder, which is effectively excess water, is then excreted back as urine into the pool. At 26 weeks the volume of amniotic fluid has risen to about 16fl oz or almost 1 pint (500ml) and the entire pool is changed or recirculated every three hours.

The fetal lungs are still relatively immature and it will be several weeks before they can breathe unaided. Nevertheless, your baby has started to make breathing movements and will practice them until the time of delivery. The lungs are full of amniotic fluid, which helps the fetus develop more air sacs (alveoli); these need to be buoyant in the amniotic fluid in order to multiply properly and later to expand. A network of tiny blood vessels around the sacs is forming; this will be essential for the transfer of oxygen to the rest of the baby's body after birth. If the water breaks before the end of the second trimester, the baby's lung development is almost always compromised and breathing difficulties after birth are invariably a problem.

TOUCHING *The hands move toward the face and touch and grasp anything they encounter.*

A VIABLE BABY

Even though the lungs are still relatively immature, the fetus has now reached a stage of potential viability, which means that it may be able to survive outside the womb, albeit with the help of neonatal medical expertise and a ventilator to assist with breathing. The limit of potential fetal viability is currently approximately 24 weeks. Babies that are born before the age of 24 weeks are very unlikely. to survive. Generally, any baby that is less than 20 weeks old when born is very unlikely to survive and will be considered either a miscarriage (*see* p.340) or a stillbirth (*see* p.341). After 24 weeks, the chances of survival begin to increase although, until the age of approximately 30 weeks, there is still a high chance of the baby suffering from a physical or mental disability (*see* p.339). Nevertheless, each day that passes after 26 weeks is accompanied by an increase in lung maturity and a reduced risk of other problems as well. As I will explain in the next section, the first few weeks of the third trimester of pregnancy are crucially importantin terms of potential fetal survival.

SKIN AND NAILS *A layer of underlying fat has been laid down, but blood vessels are still visible. Fingernails have developed and also a unique surface pattern on the fingertips.*

YOUR CHANGING BODY

DURING THE NEXT FEW WEEKS, MOST WOMEN WILL GAIN ABOUT 1LB (HALF A KILOGRAM) IN WEIGHT EVERY WEEK, ALTHOUGH, THE EXACT AMOUNT VARIES BETWEEN WOMEN AND BETWEEN WEEKS. IDEALLY, YOU SHOULD GAIN 13–14LB (6–6.5KG) DURING THIS SECOND TRIMESTER.

"...you may notice that your skin is looking particularly rosy and your hair is thick and glossy."

If you find you are putting on quite a bit more weight than is recommended during this last part of the second trimester, remind yourself that only about one pound of this weight will have gone to your developing baby. The rest can be attributed to your growing uterus and breasts and the increased blood and fluid volume that your body now contains, but also to your maternal fat stores (*see* p.42). Lots of extra pounds gained now will be difficult to shed after the birth. If your weight gain continues to be excessive as you move into the third trimester, you will be at greater risk of developing gestational diabetes (*see* p.426) and preeclampsia (*see* p.425), not to mention feeling unnecessarily tired and being troubled more than usual by backache. So try to eat a sensible balanced diet and restrict your sugar and carbohydrate intake. If you do need to control your weight, reducing your calorie intake gradually will not harm your baby's growth. Some women put on very little weight in pregnancy, but as long as their diet contains all the necessary nutrients, this is no reason for concern.

THE EXPANDING UTERUS

Your uterus continues to expand, and between 21 and 26 weeks will rise above your belly button (umbilicus). This growth has been achieved by an increase in the size of the muscles of the uterus, which are still attached to the same supporting ligaments. It is not surprising that many women experience stitch-like pains down the sides of their abdomen as the uterus expands and stretches these ligaments to their limits. The height of the fundus measures approximately 7½in (22cm) at 22 weeks; 9½in (24cm) at 24 weeks; and 10in (26cm) at 26 weeks.

To accommodate the increasing size of your uterus and baby, several other changes occur. As the uterus moves upward in your abdominal cavity, your rib cage will move upward too, by as much as 2in (5cm), and the lowest ribs begin to spread sideways. This frequently causes discomfort or pain around the ribcage and may mean that you start to feel breathless. The stomach and other digestive organs become compressed and progesterone continues to relax the muscles in the gut. As a result, it is common to experience heartburn, indigestion, and constipation at this stage in your pregnancy (*see* p.187).

A PREGNANCY BLOOM

Between 21 and 26 weeks the increase in your cardiac output continues to rise slowly but steadily, along with the volume of blood in your circulation, but your stroke volume and heart rate are leveling off and will not increase further. To deal with these cardiovascular changes, your peripheral resistance must reduce even further to ensure that your blood pressure does not alter significantly.

The up side to all of this extra blood flow and the enormous quantities of pregnancy hormones is that you will probably notice that your skin is looking particularly rosy and your hair thick and glossy. This is because women shed less hair during pregnancy and the increase in their metabolic rate means that hair also grows faster than usual. After the birth, you will start to lose hair in much greater quantities than usual — but to a large extent you are simply losing post-birth what you would normally have lost during the nine months.

CHANGING CENTER OF GRAVITY

Your posture will have changed by this stage in your pregnancy. The enlarging uterus and baby are slung forward in the middle of the body, and consequently, a pregnant woman is forced to find ways of restoring her altered center of gravity. Added to this mechanical load, the ligaments of the pelvis have been softened by the pregnancy hormones contained in the vastly increased blood flow to the pelvis. This is an essential change since the pelvis needs to relax sufficiently in order to be able to accommodate the passage of a 6½lb-plus (3kg) baby through its previously rigid walls. However, this means that your pelvis can no longer function as the stable girdle that it once was and your pregnant body must find a way of compensating for these changes to their stability. The simplest way to deal with this mechanical challenge is to lean backward, arch your back, and use a wider gait than normal, but this change in posture is frequently accompanied by backache, since the ligaments of your abdomen, back, and pelvis are placed under strain.

Your fast growing tummy is beginning to affect the way you move, sit, and lie. You will start to notice that you feel unstable wearing high-heeled shoes and that certain chairs are less comfortable than others. You may need to support the small of your back when you are sitting, and when you are lying down, there will be certain positions that are much more comfortable than others. These changes and effects are especially noticeable if you are expecting twins. You will find some practical advice on adopting a good posture and preventing back pain later in this section (*see* p.193) and more specific advice on backache later in this trimester (*see* p.218 and pp.243–44).

GOOD HEALTH *Through the second trimester of pregnancy, many women appear to be glowing with good health.*

HOW YOU MAY FEEL PHYSICALLY

EVEN FIRST-TIME MOTHERS WILL NOW BE VERY AWARE OF THEIR BABY'S MOVEMENTS EVERY DAY AND LEFT IN NO DOUBT THAT THESE SENSATIONS ARE THE WORK OF A LIVELY, GROWING BABY. I THINK THIS IS ONE OF THE MOST EXCITING MILESTONES REACHED BY WOMEN IN THEIR JOURNEY THROUGH PREGNANCY.

You will also find your baby's movement very reassuring, because you will now be able to monitor the welfare of your baby yourself, instead of having to rely solely on the information you receive from your doctor, midwife, or the latest scan report. I remember vividly my own astonishment and overwhelming joy when, during a meal one evening, a commotion in my tummy occurred, which resulted in my plate being bounced across the table in front of me.

UNWANTED ADVICE

Every woman carries her pregnancy differently, and however you are carrying yours, it is more than likely that your baby is exactly the right size. Yet it can be difficult to remember this advice when everyone seems to have an opinion as to whether your pregnancy is too big or too small for your dates. Throwaway lines such as "Goodness, you have put on a lot of weight" or "You're getting as big as a house" can be truly upsetting, particularly if you are already feeling self-conscious about the extra pounds you have put on. Conversely, "Are you sure that you are eating properly?" and "You do look small. Is everything all right?" may be well intended, but are guaranteed to alarm you at a vulnerable moment. If this constant analysis of your size in pregnancy begins to bother you, I suggest that you explain as calmly and as tactfully as you can that you find it distressing and you would prefer family, friends, and colleagues to stop. After all, people do not usually pass judgment on your body shape when you are not pregnant.

"...there is a tendency for people who have had children to forget how worrying scary stories can be..."

Another problem may arise if you are so engrossed in the subject of pregnancy that you find yourself inadvertently encouraging people to open up and recall all sorts of things about their own pregnancies that might be better left unsaid. Some of their anecdotes will be encouraging and useful (particularly if you have a specific problem that you are worried about) but others can be downright frightening. I think there is a tendency for people who have had children to forget how worrying scary stories can be for those who are currently going through a pregnancy. Again, my advice is to be honest. Gently but firmly explain that you would rather not hear another tale of a premature birth or an

PROBLEMS WITH DIGESTION

AT THIS STAGE OF PREGNANCY, PROBLEMS WITH YOUR DIGESTION BECOME MUCH MORE COMMON. YOU MAY WELL HAVE STARTED TO EXPERIENCE MILD OR EVEN SEVERE SYMPTOMS OF HEARTBURN AND INDIGESTION AND SUFFER EPISODES OF CONSTIPATION, TOO.

INDIGESTION

As your enlarging uterus begins to compress your abdominal organs, the capacity of your stomach is reduced and your whole digestive system begins to slow down. Food remains in your stomach and intestines for longer, making you prone to indigestion – a sensation of a heavy lump at the bottom of your stomach. At times you may have a constant dull or stabbing pain around your abdomen, sometimes with back pain.

HEARTBURN

You may also have heartburn due to the fact that the valve between your esophagus and stomach has become relaxed and is no longer very efficient at preventing food mixed with acid gastric juices from being regurgitated back. This irritates the lining of your esophagus, causing a searing or burning sensation behind the front of your ribcage.

As long as the symptoms pass within a couple of hours, they are not a cause for alarm. In the meantime, there are several ways to minimize your digestive problems:

▶ **Eat little and often,** avoiding heavy, fatty, highly spiced, or pickled foods, which make symptoms worse.
▶ **Drink a glass of milk** or eat natural yogurt before meals and before bedtime. This can help relieve heartburn by neutralizing stomach acid.
▶ **Sit upright** when you are eating to reduce the compression of your stomach.
▶ **Avoid lying down** for at least an hour after you have eaten and keep your head well propped up at night on several pillows to reduce the problem of heartburn.
▶ **If your symptoms** are severe, ask your doctor to prescribe you an antacid such as Gaviscon or Maalox.

CONSTIPATION

Your sluggish digestion can also make you constipated, leaving you feeling heavy and irritable. Try some of the following remedies:
▶ **Boost the fiber** in your diet by eating more fresh fruit and vegetables and wholegrain bread and cereals.
▶ **Increase your fluid intake** by making sure you drink at least 4 pints (2 liters) of water per day.

EASING HEARTBURN *Natural yogurt may help relieve symptoms.*

▶ **Exercise regularly.** As little as a 20-minute walk each day can help relieve constipation.
▶ **Bulking laxatives** such as Metamucil or Fiberall are effective because they contain complex sugar compounds, which the human gut cannot digest. They absorb water, helping produce a bulkier, softer stool that can be passed without straining and discomfort.
▶ **Laxatives** containing senna are not recommended in pregnancy because they irritate the gut, which has the potential to trigger uterine contractions.

excruciating labor. Far from being offended, most people will understand and some will also realize (and most probably deeply regret) that they have caused you unnecessary anxiety.

YOUR PRENATAL CARE

YOU WILL CONTINUE TO HAVE PRENATAL APPOINTMENTS EVERY FOUR WEEKS AT YOUR LOCAL DOCTOR'S OFFICE OR THE HOSPITAL, AND BY NOW WILL KNOW WHAT TO EXPECT IN TERMS OF THE VARIOUS CHECKS. FOR THE MAJORITY OF WOMEN, THIS STAGE IN YOUR PRENATAL CARE IS A QUIET AND ENJOYABLE TIME.

Although I feel it is important to cover the further investigations that may form part of prenatal care here, I want to add that it is very unusual to encounter any of these serious complications during this stage of pregnancy, either with your health or with that of your baby.

It is unlikely that you will undergo a further routine ultrasound scan during this period unless problems that need further investigation were identified at the 20-week scan. If the scan suggested anything abnormal in the development of your baby's organs — for example, an intestinal blockage or problems with the kidneys or urinary tract, you will have additional scans between 21 and 26 weeks, possibly at a specialist center. If the abnormality is confirmed, you may be advised to undergo a late amniocentesis (*see* pp.140–43) or fetal blood sample

PREDICTING PREMATURE BIRTH

Today, the majority of babies that are born prematurely survive and develop normally, but those that are born very premature (before 30 weeks) still have a significant risk of handicap if they survive (see p.339). Therefore, any test that may help predict which babies are at risk should always be carefully considered.

Some two percent of women have a very short cervix and it is thought that half of these may give birth very prematurely as a result. Some units are now using vaginal ultrasound scans at 23–24 weeks to help identify these and offer preventive treatments. If your hospital is participating in this research, you will have the length of your cervix checked using a vaginal ultrasound probe. If your cervix is found to be shorter than average, you will be closely monitored.

Some researchers believe that inserting a stitch in the cervix to lengthen and close it may be of help, although this procedure is not without risk. Some hospitals offer progesterone treatment to prevent contractions and/or steroid treatment to reduce the risk of breathing complications if the baby is born prematurely. It is too soon to know whether this type of prenatal screening will become routine practice, but the early results do appear to be promising.

test (*see* cordocentesis, p.143) to see whether or not the baby is affected by a chromosomal or genetic problem. The results from the amniocentesis usually take three weeks because the skin cells in the amniotic fluid have to be cultured before they can be examined for chromosomal abnormalities. This will seem like an eternity for worried parents-to-be, but new molecular biology techniques at some specialist centers can greatly reduce the time taken to establish the baby's genetic makeup (*see* p.143). The results from a fetal blood sample are also available more quickly because the white blood cells can be analyzed immediately.

If you have had a previous baby with a heart abnormality or if there is a family history of cardiac problems, specialist cardiac scans may be advised between 22 and 24 weeks because at this stage the four chambers of the fetal heart and all of its connecting pipes can be seen much more clearly; this improves the accuracy of the scan and the advice that can be offered to you.

The other type of ultrasound scan you may be offered is a Doppler blood flow scan (*see* p.257), which examines the way blood is flowing in the vessels of the uterus, placenta, and umbilical cord. Research has suggested that reduced blood flow through the uterine arteries at this stage in pregnancy may be a way of identifying women at high risk of developing high blood pressure (*see* blood pressure problems, p.425) or problems with the growth of their baby, (*see* p.214 and intrauterine growth restriction, p.428). As a result, some specialist units now screen women with Doppler scans at 24 weeks. The small minority of women (5 percent) in whom the blood flow is reduced can then be carefully monitored for changes in their blood pressure. The Doppler blood flow scan can also be used to look at the flow of blood in many of the baby's arteries and veins, which is a good indicator of the baby's general well-being.

BLOOD FLOW *A Doppler scan shows blood flowing through the major fetal vessels. The heart is seen as a large red stucture center left, and the yellow-colored blood vessels, bottom right, lead to the umbilical cord.*

COMMON CONCERNS

CONCERNS IN PREGNANCY ARE USUALLY A MIXTURE OF NAGGING COMPLAINTS AND ANXIETIES ABOUT THINGS YOU MAY HAVE HEARD OR THE WAY YOUR PREGNANCY IS PROGRESSING. I HOPE THE ADVICE HERE SETS YOUR MIND AT REST ON A FEW ISSUES BUT REMEMBER THAT YOUR DOCTOR OR MIDWIFE WILL ALSO BE HAPPY TO TALK THROUGH ANY CONCERNS THAT YOU MAY HAVE.

It is quite common to feel dizzy or light-headed when you change your position suddenly at this stage of pregnancy because of the massive changes in the way your increased blood volume is distributed in your body. A significant proportion is being directed to the uterus to support the placenta and baby and large quantities of blood are being stored in your pelvic and leg veins because of the reduction in peripheral resistance. When you stand up quickly it takes a few minutes for the blood in your pelvic and leg veins to redistribute; meanwhile, there is a shortage of blood to the brain leaving you light-headed and even inclined to faint. Similarly, if you have been standing for long periods, the extra pooling of blood in your legs may leave your brain short of blood, especially when it is hot and your blood vessels dilate even more to cool you down.

There are steps you can take to reduce these dizzy spells or, worse, fainting episodes, both of which can be quite frightening and unpleasant.

• Make sure that you do not get up too quickly from a sitting or lying position. Try to let the blood flow adjust gradually.

• Try to avoid becoming overheated, particularly in hot weather. One of the most common times for feeling dizzy or faint is when you try to get out of a hot bath too quickly because this leaves your circulation completely unable to deal with the shifts in blood volume needed to prevent you from feeling light-headed.

• Take care to eat regularly and choose foods such as complex carbohydrates (see p.44) that release energy gradually, so that your blood sugar levels are prevented from rising and then falling too quickly.

• If you feel faint or dizzy, sit down and try to put your head between your knees or lie down and raise your feet above your head or at least above your pelvis, so that the blood in your leg veins returns to your brain as quickly as possible.

Even if you suffer from dizziness regularly, your baby is not in any danger because the blood supply to the uterus and placenta is being maintained at your expense. However, when you lie flat on your back the weight of the uterus can end up pressing against blood vessels in the pelvic area, depriving your placenta (and hence your baby) of oxygen, so avoid this position.

The main danger of dizziness is if you suddenly start seeing stars while driving or getting on a train. For this reason, interrupt your travel regularly. If you have to stand for long periods, make sure that you keep shifting weight from one leg to the other. Better still, walk around if you can.

CHECKING FETAL MOVEMENTS

Many women I meet in the prenatal clinic are worried about how many fetal movements they should be feeling each day or night — anxieties that can be made worse by the doctor or midwife asking at each visit "Is the baby

PATTERNS OF MOVEMENT

You will begin to recognize your baby's patterns of movement and become alert to any changes.

moving well?" If this is your first baby it is obviously difficult for you to know, so I owe a big debt to the distressed pregnant woman who pointed this out to me many years ago when I was at the start of my training. As a result of this lesson, I changed my methods of finding out about fetal movements.

The issue of fetal movements is important in pregnancy for the simple reason that they are one of the best ways for you and your prenatal caregivers to assess the well-being of your baby. Having said that, I don't intend to offer rigid rules about how many movements you should be feeling per day or night, at any stage during your pregnancy journey. This is because every pregnancy is different and every baby develops its own pattern of movements, which can change as the pregnancy progresses. Some babies are more active than others generally and all babies go through periods in the day when they are quieter or are engaged in more vigorous pursuits. Over the weeks, you will get a feel for your own baby's pattern of activity, perhaps noticing that your baby responds with a kick when you are in a certain position or becomes still at certain times of the day. So, instead of advising that you should feel 5, 10, 20, or 50 movements every 12 or 24 hours, you should look out for any dramatic changes to your baby's pattern of movements and should one occur, consult your midwife or doctor promptly. In particular, if you do not feel your baby move during a 24-hour period, you should seek advice immediately.

"Over the weeks, you will get a feel for your own baby's pattern of activity..."

ABDOMINAL ACHES AND PAINS

Abdominal pain is always worrying and, for pregnant women, it invariably raises concerns that the baby is at risk. During the second trimester, the most likely explanation for aches in the lower abdominal area that virtually every woman experiences at this stage in pregnancy is that the ligaments supporting your enlarging uterus are being put under enormous strain. However, if you develop regular abdominal pain, or notice that your entire abdomen has become too tender to touch, tell your caregivers immediately so that it can be investigated promptly. There are several possible causes and, although uncommon, they can have potentially serious consequences. The most serious is pain in the uterus itself, which may be the first signs that you have had some bleeding behind the placenta from a placental abruption (*see* p.427) or are at risk of premature labor (*see* p.340). The pain may be sharp and stabbing or a dull, constant ache and may or may not be accompanied by vaginal bleeding. Whichever, your midwife or doctor will want to examine your uterus.

A uterine fibroid (*see* p.422) is a benign mass of muscle in the uterine wall, which may cause problems in the second trimester because high levels of

"You should always try to avoid lifting heavy weights in pregnancy but if you have young children, this is likely to be impossible at times."

estrogen and progesterone encourage the fibroid to grow along with the rest of the uterus. Occasionally, this rapid growth causes the center to degenerate, resulting in severe pain in the uterus and abdomen, localized to a particular spot. Pain from fibroid degeneration is very unpleasant, but usually disappears with bed rest and pain medication without causing any problems to the baby. Occasionally, large fibroids positioned in the lower part of the uterus or beside the cervix will lead to problems near the time of labor if the baby's head does not have sufficient room to descend into the pelvis.

Nausea, vomiting, and/or diarrhea accompanied by abdominal pain is uncommon in pregnancy, but is almost always due to food poisoning or viral gastroenteritis. It is usually self-limiting and, although very unpleasant, disappears quickly with no harm to you or your baby. There is no need for medical treatment apart from making sure to drink plenty of fluids to replace those you have lost. If the nausea and vomiting persists or is accompanied by abdominal pain, consult your physician. Very occasionally, symptoms may be due to listeria infection (*see* p.50 and p.412), which is a potential cause of late miscarriage and intrauterine death and is best treated with penicillin antibiotics.

Appendicitis is another rare, but important cause of persistent abdominal pain in the second trimester of pregnancy. However, it can be very difficult to make the diagnosis in pregnant women, since the appendix is no longer in its usual position in the lower right corner of the abdomen but has been displaced by the growing uterus.

Urinary infections are another important and common cause of abdominal pain in the second trimester. It is usually felt in the lower part of your abdomen, above the pubic bone and is likely to be accompanied by discomfort when passing urine. Remember that you may not notice the early symptoms of a urinary infection, such as cystitis, before organisms have traveled up the dilatedurinary tract to the kidneys and developed into pyelonephritis. In mid- and late pregnancy, urinary infections can lead to irritability of the uterus and premature contractions, not to mention long-term damage to your kidneys if left untreated. For this reason, if you have abdominal pain in pregnancy, your urine will be tested and you will probably begin a course of antibiotics while you wait for the results. These medications will not affect or damage your baby. If you do have a urinary infection, it is essential to finish the course, even if symptoms disappear quickly, and have a further urine sample examined to make sure the infection is gone. Urinary infections that are inadequately treated will recur and, worse still, may then become resistant to the usual antibiotic treatments.

PREVENTING BACK PAIN

BACK PAIN IS SO COMMON IN PREGNANCY IT IS UNUSUAL FOR A WOMAN NOT TO SUFFER FROM IT.

YOU ARE LIKELY TO BEGIN TO NOTICE IT AROUND THE END OF THIS TRIMESTER, SO HERE ARE

SOME TIPS THAT MAY HELP REDUCE ITS SEVERITY AND PREVENT IT FROM BECOMING WORSE.

▶ **When you are upright**, adopt good posture: stand tall, and hold your shoulders back (your back should always be in a straight line). Remember that if you slouch over your expanding tummy, your back will arch and this will aggravate your lower back pain. Try not to stand for long periods of time.

▶ **Invest in some good flat or low-heeled shoes**, preferably with support for the arches of your feet and sturdy soles. Wearing high heels from this point onward will make you feel more unstable and increase the strain on your back.

▶ **Sit well: this is particularly important** if you spend long periods working at a desk. Make sure that both shoulder blades and the small of your back are against the chair back and that the seat supports your thighs. The chair should be at the right height for you to keep your feet flat on the floor and the computer screen should be at eye level.

▶ **When you are driving** check that the car seat supports the small of your back and that you can reach the hand and foot controls easily. Your seatbelt may feel uncomfortable but you must wear it for every trip.

▶ **When you are resting,** raise your feet and legs to take the pressure off your back and pelvis. Later on in pregnancy you may need a firmer mattress to help support your back. You will also find that sleeping on your side will help reduce the strain in the ligaments of your back.

▶ **When you get out of bed,** first turn on your side and, keeping your back straight, swing your legs over the side of the bed. In this position you will be able to push yourself upright using the strength of your arms without placing any strain on your back.

▶ **Regular gentle back exercises** will help the muscles and ligaments of your back stretch and become more supple. Pelvic tilt exercises are especially helpful, as are exercises that help strengthen the muscles of your back (see p.219).

▶ **Try not to gain too much weight** — every extra pound places further strain on your back.

LIFTING HEAVY WEIGHTS

You should always try to avoid lifting heavy weights in pregnancy but if you have young children, this is likely to be impossible at times. When your toddler needs to be carried use this method. Squat down and hold him close to you. Keep your back straight and use the muscles in your legs to push yourself upward as you stand. Use the same technique to lift any heavy weight.

DENTAL HEALTH

In addition to visiting the dentist regularly, it is often a good idea to see a dental hygienist for some general advice on gum care. Sore gums that bleed when you brush or floss your teeth are very common; they become soft and spongy thanks to the increased blood supply and hormones of pregnancy. To help firm your gums and prevent bacteria from infecting the broken skin, increase the number of times you brush your teeth. Recent research has suggested that gum disease in pregnant women may contribute to the development of problems such as late miscarriage and premature labor. Although the mechanisms are not completely understood, it is possible that a constant focus of inflammation or infection in the mouth can result in complications in other areas of a pregnant body.

THINGS TO CONSIDER

I HOPE THAT YOU HAVE ALREADY ENROLLED IN A PRENATAL OR BIRTHING CLASS BECAUSE THE BEST ONES TEND TO FILL UP WELL IN ADVANCE. IF YOU HAVEN'T FOUND A PLACE YET, MAKE IT A PRIORITY TO DO SO NOW.

The more knowledgable and prepared you are for labor, the more relaxed and confident you will feel; in addition to this, you will find that the opportunity of sharing concerns, feelings, and experiences with other parents-to-be is a source of comfort and relief. Even if this is not your first baby, do sign up for a refresher course — you will be surprised how quickly you have forgotten the details of labor and breathing techniques. Also, there is a constant evolution in how a hospital deals with labor and what sort of pain relief it can offer, so even if you had your first baby in the same hospital, there may have been changes of which you are unaware.

PARENTS AND IN-LAWS

If you are one of those lucky individuals who usually enjoys an uncomplicated relationship with their parents and in-laws, or step-parents for that matter, you may be surprised to find that things are not quite as straightforward as they were before you became pregnant. There are so many different permutations of a

"Your mother may be offering all sorts of advice about pregnancy and child-rearing already and may be put off if you plan to deal with your pregnancy and newborn differently."

family unit today that I could not begin to cover them all but I think it is useful to reflect on the fact that, although pregnancy invariably brings joy to a family, or extended family, it can also give rise to conflicting emotions that can reverberate upward through the generations as well as downward.

Your mother may be offering all sorts of advice about pregnancy and child-rearing already and may be a bit put off if you are taking the view that life has moved on in the intervening years and that you plan to deal with your pregnancy and newborn baby differently. Similarly, your mother-in-law will have her own views, too, that don't always jibe exactly with those of your own mother. Both are capable of loaded questions such as, "Why are you working so hard?" or, "Are you planning to give up work after the baby is born?" If these are beginning to bother you, ask your partner for help. Presenting a united front and demonstrating clearly that you are making decisions together about issues such childcare and work may help silence the critics in the family.

NEW ADDITION *An older child may want to ask exactly how his new brother or sister will arrive in the outside world.*

TELLING CHILDREN ABOUT THE BABY

If you already have a child or children, the other delicate issue you will shortly have to address, if you have not already done so, is when to tell them that they will soon have a baby brother or sister. Of course the timing depends, to a large extent, on the age of the child. A two-year-old may not have noticed your changing shape and will certainly not have linked it to the fact that there is a baby growing inside you. However, older children will be aware of your altered appearance, so it is much better that they hear the news from you instead of accidentally from someone else.

If you have not told them already, reflect for a moment on why you have not. I suspect that this will be because you are worried that any existing children may fear they are going to lose some of your love and attention by having this new person in the family. This is a logical concern for a small child who cannot yet know that parents have limitless love when it comes to their children. So you need to constantly reassure them.

The other thing to remember about young children is that they have little perspective of time and have no way of understanding that your pregnancy is going to continue for another six months or so before they see the end product. Children absorb most information they are given but often choose to process it in their own time, usually at a later date. So, when you are trying to have a sensitive conversation about the future baby, do not worry if your toddler appears to have no interest in the subject and suddenly interrupts to ask if he can have a snack. Equally, do not be surprised when the next day, or the next week, he returns to the subject of the future baby without any warning. Just pick up the threads of the conversation and continue to reassure him.

YOUR GIRLFRIENDS

During the second trimester of pregnancy, your relationship with girlfriends who don't have children or are not planning to have them in the near future can become strained. Now that your attention is focused on visits to the prenatal clinic, how many times a day you can feel your baby kick, and which parenting class you want to join, your friends may find your new topics of conversation rather limited. They may be wondering what happened to the prepregnant you and whether that person will ever reemerge.

The reality is that you are moving on to a different phase of life, and this change in your relationship will be even more noticeable after your baby is born. But there is no reason why a close friend cannot be equally important to you, just because your lifestyle has taken on a new direction. If you value your friendships, there is every good reason to continue them.

As far as nights out are concerned, whiling away an evening in a crowded, smoke-filled club may no longer be an attractive option in pregnancy but you can make the most of meals out and get-togethers at friends' homes while you still have the freedom to do so. Reassure them that there will be nights out after the birth even if they end a little earlier, either because you need to get as much sleep as possible or because your babysitter will want to go home. Having a baby does not mean that you do not want to see your friends, or that you have to become such a bore that you are no longer able to involve yourself in their lives and concerns or listen to their current news.

WHAT'S IN A NAME?

Before pregnancy, you might have assumed that the only possible difficulty in choosing a name would be to whittle down a long list of names to a few contenders.

GIRLFRIENDS *Your relationship may change but you don't need to lose touch with your nonpregnant friends.*

Now that you are pregnant, you may be surprised to find that the whole exercise is more complex than you had imagined.

Part of the problem may be that you find it difficult to relate to your baby at this stage. Some mothers-to-be start chatting away happily to their baby when it is only a few inches long, but believe me, there is no need to feel disturbed if it is taking you a little longer to develop the relationship. Knowing the sex of the baby at the earliest possible opportunity helps some parents think about their unborn baby as a real person and this may also help when it comes to choosing a name; others feel this takes away some of the excitement of the birth. For the latter group, choosing two sets of possible names for their baby boy or girl can be one of the magical parts of the pregnancy.

The next problem is that you may soon be feeling pressurized by suggestions from family and friends. Some women deal with the issue by inventing a completely absurd name, which shocks their relatives into silence; others opt for a vague, noncommittal approach. Having said that, it is also common for parents to make their final choice during the birth, or days, or even weeks afterward when the legal requirement to register the child's name forces them to make a decision. There are only two outcomes I can guarantee: the first is that, as you watch your baby grow, you will not be able to imagine your child being called anything other than the name you chose. Second, when your child grows up, she will tell you how she wished you had given her a different name.

CHOOSING A NAME

Sometimes the perfect name does not become apparent until you meet your baby face to face.

The last name dilemma

If you are married or in a long-term relationship, the issue of which last name your baby uses may be open for debate. Although the assumption is that the child will take the father's last name, there is no legal reason why this should be so and you may have strong feelings that your own last name should be used. One increasingly favored option is either to combine the last names or to use the mother's name as an additional first name.

My personal view is that life is quite complex enough for young children today without adding unnecessary speculation from outside parties about the identity of the parents. Call me old-fashioned, but I have always found that being known as Mrs. Summerfield at home and at the girls' school and Professor Regan at work has had some very positive advantages and has never given rise to any uncertainty for my children.

THE THIRD TRIMESTER

Your baby is capable of surviving if delivered now, albeit with medical assistance, but the remaining weeks in the uterus are vitally important. Your baby's development is now focused on maturing the lungs, digestive system, and brain so that they can function in the outside world. As your abdomen expands to accommodate your growing uterus and baby, your thoughts increasingly turn toward the birth.

CONTENTS

WEEKS 26–30

202 The developing baby

206 Your changing body

209 How you may feel physically

210 Your emotional response

212 Your prenatal care

215 Common concerns

220 Things to consider

224 Shopping for your baby

WEEKS 30–35

230 The developing baby

234 Your changing body

236 How you may feel physically

238 Your emotional response

240 Your prenatal care

242 Common concerns

245 Things to consider

256 Specialized prenatal monitoring

WEEKS 35–40

260 The developing baby

263 Your changing body

264 How you may feel physically

266 Your prenatal care

271 When your baby is overdue

275 Things to consider

YOUR BABY
IN THE THIRD TRIMESTER

WEEK 27 THE BABY BEGINS TO
DEVELOP A PATTERN OF REST AND SLEEP
ALTERNATING WITH ACTIVE PERIODS.

WEEK 28 SKIN CREASES ARE
VISIBLE ON A CHUBBY HAND WITH
PERFECTLY FORMED FINGERNAILS.

WEEK 29 MOVEMENTS ARE STRONG AND
PURPOSEFUL AND INCLUDE HEFTY KICKS,
PUNCHES, AND RAPID CHANGES IN POSITION.

"During the weeks between now and delivery,
the baby's body systems are becoming ready
for life outside the uterus."

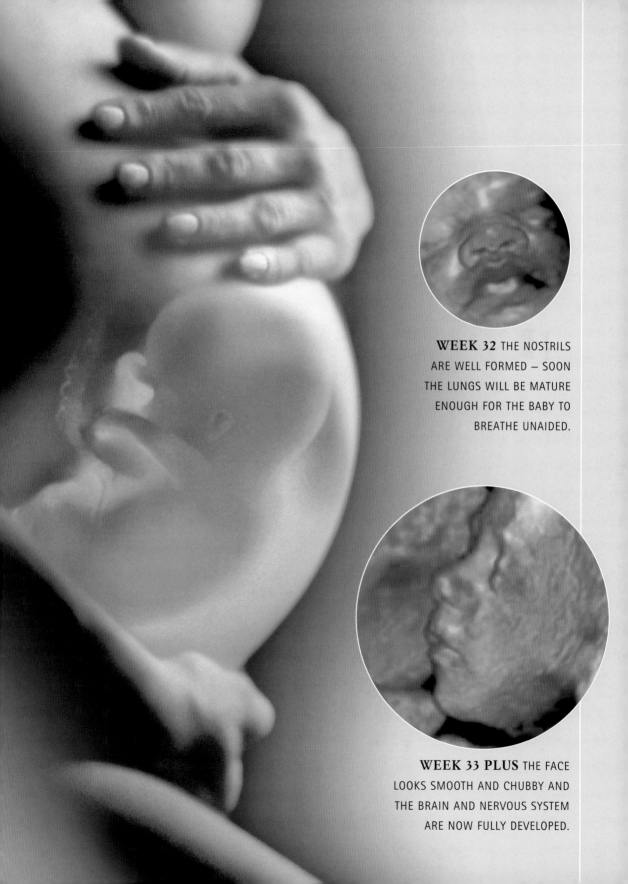

WEEK 32 THE NOSTRILS ARE WELL FORMED – SOON THE LUNGS WILL BE MATURE ENOUGH FOR THE BABY TO BREATHE UNAIDED.

WEEK 33 PLUS THE FACE LOOKS SMOOTH AND CHUBBY AND THE BRAIN AND NERVOUS SYSTEM ARE NOW FULLY DEVELOPED.

WEEKS 26–30

THE DEVELOPING BABY

DURING THE NEXT FEW WEEKS, YOUR BABY CONTINUES TO GROW IN LENGTH, WHILE THE BODY WEIGHT INCREASES QUITE SIGNIFICANTLY BECAUSE WHITE FAT IS BEING DEPOSITED UNDER THE SKIN. THE BABY NOW LOOKS PLUMPER AS THE ABDOMEN AND LIMBS FILL OUT AND THE SKIN STARTS TO LOSE ITS WRINKLY APPEARANCE.

Subcutaneous fat helps your baby regulate its own body temperature, an essential development for life after delivery, although this ability is only partially acquired in the uterus, and newborn babies still lose heat very quickly. As the fat is laid down, the lanugo hair becomes sparser and soon only a few patches over the back and shoulders will remain, although the coating of white vernix will stay until about 36 weeks. The hair on the scalp will lengthen and the eyebrows and eyelashes will become fuller. Skin creases can be seen on the hands and feet, and little fingernails and toenails are also clearly visible. The testes of male babies start to descend into the scrotum.

Now that the eyelids are open, your baby will start to blink and will become much more aware of differences in light. This new sense allows the baby to be more responsive to external stimuli; many mothers notice their baby has developed a distinct pattern of rest alternating with activity. The baby is also able to start focusing its eyes at this stage, although the distance is limited to about 6–8in (15–20cm) until after birth.

GETTING READY TO BREATHE

From now until the end of the pregnancy the further development of the lungs is vitally important. By about 29 weeks, most of the smaller airways (bronchioles) are in place and the number of alveoli (little air sacs), which lie at the end of the bronchioles, are increasing. The formation of alveoli continues throughout pregnancy and after birth. In fact, the lungs do not become fully matured until a child is eight years old, which is why many childhood respiratory problems disappear or improve as children get older.

The next step in lung maturity is the production of a lipid called surfactant, made by the lining cells of the lung, which coats the air sacs in a very thin film. The surfactant works by reducing the surface tension inside the alveolar air sacs, in much the same way that dish soap disperses grease on dishes. This process is

◀ *By 27 weeks, the eyelashes and eyebrows are fuller and the fetus can blink.*

	WEEKS
FIRST TRIMESTER	▸ 1
	▸ 2
	▸ 3
	▸ 4
	▸ 5
	▸ 6
	▸ 7
	▸ 8
	▸ 9
	▸ 10
	▸ 11
	▸ 12
	▸ 13
SECOND TRIMESTER	▸ 14
	▸ 15
	▸ 16
	▸ 17
	▸ 18
	▸ 19
	▸ 20
	▸ 21
	▸ 22
	▸ 23
	▸ 24
	▸ 25
THIRD TRIMESTER	▸ 26
	▸ 27
	▸ 28
	▸ 29
	▸ 30
	▸ 31
	▸ 32
	▸ 33
	▸ 34
	▸ 35
	▸ 36
	▸ 37
	▸ 38
	▸ 39
	▸ 40

not life size

PRACTICE BREATHING *The flow of amniotic fluid in and out of the baby's mouth as it practices breathing movements is seen as red patches on this color Doppler scan.*

important because when the baby takes a first breath of real air, the air sacs need to be as elastic as possible to be able to expand successfully. When the first breath is exhaled, the air sacs must be prevented from collapsing in readiness for the next lungful of air. A baby born before 35 weeks cannot yet produce sufficient quantities of surfactant and this, coupled with the inadequate development of the bronchioles and alveoli, the newborn baby's lungs are too rigid to deal with the constant flow of air entering and leaving them. Should you be unlucky enough to have a premature birth, you will probably be given an injection of steroids before the baby is born; this helps to stimulate the lungs to produce surfactant (*see* p.342). The neonatal doctors may also decide to spray artificial surfactant into your baby's lungs after he or she is born in order to make them more elastic.

Of course, your baby is not breathing air at present because the placenta is still supplying all its oxygen requirements. Nonetheless, your baby will have started to make rhythmic breathing movements as it continues to develop its lungs in preparation for birth. These movements of the chest wall can be seen on an ultrasound scan and explain the "hiccups" you sometimes feel — short jerky movements that are quite different from other activity you can feel going on inside you.

YOUR ACTIVE BABY

You will be very aware of fetal activity between 26 and 30 weeks. Although conditions inside the uterine cavity are becoming cramped, there is still enough room for the odd somersault and complete change of position. The amniotic fluid is not being produced at the same rate as a few weeks ago so movements are no longer well cushioned and hence more noticeable than previously. It is very common to see dramatic changes in the shape of your abdomen when the baby heaves itself into a different position. Some women worry that they will be damaged or that their baby will suffer an injury as a result of all this vigorous activity. Neither will occur. There is still enough amniotic fluid to protect the baby and the thick muscular wall of your uterus is more than enough to prevent damage to your internal organs. Before leaving the subject of movements, I want to remind you that there is no correct number of movements or kicks that you should experience every day (*see* pp.190–1) but any sudden changes in your baby's regular pattern of movement needs to be reported to your doctor or midwife immediately, just in case your baby is in trouble.

There is no correct position for the baby to be in at present but many babies at this stage are still lying with their head uppermost. This often results in the mother feeling the head butting against her ribcage, which can be quite unpleasant and can sometimes be the cause of quite sharp pain. Like every other problem in pregnancy, it will not last forever. Most babies turn around to embark on their journey into the outside world head first.

not life size

MATURING SYSTEMS

Your baby's nervous system continues to become more intricate and sophisticated. Constant movements of the muscles help make movements and reflexes more coordinated. Your baby will practice the sucking reflex on a thumb or fingers whenever the opportunity presents itself but the ability to suck from the breast will not be fully developed until 35–36 weeks.

At the start of the third trimester, an average fetus measures about 10in (25cm) from crown to rump and weighs just about 2lb (1kg). By 30 weeks, its length is about 11in (28cm) and it weighs about 2–3lb (1–1.5kg).

The fetal bone marrow has now taken over as the main producer of the baby's red blood cells. This will help your baby become independent after delivery because these cells will transport oxygen around the blood stream. A simple immune response to infection is now in place.

As your baby reaches 30 weeks, its ability to survive in the outside world has improved dramatically and, as a result, the vast majority of babies that are born at this gestation will cope extremely well, with a bit of help from the special care baby doctors. From now onward, every day spent in utero reduces the time that your baby would need to spend in a neonatal unit. Even though the baby's physical size is not changing dramatically, its functional maturity is taking a considerable leap forward.

By 30 weeks, the placenta will weigh just under 1lb (450g), which is a massive increase compared to the 6oz (170g) it weighed at 20 weeks. Every minute, it receives about 16fl oz (500ml) of blood from your circulation.

YOUR BABY'S BRAIN

The brain grows in size and now starts to fold over to fit inside the bony skull. An anatomical slice through the upper part (cortex) of the fetal brain now looks like a walnut or a map of the Scandinavian fjords, with lots of little inlets and inward projections. The protective myelin sheath that began to form around the nerves of the spinal cord many weeks ago now extends to the nerve fibers entering and leaving the brain. As a result, nerve impulses can now travel much faster from the brain to the rest of the body. This ensures that, in addition to more intricate movements, the baby is now able to learn new skills.

YOUR CHANGING BODY

YOUR UTERUS IS CONTINUING TO EXPAND AT A STEADY PACE. BY 26 WEEKS IT HAS REACHED ABOVE YOUR UMBILICUS OR BELLY BUTTON AND DURING THE NEXT FEW WEEKS YOU WILL NOTICE THAT YOUR ABDOMEN IS ENLARGING BOTH UPWARD AND SIDEWAYS.

By the 30th week, the height of the uterine fundus measures approximately 12in (30 cm) from your pubic bone. I say approximately because there is much individual variation and it is important not to become worried if your fundal height is a few inches lower or higher than the standard textbook measurements. Your doctor and midwife will measure your uterus at each visit and if there is any serious discrepancy in size, they will arrange for you to undergo a series of ultrasound growth scans (*see* p.214) together with some other investigations to ensure that all is well with your developing baby (*see* pp.256–9).

CRAMPED INSIDE

In order to accommodate this enlarging mass, your other body organs need to make a few adjustments so you may experience some new symptoms or an exaggeration of some previous ones. The intestines and stomach become further compressed upward because they can no longer fit themselves comfortably around the sides of the uterus. This upward displacement often results in heartburn and/or indigestion: look back to the feature on page 187 for the best ways to deal with this. Similarly, even if you had a healthy appetite during the second trimester of pregnancy, you will probably find that you can no longer manage to eat a large meal at one sitting.

Your bladder is also unused to this extra pressure in the abdominal cavity and can no longer hold the quantities of urine it used to be able to cope with; this causes its own set of irritations (*see* p.215).

You may also experience some rib pain or discomfort, since your ribcage is now pushed outward to make more room for the increasing contents of your abdominal cavity. Some women are lucky and go through the whole of their pregnancy without any rib pain. However, if your body frame is smaller than average or you are carrying twins or triplets then you are very likely to notice rib discomfort. It will be made worse if your baby is an especially strong kicker or spends a lot of time

INSIDE YOUR ABDOMEN
Your uterus grows both upward and outward, reducing the available space for your stomach and intestines.

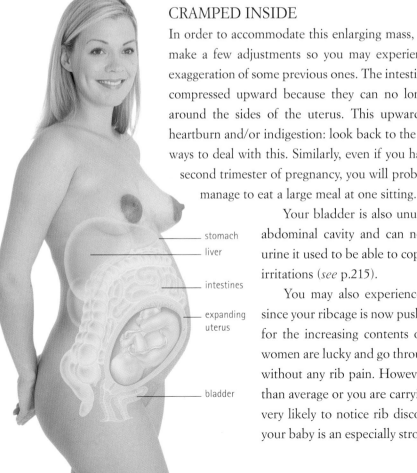

stomach

liver

intestines

expanding uterus

bladder

SHORT OF BREATH

You will notice a definite change in your breathing pattern during the third trimester. There are several reasons for this:

▶ The high levels of progesterone increase your body temperature and breathing rate.

▶ In addition, as your ribs flare outward, your diaphragm has to stretch further and in the process becomes less flexible. This reduced movement of the diaphragm forces you to try to breathe more deeply.

▶ Last, the expanding uterus pushes the abdominal contents up against the diaphragm leaving the lungs with less room to expand when you try to take a deep breath.

With all these conflicting pressures it is hardly surprising that pregnant women frequently experience episodes of breathlessness, dizziness, and light-headedness toward the end of their pregnancy. If you look back to page 190 you will find practical advice on ways to reduce some of these symptoms.

in the breech position (*see* p.269) because the fetal head will bump up against your diaphragm and ribcage. You may be particularly uncomfortable when you are sitting down, because this compresses everything even more. If you have a desk-bound job, it is sensible to make a few adjustments to your routine. Try to ensure that you get up and walk about regularly. When you are feeling particularly uncomfortable, keep changing your sitting position until you find a better one. Make a determined effort to maintain good posture.

A SURGE IN CIRCULATION

From 26 weeks onward, your circulatory system embarks on another surge. The total blood volume is now about 11 pints (5 liters) — a 25 percent increase over normal, although the maximum blood volume will not be reached until about 35 weeks. This increased blood volume means that your cardiac output (the quantity of blood pumped by the heart at each beat) continues to increase during the next few weeks. However, further relaxation of the blood vessels around your body is no longer an option because all your blood vessels are now at maximum capacity. In fact, from this point onward, your peripheral resistance will have to increase slightly and your blood pressure will start to rise, although this should be a small and very gradual change.

Your body tissues also become thicker because there is so much fluid on board that it has to be accommodated somewhere — so it is very common and perfectly normal for your fingers and legs to become slightly swollen. Having said that, if you notice that your face, fingers, or legs have suddenly become much puffier or swollen, these may be early signs of preeclampsia (*see* p.425) and you need to be seen urgently. Although preeclampsia usually develops after

CIRCULATION CHANGES

The graph shows a steep rise in cardiac output and blood volume from mid-pregnancy onward and a corresponding dip in the peripheral resistance of the body's blood vessels.

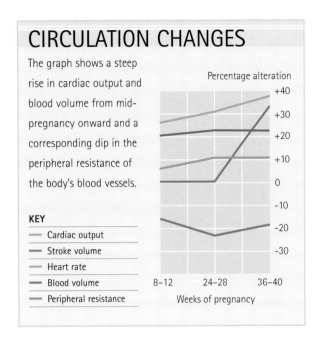

Percentage alteration

+40
+30
+20
+10
0
-10
-20
-30

8-12   24-28   36-40

Weeks of pregnancy

KEY
- Cardiac output
- Stroke volume
- Heart rate
- Blood volume
- Peripheral resistance

30 weeks and then only in a minority of women. Rarely, it develops earlier and in such cases, it is likely to become severe.

The continuing changes in your circulatory system means that the blood flow to your skin and mucus membranes is increased. In response, the peripheral blood vessels dilate and this is why pregnant women in the third trimester notice that they "feel the heat" and sweat more easily, sometimes profusely. Many women also find that the palms of their hands and the soles of their feet are red in color and feel as if they are on fire. This is called palmar erythema. All of these skin changes are entirely normal and will disappear after you have delivered. They merely reflect the fact that you need to get rid of the extra heat that your increased metabolism and your baby's metabolism is generating. If the blood vessels in your skin did not dilate, you would not be able to maintain your body temperature or your baby's at a constant level and you would literally overheat — just like a car with a broken radiator.

BREASTS AND COLOSTRUM

Your breasts will feel a lot fuller by now, due to the combined and continued action of the hormones that are responsible for breast growth in pregnancy. The veins on the surface of your breasts become more prominent and more visible during this last trimester and the nipples and areolae continue to darken.

Under the influence of these hormones, the internal structure of your breasts has been changing and developing ready for lactation and breastfeeding (*see* p.396) While the placenta is still in the uterus, high levels of estrogen and progesterone block the key hormones that trigger milk secretion but you may notice from this stage onward that you are producing a clear liquid, which leaks from the nipple at all sorts of strange times, for example, when you are in the bath or making love. This liquid is called colostrum and it is the fluid that your baby will suckle for the first few days of life, before your real milk comes through. Colostrum contains sugar, protein, and antibodies — in fact, all your baby's nutritional needs — and the most likely reason it has started to be produced now is to cater for those babies that decide to make an early appearance into this world. Having said that, please do not worry if you do not see any colostrum throughout your entire pregnancy. I can assure you it is there, it is just that you are one of the fortunate women from whom it has not actually leaked out.

HOW YOU MAY FEEL PHYSICALLY

YOU ARE LIKELY TO BE ACTUALLY ENJOYING YOUR ENLARGED SIZE BY NOW, EVEN IF AT TIMES YOU FEEL RATHER COMPROMISED BY IT. REMEMBER TO WALK TALL AND KEEP YOUR BACK STRAIGHT, SINCE BAD POSTURE WILL PUT A LOT OF PRESSURE ON YOUR LOWER BACK DURING THESE LAST THREE MONTHS.

I think it is useful to make a few suggestions here about how you can address the predictable fatigue and loss of energy that may have started by now. Many pregnant women tell me that, however much they rest, they are still tired and lacking in energy. The usual advice is to spend time with your feet up but this is more difficult to do when you have a job and/or other children, not to mention the rest of your life to run. So the message needs to be — think realistic, not idealistic. Try to find ways to reduce your commitments at work and at home.

Delegation is often the answer and I suspect that you will be pleasantly surprised by how receptive your colleagues and your family are if you just give them the opportunity to help you. So instead of trying to be superwoman, identify someone else to go to the extra committee meetings at work. Ask your partner to go to the school parents' evening, or send your apologies. Look at the household chores with a fresh eye. Do they really need to be done or could they be left to a later date when you are feeling more energetic? If the answer is yes, as may be the case with basic shopping and housework, then think about ways to employ someone to do them. If this is not possible, then you will need to ask your partner, another family member, or a supportive friend for help.

As any mother of more than one child will tell you, there can be real problems dealing with your first child or other children when you are heavily pregnant. When your two-year-old toddler is having a tantrum and refuses to have a bath, you need to step back a few paces and give yourself a break. Ask yourself — is this bath really necessary? If the answer is no, then skip the bath. If the answer is yes, go for a compromise of using a sponge on the face and grubbiest parts of your child. Remember that becoming fraught about daily domestic issues will help no one and you need to make sure that you conserve your physical and emotional energy for things that really do matter.

"When your two-year-old toddler is having a tantrum and refuses to have a bath, you need to step back a few paces and give yourself a break."

YOUR EMOTIONAL RESPONSE

YOU ARE DEFINITELY IN THE HOME STRETCH NOW — WELL PAST THE HALFWAY MARK IN THIS PREGNANCY JOURNEY. THIS IS A REAL TRANSITION PERIOD IN EMOTIONAL TERMS, BECAUSE THE BIRTH OF YOUR BABY, WHICH USED TO BE A RATHER ABSTRACT NOTION, SUDDENLY BECOMES VERY REAL.

Your baby has a very good chance of survival now, so you may be starting to become impatient, wishing away the next few months. At the same time you may be experiencing contradictory feelings of panic at the thought of having a baby to look after in the near future. If this is your first baby, you are probably starting to worry about how qualified you are to be let loose on a newborn infant. After all, many women have never changed a diaper, let alone held a very young baby, before they are handed their own in the delivery room. If this is not your first child, you will understandably be concerned about how your other children will adapt to the challenge of another little person who will have demands on your time and attention. You may also worry about how this new baby will fit into your already hectic life.

Since the possibility of birth now exists for real, you are probably also starting to think about how you will cope with labor and delivery. If this is your first birth, you will be conscious that you are about to sail into uncharted waters. If you are reading this book stage by stage, I would suggest that now is the time to jump ahead and read the sections on pain relief, labor, birth, and life after birth to equip yourself with the practical and emotional aspects of childbirth and beyond. Like most other important events in our lives, the better informed you are, the more capable you will be at dealing with the challenge positively and confidently. Make sure that you start your prenatal or parenting classes now, if you have not already done so.

"Some women who are normally slender and weight-conscious feel suddenly liberated by their large, rounded belly."

A POSITIVE BODY IMAGE

If you are normally a fit, healthy woman, the physical downside of pregnancy can come as something of an emotional shock. You may become increasingly frustrated by your growing bulk, which is preventing you from leading your life as you used to. On the other hand, you may be loving every minute of your new-found voluptuousness. Some women who are usually very slender and weight-conscious tell me that they feel suddenly liberated by, and enormously proud of, their large, rounded belly. They view their body as an affirmation of their sexuality, especially as it might be the first time that they have ever had a generous cleavage! Similarly, women who have previously been worried about their body size may for once be reconciled with their larger shape and positively enjoying it. The truth is that the way we feel about our heavily pregnant bodies has a lot to do with how well we feel on a day-to-day basis during the latter stages of pregnancy and the way in which our partners react to our distended bellies and swollen breasts (not to mention extra all-round weight). Some women become deeply attached to their growing bump and a little sad at the prospect of losing it, while others feel that the day it disappears cannot come quickly enough.

INVOLVING YOUR PARTNER

Some men are closely involved in their partner's pregnancy from the beginning, but many more do not show much interest in the details of pregnancy, labor, and life after birth until rather late in the day. If this is the case with your partner, you may be starting to feel concerned that he is still not as involved in your pregnancy as you might have wished. Indeed, some men are reluctant to become demonstrably involved at all. They are not necessarily being unsupportive, it is just that men and women tend to be on different wavelengths during this unique time.

Women tend to immerse themselves totally in their pregnancy, because it is both physically and psychologically part of them. It is not surprising that men are less able to do the same, since they are, by definition, physically detached. Many tend to carry on with their lives as if nothing has changed. Although they may recognize that life will change dramatically after the baby arrives, it may be difficult for them to translate this somewhat abstract notion into the day-to-day reality.

If you are first-time parents, pregnancy provides you with the opportunity to start shifting your relationship from the couple that you currently are, to the family that you will shortly be. However, I do think it is important to remember that trying to change your partner into your ideal of what he should be during your pregnancy is unlikely to be successful. He is going to need to adapt in his own way and in his own time — albeit with a few prompts from you. He is undoubtedly just as eager as you are that everything goes smoothly during labor and after, so perhaps the most important thing that you can do now is to ensure that he is sufficiently informed to offer you practical and emotional help throughout. Then he will be able to look back on the event and feel he was as involved in the birth of his child as he wanted to be.

POSITIVE BODY IMAGE

How you feel about your heavily pregnant body is usually a reflection of your overall health and well-being at this stage of pregnancy.

CHECKING YOUR BABY'S GROWTH

AT EACH PRENATAL VISIT, YOUR CAREGIVERS MONITOR THE GROWTH OF YOUR BABY BY
PALPATING YOUR ABDOMEN AND MEASURING THE FUNDAL HEIGHT OF YOUR UTERUS. IF A MORE
DETAILED CHECK IS NEEDED, IT IS USUALLY DONE WITH A SERIES OF ULTRASOUND SCANS.

GROWTH SCANS

Fetal growth scans are revealing because most problems at this stage in pregnancy are likely to affect the rate at which your baby is growing. The size of the baby's head, limbs, and abdominal girth will be recorded, and the relationship between the various measurements examined carefully because late pregnancy problems may not affect all aspects of growth equally.

IDENTIFYING THE PROBLEM

Intrauterine growth restriction (IUGR) manifests itself in different ways depending on the cause (see pp.256–57 and p.428). For example, if the placenta is not working well (as can be the case if the mother has high blood pressure or preeclampsia) the growth of the baby's head will be maintained but usually at the expense of the growth of the baby's abdomen. This is because the blood supply carrying oxygen and nutrients from the placenta will be diverted to baby's brain, and the abdominal organs receive less. To compensate, the baby's liver will start using fat stores causing the liver (and

abdominal girth) to become smaller. This growth pattern is known as "head sparing growth retardation" — a rather frightening term, but one that sums up a clever survival mechanism that ensures that the fetal brain is protected in a potentially difficult situation.

COMPARING MEASUREMENTS

Your baby's measurements will be compared with previous and future measurements because the rate of growth over time is what determines whether it is safe to leave the baby in utero or whether the baby needs to be delivered immediately.

If your baby is not growing very well but is not in distress, you will be asked to return for another scan in 7–10 days. This may seem a long time to wait, but it is difficult to interpret changes in measurements within a shorter interval of time.

INTERPRETING GROWTH CHARTS

ON EACH GRAPH *the 50th percentile (red line) is the average and the 90th percentile line (above) and the 10th percentile line (below) represent the upper and lower ranges of normal growth. On the head circumference graph, the baby's head is growing steadily. On the abdominal circumference graph, the velocity of growth of the abdomen is showing a decline, possibly because blood and nutrients are being directed to the heart and brain at the expense of organs in the abdomen.*

COMMON CONCERNS

THIS IS A WEIGHTIER SECTION, NOW REFLECTING THE FACT THAT PREGNANCY-RELATED PROBLEMS AND IRRITATIONS ARE MORE NUMEROUS IN THE THIRD TRIMESTER. FORTUNATELY, THERE ARE REMEDIES AND STRATEGIES THAT WILL HELP REDUCE SOME OF THEIR EFFECTS.

Urinary frequency during the day is common — the usual reflex signals that start when the bladder is full occur much earlier when there is an increasingly heavy baby pushing down on it from above. Although there is nothing that can be done about this further mechanical design fault of pregnancy, do remember that, if you need to pass urine very frequently and can only expel a tiny amount on each occasion, you may have developed a urinary infection and need to make sure that your urine is properly tested (*see* p.192).

You may have started to leak small quantities of urine when you sneeze, cough, or laugh; this is called stress incontinence and is common toward the end of pregnancy. Renewed attention to Kegel exercises can reduce the problem as can cutting out tea, coffee, and colas, which have a diuretic effect.

Sleep patterns in the third trimester are often disturbed and your bladder will make a significant contribution to this by ensuring that you have to get up several times a night to use the bathroom. Several of my patients have suggested that these nightime interruptions are designed to help you adjust to the inevitable lack of sleep after the baby is born. They may be right, but when I was pregnant I would have preferred to sleep undisturbed at night between 26 and 40 weeks and find out about nightime vigils at a later stage.

VAGINAL INFECTIONS

It is normal for vaginal discharge to increase from the second trimester of pregnancy onward. However, it should always remain clear and mucuslike, odorless or just mildly smelling — similar to the discharge you may have experienced before the start of your menstrual period. You may find that you need to use a thin panty liner. If the discharge becomes yellow-green, develops a stronger smell, or your vulva, vagina, and anal region become reddened and painful, particularly when you urinate, tell your prenatal caregivers. They will take some swabs to check for vaginal infection, which if left untreated may increase your risk of going into premature labor.

bladder

pelvic floor muscles

BLADDER PROBLEMS
During a cough or sneeze you may leak urine. The problem is due to the weight of the baby pressing on your bladder and also weak pelvic floor muscles, shown above as a solid line (with a dotted line indicating their pre-pregnancy position).

DEALING WITH YEAST

Many pregnant women are troubled by yeast (candidiasis) in pregnancy. The following remedies may help relieve symptoms:

▶ **Cream and suppository remedies** can be bought over-the-counter or prescribed by your doctor. Suppositories, inserted into your vagina, are the most effective because they tackle the root cause of the infection by increasing the acidity of your vaginal secretions. They will not harm your pregnancy, and a single pessary may resolve the problem. Creams applied to the vulva may reduce the discomfort temporarily, but they won't cure the underlying problem.

▶ **Personal hygiene** is important. Make sure that you always wipe your anal region from front to back (rather than back to front) after passing a stool. Bathe regularly and keep your vulva clean and dry. Avoid highly fragranced soaps and bubble baths, particularly if the vulval skin is reddened and sore.

▶ **Adding a few drops of vinegar** to your bath or bathing the vulval area with a weak solution of cider vinegar may relieve symptoms. Alternatively, you could try live yogurt to balance the body's natural bacteria and fight fungal infections. You could try smearing the yogurt into the vaginal entrance to relieve the itching.

▶ **Wearing cotton underwear**, and avoiding tights or tight-fitting jeans will give the skin around your genital area more air to breathe.

▶ **Reducing your intake of sugar and yeast** may prove useful if you have recurrent episodes of yeast infections, since they can both aggravate the problem.

Most itchy vaginal infections are due to yeast (candida infection), which is an innocent, albeit uncomfortable, side effect of pregnancy. You will notice an itchy, curdlike discharge (which looks a bit like cottage cheese) around your vagina. Yeast is not a cause of preterm delivery and most women experience at least one episode of it during pregnancy. It is largely due to the vaginal environment becoming less acidic during pregnancy thanks to the effects of hormones, and this encourages the growth of the yeastlike fungus (*Candida albicans*), which is normally present in small numbers in the vagina and gut. Another common cause of yeast in both pregnant and nonpregnant women is antibiotic treatment because the antibiotics kill off some of the normal housekeeping bacteria in the gut and vagina, allowing the candida organisms to gain a hold.

HEADACHES

Headaches are very common in pregnancy and are usually nothing to worry about. However, some women suffer from migraine attacks that can leave them quite debilitated. If you are suddenly experiencing severe headaches, report them to your doctor or midwife promptly. Please do not be tempted to wait until your next prenatal appointment, because severe headaches at this stage in pregnancy can be a sign that your blood pressure is too high (*see* p.425). Even if your headaches prove to be nothing serious, your doctors will be able to suggest some safe remedies.

ITCHING SKIN

By the end of pregnancy your skin will have stretched by an extra 150–290 square inches (77–155 square cm) and can become dry and itchy as it becomes increasingly taut over your enlarging tummy. Stretchmarks — which often make their appearance around now — can make the problem worse. Expensive creams marketed specially for pregnant women, to prevent or reduce stretch marks, are unlikely to do more than relieve dry itchy skin temporarily. I can promise you that cheaper remedies — simple, unscented emollient creams or oil such as baby oil or olive oil — are just as effective at keeping your skin supple and well hydrated. The other practical step you can take to reduce the itchiness is to start wearing cotton clothes, which help keep the skin cool.

HEMORRHOIDS

Many women become troubled by hemorrhoids by this stage in pregnancy. These are dilated veins around the inside and outside of the anus, or back passage, which are caused by the pressure of the baby's weight in your pelvis. Hemorrhoids frequently cause throbbing pain and itching around the anal area and they may also bleed. You may find that you can feel a swollen tender vein protruding out of your anus or notice some light red bleeding on the toilet paper after you have passed a stool. If you are constipated, you are more likely to strain in an attempt to empty your bowels and this can cause the hemorrhoids to swell further, so make sure you drink plenty of water each day, increase your intake of dietary fiber and exercise regularly. Lifting heavy weights can aggravate the problem. Over-the-counter creams that contain a lubricant and a light local anesthetic will help relieve the discomfort as can icepacks, particularly when you have had a long and tiring day.

LEG CRAMPS

Many pregnant women suffer from leg cramps, particularly at night. You may find that you wake up suddenly, gripped by painful, violent spasms in one of your legs or feet. Some doctors think that the pressure of the uterus on certain nerves in the pelvis may be the trigger while others suggest they may be due to low calcium or salt levels, or an excess of phosphorus. However, none of these theories has been proven so don't even consider trying to adjust your levels of

"If you are suddenly experiencing severe headaches, report them to your doctor or midwife promptly."

RELIEVING BACK PAIN

WOMEN USED TO BE TOLD THAT THEY HAD TO PUT UP WITH BACKACHE IN PREGNANCY BECAUSE NOTHING COULD BE DONE ABOUT IT. IN FACT, THERE ARE SEVERAL PRACTICAL MEASURES THAT HELP RELIEVE SYMPTOMS — YOU DON'T HAVE TO PUT UP WITH DEBILITATING PAIN.

The kind of back injury that tends to occur at this stage of pregnancy is generalized back pain. Later in the trimester you may develop more specific back problems, such as sciatica, pubic symphysis dysfunction and sacroiliac joint pain — these are covered in detail on pages 243–44.

First of all, make sure that your doctor identifies exactly what the problem is: the back is such a complex area that pain could be due to any number of causes. It is not sensible to embark on a series of treatments that are at best inappropriate, at worst dangerous.

Consider consulting a chiropractor, but make sure that you choose a trained practitioner (see pp.436–38). A skilled chiropractor will relieve symptoms of back ache (or joint pain) by gentle manipulation and massage but you should never agree to any realignment of vertebra — especially in the lower spine — by "clicking" them into place or using short, sharp, manipulations.

Once your doctor has made a diagnosis, back exercises designed for pregnancy may be helpful (some of are shown here).

PROTECTING YOUR BACK

Because your belly now weighs more than usual, you may find that walking even short distances can pull on your abdominal ligaments or give you lower backache. Your pelvic ligaments are under more strain than ever and, and because they are more elastic than usual, it is inevitable that they will complain when made to work harder. Turn to the tips on page 193 to remind yourself how to protect your back when lifting and how to support your back while you sleep.

STRENGTHENING MUSCLES

Regular exercise will help build stronger back muscles and improve your posture and, as a result, support your spine and lumbar region and help reduce — if not prevent — back pain. Physical activity will also help you sleep better since you will feel calmer, thanks to endorphins released during exercise, which have a slight painkilling and mood-enhancing effect.

AN ORTHOPEDIC BELT

Another practical way to reduce back strain is to wear an orthopedic belt

SUPPORT *A belt may bring instant relief.*

(these are usually advertised as maternity belts in magazines and on the Internet). The belt is positioned just below your belly and straps around your pelvis with velcro fastenings. Wear it during the day and take it off at night. I remember how important my belt was to me at this stage in pregnancy. I was carrying twins, and am short (about 5ft 2in or 1.5m), which meant that by 26 weeks, I was feeling extremely unsteady on my feet and the backache was awful. As soon as I put on my belt, the relief was immediate. Why they are not regularly recommended to pregnant women is a mystery to me.

BACK EXERCISES

If your back is giving you problems, try some of the exercises below. They will help strengthen the muscles that give support to your spine and pelvis and will keep you supple, which will be of great benefit during labour. As always, stop exercising if you feel any discomfort, and if you are unsure about any specific exercise, ask the advice of an obstetric physical therapist (contact him/her through your midwife or doctor).

▶ **Knee hug** Lie on your back with your arms hugging your knees (make space for your bump) and gently roll a little from side to side to release tension in your lower spine and pelvis. This is very soothing for your lower back.

▶ **Spinal twist** Lie on your back with your knees bent and feet together, arms out at shoulder height. Slowly drop your knees to one side, while turning your head to look in the opposite direction. Feel your spine twisting gently. Raise your knees back up and repeat on other side.

▶ **Spinal relaxation** Lie on your back, with your knees bent, shoulder-width apart, with your arms at your sides. Push up on your legs so that your thighs, pelvis, and back as far as shoulder blades are lifted off the floor. Lower your back down slowly, exhaling at same time. Repeat five times.

▶ **Pelvic tilts** Lying on your back with your knees bent, pull in your lower abdominal muscles, squeeze your buttocks, and press the curve of your back into the floor. Hold for 10 seconds (don't hold your breath) and release slowly. Repeat five times, building up to 10.

▶ **Knee squeezes** Lie on your back, with your knees bent and your feet together. Squeeze any object roughly the size of your fist between your knees (such as a can of beans). Hold the contraction for 10 seconds and repeat 10 times, twice a day. Progress to an object the length of your forearm (such as a paper towel roll) only when the previous exercise is absolutely painless throughout the contraction. This exercise is particularly good if you are suffering from pubic symphysis dysfunction.

KEY BACK STRETCHES

SPINAL STRETCH *Sitting down on bent knees, legs slightly apart to make way for your belly, stretch your arms out in front of you along the floor. Feel the stretch all along your spine.*

CAT STRETCHES *Kneeling on all fours, knees and arms shoulder-width apart, arch your back into a hump, clenching your buttock muscles and tucking your pelvis in. Hold, then release slowly until your back is flat again. Repeat five times.*

> "You may be anxious to ensure that you are not regarded simply as a mother-to-be but also as a working woman and colleague."

these minerals with supplements or dietary changes. When you get a cramp attack, simply flex the leg, calf, or foot in the opposite direction. So if your calf cramps, for example, stretch it out by straightening your leg and flexing your foot towards you as you simultaneously massage the calf area until the pain fades away. Although leg cramps are uncomfortable, they are nothing to worry about, since they are temporary ailments that will disappear after your baby is born. However, constant leg pain should always be investigated because of an increased risk of deep vein thrombosis (DVT) in pregnancy (*see* p.423).

CARPAL TUNNEL SYNDROME

Some of my patients become alarmed because their fingers sometimes feel tingly, as if they had pins and needles in them. Occasionally, they might even feel a little numb or weak, as if they have lost sensation. This common ailment is caused by fluid retention, which swells the band of tissue (carpal tunnel) at your wrist and puts pressure on the nerves and ligaments that lie in this tunnel, before they enter your hand. The symptoms will disappear after the birth of your baby, because you get rid of all the excess water that has accumulated. In the meantime, if you become seriously uncomfortable, your doctor will refer you to a physical therapist, who may prescribe a splint to support your wrist. You could also try sleeping with the affected arm propped up on a pillow, to help drain the excess fluid. Remember that diuretic drugs used to get rid of excess body fluid should not be used in pregnancy.

THINGS TO CONSIDER

IF YOU ARE WORKING, YOU SHOULD MAKE SURE THAT YOU AND YOUR EMPLOYER ARE AGREED ON ALL OF THE SPECIFICS OF YOUR MATERNITY LEAVE (*SEE* P.63). YOUR DOCTOR OR MIDWIFE CAN GIVE YOU A COMPLETED FORM CONFIRMING YOUR PREGANCY AND DUE DATE IF YOU NEED ONE IN ORDER TO QUALIFY FOR MATERNITY PAY AND LEAVE .

Like many women, you may be hoping to continue working as long as possible to maximize your maternity leave after your baby is born. However, if you need to stop work for medical reasons, you can obtain a letter from your doctor so that you will qualify for short-term disability.

If you work in an office where certain styles of clothing are not permitted or are frowned upon, clothes can be a major issue as you near the end of your pregnancy. Although anyone who sees you will probably instantly realize you are pregnant, you may be anxious to be sure that you are not regarded simply as a mother-to-be but also as a working woman and colleague. If slipping into comfortable leggings and baggy T-shirts is not an option, then you will have to struggle on with wearing a jacket or similar business casual attire for as long as you can bear it. Borrow or buy a few outfits that will fit the bill.

If you are heavily pregnant during the summer, it may be quite difficult to find clothes that can keep you both cool and decent. You feel like a furnace for much of the time and if it is summer or you are living in a hot climate, you may feel unbearably hot, puffy, and sweaty. Heat rashes form in all sorts of recesses of your body (under your arms, under your breasts, between your legs). If your feet and hands have swollen, shoes start to pinch, and finger rings may become so tight and uncomfortable that they are impossible to wear. There is not much you can do about this, other than avoiding situations where you will feel particularly hot, such as overcrowded restaurants or stuffy theaters, and by wearing loose, light clothes made of natural fibers such as cotton.

STARTING PRENATAL CLASSES

You will probably be starting your birthing classes now — most hospital-run classes have start dates every four weeks and recommend women start their course between 26 and 30 weeks. Monthly start dates are also the norm for some other forms of prenatal classes. If you do have a choice of when to start, always opt for the earlier date since you never know what might happen. You need to make sure that you attend the all-important sessions on labor and pain relief, before you are forced to find out all about it first-hand in the delivery room. For exactly the same reason, you want to avoid missing the formal visit to the maternity ward, if you have not already been shown around. This is especially important if this is your first birth, if you are expecting twins (50 percent of twins are delivered before 35 weeks), or if you have had a previous premature delivery.

Your partner may not want to attend all of the classes, but make sure that he at least knows when the special session for fathers is and encourage him to attend this one. It is far better that he has prior warning about the role you would like him to play, rather than leaving him to find out for himself during labor.

PREPARING FOR BIRTH

Breathing and relaxation classes will help focus your attention on and prepare you for the next stage — your baby's birth.

YOUR SEX LIFE

A couple's sex life is often revitalized in this period of pregnancy since most women are feeling both physically and emotionally well. You may be conscious that time is running out before the birth of your baby, with the inevitable disruption that this will bring to your night's sleep and, as a result, to your sex life. Tiny babies are not very considerate about their parents' need for intimate times together alone. The only thing that may hinder your sex life at this stage are nagging doubts so let me deal with a few of them.

• Although rarely discussed, the fact that you may feel the baby moving inside you while you are making love can make you feel inhibited, or it can make you laugh. Although the sensation may be disturbing, it is certainly not a sign that your baby is upset by your lovemaking.

• You may both be worried that you will harm your baby by having penetrative sex or concerned that sex could trigger labor inadvertently since your partner's semen contains prostaglandin (a hormone used to induce labor). In addition, orgasm causes the uterus to contract.

The reality is that no amount of sexual activity will harm your unborn child or trigger labor in a normal pregnancy, so you can continue an active sex life unless you have been told to stop because of a potential problem or complication. Examples include a previous premature delivery or a risk factor for premature labor such as a short or slightly dilated cervix (*see* p.188); threatened premature labor (*see* p.340); recent bleeding and/or a low-lying placenta (*see* placenta previa, p.240 and p.427); and ruptured membranes.

"...disturbing dreams are a way of sifting through any negative emotions without having to experience them in reality."

DISTURBING DREAMS

On a different note, many women report that they experience strange dreams during late pregnancy. They may be sexually explicit dreams or disturbing dreams involving the death or illness of babies and children. Both are common and can cause great anxiety, since you will undoubtedly start to wonder about their meaning. So it is important to remember that they are not an omen of awful things to come. Like all good and bad dreams (most of which we do not remember because we do not wake through the dream phase of sleep) they are a method of coping with day-to-day concerns and fears. Think of them as a way of sifting through negative emotions without having to experience them in reality. One of the reasons these dreams seem more common during the last trimester is that you wake much more often (either because you need to go to the bathroom or because you are uncomfortable) and are more likely to recall them.

DIET AND EXERCISE

IN THE THIRD TRIMESTER, EATING NOURISHING FOOD AND MAINTAINING YOUR FITNESS HAS A DUAL PURPOSE. BOTH WILL HELP REDUCE FATIGUE AND BOOST YOUR WELL-BEING AS YOU ENTER THE LAST STRETCH OF PREGNANCY AND BEGIN TO BUILD YOUR STRENGTH FOR LABOR.

GOOD EATING

Your diet is less crucial to your baby's well-being than in the first trimester, and unless you are surviving on a diet of chips and sodas, your baby is likely getting everything it needs.

▶ **Your weight gain should be** around 1–2lb (0.5–1kg) per week during the final three months *(see p.42)* although it may be minimal in the final weeks.

▶ **Your daily calorie intake** in the third trimester can increase by 300– 500 calories, which sounds like a lot, but a typical candy bar contains 300-odd calories. An extra healthy snack (the odd treat is okay, but try to avoid satieting your increased hunger with sugary treats) each day will supply all you need.

▶ **You may need to eat more frequently** during the last few weeks because you feel the need to snack regularly. Your body is most likely laying down some final, extra stores in preparation for labor, so choose foods that are nutritious and will give you vital energy. Since you never know when you will go into labor, the better your diet in the weeks ahead, the better your ability to cope physically with the demands on the day.

▶ **Maintain your fluid intake** (at least eight glasses a day) to ensure that your body is fully hydrated; this will give you more energy. It may seem obvious, but if you haven't stopped smoking yet, you should now: smoking starves the placenta, and thus your baby, of oxygen.

FIT FOR LABOR

There is no reason why you should discontinue to exercise until the day you deliver, unless your doctor has specifically told you to stop.

▶ **Certain activities will now be difficult or uncomfortable** – the chances are that you will have given up white-water rafting, horseback riding, and running by this point!

▶ **If you are accustomed to a particular sport,** you may be able to continue for a little longer, albeit at a gentler pace, provided you feel well and your doctor gives you the green light (although I'm sure you will know when things are becoming more than you can manage).

▶ **If you haven't tried swimming, pregnancy yoga, or exercise classes yet,** try to find time to do so soon. You will be surprised by how good they make you feel.

▶ **Whatever your chosen method of exercise,** make sure that you are doing your Kegel exercises regularly *(see p.165)* and paying attention to your posture.

SHOPPING FOR YOUR BABY

There are no fixed rules about what to buy for your baby, but from my own experience and that of the many pregnant women I have talked to over the years, there are certain items that are more essential than others. Broadly speaking, there are two main areas to think about when choosing what you need for your baby's first few months: clothes and equipment.

CHOOSING BABY CLOTHES

Young babies cannot regulate their temperature very well, so they need to be kept covered during the early weeks, but not so much that they start to overheat. The general rule of thumb is that, for the first two months, babies need one more layer than you would wear on any given day (although this varies depending on the time of year and on

THE RIGHT SIZE *Most babies grow so fast they only wear newborn-sized clothes for a matter of weeks.*

the baby, since some feel the cold more than others). Remember also that babies have little or no hair, so on cooler days they will need to wear a bonnet or hat outdoors (never indoors) and, if it is sunny, they must have a hat that protects their head, neck, and face.

Comfort, practicality, and ease of washing are the main criteria when choosing baby clothes. Look for clothes that do not restrict your baby's movements; that can be put on and taken off easily without causing your baby discomfort; that do not have bows, ribbons, and lace that will catch fingers; and that allow the skin to breathe. Babies grow so fast that clothes for newborns may only last a couple of weeks and, if you and your partner are taller than average, you may even have a baby who at birth is already wearing clothes for older infants. So, apart from two or three all-in-one stretch suits for newborns, I would advise you to go straight for the next size up when choosing your baby's clothes. Don't feel shy about borrowing newborn clothes if they are offered — they get very little use and can be handed back within a month of the birth.

Make sure that the clothes you buy are made of a breathable fabric that can be machine washed at a reasonable temperature (minimum 100°F) and tumbledried. Cotton is the best fabric for breathability, comfort and ease of washing; synthetic-only fabrics are less suitable, particularly in the early weeks. Wool is good in winter, but it can be irritating worn next to a baby's delicate skin. Make sure all-in-one suits are quick and easy to undo — in the early months, you will be changing at least 10 diapers in a 24-hour period. Go for the styles that have snap fastenings around the bottom to ensure that your baby is not put through the unnecessary contortions of taking the whole garment off for every diaper change. All-in-one suits without feet have the advantage that they will not cramp the growth of your baby's toes.

If you are having an autumn or winter baby, you will need some warm outerwear, too. All-in-one suits, with integrated hoods and booties are ideal. Pay attention to the outer fabric and inner lining since some suits are warmer than others. Your baby will also need a warm hat (babies can lose most of their body heat very quickly from an uncovered head), and several pairs of mittens and booties to keep hands and feet warm. Young babies can be relied upon to regularly lose these items by pulling or kicking them off. You will find countless varieties of shoes for babies in stores — all of them unnecessary and potentially harmful if they cramp your baby's toes. Your baby will only need shoes (properly fitted in a children's shoe department) for later walks outside.

Most importantly, remember that you will be given many clothes as presents so try not to buy too much now. Your newborn can only use a few outfits per day even for the sort who throws up after every feed. Before you can blink, clothes will no longer fit, which is why it is much better to stock up on missing items later on.

NATURAL FIBERS *Clothes made of cotton and wool allow your baby's skin to breathe.*

ESSENTIAL BABY CLOTHES

▶ Six cotton shirts with wide necks

▶ Six all-in-one suits

▶ Two cardigans (fleece-backed cotton or wool for winter, lighter cotton for warmer days)

▶ Two pairs of socks or soft cotton booties

▶ One shawl or cotton blanket

▶ One bonnet or sunhat, which shades eyes and neck

▶ One outdoor coat, including hood and booties, or one all-in-one outdoor suit, depending on season

▶ One pair of mittens, depending on season

CHOOSING A STROLLER

I cannot recommend a particular stroller (it would be out of date before you had finished reading this section), but I can offer a few points to keep in mind when you are choosing transport for your newborn:

▶ For the first few months, your baby's spine needs proper support and he will need to lie totally flat. Any stroller that does not have a flat position should be rejected. If you buy a travel system, you can use the car seat clipped onto the stroller but only for short trips.

▶ Think about where you live. Some of the fanciest strollers have a very long chassis and big wheels — ideal for cross-country jogging but hard to maneuver up and down steps and in stores and on busy streets.

▶ For winter babies, look for a carriage that is well insulated and offers protection from the elements.

▶ Whatever time of year you give birth, you will need to have a rain hood but, unless you are having your baby in spring or summer, you will not need a sunshade for the time being.

▶ Do make sure that the folded-up stroller or carriage fits inside your car trunk and the car seat fits in your car. Most baby equipment stores and department stores will let you try them out before you buy them.

BUYING BABY EQUIPMENT

When you become pregnant for the first time, you discover a whole new world of products aimed at mothers, parents, and children. If you have had little contact with babies up until now, you might be astonished at the variety of what is available and even if this is not your first child, you may be surprised to see items in the stores this time round that were not around as recently as 18 months ago. Undoubtedly, many of these so-called "essential" products are conceived by the fertile imaginations of those who work in the baby and childcare industries, aided and abetted by all kinds of marketing wizardry.

Go to any baby section in a department store or leaf through any mother and baby mail- order catalog and you are suddenly confronted with everything from endless varieties of strollers and carriages — with horrifying price tags to match — to a plethora of little gadgets, which may or may not be of any use. After all, you ask yourself, how important is an in-car bottle and jar warmer? While there is no denying that many products are genuinely helpful and make our lives easier, it can be very difficult for a first-time parent to distinguish between what is a true must-have and what is a nice, but entirely optional, extra.

Strollers and carriages

The choice of stroller or carriage is probably the most important and costly item. Technically, a carriage is a crib on a chassis that can then be taken off and used for the baby to sleep in at night because it has sufficient depth to accommodate a mattress. A stroller may allow the baby to lie completely flat but it cannot be used for him to sleep in at night because it cannot be taken off the chassis and, crucially, it lacks the depth to accommodate a mattress.

Whether you go to a specialized baby store or a department store, the sales assistant is likely to blind you with particulars as he or she demonstrates how the various models work. Before you know it, like a child's transformer toy, travel systems, strollers, and carriages are being assembled, folded, or taken apart to become forward and back facing strollers, car seats, and more. Some of the new generation of strollers and carriages now have four-wheel mechanisms and larger wheels allowing you to jog with your baby across the most rugged terrain.

As with all aspects of buying equipment, speak to as many people as you can who have recently had babies, since their advice will be unbiased and they can explain the pros and cons before you begin to look in stores. You will then have a clearer idea of what you are looking for and what your main criteria are.

If the price tags of strollers is alarming (and they often are) grandparents-to-be might like to contribute; alternatively, consider borrowing one from a friend or relative, or buying second-hand. Because of the high price and high turnover of nursery equipment, there is a thriving second-hand market in all these goods.

A baby sling is a useful and inexpensive addition to having a stroller. It allows you to keep your baby close to you (with the bonus of a peaceful nap for your baby through any trips) and to have both hands free. It also saves the bother of hauling your carriage in and out of stores and people's houses. Slings range from traditional hammocks that lie across the body to high-tech sport models with adjustable straps and back supports. Whichever one you choose make sure it supports your newborn baby's head. Try the sling on before you buy it to make sure that you can put the baby in it and fasten it by yourself.

Car seats

The other essential item you will need is a car seat: in fact, if you give birth in a hospital, you will not be allowed to leave unless you have one properly installed in your car. Some are part of a travel system — a suite of items that attach to a stroller base; or can be lifted out of the car and used as a babyseat. Many car seats for newborns are designed to last only around six months, so this is an item that you could consider borrowing from a friend if you know its history. If you buy a second-hand seat, check that it has not been involved in a serious accident, because there is a risk that it may no longer be safe as a result.

BABY SLING *The most comfortable slings have wide straps that support your back and shoulders and well-placed head support for your baby.*

Cribs and beds

What will your baby sleep in at home? There are various options, from bassinets, cradles, and cribs to full-sized beds. Essentially, all options are fine from the start and, to be honest, many babies spend their first few weeks in simpler beds and are none the worse for it. The important thing is to buy a new mattress. A few years ago, there

CRIB SAFETY *Your baby is safest with his feet near the base of the crib so that he cannot slip under the blankets.*

was a crib death scare that suggested a link between old mattresses and an increased risk of Sudden Infant Death Syndrome (SIDS). This theory has now been discredited but there is still a good reason for buying a new mattress: a second-hand one will have an indentation from the previous baby and will not give your newborn adequate spinal support. Some parents keep their babies in a cradle during the day, then transfer them to the crib at night, with the idea that the baby will gradually recognize that the latter is specifically for a long sleep at night. This is certainly worth a try, although it may make little difference before the baby is around three months old, by which time, he will have outgrown a cradle anyway. Babies move more freely and sleep better in a full-sized crib from the start, so there is really no need to invest heavily in the other options because you will soon be dispensing with them.

As far as bedding is concerned, cotton is best, but it is important not to let your baby overheat by piling on layers of woolen blankets. You can check if your baby feels cold by feeling the nape of his neck: if it feels warm, then he is fine. For each type of bed, you will need a minimum of two thermal blankets, two fitted sheets, and two top sheets. Babies should not have pillows, because their heads need to lie flat on the mattress. Even though crib bumpers, quilts, and comforters are widely available in stores, they are not recommended for small babies because they may move over the baby's head and restrict breathing

DIAPER-CHANGING AND FEEDING EQUIPMENT

Regarding smaller items of baby equipment, you will need a plastic covered changing mat and a plastic bucket or bin (with a lid) in which to put disposable or reusable terrycloth diapers. Disposal units store used disposable diapers in a sealed, fragranced container until you are ready to empty them. This is hardly an essential item but it reduces the amount of times you have to empty the trash and avoids unpleasant smells. A baby bath can make bath time easier on your back and nerves as you struggle with a small, slippery baby.

If you plan to use terry cloth reusable diapers, which are much more environmentally friendly than disposables, you will need to buy at least 30 of them to accomodate as many as 10 changes a day, together with plastic pants, pins, and diaper liners. They may appear to cost less than disposables but you need to take into account the fact that they need laundering either by you (make sure you have a good washing machine and dryer) or by a diaper laundering service (this latter option works out at roughly the same cost as using disposables). The more modern-shaped reusable diapers are fully washable and tend to fit better than the terry cloth styles because they come in different sizes, although all types require a liner (and plastic pants to protect clothes from soiling). You will find more information about the baby products you may want to buy closer to your delivery date on pages 224–27.

Feeding equipment

If you plan to bottle-feed from the start, you will need at least six bottles because you will be feeding your baby up to seven or eight meals per day (or at least making up that many feedings). If you plan to breastfeed, you should still buy two or three bottles so you will be prepared if or whenever you decide to start using bottles. Remember that babies can take your expressed milk, as well as formula milk, from a bottle. Buy slow-flowing nipples; otherwise, your baby will struggle to swallow fast enough.

You will need to sterilize bottles until your baby is six months old using one of the following:
• A sterilizing tank uses water and sterilizing agent in tablet or liquid form. Bottles and nipples have to be submerged for several hours.
• The newer electric or microwave steamers use steam to sterilize bottles and nipples in a matter of minutes. Most kits are sold with bottles.

These are the essential items to have ready before your baby's birth but by all means go out and buy whatever seems useful afterward. The early weeks and months are about making life easier and, within reason, you should look for anything that helps you do just that.

ESSENTIAL EQUIPMENT

▶ Stroller or carriage that allows baby to lie flat
▶ Rain hood
▶ Crib or cradle with a new mattress
▶ Cotton bed sheets, including, for each size of bed:
  Two fitted sheets
  Two top sheets
  Two thermal blankets
▶ Rear-facing car seat
▶ Plastic changing mat and plastic diaper bucket (with lid)
▶ Bottles (six if bottle-feeding, two if breastfeeding) plus slow-flow nipple.
▶ Sterilizing equipment
▶ Baby sling with good head support

WEEKS 30–35

THE DEVELOPING BABY

YOUR BABY IS CONTINUING TO GROW IN LENGTH, BUT THE REALLY NOTICEABLE DIFFERENCE IS YOUR BABY'S WEIGHT. THE LAYER OF SUBCUTANEOUS FAT IS INCREASING AND THE SKIN NOW LOOKS PINK AND LESS WRINKLED, ESPECIALLY IN THE FACE, WHICH NOW LOOKS SMOOTH AND CHUBBY.

From 28 to 32 weeks the weekly weight gain is as much as 17oz (500g) and continues at a rate of about 9oz (250g) per week between 32 and 35 weeks, which means that the average baby weighs 5½lb (2.5kg) at 35 weeks. A baby born around this time will still look a little on the lean side but will no longer have the wrinkly, red, emaciated look of a few weeks ago. The surface coating of white waxy vernix will be very thick, but the lanugo hair is fast disappearing and will probably be present only in patches on the shoulders and back. If delivered now, your baby will be in less need of these protective mechanisms to combat the cold since its control of body temperature is becoming much more reliable.

Your baby's eyes are opening and closing now, blinking and learning to focus, since the pupils are able to contract and dilate in response to differences in light filtering through the wall of the uterus. The brain and nervous system are also fully developed, although some of the reflexes and limb movements will still be poorly coordinated if the baby is born now. The fingernails extend to the end of the fingertips, but the toenails will need a few more weeks to reach the end of the toes.

The sucking reflex becomes properly established at this stage and the baby will be repeatedly sucking on its thumbs and fingers. However, most babies born before 35 or 36 weeks still need a little more practice, which can mean that breastfeeding is more difficult to establish. This is one of the reasons why the definition of a premature baby is still, strictly speaking, a baby born before 37 weeks. Although most babies born after 28 weeks have an excellent chance of survival, thanks to the special care they receive after the birth, there is no technical advance that can make a premature baby suck as effectively as a full-term baby. So if your baby is born at or before 35 weeks, you will probably need some specialized help from midwives and breastfeeding counselors.

The lungs are maturing so fast between 30 and 35 weeks that every passing day reduces the time that your baby is likely to need assistance to breathe. In practical terms, a baby born at 34 weeks may need some help breathing, for days

◀ *At 30 weeks the eyes can open and respond to changes in light.*

	WEEKS
FIRST TRIMESTER	▶ 1
	▶ 2
	3
	▶ 4
	5
	6
	▶ 7
	8
	▶ 9
	10
	11
	12
	13
SECOND TRIMESTER	14
	15
	16
	17
	18
	19
	20
	21
	22
	23
	24
	25
	26
THIRD TRIMESTER	27
	28
	29
	▶30
	▶31
	▶32
	▶33
	▶34
	▶35
	36
	37
	38
	39
	40

not life size

not life size

By 30 weeks, the fetus is about 11in (28cm) long and weighs about 2¼–3⅓lb (1–1.5kg). At 35 weeks its weight has increased to about 5½lb (2.5kg) and the fetus now measures 13in (32cm) from crown to rump and as much as 18in (45cm) from head to toe.

or even weeks, whereas one born at 36 weeks is almost always able to breathe unaided. In these next few weeks your baby crosses the divide; its lungs undergo the final steps of maturation that allow them to function independently.

The fetal adrenal glands, on the top of the kidneys, are pumping out cortisol to help stimulate the production of surfactant in the fetal lungs. They are working so hard that they are the same size as the adrenal glands of an adolescent and are producing 10 times the quantity of cortisol as those of an adult. Soon after your baby is born they will shrink back down and only become active again at puberty.

SEX HORMONES

In boys and girls, the fetal adrenal glands continue to produce large quantities of an androgen-like hormone (DHEAS), which has to be processed by enzymes in the fetal liver before it can be passed on to the placenta for final conversion to estrogen. In boys, the fetal testes are producing testosterone and some is converted by special target cells in the genitals to DHT (dihydrotestosterone) essential for the development of the external genitals. It is quite common for these high levels of hormones to result in the external genitals of both boys and girls appearing large and swollen at birth. In the case of boys, the scrotal skin that surrounds the testes can be darkly pigmented. All of these changes disappear in the next few weeks as hormone production settles down.

3-D ULTRASOUND AT 30–35 WEEKS

REFLECTIVE *Images of a perfectly formed face begin to reveal a suggestion of the personality within.*

SLEEP PERIODS *Movement is now restricted by space and during quiet periods, the baby sleeps.*

TWIN PREGNANCY *An X-ray of a twin pregnancy reveals both babies lying transversely across the abdomen with both heads close to the mother's spine. Unless they change position, this will cause problems in normal labor and vaginal delivery. A cesarean section is the most likely option to deliver the babies safely.*

MOVEMENTS AND LIE

Your baby's movements will be strong but most probably slower than before for the simple reason that the baby can no longer move around as freely because space inside the uterus is now at a premium. However, if your baby's movement pattern changes from being very active to very quiet, or vice versa, seek advice immediately. Mothers-to-be are usually the best judge of whether problems are brewing in utero and you should never be worried that you are bothering people unnecessarily. It really does not matter how many false alarms there are.

Most babies are lying longitudinally (vertically) by week 35, but there are situations in which the baby may be transverse (horizontal) or oblique (diagonal). The risk of an abnormal lie is increased when the amniotic fluid level is high (*see* polyhydramnios, p.426); when the placenta is in the lower segment of the uterus (*see* placenta previa, p.240 and p.427); or when there is more than one baby.

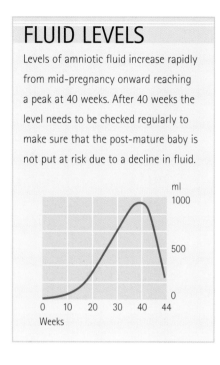

FLUID LEVELS

Levels of amniotic fluid increase rapidly from mid-pregnancy onward reaching a peak at 40 weeks. After 40 weeks the level needs to be checked regularly to make sure that the post-mature baby is not put at risk due to a decline in fluid.

Your baby's presentation is determined by which part of the baby is closest to your pelvis: head down is described as a cephalic presentation while bottom down (and head up) is called a breech presentation (*see* p.269). Cephalic is the most common presentation and by term, 95 percent of babies are in this position. At 32 weeks, as many as 25 percent of babies are breech, but this percentage has dropped to just 4 percent by 38 weeks. After 35–36 weeks the baby is much less likely to change presentation because the lack of space prevents major movements.

THE AMNIOTIC FLUID

Your baby excretes about 16 fl oz (half a liter) of urine daily and at 35 weeks the amniotic fluid reaches a peak volume of 2 pints (1 liter). After this time the volume starts to decline and can be as little as 3.5–7fl oz (100–200ml) in a pregnancy that is post mature (overdue). Low levels of amniotic fluid (*see* oligohydramnios, p.426) can be a sign of a growth-restricted baby or a baby with kidney problems, while excessive amniotic fluid, or polyhydramnios (*see* p.426), may be seen in twin pregnancies and is sometimes associated with physical abnormalities in the baby or diabetes in the mother.

YOUR CHANGING BODY

NOW AND FOR THE NEXT FEW WEEKS, THE HEIGHT OF THE FUNDUS MEASURED IN CENTIMETERS WILL BE ABOUT THE SAME AS THE STAGE OF YOUR PREGNANCY IN WEEKS. THIS CHANGES SLIGHTLY WHEN THE BABY'S HEAD DESCENDS AND CAUSES THE HEIGHT OF THE FUNDUS TO DROP SLIGHTLY IN MOST PREGNANCIES.

Whatever the exact measurements at this stage, your uterus has expanded your abdomen so much that your belly button may have become inverted, giving it quite a prominent appearance. If this coincides with summertime and light clothing, it is often clearly visible through your clothes. Its change in appearance is not permanent; it will pop back into place once your baby is born.

Your blood volume will probably reach a peak of 10½ pints (5 liters), although some women will have a further increase between 35 and 40 weeks. Most of the increase is due to the plasma or fluid content in your bloodstream, but the number of oxygen-carrying red cells does not increase at the same rate. This dilution of red cells by the increasing plasma fluid is a common cause of anemia in late pregnancy (known as dilutional anemia). Certainly, your blood count will be checked during this stage of pregnancy. However, rarely there is a serious problem as a result of lack of red blood cells, because the amount of hemoglobin (oxygen-carrying pigment) is now much higher than before you became pregnant. Rest assured, your baby is happily making use of the oxygen and nutrients it needs.

VARICOSE VEINS

If you are going to be troubled by varicose veins, this is the stage in pregnancy when you are most likely to notice them. Varicose veins are dilated veins just under the surface of the skin, most of which occur in the legs and anal region (*see* hemorrhoids, p.217). Wherever they pop up in pregnancy, they are caused by an unavoidable mechanical problem — the weight of your enlarging uterus pressing down on the main veins in your pelvis. These veins feed blood back to your heart and lungs, but they are now very dilated by your increased blood volume. When they meet a large obstacle in their path, such as your expanded uterus, the back pressure that develops forces your blood to pool in the dependent (smaller) veins in your legs, vulva, and anal region. Since your baby is going to get bigger over the next few weeks the discomfort from varicose veins is likely to get worse. Symptoms usually improve after the delivery of your baby but for some women varicose veins become a long-term problem.

Varicose veins in the vulval area are not as common, but they are often a cause of concern because they look unsightly and can become tender and uncomfortable. The symptoms are best treated in the same way as hemorrhoids. Although there is the potential for vulval varices to bleed heavily if damaged at the time of a vaginal delivery, this is only very rarely a problem. Furthermore, they usually completely disappear after the birth.

TIPS FOR DEALING WITH VARICOSE VEINS

▶ **Buy support pantyhose.** For maximum relief, put them on in the morning before you get out of bed.

▶ **Rest with your feet up** as high as possible whenever you can. This will help blood drain from the veins in your legs.

▶ **Walk briskly.** This will keep the muscles in your legs working and help return blood to your heart.

▶ **If you have to stand** for any period of time, keep shifting your body weight from one leg to another, instead of distributing it equally between both.

▶ **Keep a check on your weight gain.** Carrying extra pounds puts even more pressure on your legs.

HOW YOU MAY FEEL PHYSICALLY

IT IS VERY COMMON FOR WOMEN TO FEEL UNCOMFORTABLY LARGE AND UNWIELDY AT THIS STAGE OF PREGNANCY, PARTICULARLY IF IT HAPPENS TO COINCIDE WITH THE SUMMER MONTHS WHEN HOT WEATHER INCREASES THE RISK OF DEVELOPING SWOLLEN HANDS, FEET, AND LEGS.

Even if you do not feel like the proverbial beached whale, you may well be moving around more slowly and laboriously than you normally do. Day-to-day tasks such as getting out of the car or putting on a pair of socks require a radical alteration of your usual technique. Although nobody likes to feel physically compromised and dependent on others for help, the best way to deal with these situations is to maintain your sense of humor and keep reminding yourself that this is temporary. If you are philosophical about your restricted movement now, it will also help to prepare you for the fact that young children will inevitably slow you down. After the birth, you will no longer be able to rush out of the house in three seconds flat, grabbing your car keys and bag as you go. You will just have to take things a bit slower. Try, though, to stay as active as possible during this last stage of your pregnancy — it will help you feel physically and mentally prepared with the challenges ahead of you, especially labor.

HARD TO SLEEP

By now, you may not be sleeping well and this will affect how you physically feel during the day. It becomes increasingly difficult to find a comfortable position at night. Lying on your back should be avoided, because the weight of your uterus will press on the major veins returning blood to your heart, making you feel very faint and reducing the blood supply to your baby. The possibility of lying on your front disappeared some weeks ago and it is likely that your only practical option now is to lie on your side with your upper leg bent forward at the knee and, if necessary, supported by a pillow. However, you cannot stay in the same position all night, and as you near term, turning over in bed becomes a major operation,

FINDING A POSITION *You may be most comfortable lying on your side with cushions supporting your belly and upper leg.*

MOVING SAFELY

Getting up from the floor or bed after relaxation or exercise can put strain on your abdominal muscles, which are already stretched to full capacity. Your altered center of gravity will also make large-scale movements difficult.

The following technique has been devised by yoga teachers to help you get to your feet safely. As with any strenuous maneuvers at this stage of pregnancy, move slowly and remember to breathe throughout.

STEP ONE *With your knees bent, roll onto your right side bringing your the knee beneath you up to waist level. Keep your left hand aligned with your bent knee.*

STEP TWO *Shift your weight onto your left hand and knee. Position your right knee under your right hip and your right hand under your shoulder and come up slowly on all fours.*

involving shifting your increasing bulk, not to mention the supportive pillows around the bed. Added to which, your bladder is giving you regular wake-up calls and your baby may be continuously kicking and wriggling.

The lack of sleep can make you extremely tired and irritable, which is why it is so important to try to find time to rest during the day. Even if you are still working full time, make sure that you reserve half an hour per day to sit down with your feet up. If you are at home, an hour's nap on your bed after lunch will really help make up for the poor quality sleep at night. If you establish a routine in which you break off from your tasks to rest during this prenatal period, it will be easier to continue after the birth when fatigue and lack of sleep are inevitable. You are going to need to train yourself to take advantage of the times when your newborn is sleeping to catch up on some rest or sleep for yourself and restore your energy and sanity.

BRAXTON HICKS' CONTRACTIONS

From now until the end of your pregnancy, the uterus starts to practice contracting mildly in preparation for labor. These painless tightenings, called Braxton Hicks' contractions, start at the top of the fundus and travel down the uterus causing it to harden for about 30 seconds. The 19th-century obstetrician John Braxton Hicks, from St. Mary's Hospital, London, was the first to describe them. He realized that this painless activity toward the end of pregnancy gave

BREATHING *Practicing deep, slow breathing can help you get rid of tension and regain control between contractions.*

BEARING DOWN *Exhaling with your knees wide apart and your head and elbows supported can help you prepare for second-stage contractions.*

the uterus the practice it needed to contract strongly enough to expel a baby through the birth canal and into the outside world. The contractions also help direct more blood into the placenta during the last few weeks of pregnancy.

Although some women are completely unaware of having Braxton Hicks' contractions, for others they can become quite strong and uncomfortable toward the end of pregnancy. If this is the case for you, try changing your position, getting up and walking around, or having a warm bath, since these simple remedies can help relax the uterine muscles. Practicing some relaxation and breathing techniques you are preparing for labor are also likely to be of benefit, as will back massage.

If this is your first pregnancy, it may be difficult for you to know whether you are having strong Braxton Hicks' contractions or early labor pains so the rule here is that if you are not sure, go to your midwife or nearest obstetrician for help. Similarly, it is essential to report any prolonged or painful uterine activity immediately, particularly if it is accompanied by lower backache, since you may be threatening to go into premature labor. As the mother of premature twins who spent a month in special care after delivery, I can assure you that this is a frightening and distressing experience for every parent, so make sure that you take every precaution to avoid delivering prematurely. Another possible cause of uterine pain and low backache is placental abruption (*see* p.427), which requires urgent medical attention.

YOUR EMOTIONAL RESPONSE

AT THE TOP OF THE LIST OF ANXIETIES THAT PATIENTS SHARE WITH ME AT THIS STAGE IS THE FEAR THAT THEIR LABOR WILL BE DIFFICULT, THAT IT MAY GO DISASTROUSLY WRONG, OR THAT THEY WILL DISGRACE THEMSELVES DURING THE DELIVERY (*SEE* Q&A OPPOSITE).

As always, the fear of the unknown is far more difficult to deal with than the reality. So once again, try to discard any horror stories that you have heard and hold on to the fact that most pregnant women are extremely healthy and their babies have a trouble-free entrance into this world.

Another common feature of late pregnancy is that women often find it hard to concentrate on specific tasks. Many of my patients tell me that their minds repeatedly wander off to baby-related issues, and for those of you who are still at work, this can be quite a problem. It may come as a bit of a shock to find yourself dreaming the days away and unable to focus on the job at hand. Tasks that used to demand high priority may no longer seem very important. I think the best way to manage this situation is to identify key tasks and ensure that they are finished, sideline non-essential jobs, and make sure that you do not take on anything new that is challenging or unlikely to be accomplished within a short time span. You should then be able to leave work comfortable in the knowledge that you have left things in a reasonable state.

Another feature of this last trimester is that sad or bad news tends to affect you more than usual. There is no doubt that pregnancy triggers intense emotional responses in many of us and makes us much more vulnerable to sad situations, particularly those involving children. Watching a TV program about any form of child deprivation or the loss of a child, for example, is likely to reduce you to a flood of tears, even if in the past you were able to take such things in stride. The only practical advice that I can offer is to try to limit your exposure to situations that are likely to make you feel distressed.

EMBARRASSING SITUATIONS

▶ **I hate feeling out of control. How can I avoid disgracing myself during labor?**

Nothing you do during your labor and delivery will be considered disgraceful. This will be one of the few times in your life when you cannot be totally in control of your body, so instead of feeling embarrassed and agitated, just accept it. As for anyone in the delivery room being horrified or disgusted by anything that happens or upset by you groaning, swearing, or shouting at them — forget it; the midwives and doctors have seen and heard it all before. They would not be doing their chosen job if they did not understand the practicalities of what happens

when a 7½-lb (3.5-kg) baby is pushed through a woman's birth canal.

▶ **What if my water breaks when I am in a public place?**

It is unlikely that your water will break in the middle of the supermarket or other public place but even it does — so what? I have never heard anyone complain about having to help a pregnant woman whose membranes ruptured unexpectedly. But I have heard lots of people talk about how pleased they were to be able to help when this entirely natural event occurred. The reality is that it is very rare for the amniotic fluid to gush out — it is usually a trickle because most babies are head

down, pressing on your cervix and preventing too much liquid from escaping.

▶ **I am worried that I might have a bowel movement during labor. Should I have an enema?**

Having a bowel movement during labor can happen because of the baby's descending head placing pressure on the rectum. However, it is unlikely that there will be much stool in front of your baby's descending head, so any problem is likely to be minimal. Compulsory enemas in early labor were routine practice years ago but are increasingly rare in modern-day maternity units.

YOUR PRENATAL CARE

YOUR DOCTOR OR MIDWIFE WILL WANT TO MONITOR YOU MORE CLOSELY TOWARD THE END OF YOUR PREGNANCY. FROM ABOUT 36 WEEKS ONWARD, YOUR PRENATAL APPOINTMENTS WILL BE EVERY WEEK.

The usual routine checks will be performed, but your caregivers will be especially alert to signs of late pregnancy complications such as gestational diabetes (*see* p.426) or slow growth of your baby (*see* intrauterine growth restriction, p.428). Preeclampsia (*see* p.425) becomes increasingly common after week 30. Although it may develop without symptoms, there are usually some indicators. Any of the following should prompt you to see your doctor or midwife urgently to check for protein in your urine:

• Rings are too tight for your fingers and your feet too swollen for your shoes.

• Your face becomes puffy and swollen.

• Headaches have become constant or unbearable and you have flashes of light at the edge of your field of sight.

The height of your uterine fundus will be measured and if it is higher or lower than your dates suggest, you may be advised to have an ultrasound scan to check the size and health of your baby. If it shows that the baby is too small or too large for your dates, or if the amniotic fluid volume is increased or reduced, further investigations (*see* pp.256–59) will be arranged. It may even be necessary to make plans to induce early delivery of your baby.

PLACENTA PREVIA

A placenta that remains low in the uterus causes problems if all or part is in front of the baby's head, overlapping or covering the internal part of the cervix (the cervical os). The first sign is often one or more episodes of painless bleeding, sometimes as early as 30 weeks, which must be assessed immediately in the hospital. If only the lower edge of the placenta approaches the cervix (marginal placenta previa), the baby's head may be able to pass through the dilated cervix and a vaginal delivery may be possible. If the placenta is lying centrally over the cervix (partial or complete placenta previa), there is a high risk of hemorrhage before or during labor. A cesarean section is the only safe option (*see* p.427).

MARGINAL   **COMPLETE**

Palpating your abdomen will enable your caregivers to determine the position in which your baby is lying. If your baby is breech (bottom down) it still has time to turn around and adopt the cephalic (head down) position, which is the best position for a normal vaginal delivery. However, if the baby's position persists as breech, you may be advised to undergo external cephalic version (ECV), a manual procedure to turn the baby around in the womb, which is usually performed after 35 weeks (*see* p.271). Do remember that even the most skilled doctors and midwives can get the position of your baby wrong. Any obstetrician who says that he or she has never missed a breech presentation is either untruthful or has not been doing the job for long enough to have it happen!

A **further ultrasound scan** will be carried out at about 32 weeks if you were found to have a low-lying placenta earlier in your pregnancy. This is done to determine whether its position has changed. Even if the scan shows that your placenta is low, there are still several more weeks during which the lower segment of the uterus will continue to develop, so the chances of a low placenta causing problems at the time of delivery are reduced as the pregnancy becomes more advanced. The incidence of placenta previa (*see* left) is only 1 in 200 at term, whereas before 32 weeks it can be as high as 20 percent.

A **complete blood count** is usually performed at about 34 weeks to check for anemia (*see* p.423). The same blood sample will be used to check that you have not developed unusual red blood cell antibodies that might cause problems at a later stage, should you require a blood transfusion, for example, if you bleed severely during the delivery (*see* p.424). If you are Rhesus negative (*see* p.128 and p.424) you will be given a Rhogam injection and your blood will be checked to make sure no rhesus antibodies have been produced.

DIABETIC PREGNANCIES

All diabetic pregnancies will be closely watched from 35 weeks for late pregnancy problems (*see* p.408 and p.426). Poorly controlled glucose levels result in the baby being overweight (macrosomia), which increases the risk of shoulder dystocia (*see* p.429), birth injuries, and stillbirth. If your diabetes is well controlled and your baby's growth is normal, you may be able to wait for labor to begin and have a normal vaginal delivery. In uncomplicated diabetic pregnancies, there is no indication that an elective cesarean section improves the outcome.

However, many maternity units have a policy of induction (*see* p.294–97) for diabetic mothers at 38–39 weeks, using continuous fetal monitoring and regular checks on the mother's blood sugar levels throughout labor and delivery.

"Remember that even the most skilled doctors and midwives can get the position of your baby wrong."

After 38 weeks, diabetic pregnancies are at increased risk of birth trauma, stillbirth, and neonatal complications. If fetal distress develops or there is poor progress in labor, an emergency cesarean section is sometimes required. After birth, babies born to diabetic mothers are thoroughly assessed because they can develop hypoglycemia (low blood sugar levels) during the first hours of life. They are also at increased risk of respiratory distress syndrome (*see* p.373), particularly if they are delivered prematurely.

COMMON CONCERNS

MOST OF THE PHYSICAL AILMENTS EXPERIENCED IN LATE PREGNANCY ARE RELATED TO YOUR INCREASING SIZE AND ARE UNLIKELY TO GET BETTER UNTIL YOUR BABY IS DELIVERED. THAT SAID, IF YOUR BABY'S HEAD ENGAGES IN THE PELVIS BEFORE YOU GO INTO LABOR, YOU MAY HAVE SOME RELIEF FROM THEM.

"If you have been bothered by backache, this may get worse over the next few weeks."

If you are seriously troubled by breathlessness, try to cut down on unnecessary exertion while remaining reasonably active. Lying down flat often makes breathlessness worse, so you may find that you need to rest and sleep in a semi-propped-up position during the last trimester of pregnancy.

PALPITATIONS

Missed heartbeats, a short run of fast heartbeats, or just being acutely aware of your heartbeat (often loosely referred to as palpitations) are common in late pregnancy. Normally they are nothing to worry about and are simply the result of changes in your blood circulation coupled with the mechanical disadvantages of having a large mass in your abdominal cavity. However, if you develop chest pain or severe breathlessness with palpitations or if they are occurring more and more frequently, you should consult your midwife or doctor.

SEVERE ITCHING

It is very common to develop patches of dry, flaky, skin in late pregnancy but some women suffer from a severe form of itching on their abdomen and especially on the palms of their hands and soles of their feet, which does not respond to the usual moisturizers. Occasionally this is the first sign that you are developing cholestasis of pregnancy (*see* p.423), which is a rare condition in pregnancy caused by bile salts deposited under the skin. If it is severe, it can lead to maternal jaundice, liver failure, premature delivery, and even stillbirth so it is important to report severe, persistent itching to your prenatal caregivers quickly.

LOSING FLUID

If you experience small gushes of fluid from your vagina when you make a sudden movement, it is most likely due to stress incontinence. However, at this stage of pregnancy, you should also consider the possibility that your membranes have ruptured (your water has broken) and you are leaking amniotic fluid. If you are unsure, save a sample in a clean container and seek advice from your midwife or doctor. They will examine you and test the fluid to determine whether it is amniotic fluid or urine. If your membranes have ruptured, both you and your baby are at risk of developing an infection so if there are no signs of uterine contractions developing within 24 hours of this occurring, most prenatal caregivers will suggest that you are induced (*see* pp.294–97) as long as you are at least 34 weeks pregnant.

LOCALIZED BACKACHE

If you have been bothered by backache, this may get worse over the next few weeks. In addition to the generalized discomfort you have probably experienced up until now, you may find that mild, generalized lower backache has been replaced by specific and clearly localized pain caused by a specific disorder such as sciatica that develops toward the end of pregnancy (*see* below). Although back pain is common during pregnancy, it is important to take severe lower back pain seriously and seek advice from your midwife or doctor.

Sciatica is characterized by a sharp, constant, or intermittent pain in the lower back or buttocks, which sometimes shoots down the back of one or both legs. The sciatic nerve is the largest nerve in the body and runs from the spinal cord, through the buttock and into the back of the leg. When crushed or compressed by your baby's head anywhere along its route, the sharp pain is frequently accompanied by numbness, tingling, weakness, and occasionally, a burning sensation. If the pain or weakness becomes severe, you will need to see your doctor to rule out the possibility of a slipped disk.

Gentle maneuvers to encourage the baby's head to change position and relieve the pressure on the sciatic nerve can be helpful, although it is sometimes easier said than done. Improving your posture and performing regular pelvic tilt exercises will bring relief (*see* p.219), as will yoga and stretching exercises, such as lying down flat on a firm mattress and trying to lengthen your spine by raising your head on pillows or books.

Coccygeal pain is pain in the very lowest part of your spine and tenderness when you press into the natal cleft of your buttocks. The coccyx is a sort of hinged appendage made up of four tiny bones at the end of your sacrum (the

LOCATING THE PAIN

Severe pain in your lower back is likely to have a specific cause and needs appropriate treatment.

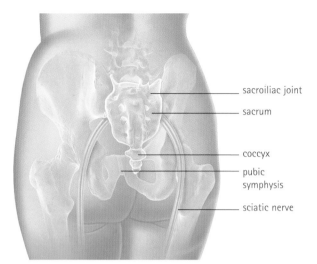

sacroiliac joint

sacrum

coccyx

pubic
symphysis

sciatic nerve

TROUBLE SPOTS *Localized back problems are usually due to the softening of ligaments supporting the sacroiliac joint (the pubic symphysis joint between your pubic bones or the coccyx). Pain that radiates down one leg may be due to the baby's head pressing on a sciatic nerve.*

large triangular bone at the base of the spine). Lax supporting ligaments can cause the coccyx to become displaced from the sacrum during late pregnancy and during delivery. A previous bruising impact injury to the area, such as a fall, often contributes to the problem. The pain can be excruciating, particularly when sitting, and if this is the case, try applying local heat such as a compress and hot water bottles, or taking a hot bath. You can also take analgesics but try to limit them to times when nothing else brings relief.

Sacroiliac pain is usually experienced as a steady pain in the middle or lower back. At the lower end of the spine your sacrum interconnects with the left and right iliac bones at the sacroiliac joints (*see* picture), to help provide you with a stable pelvic girdle with which to walk and maintain an upright posture. Toward the end of pregnancy, hormones relax the ligaments to prepare for the passage of your baby through the pelvic canal and this, together with the increasing weight of your uterus, can make the sacroiliac joints unstable. This can result in severe pain, especially when walking, standing, or bending. You may need to see your doctor, physical therapist, or osteopath. Meanwhile, wear comfortable, low-heeled shoes and make sure you maintain good posture — keep your shoulders back, walk tall, and don't lean backward.

Pubic symphysis dysfunction is pain affecting the symphysis pubis, the narrowest point of your bony pelvic girdle lying just in front of your bladder. As the ligaments around the joint loosen in late pregnancy, the two pubic bones (pubic rami) may rub against each other uncomfortably when you walk and particularly when your legs rotate outward or your knees move wide apart. If you are suffering from this type of pain, avoid straddling movements by keeping your knees together and swinging your legs around from the hips when you get out of the car, bed, or bath. Ice packs over the painful area under your underwear for 10 minutes every three hours may reduce the swelling and pain. Knee squeezing and pelvic tilts will also help (*see* p.219) if you practice them regularly. If the two pubic bones actually separate from each other (a condition called diastasis of the symphysis pubis) the pain can be very severe. Although bed rest and local heat treatment can help, most women who develop this rare complication in late pregnancy are forced to limit their weight-bearing activities and often need to use crutches to move around.

THINGS TO CONSIDER

BY THIS TIME YOU WILL PROBABLY HAVE STARTED TO DEVELOP VIEWS ABOUT HOW YOU WOULD LIKE YOUR IDEAL LABOR AND DELIVERY CONDUCTED. YOU CAN TALK TO YOUR MIDWIFE OR DOCTOR ABOUT YOUR PREFERENCES OR CONSIDER WRITING A BIRTH PLAN.

To make the process simpler, I have included a brief summary of the major childbirthing philosophies as well advice on compiling your own list of birth preferences, which can be incorporated in your hand-held notes. However, before you make any decisions about the way you would like your labor and delivery handled, I suggest that you read the sections on pain relief, monitoring, labor, and birth to form a clear idea of what might be available and what to expect.

The change of title from the more usual "birth plan" is deliberate because I think that it is more useful to think of this document as a list of preferences. To me, a birth plan implies a rigidity of approach — as if it is a set of rules and commandments to which you and your medical and caregivers must comply.

TOPICS FOR YOUR BIRTH PREFERENCE PLAN

Today, most maternity units make great efforts to help women fulfill their wishes during labor and delivery. Good communication with your caregivers will help them work toward your requests wherever possible and prevent disappointments and unrealistic expectations.

THINGS TO CONSIDER

▶ Who would you like to be with you during labor and birth — your partner, your mother, or friend? Usually this person has attended childbirth classes with you.
▶ What are your views on being cared for by student midwives and doctors (interns and residents)?
▶ Are you prepared to have your membranes ruptured and to receive medications to speed up your contractions (see pp.294–97)?
▶ What are your views about fetal monitoring (see pp.291–92)?
▶ How active or mobile do you wish to be during labor?
▶ Would you want your partner to be with you during a cesarean delivery (see pp.360–69)?
▶ Do you have views on episotomies or perineal tears (see p.330–31)?
▶ Do you want to hold your baby immediately following the birth or after first checks have been made?
▶ Who do you wish to cut the umbilical cord?

QUESTIONS TO ASK

▶ Will you be allowed to eat and drink normally in early labor?
▶ Is it OK to wear your own clothes?
▶ Will you have access to a bath, shower, or birthing pool?
▶ What types of pain relief are available and if there is a 24-hour epidural service (see pp.311–15)?
▶ Are different positions encouraged during delivery?
▶ Is there a time limit for the second stage of labor, even if progress is being made?

As we all know, the most carefully laid plans can go awry and labor can take an unpredictable turn, so the best way to avoid distress and disappointment about the final outcome is to be as flexible as possible.

At my hospital, we offer women a double-sided sheet of paper with a selection of issues that they may find helpful to consider. The points are arranged in boxes with space provided for women to make notes after they have considered the issues. We then encourage them to discuss their ideas with their midwife or doctor before drawing up a list of preferences. There are some distinct advantages to this method:

• Your list sends a message to the team delivering your baby that you have thought about your labor and want to participate in the decision-making.

• Drawing up your list of preferences will help you feel more composed, because you will spend time thinking about your views on labor and delivery. If you find that you need more information about the many eventualities that could occur there is still time to seek out the missing facts.

• Early planning also gives your partner the chance to understand your preferences, to know what you expect of him during labor, and, if necessary, to speak on your behalf during labor and delivery.

UMBILICAL STEM CELL COLLECTION

Stem cell collection is a new service that is available to parents. I mention it here simply to provide information rather than serving as an advocate for the procedure. At a cost of around $1,250 for collection and around $120 per year for storage, it offers parents the opportunity to have stem cells harvested from their baby's umbilical cord and stored as an insurance against potential illness in later life. Stem cells, which are found in embryonic tissue as well as umblical cord blood, have the potential to develop into different types of body cells. Although stem cell treatment is still in its infancy, its most promising uses are in diabetes, in degenerative disorders such as Alzheimer's disease, and as a substitute for bone marrow in diseases such as leukemia.

You can find brochures advertizing umbilical cord sampling in some maternity wards and on the Internet. You will need to make arrangements several weeks before the birth. You will be sent a collection kit to take with you to the hospital and after the birth the sample will be sent to a laboratory to be frozen and stored for possible future use.

TESTING CELLS *Stem cells found in the umbilical cord blood can develop into white and red blood cells and platelets. White blood cells from a sample are being tested here.*

Disadvantages of birth plans

The sheer length of your birth plan document can be a problem so bear in mind that three closely typed pages of detailed instructions will be harder for your caregivers to absorb and follow than a single page of succinct bullet points. When you are putting together your wish list, try to take a positive approach and focus on what you would like to happen during the birth rather than making a negative list of things that you do not want to happen. Some doctors and midwives will even be put off by a lengthy list of "Don't do this and don't do that." However, there are other important reasons why birth plans can end up being counterproductive:

• There are so many different ways of experiencing labor that no birth plan can possibly anticipate them all. Indeed, I think that the more detailed the birth plan, the more likely it is for events to fall short of expectations.

• Some women who have spent a lot of time and effort constructing a "natural" birth plan feel desperately distressed and disappointed if their labor takes an unexpected turn and requires sudden medical intervention. I understand their disappointment but when they tell me that they now feel a failure as a woman because they were unable to deliver their baby naturally, it becomes my turn to feel distressed. No one who nurtures a baby in their womb for the best part of a year and then delivers it safely into the outside world, by whatever route, can be considered anything other than extraordinarily successful. Similarly, when I hear comments such as, "control was wrested away from me by the doctors as if I did not matter," I do not feel defensive or angry. My immediate concern is that this woman is at greater risk of developing postpartum depression because she feels so negative about her birth experience and believes that she has been let down by her caregivers and by herself.

• Every person who is involved in the delivery of your baby (including you) has a common goal: the safe delivery of a healthy baby to a healthy mother. Although your prenatal caregivers want to help you experience the delivery of your dreams, there may be occasions when your wishes and expectations are just not compatible with protecting your safety and that of your baby. In such situations it is really important that you listen to the advice offered by the experts and understand why it may be necessary to override your birth plan.

My personal view is that ensuring that your medical team understands that you want to be involved in any decision-making is far more important than any written statement. Women give birth every minute of the day with no birth plan whatsoever — they simply use their voice to express their preferences.

"Women give birth every minute of the day with no birth plan whatsoever — they simply use their voice to express their preferences."

BIRTH POOLS *Spending your labor in water is now an option in some maternity units although there may be only one birthing pool available.*

WATER BIRTHS

Birthing pools and water-assisted births have become increasingly popular over the last 5 to 10 years, largely out of enthusiasm for gentle birth ideas of French obstetrician Dr. Leboyer, but also because they can be effective as a method of pain relief (*see* p.319–20); so much so, that many maternity units have installed birthing pools where you can spend some or all of your labor. My own hospital recently overcame the plumbing problems of an old Victorian building and installed one in our labor ward, and it has proved to be very popular. Many obstetricians and midwives recommend that you not enter the pool until you have reached 5cm dilation for the most efficient labor, and that you leave the birthing pool for the third stage of labor because the relaxing effects of the water could theoretically increase bleeding after delivery or encourage retention of the placenta. Some mothers, however, do choose to remain in the water throughout the birth and feel very positive about their experience (*see* p.321).

If you think that you might like a water-assisted birth, check whether your hospital provides this facility and how likely it is that you will be able to use it (most birthing centers and an increasing number of hospitals have water-birthing rooms). Remember that a single pool will probably be allocated on a first-come-first-served basis, and it is difficult to predict exactly when you might go into labor. If you are hoping to rent a pool for a home birth, make sure the floor of the room that you are going to use will sustain the weight of a full birthing pool. The water should not be above body temperature (98.6° F/37° C); if it is hotter, you may become dehydrated or be at risk of high blood pressure. You will need to set it up close to where you wish to give birth and ensure that you have facilities both to fill it and, especially, to empty it after the delivery.

THE NESTING INSTINCT

With D- (delivery) day approaching, you may develop an urge to sort out and tidy up everything around the house, in preparation for the birth of your new baby. Although aiming to conserve your energy in preparation for the birth would seem the best plan, many of you will be rushing around, trying to get the house ready. This strange compulsion, known as the nesting instinct, grips many women as the end of their pregnancy approaches. So don't be surprised if you find yourself steam-cleaning the carpets, clearing out the kitchen cabinets, attempting to dust the tallest bookshelves, or suddenly feeling inspired to repaint the living room.

I suspect that this nesting instinct is one of the means we use to help ourselves psychologically prepare for the birth. Many women tell me that they are only able to fully relax when they know that the house is completely ready for the new baby's arrival. Such is the enormous emotional relief and mental release from knowing that things are well prepared that some find they go into labor as soon as they feel their home is ready. Interestingly, women who deliver prematurely sometimes find the adjustment to the practicalities of motherhood more difficult and this may be because they have not had sufficient time to prepare for their baby.

AIR TRAVEL IN LATE PREGNANCY

If you are planning a trip abroad at this stage of your pregnancy you may have some concerns about the safety of air travel and at what point an airline may refuse to carry you. Generally speaking, most airlines do not accept pregnant women after the 34th week of pregnancy, but individual airlines vary. Although many people assume this is because the reduced cabin pressure in an aircraft can induce labor or harm the baby, there is no hard, scientific evidence to support this view. It is my belief that the ruling is based on the fact that some 10 percent of pregnancies are going to deliver prematurely, and airlines want to reduce the likelihood of having to deal with a woman in labor during their flight. Indeed,

"This strange compulsion, known as the nesting instinct, grips many women as the end of their pregnancy approaches."

this is an ordeal that you probably do not want to willingly inflict on yourself either. Should labor start, there is a small chance you might give birth on the plane (on a long haul flight) and an even greater risk that you would be faced with the prospect of seeking help from doctors and midwives in a strange place.

If you do decide to fly in your last trimester, make sure that you have taken the precaution of finding out where the maternity units are located at your destination. You should also make sure that the airline is prepared to fly you not only on the outward journey, but on the return one as well.

PLANNING CHILDCARE

Without a doubt, one of the biggest financial outlays for working parents is that of childcare. Nurseries are not available in every area, and good ones can be heavily over-booked. As a result, many women have to find a childcare professional or nanny to look after their children, particularly if their working life involves anything other than a strict nine-to-five day. Not surprisingly, many women are forced to conclude, after calculating the full costs of childcare, that it is financially not worthwhile to work. This situation needs to change!

Although it may seem premature to be discussing childcare before the baby has arrived, I can assure you that it is never too early to give thought to this crucial issue. If you are planning to go back to work, it is particularly important that you give thought to the sort of childcare that you would both prefer now, so that you have time to prepare while you are on your maternity leave. You will most likely be considering one of the following options:

Maternity nurses are usually employed to live in your home for a few 4–6 weeks after the baby is born. They will help you with the practicalities of the 24-hour demands of your new baby, including feeding, diaper changing, doing the baby's laundry, and ensuring that you have regular rest periods and a good night's sleep. However, their most important role is to help teach you how to work out a future routine for caring for your baby. Some women will welcome the organization and routine that a maternity nurse aims to provide, whereas others may find them intrusive, preferring to muddle through in the first few weeks, learning the ropes by themselves. There are plenty of private agencies offering maternity nurses, but a personal recommendation will be the best route to follow. If you decide to employ one, you will need to work out exactly what you want her to do for you and your family. They are invariably expensive.

Nurseries or childcare centers are run either privately or by the state, and their hours and flexibility vary considerably. As mentioned above, they may be hard to come by, especially good ones, and you will need to research

> "Without a doubt, one of the biggest financial outlays for working parents is that of childcare."

what is available locally at the earliest opportunity. All nurseries and adhere to strict legal requirements concerning safety, the ratio of caregivers to children, the suitability of the location, the space available, and the equipment they provide. All of the above points need to be considered carefully but friends' recommendations are also invaluable.

Family daycare will look after your child in their own home and are often paid per child and per hour, so although childcare is usually cheaper than a nanny for just one child, if you are asking them to care for two or more children, they can become as expensive as a full-time nanny. Family daycare tends to be less flexible because they often have other children to look after, including, though not always, their own. So if your child gets sick, they may not be able to look after him — a situation that also applies to nurseries. In addition, if you work irregular hours or sometimes have to stay late unexpectedly, the daycare may not be able to accommodate your individual needs, in which case you will have to pay for additional childcare to fill in the gaps. Local referring agencies can help you find a licensed child care provider. Licensing regulations for family daycare vary from state to state.

A nanny will look after your child in your own home. Nannies can either live in or live out, they can work for you alone or you can share them with another family. You will need to determine clearly the hours that they work during the day and whether you wish them to undertake other duties, which may include one or two evenings a week babysitting. Speaking from practical experience, the most important thing about employing a nanny is to make sure that you are completely up front about what you expect him or her to do for you. As with all employee/employer relationships, trust and good communication are crucial. No one can completely protect their family from the proverbial nanny from hell, but you can take some careful steps to make sure this is unlikely to happen to you.

In general terms, live-in nannies earn less money than live-out nannies because you also provide them with board and lodging. However, when you add up the additional costs of having another adult living in

BACK TO WORK *Leaving your baby for the first time is a little easier when you are totally confident in your childcare provider.*

your house, not to mention the extra bills, you will probably conclude that the overall outlay for a live-in nanny is higher than you originally thought. For some couples, the advantage of a live-in nanny is that they have someone in the house to call on in an emergency, whereas others find that another person in their home is an intrusion. Whatever the case, it is important to remember that if you are repeatedly late home from work, frequently expect them to help out on their weekend off, or fail to pay them for the extra hours they work, you will soon find that your nanny has become disgruntled and is looking for another job.

A live-out nanny is generally the most expensive childcare option in terms of the salary you pay, but she goes home at the end of the day and you have your home to yourselves. When you are considering the financial implications of employing a nanny, it is important to remember that most nannies will expect you to deduct federal and local taxes from their salary. Setting up a nanny-share arrangement with another family is one way of reducing the expenditure but this requires a good deal of flexibility.

Start by buying an updated copy of *The Nanny Book: The Smart Parent's Guide to Hiring, Firing, and Every Sticky Situation in Between* by Susan Carlton and Coco Myers and follow up by getting advice from as many friends and acquaintances as possible, even those who are not currently using any childcare. Above all, aim to have clear ideas about what you are looking for before you start to advertise. Even if you decide to pay an agency to find a suitable nanny for you, you must make sure that you interview them and contact their references personally before you agree to employ them. Advertising and interviewing for a nanny is a time-consuming business, so plan ahead to make sure that he or she can start work on your preferred date. Resist the temptation to ask your new nanny to shorten the notice that she gives to a current employer and start sooner. If he or she does this for you, then they can just as easily leave you at short notice in the future.

Au pairs are another possible source of childcare and are usually much less expensive. In exchange for a room, board, and some pocket money they will help you look after your baby or children and undertake light housework duties. However, since they are usually young people from abroad with limited English skills and, quite possibly, no experience of caring for babies or young children,

"...the most important thing about employing a nanny is to make sure that you are completely up front about what you expect him or her to do for you."

I think this option is much more suitable for school-age children rather than a newborn baby, particularly since many au pairs want to attend a language school for several hours every day. It is vital that you have total confidence in the person to whom you entrust your child or children and it is unlikely that a young au pair will fulfill your needs in that respect.

Younger grandparents with time on their hands are sometimes more than willing to care for a baby for one or two days a week so this may be an option, especially if you plan to work part-time. There are rich rewards in terms of the close bond that they will develop with their growing grandchild, but you need to be sure that you are not asking more of them than they can manage. Remember, too, that parenting styles differ: their views on, for example, feeding, sleep, crying, and snacks may conflict with your own and it is usually more difficult to address a problem with a relative than it would be with a professional caregiver. Much will have changed over the years since your own parents or in-laws were bringing up a small baby and they may need a refresher course on the complexities of strollers and car seats and on important safety issues, especially if they plan to care for your baby in their own home.

GRANDPARENT CARE *When it works well, grandparent care can be a rewarding experience all around.*

If you only need a few hours to yourself for one or two days a week, reciprocal arrangements with a friend with children may be an option, but bear in mind that you will be caring for two or more children rather than just your own on your days off.

Whichever childcare option you choose, you will need to invest a significant amount of time and effort into finding the best affordable solution for you and your family. Start thinking about the options now, since you need to be very clear about what you require and the timeframe involved to find them when you actively start looking. This is usually two to three months before you plan to return to work if you decide on a nanny or daycare facility, but can be considerably longer if you are looking for a place in a popular nursery.

SPECIALIZED PRENATAL MONITORING

Most women and their babies are generally fit and healthy in late pregnancy and are unlikely to need any form of specialized monitoring. However, if your pregnancy goes past its term or you have developed, or are at risk of developing, a late-pregnancy complication, your caregivers will arrange for you to have some specialized tests.

The kinds of problems that are likely to involve specialized monitoring include high blood pressure; a baby that is not growing well; reduced fetal movements; gestational diabetes that is poorly controlled; or a pregnancy that has gone past the due date (to mention just a few). Of course, the exact tests that you are offered will be determined by the particular problem, but on most occasions you will undergo an ultrasound scan to assess your baby's growth together with a general assessment of the baby's well-being, called a biophysical profile. This will include a non-stress test (NST) and an electronic trace of the baby's heart rate. Many units will also perform a Doppler ultrasound scanning of the blood flow in the uterus, placenta, and in the baby's major blood vessels.

Most maternity units have facilities that provide detailed monitoring tests. The emphasis is on trying to keep the mother-to-be safe in an outpatient setting, albeit under careful scrutiny.

FETAL GROWTH MONITORING

If a problem with your baby's growth is suspected, you may be offered ultrasound scans at regular intervals to establish the exact nature and cause. Your baby's head circumference and abdominal circumference will be measured as well as the length of the femur (thigh bone), another good indicator of growth

There are several types of intra-uterine growth restriction (IUGR, *see* p.428) each with different causes and effects on fetal growth.

SPECIAL TESTS *Usually these are performed in an outpatient setting avoiding the need for prolonged stays in the hospital before your delivery date.*

DOPPLER ULTRASOUND SCANS

This highly sensitive form of scanning is performed like a normal ultrasound scan to assess the amount of blood flowing through the blood vessels in the uterus, placenta, umbilical cord, and in the baby's head.

▶ **When blood flow is being diverted to the brain and heart** and away from less vital body organs, the main blood vessels in the brain, particularly the middle cerebral artery, dilate (become less resistant) to accommodate the extra volume. This change can be detected by a scanner and gives a clear message that the baby is exposed to stresses such as low oxygen levels (hypoxia), and that action is needed in the near future.

▶ **Reduced blood flow in the umbilical artery** is a useful predictor of risk when a baby is growing slowly. On a normal Doppler scan blood pressure falls at the end of each heart pumping cycle but the supply to the

high pressure at start of heart pumping cycle   low pressure at end of heart pumping cycle

NORMAL *Although the blood flow to the baby dips at the end of each heart pumping cycle it never stops. The supply is continuous.*

baby is maintained. However, if the blood flow is interrupted at the end of each cycle, it is a sign that the baby is suffering from a lack of oxygen. If the scan shows blood flowing backward, immediate intervention is required.

high pressure at start of heart pumping cycle   absent flow at end of heart pumping cycle

ABNORMAL *Small gaps between the peaks and troughs show an absence of blood flow to the baby at the end of each pumping cycle.*

In symmetrical growth restriction, growth is restricted early in pregnancy and the baby's head and body are equally affected. Symmetrical growth restriction can be caused by congenital abnormalities, infections such as rubella cytomegalovirus and syphilis (*see* pp.411–13), and toxins such as alcohol, cigarette smoke, and heroin.

Asymmetrical growth restriction occurs after 20 weeks and is often referred to as placental insufficiency. It develops when a maternal or fetal problem affects placental function, and blood flow becomes insufficient to meet the needs of the growing baby. Examples include preeclampsia (*see* p.425), twin pregnancies, and some fetal abnormalities (*see* pp.415–21). The baby responds by diverting blood to the brain and heart to protect the growth of these vital organs and the head becomes relatively larger than the abdomen as fats stored in the liver and abdomen are used up. Subcutaneous fat is also absorbed and, as a result, the fetal limbs may become scrawny.

If your baby is growing too slowly with a head-sparing pattern, you may be offered a Doppler ultrasound scan (*see* above) to assess the severity of the situation. If there is no immediate danger, you may return for further growth scans at 7–10 day intervals. If a subsequent scan confirms that there has been no further growth or that your baby is growing very slowly, you will probably be advised to have an labor induced (*see* pp.294–97). In some cases, urgent delivery by cesarean section is needed.

FETAL HEART RECORDINGS

Non-stress tests (NSTs) are pictorial printouts generated by an electronic machine that assess your baby's heart rate as well as the activity of the muscles of your uterus. NSTs are most commonly used during labor to assess how the baby is coping with contractions.

Two belts are strapped around your abdomen: one picks up any activity in your uterine muscles, while the other records your baby's heart rate. The combined trace shows whether the baby's heart rate pattern is normal or abnormal, and whether your uterus is actively contracting or quiet.

Computerized NSTs

This monitoring, for example, the Oxford NST, is used as a guide to the baby's general state of health and is usually reserved for specialized monitoring in labor and delivery. The Sonicaid System sets out a list of criteria that have to be met by the fetal heart rate pattern during a certain time interval. These might include a minimum baseline heart rate, episodes of high and low variability, presence of accelerations, lack of deep decelerations, and fetal movements. It is very reassuring when these criteria are met within a short space of time. The maximum recording time is 60 minutes, but the

---

INTERPRETING AN NST

Babies in utero normally have a baseline heart rate of 120 to 160 beats per minute. This varies constantly by 5–15 beats, except during periods of sleep that last about 30 minutes. This variability is an important sign of well-being: if there is a lack of variability for more than 30 minutes, the baby may be experiencing stress.

Healthy babies also have frequent accelerations or increases in their heart rate (defined as an increase of more than 15 beats per minute for more than 15 seconds), which are usually associated with fetal movements and are sometimes provoked by external stimuli, such as firmly prodding your abdomen, and uterine contractions.

Decelerations in the heart rate are also very common following fetal movements or uterine contractions. However, repeated decelerations of more than 15 beats per minute for more than 15 seconds are another sign of possible fetal distress, particularly when they have not been provoked by contractions. That said, there are often variations in the way individuals interpret NSTs, which is one of the reasons for developing computerized analysis of the tracings.

GOOD VARIABILITY *The peaks and troughs on this NST show a healthy pattern of accelerations and decelerations in the fetal heartbeat over a short period of time.*

POOR VARIABILITY *An NST showing little variation in the fetal heartbeat over a period of more than 30 minutes suggests that the fetus may be suffering from stress.*

computer starts analyzing the NST after 10 minutes. If the criteria have been met, the analysis stops and it is unlikely that another NST will be necessary.

If the criteria are not met within 10 minutes, the computer will continue analyzing the signals every two minutes, until criteria are met. If this does not occur within 60 minutes of recording, this will cause concern about the baby's well-being.

As with all forms of testing, the computerized analysis may produce a false positive result, suggesting that there may be a problem when none exists. Although this invariably causes alarm, on balance I think it's much safer to use a test that eliminates the risk of caregivers failing to identify a baby in distress needing immediate help — even if it does throw out the occasional false positive.

Contraction stress test

If the NST shows no change in the fetal heart rate when the fetus moves, a method called the contraction stress test will probably be used to check how the baby is coping. This test measures the reaction of the fetal heart rate to contractions of the uterus. When the uterus contracts, the blood flow to the placenta decreases for a short time. Under normal conditions the fetal heart rate is not affected, but the contraction can decrease the oxygen flow and cause the fetal heart rate to drop if the baby has a problem or if there is something wrong with the placenta.

To make a woman's uterus contract mildly, she is given oxytocin. The response of the fetal heart rate to the contractions is measured by Doppler ultrasound. For results to be obtained, three contractions must take place over about 10 minutes, and each must last about 40 seconds. If the response is abnormal, further testing or treatment is needed.

AMNIOTIC FLUID VOLUME

The volume of your amniotic fluid is usually assessed by measuring the depth of the pools around the baby using ultrasound scanning. When the maximum depth is less than 1in (2–3cm) or the sum of the depths of the pools in four separate areas measures less than 3in (7.3cm), intervention and prompt delivery is necessary.

Exactly why fluid volume surrounding a baby near to term is so important in determining the outcome of pregnancy has been difficult to establish scientifically. The logical explanation is that increased or reduced fluid volume are indications that the fetal kidneys and metabolism are not working optimally, but testing these important functions while the baby is still in utero is nearly impossible. Nonetheless, my personal experience is that evidence of reduced fluid volume should always be taken seriously. When a pregnancy is near term or past its due date, I almost always make the decision to deliver the baby when the fluid volume is very low.

BIOPHYSICAL PROFILE

This used to be the first test to recognize the importance of using a combination of factors to estimate fetal well-being. It uses a scoring system to assess fetal breathing movements, body movements, muscular tone and posture, the volume of amniotic fluid, and the results of an NST. Today, a reduced volume of amniotic fluid and sub-optimal NST analysis are considered the most important indicators that a baby may require prompt action. If, for example, your fluid volume is low but the NST is fine, your caregivers will automatically look at additional parameters to help them decide whether they should watch and wait or if they should intervene.

WEEKS 35–40
THE DEVELOPING BABY

YOUR BABY IS QUITE A SNUG FIT INSIDE YOUR UTERUS NOW. THE BABY IS USUALLY CURLED UP TIGHTLY, HEAD POINTING DOWNWARD, WAITING FOR LABOR TO START. MOVEMENTS ARE MORE LIMITED BUT YOU WILL PROBABLY NOTICE REGULAR CHANGES IN THE CONTOURS OF YOUR TUMMY AS THE BABY SHIFTS POSITION.

Your baby continues to gain weight steadily during this final stage of pregnancy, almost entirely due to more fat being laid down under the skin, around the muscles, and around some of the abdominal organs. The average full term baby will have a plump rounded appearance and will weigh 6½–9lb (3–4kg); it is common for boys to weigh a little more than girls. Although your baby is too cramped to move freely now, you should still be able to feel movement and you may experience the odd sharp twinge as your baby throws a punch and indents the uterine wall. Remember that any sudden change in the pattern of your baby's movements needs to be investigated urgently.

Most of the lanugo hair has disappeared, although some slippery vernix is still present to help the passage of the baby through the birth canal. Post-mature babies commonly have cracked and peeling skin because they have been without their protective coating of vernix for longer periods of time; some even have scratch marks on their faces from their long fingernails. The amount of hair babies have at birth is variable, ranging from completely bald, to downy patches to a complete head of hair. Most of it is lost in the first weeks but this will hardly be noticable because it is replaced simultaneously with more hair.

READY FOR BIRTH
The lungs are now fully mature, and the baby continues to produce large quantities of cortisol to provide plenty of surfactant in the lungs and make sure that the transition to breathing air in the outside world goes smoothly. The heart is beating at a rate of 110–150 beats per minute. Dramatic changes will occur in the heart and circulatory system at the time of delivery when the baby takes the first breath (*see* pp.378–79).

The digestive system is now ready to accept liquid foods. The intestines become filled with a dark green sticky substance called meconium, which is made up of dead skin cells, remnants of lanugo hair, and secretions from the

◀ *Close to full term, the baby is very short on space.*

WEEKS

FIRST TRIMESTER ▸ 1
▸ 2
▸ 3
▸ 4
▸ 5
▸ 6
▸ 7
▸ 8
▸ 9
▸ 10
▸ 11
▸ 12
▸ 13
SECOND TRIMESTER ▸ 14
▸ 15
▸ 16
▸ 17
▸ 18
▸ 19
▸ 20
▸ 21
▸ 22
▸ 23
▸ 24
▸ 25
▸ 26
THIRD TRIMESTER ▸ 27
▸ 28
▸ 29
▸ 30
▸ 31
▸ 32
▸ 33
▸ 34
▸ 35
▸ 36
▸ 37
▸ 38
▸ 39
▸ 40

not life size

not life size

At 38 to 40 weeks your baby will weigh between 6½ and 9lb (3–4kg) and will measure as much as 20in (50cm) from the crown of the head to the tip of the toes.

baby's bowel, liver, and gall bladder. This meconium plug will normally be passed in the first few days of life, but if your baby becomes distressed or frightened before delivery, it may have a bowel action into the amniotic fluid. If meconium is seen in the amniotic fluid after the waters have broken, it is evidence that the baby has already been put under stress and may need to be monitored closely during labor (*see* pp.291–92). For boys, the testes descend into the scrotum during this period, which explains why premature babies are often born with undescended testes.

Your baby's immune system is now capable of protecting against a variety of infections, but this is mainly due to the transfer of antibodies from your own blood. After birth, babies continue to receive antibodies from breast milk. One of the main reasons for trying to establish successful breastfeeding is that you can continue to give your baby protection against infection in the first few months of life, before he or she is capable of producing antibodies.

HOW THE HEAD IS ADAPTED

Your baby's head is relatively much smaller than it was earlier in the pregnancy, but the circumference is still as big as its abdomen. By full term, the head remains one of the largest parts of the baby's body, so delivering it safely through the birth canal during labor is an important consideration. This is one of the reasons why the fetal skull bones do not fuse together until much later in neonatal life. Although the baby's brain needs to be protected by bone, these are quite soft compared to an adult skull and can slide over each other and overlap. This allows the head to adapt to the shape of the mother's pelvis and greatly eases the passage through the birth canal and vagina.

In a normal pregnancy, the fetal head will move down into the pelvic brim and become engaged in preparation for the start of labor. In first pregnancies, head descent can start as early as 36 weeks, whereas in second or third pregnancies, the fetal head may not engage in the pelvis until immediately before labor starts.

THE PLACENTA AT TERM

Your placenta now looks like a discus and measures about 8–10in (20–25cm) in diameter and is about 1in (2–3cm) thick. This large surface area facilitates the transfer of oxygen and nutrients to your baby and the passage of waste products from baby back to mother. At term, the placenta will weigh around 1½lb (700g), just less than one-sixth of the fetal weight. Although nearly 45 percent of pregnancies are undelivered at 40 weeks, it is unusual for doctors and midwives to let the pregnancy continue after 42 weeks. At this stage, they will probably suggest an induction of labor (*see* pp.294–97) because the placenta will no longer be functioning effectively. Its reserves are now pretty well exhausted, which is why the risk of having a stillborn baby is increased in post-mature pregnancies. After 42 weeks, your baby can be more reliably cared for in the outside world.

YOUR CHANGING BODY

IF YOUR BABY'S HEAD HAS STARTED TO ENGAGE, OR SETTLE INTO THE PELVIS, YOUR BUMP WILL APPEAR TO BE LYING LOWER IN YOUR ABDOMINAL CAVITY. THERE IS SOMETIMES QUITE A NOTICEABLE CHANGE IN YOUR BODY SHAPE AND YOU MAY HEAR PEOPLE REMARKING THAT YOU HAVE "STARTED TO DROP."

READY FOR BIRTH

A color-enhanced X-ray shows a full term baby with its head down and engaged in the mother's pelvis.

This does not mean that you are about to go into labor and literally drop your baby; you may still have several weeks to go. It is merely an indication that your uterus and your baby are both getting prepared for labor. As I mentioned earlier, if this is your first baby, engagement is likely to occur sooner rather than later. This is because the muscles of your uterus are tight since they have not been stretched by a previous labor and are able to exert more pressure on the baby's head. Also, the arrangement of the pelvic bones is slightly altered after a previous vaginal delivery and this may delay engagement.

If your baby's head has started to engage, your breathing may be easier now and the decrease in pressure under your diaphragm and ribs may make it possible to eat a complete meal. This is why engagement is sometimes referred to as lightening (of the abdominal pressure). The downside to this change is that the baby's head (if head down) is pressing directly on your bladder. You will need to urinate frequently, and at night your increased bulk will make getting in and out of bed to visit the toilet a major undertaking.

Further loosening of your pelvic ligaments and joints will occur in preparation for the birth and can result in a variety of aches and pains in the pelvic area and an increasingly sore lower abdomen. The problem is made worse because your posture changes again as your baby moves into your pelvis. Your own weight gain usually slows down and may even stop during the final few weeks of pregnancy although the baby can put on as much as 2¼lb (1kg). But if you suddenly feel swollen and puffy, see your midwife or doctor urgently to check that you are not developing preeclampsia (*see* p.425).

HORMONE EFFECTS

The pregnancy hormones produced by the placenta will bring about further changes to your body. Your breasts will swell even more and may fill up with milk, even squirting small quantities at unexpected times. However, not every woman experiences this symptom and you may never see a drop of milk or colostrum leaking from your breasts until after the baby has been born and you start to breastfeed. Many women notice an increase in their vaginal discharge, which may look slightly brown or pink, particularly if you have had sex recently. This is usually nothing to worry about and is merely a further sign that your cervix has become softer because of the increased blood supply it is receiving. As a result it can become bruised and bleed slightly even with light contact. However, any bright red vaginal bleeding, particularly if it is accompanied by pain, should be reported urgently.

HOW YOU MAY FEEL PHYSICALLY

"...this is not the time to worry that you cannot bother your midwife again because you have already called her three times this week..."

YOU HAVE NOW REACHED YOUR MAXIMUM SIZE AND FIND THAT YOU BUMP INTO THINGS AND FEEL QUITE CLUMSY. YOU NEED TO TAKE CARE WHEN GOING UP AND DOWN STAIRS BECAUSE YOUR CENTER OF GRAVITY HAS ALTERED SIGNIFICANTLY AND YOU CAN NO LONGER SEE YOUR FEET.

During these last few weeks of your pregnancy, Braxton Hicks' contractions (*see* pp.237–38) will be a constant reminder of the fact that labor could start at any time. True labor contractions are much stronger and more painful, but if you doubt what you are experiencing, always seek advice. Your doctor or midwife will encourage you to come into the maternity unit and be checked over, rather than stay at home feeling anxious. This is not the time to be ignoring abdominal pain and hoping that it will go away. Nor is it the time to worry that you cannot bother your midwife again because you have already called her three times this week with the same symptoms. It does not matter how many false alarms there are, it is essential that uterine pain is always investigated promptly and carefully.

No matter how much you are trying to rest at this stage, you will probably still be feeling tired because you are unlikely to be getting enough of the continuous, uninterrupted sleep that you need to restore your mental and physical energy. Quality sleep involves cycles of four different stages from light sleep to deep sleep followed by REM (Rapid Eye Movement) sleep, which is when you dream. If you wake up during any of these stages, the sleep cycle goes back to stage one. As a result, you miss out on important deep sleep and REM stages and wake feeling fatigued. Even if you manage to doze and sleep for long stretches of time, the repeated lack of quality rest will mean that you become progressively weary and exhausted.

IMPATIENCE AND FRUSTRATION

The most common emotions women experience at this late stage of pregnancy are impatience that they are still waiting for D–day to arrive and frustration because there is no way of knowing when it will occur. By now, many women feel desperate to reach the end of their pregnancy, however enjoyable it has been.

If you are feeling like this, remind yourself that the end is in sight. Even if you are overdue, there is only a set number of days left to go (*see* below). Nevertheless, one of the other pressures you will have to deal with at this point is that the closer you get to your due date, the more you will have to field questions about when you are due, and telephone calls asking if you have had the baby yet. Your friends and family obviously mean well when they show such interest, but many of you will feel even more irritated by being constantly reminded that your long-awaited baby has still not arrived.

Labor represents an enormous emotional and physical challenge and I suspect that many of you will view it with a mixture of excitement and apprehension, since it is almost impossible to predict exactly how it will proceed and how your body will respond. As several women have commented to me recently, it is easier to train for a marathon than for labor. If you still feel seriously apprehensive, have a detailed discussion with your caregivers so that they can understand and address your fears.

MAGNIFICENT *By the end of your pregnancy, your belly can be a source of amusement coupled with sheer amazement.*

YOUR PRENATAL CARE

DURING THE LAST WEEKS OF PREGNANCY, YOU WILL HAVE CHECKUPS EVERY WEEK. BE SURE TO TELL YOUR DOCTOR OR MIDWIFE ABOUT ANY NEW OR UNUSUAL SYMPTOM, ANY ISSUES THAT ARE WORRYING YOU, OR ANYTHING THAT DOES NOT FEEL QUITE RIGHT WITH THE BABY, EVEN IF YOU CANNOT PUT YOUR FINGER ON THE EXACT PROBLEM.

"...a deeply engaged head is usually a good sign that labor will be swift and un-complicated."

The usual prenatal tests will be performed and you may have another blood count if you have been feeling very tired, or have been taking an iron supplement for anemia that has been previously diagnosed. Your caregivers will look for obvious signs of severe fluid retention (edema) and if you have noticed any sudden swelling in your fingers, ankles, or face and there is any suspicion that you might be developing preeclampsia, they will arrange for blood tests and more frequent checks of your blood pressure. Women with late pregnancy complications are usually asked to come to an outpatient center or a special area in the unit which provides more detailed monitoring (*see* pp.256–59).

Your doctor or midwife will palpate your abdomen carefully at each of your prenatal visits and record the findings in your medical reports. At this stage of your pregnancy, it becomes important to assess the lie and presentation of your baby and whether the presenting part has started to engage in the pelvis. These findings influence the plans that are made for your labor, may determine the type of delivery that is best for both you and your baby, and will help your prenatal caregivers assess your progress when labor is underway.

IS THE HEAD ENGAGED?

Pregnant women are often unsure about what the term "engagement" means, so a brief explanation of engagement and the terms used to describe it in your medical records may be useful. Strictly speaking, the baby's head is not properly engaged until more than half of it (three-fifths of the head) has passed through the pelvic brim in the mother's abdomen. The best way to assess engagement is with an abdominal palpation.

• **(High)**: if your caregivers can feel all of the head in the mother's abdomen, the baby's head is high or free.

• **(Non-engaged)**: when they can feel more than half (three-fifths or four-fifths) of the head above the pubic bone, they will either write in the notes that the baby is not engaged in the pelvis or state exactly how much of the head is palpable abdominally, for example, 3/5 or 4/5.

• **(Engaged)**: when they can feel less than half the head (just two-fifths of it) above the pubic bone, the baby's head is engaged. If there is only one-fifth or no fifths left to feel, the notes will record that the head is deeply engaged.

The other way to assess engagement is by performing a vaginal examination. Today, these are rarely done in the prenatal clinic, although they are performed regularly during labor to monitor the progress of your baby's downward descent through the pelvis. However, there may be occasions when an prenatal vaginal examination is helpful. For example, it can be difficult to assess the height of the head abdominally in very overweight women near full term. Similarly, when the baby's head is very deeply engaged and the shoulder is positioned just above the pelvic brim, it can be difficult to decide which part of the baby is being palpated. Accuracy is important here because, if you go into labor with your baby's head high and free, there is the potential for serious complications such as cord prolapse (*see* p.429). On the other hand, a very deeply engaged head before labor is usually a good sign that the labor will be swift and uncomplicated.

If you are a first-time mother and your baby's head is still not engaged, you will probably have an ultrasound scan to check that there is nothing preventing your baby's head from engaging, such as a low-lying placenta, uterine fibroid, or ovarian cyst. If the baby's head cannot travel past the obstruction, delivery usually has to be by cesarean section. Occasionally, the high head may be because your pelvis is too small to allow the fetal head to engage — the medical term for this problem is cephalopelvic disproportion (CPD). This is always a relative diagnosis: a woman with an average-sized pelvis may develop CPD if her

ENGAGEMENT

NOT ENGAGED

ENGAGED

NOT ENGAGED *The baby's head is still at the brim of your pelvis and the uterus is at its maximum height.*

ENGAGED *The baby has dropped into the pelvis, producing a sudden change in the outline of your belly.*

and cons of induction (starting labor artificially) versus waiting a little longer.

• If you decide to wait, you will probably be asked to visit the maternity outpatient unit for a post-maturity assessment (*see* below) after 41 weeks and 3 days. If the assessment is satisfactory and no problems are found, you may wish to continue your wait, in which case your baby will be assessed again at two-day intervals until 42 weeks, when you will most likely induce labor. In my experience, it is unusual for women to choose to continue beyond 42 weeks, but if they do, regular fetal heart traces and biophysical profile scoring will be needed.

• If at any stage, your post-maturity assessment is abnormal in any way, your caregivers will discuss the need to induce labor and deliver your baby. Although research shows that induction is likely to result in a higher incidence of prolonged labor and instrumental deliveries, there are conclusive studies showing that it does not increase cesarean section rate. On the other hand, leaving the pregnancy until the end of 42 weeks may increase the risk of fetal distress or unexplained stillbirth if the placenta stops functioning well. Even when the placenta is working well and the baby is continuing to grow after 41 weeks, there is also the risk of a difficult or obstructed labor if the pregnancy is left too long because the baby becomes increasingly large.

It is unusual for the assessment findings to be so dramatic that they prompt an immediate decision to deliver the baby but, if this is the case for you, you may be advised that cesarean section is the safest course of action. That said, everyone involved in looking after you will do his or her very best to achieve an induction of labor and vaginal delivery if this is what you prefer.

• If you need to have a post-maturity assessment, your caregivers will start by checking the exact size of your baby (*see* p.256–57) and the amount of amniotic fluid in the uterine sac (*see* p.259). The results may prompt them to perform a detailed Doppler blood flow assessment (*see* p.257). The scanners will also perform a biophysical profile of the baby (*see* p.259) looking carefully at limb movements, muscular tone, breathing movements, and heart rate pattern in order to help assess the baby's general well-being. Most units will also offer a computerized fetal heart trace (*see* pp.258–59), a pictorial printout generated by an electronic machine that assesses your baby's heart rate to see whether the criteria for a healthy baby are met within a certain period of time. They will also look at the placenta and grade its appearance and texture, which will give a rough indication of how well it is working. All of these tests are prone to error and should be considered as indicators, rather than as definite diagnosis.

"Having sex is another option that, theoretically, should encourage labor to start..."

COMMON QUESTIONS IN LATE PREGNANCY

▶ **How can I prepare for the pain of labor?**

If you have been feeling frightened about imminent labor and delivery, have a detailed discussion about your anxieties with your midwife and doctor so that they understand exactly what your fears are and respond to them individually. I hope that you will have already had plenty of conversations with your midwife and birthing instructors about different options for pain relief available to you during early labor (see pp.308–23). In early labor, many women find TENS machines, breathing exercises, massage, and having a long soak in a warm bath especially soothing and relaxing.

▶ **My baby seems less active than before. How can I be sure that everything is OK?**

Many babies become less active during the last few weeks of pregnancy, usually because there is no longer sufficient space in your uterus for them to move around and kick as freely as before. If you have not felt the baby moving during the last few hours, try provoking a kick or jolt by prodding your abdomen, coughing, or changing your position. If this does not work, then you need to seek advice immediately. You will most likely be advised to visit the maternity unit for a fetal heart trace (see pp.258–59), to make sure that all is well. You may also be given a fetal movement or kick chart to fill in over the next couple of days but, as I have mentioned before, I have mixed feelings about these because I firmly believe that babies develop their own individual patterns of movement late in pregnancy, and it is a change in this pattern that needs to be reported to the caregivers and investigated promptly, not the actual number of movements or kicks.

▶ **I have had enough of being pregnant. What can I do to help start my labor?**

Although the following ideas are by no means proven, some are worth a try. Eating spicy food is traditionally thought to help initiate action, presumably because it may encourage a bowel movement. Taking castor oil is a much less enjoyable version of the same idea.

If you have not felt like moving around much for the last few weeks, some exercise may help move the baby down a bit inside your pelvis. The more pressure exerted on your cervix, the more likely that labor will start. Try taking a long walk to see if this helps start labor.

Having sex is another option that, theoretically, should encourage labor to start, because semen contains prostaglandins – chemicals similar to those in the pessaries used to induce labor. So if you're not too exhausted, give it a try. Nipple stimulation is often cited as a way of inducing labor because it releases oxytocin, which stimulates the uterus. That said, you or your partner would need to stimulate your nipples for around one hour, three times a day, to have any significant effect, so I suspect that this is not likely to be the most helpful option!

▶ **How can I distinguish between vaginal bleeding and a show?**

The simple answer is that you cannot know until you have been fully checked out, so speak to your midwife or doctor immediately. A typical show includes the loss of a mucuslike plug, mixed with fresh red and old brown blood, but it is always best to make sure that there is no other cause of fresh bleeding, particularly if it is accompanied by sudden abdominal pain. (See placenta previa, placental abruption, and prepartum hemorrhage, p.427).

PREPARING FOR A HOME BIRTH

IF YOU ARE PLANNING A HOME BIRTH, MAKE SURE THAT THE PRACTICAL ARRANGEMENTS ARE NOT LEFT TO THE LAST MINUTE. YOU DON'T WANT TO FIND YOURSELF HUNTING FOR TOWELS AT THE BOTTOM OF THE LAUNDRY BASKET IN THE MIDDLE OF A CONTRACTION.

The midwife who will attend to your delivery will bring all the necessary medical equipment with her (*see* list, right) but make sure you have discussed with her, several weeks before the expected date, exactly what she expects you to provide. She will also be able to give you some useful tips about additional, non-essential items that you may find helpful during your labor and delivery.

PACK A MATERNITY BAG

You might think this is a strange idea since you are not actually going to the hospital, but packing a maternity bag (*see* p.277) is a good way to be sure that your essential personal items are gathered together in one place, ready for when the time comes. This will also be useful if things do not go according to plan and you end up in the hospital for any reason.

ORGANIZE YOUR BABY EQUIPMENT

Assembling a bag or assigning a drawer or cabinet for all the basic items you will need for the new baby is a sensible idea. You may be planning to deliver at home, but very soon you will be going out with your new baby, so don't forget to set up a portable crib or cradle and car seat.

PLAN WHERE YOU WANT TO DELIVER THE BABY

The essential requirements are comfort, warmth, and cleanliness. Make sure that you have plenty of plastic sheeting to protect bedding, mattresses, chairs, and the floor and large plastic bags to clean up any trash. You will also need lots of towels, hot water, soap, bowls, and sponges. If you are going to use your bed, it should be easily accessible to your midwife from both sides. Several changes of bed sheets will come in handy, together with extra pillows or cushions.

EXTRA COMFORTS

You may want to have a bean bag or large floor cushions available to you during labor. There is no reason why you should not use a birthing pool at home, but this will have to be organized well in advance. Although you may prefer to have dim lighting to help relax during labor, your midwife will need a good source of light to see what she is doing, especially after the delivery when you may need stitches, so have a portable, directable lamp close at hand.

MIDWIFE'S DELIVERY PACK

BASIC ITEMS
- blood pressure monitor
- thermometer
- fetoscope
- fetal Doppler
- gloves

PAIN RELIEF
- gas and air cylinder
- opiate drugs such as fentanyl
- local anesthetic

EMERGENCY EQUIPMENT
- oxygen cylinder
- baby resuscitation equipment
- antiseptic solutions
- intravenous drip set
- urine test sticks
- scissors
- stitching equipment

THINGS TO CONSIDER

MOST OF THE CONSIDERATIONS AT THIS STAGE OF PREGNANCY TEND TO BE PRACTICAL, CONCERNING PREPARATIONS FOR THE BIRTH AND THE PERIOD AFTERWARD. THAT SAID, YOUR MOST PRESSING CONCERN IS LIKELY TO BE KNOWING FOR SURE WHEN YOUR LABOR HAS REALLY BEGUN.

There are lots of possible indicators but no hard and fast rules so interpreting exactly what is happening to you when you are in labor, especially if it is the first time, is not easy. I've included the key signs and symptoms at the beginning of the Labor and Birth chapter (*see* pp.283–86) so I suggest you turn to those pages now. As always, seek advice and reassurance whenever you feel unsure — no one will accuse you of wasting time if your symptoms turn out to be a false alarm.

CLOTHES FOR COMFORT

In the last few weeks of the third trimester, you may find it useful to buy some special maternity panties in order to accommodate your vastly enlarged abdomen. These garments will never win any fashion prizes, but they can make a world of difference for your comfort, particularly if you have been suffering with underwear that is continually slipping down or riding up in uncomfortable positions. Some women also find that wearing a light girdle, positioned under their belly (not constricting it), helps support their abdomen and reduce symptoms of backache and weariness. Both of these items can be found in maternity shops and specialist mail order catalogs.

If you are planning to breastfeed, you will need a couple of good feeding bras so that you are comfortable in the hospital and when you return home. These need to be properly fitted in a specialist store or department store by trained fitters know how much room to allow since your breasts will expand when your milk comes in. You will also need to find nightgown with a low button opening on the front that will allow you to breastfeed. This may sound overly complicated, but breastfeeding really does become easier if you feel comfortable and at ease. If every meal involves struggling in and out of your clothing, you will become increasingly irritated — especially when you are embarking on your third meal of the night at five in the morning.

This is a good time to choose clothes to wear into the hospital — something comfortable that you do not mind getting dirty — a loose-fitting dress, or a baggy T-shirt with sweatpants. You will also need a fresh set of pajamas for after the delivery and a bathrobe and slippers for the postnatal ward.

"...maternity panties will never win any fashion prizes, but they can make a world of difference for your comfort."

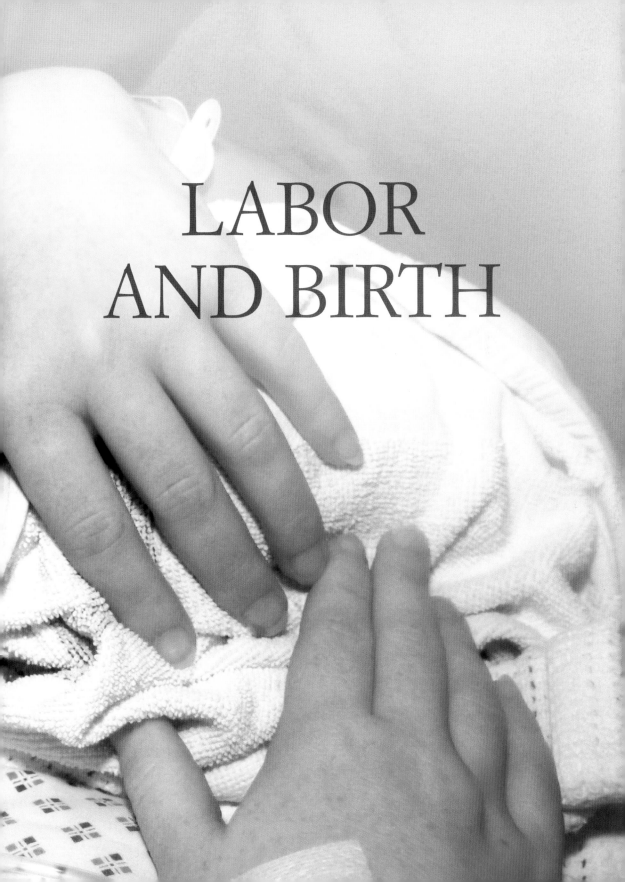

LABOR
AND BIRTH

THE STAGES OF LABOR

The only predictable thing about pregnancy is that it always comes to an end—in the majority of cases with the delivery of a healthy baby to a healthy mother after normal labor and a vaginal delivery. I regularly reflect on the fact that this is an extraordinary achievement, since decades of research have failed to establish exactly what triggers labor. Indeed, if we better understood this process, we would be better able to predict when it will happen and take steps to prevent it from occurring prematurely.

CONTENTS

THE FIRST STAGE

287 Going to the hospital

294 Induction of labor

298 Established first stage

305 Prolonged labor

308 Pain relief in labor

321 Birth story

THE SECOND & THIRD STAGES

326 The second stage of labor

330 Episiotomies and tears

332 The third stage of labor

THE FIRST STAGE

Going into labor is always an exciting time as your pregnancy nears its end and you embark on the next steps of this amazing journey. During the first stage, your uterus will contract repeatedly, causing your cervix to thin, shorten, and dilate. Only when your cervix is fully dilated can your baby's head pass into the birth canal for delivery.

There is no right or wrong way to go into labor. Every woman does it differently and no two labors are the same. Interestingly, toward the end of pregnancy, women are often more concerned about the symptoms and signs that they are likely to experience before labor and during early phases of giving birth than in the three stages of established labor. The questions they ask are not simple to answer, because the pre-labor stage can last for days or you may skip it completely and become dilated 5cm before you know it.

SYMPTOMS AND SIGNS OF EARLY LABOR

There are various signs and symptoms that indicate the end of pregnancy and that the start of labor is not too far away.

Engagement of the baby's head is one of the signs that labor is likely to occur soon for first-time mothers. During the last few weeks of pregnancy your prenatal caregivers will be assessing the position and descent of your baby's head into the pelvis. When it engages (*see* p.267 and p.302) you will probably notice that your breathing becomes easier and that your indigestion and heartburn have disappeared now that the pressure on your abdomen has been somewhat relieved. Instead, you will be feeling a new pressure in your pelvis and it is likely that you will need to urinate frequently. However, if this is not your first baby, engagement of your baby's head may not occur until shortly before, or even after, labor starts.

Braxton Hicks' contractions (*see* p.237) are likely to become stronger and more frequent in the prelabor stage. They are usually painless, although some women may find them uncomfortable. It is easy to mistake them for real labor contractions, particularly if they are strong and this is your first baby. However, Braxton Hicks' contractions occur irregularly, rarely more than two per hour,

"...every woman goes into labor differently and no two labors are the same."

and then fade away, whereas labor pains start slowly but gradually build up in strength and frequency.

Your cervical canal has contained a plug of mucus throughout pregnancy, designed to prevent infection from ascending from the vagina into the uterus. As the cervix starts to soften, shorten, and dilate, this plug becomes dislodged and the thick discharge that results is referred to as the "show." It is frequently tinged with small quantities of blood, since the mucus plug was attached to your cervical canal by small blood vessels (capillaries). The appearance of the show is often interpreted as a sign that labor is imminent. The reality is that you can have a show and still remain pregnant many days later. Nonetheless, loss of the cervical plug is a demonstration that your cervix is changing and a sign that the end of pregnancy is near.

If your vaginal discharge becomes watery or you pass a gush of clear fluid, your water may have broken (ruptured membranes) or you may have merely leaked some urine. It is important to find out which has occurred so put on a sanitary pad to soak up any further fluid and contact your midwife or doctor immediately. One of them will examine you to decide whether you are leaking amniotic fluid or urine (*see* p.286).

The prelabor emotional symptoms experienced by pregnant women vary. Some women find that their nesting instinct goes into overdrive and they rush around finishing as many tasks as possible. Others prefer to avoid venturing too far from home in case anything happens. This is undoubtedly a strange and unpredictable period of time, during which you may feel as if you are in limbo. This can give rise to feelings of anticipation, excitement, impatience, anxiety, and fear. The fear is usually focused on what might happen during labor and, in particular, on how you will deal with the pain. Reading about the available methods of pain relief (*see* pp.308–23) will help you feel more relaxed, confident, and in control of the exciting developments ahead.

> "...you can have a show and still remain pregnant many days later."

RECOGNIZING LABOR

This is one of the biggest concerns for many women. Thinking that labor has started only to be sent home by the hospital is disappointing. But remember, your prenatal caregivers deal with these uncertainties on a daily basis and it does not matter how many false alarms there are, as long as you and your baby are safe. Most pregnant women experience symptoms and signs that suggest they have begun labor (*see* box opposite) and need to seek advice. However, these signs come in no specific order and you may not experience all of them.

It is also important to remember that early labor does not always progress at a steady rate. You might experience one or several symptoms followed by hours of no activity at all, only for events suddenly to pick up speed again. Overall, there will be a tendency for your uterine contractions to become gradually stronger and more painful, but this increase in strength does not necessarily occur steadily. It is quite common to experience a period of painful contractions followed by a series that are less intense in strength.

Most first-time mothers are very aware when they are in labor because the contractions take longer to establish since the uterus has never attempted to expel a baby before. In second and subsequent births, labor can be quick and if the contractions have been bearable throughout, there are occasions when the mother will not realize she has reached full dilation until she experiences an overwhelming urge to push the baby out. However, it is unusual for women not to make it to the hospital in time, or to find themselves delivering on their own at home before the midwife arrives (*see* p.289).

SIGNS OF LABOR

▶ Your contractions are occurring every 15 minutes or so (time them).

▶ Your contractions are getting longer, stronger, and closer together.

▶ Walking around or changing positions does not make your contractions go away.

▶ You have pain in your lower back, instead of your lower abdomen.

▶ You feel the need to empty your bowels.

▶ You are passing fluid which you don't think is urine (ruptured membranes, *see* p.286).

CONTACTING YOUR MIDWIFE OR PHYSICIAN

Any time you are worried or unsure about what is happening or what you should do, contact your midwife or maternity unit. Your prenatal caregivers are there to give you advice and practical help and are available 24 hours a day. Whether or not you are advised to go to the hospital will depend on many factors:

• whether this is a first, second, or subsequent birth
• the strength and frequency of your contractions
• how you are dealing with contractions at home
• if you have had any vaginal bleeding (more than a show)
• how far you live from the hospital
• whether your water has broken
• whether your baby's movements have changed significantly.

Broadly speaking, if you have not had any complications during pregnancy and this is your first baby, your midwife or physician will probably advise that you stay home until your contractions are regular. There are no hard and fast rules but if the contractions are occurring every 15 minutes, lasting for about one minute (time them), and are so uncomfortable that you are forced to stop what you are doing, you should be thinking about going to the hospital. If you live far away from the maternity unit or are likely to meet difficulties or delays on the journey, you should allow plenty of time to get to the hospital.

Another important consideration is how you are coping with the contractions and whether you will need pain relief. Many women feel more comfortable, both physically and emotionally, with the knowledge that a variety of pain relief is close at hand once they reach the hospital (*see* pp.308–23).

WATER BREAKING

"...if your water breaks before your contractions start, this invariably jump-starts labor."

If your water breaks (membranes rupture) before the onset of regular or irregular uterine contractions, it is sensible to seek advice from your midwife or doctor. If you are near to term and you and your midwife know that the baby's head is deeply engaged, you may not need to be checked over and can safely wait at home for several hours to see what happens. However, now that the protective amniotic seal around your baby has been broken, you should not take a bath (shower instead) and make sure that you clean yourself carefully after passing a stool to reduce the risk of infection developing in the uterus.

If, on the other hand, your water breaks before 37 weeks or if the amniotic fluid is not pale yellow, but is tinged green or black, you need to contact the hospital immediately. This is a sign that your baby is or has been excreting meconium into the amniotic fluid, which invariably means that he has been exposed to stress and delivery should be sooner rather than later. Meconium is a thick sticky substance present in the baby's digestive system during pregnancy. If the baby is distressed, the response of the nervous system affects the digestive system, causing meconium to be expelled from the gut into the amniotic fluid.

In fact, in only 15 percent of pregnancies does the water break before contractions have started, and when this does happen it invariably jump-starts labor. Bear in mind, however, that once the membranes have ruptured, there is a greater chance of an infection developing and affecting the baby in the uterus. As a general rule, most hospitals advise women who have reached 35 weeks or more to have labor induced if uterine contractions have not started within 24 hours of the water breaking (*see* pp.294–97).

Finally, if you see a lot of blood mixed with the fluid that you are passing, or have bright red, fresh bleeding that continues after the water has broken, you must treat this as a potential emergency. Always call your midwife or doctor and go to the maternity unit immediately.

GOING TO THE HOSPITAL

THE FIRST THING TO DO ONCE YOUR MIDWIFE OR PHYSICIAN HAS ADVISED YOU TO GO TO THE HOSPITAL IS TO PICK UP YOUR MATERNITY BAG AND YOUR PRENATAL RECORDS IF YOU HAVE THEM.

As for the trip to the hospital, if you are planning to travel by car, make sure you and your partner have worked out the route well in advance and know how long the trip will take at any given time of day. It goes without saying that you should not drive yourself to the hospital, except in very unusual circumstances. Strong uterine contractions are distracting and totally incompatible with the concentration necessary for safe driving.

It is a good idea to have also checked out the parking facilities at the hospital or maternity unit and to have some loose change in your maternity bag for the parking garage or street meters. If you arrive in a hurry or in an emergency situation, it may not be possible to park the car as you had planned. In this case, your driver should leave a note behind the windshield and let the hospital security desk know that you need to get to the labor ward urgently and somebody will attend to the car as soon as possible.

"...It goes without saying that you should not be driving yourself to the hospital..."

If you don't have access to a car, you will need to call either a taxi or an ambulance to transport you to the hospital. Make sure that you give the dispatcher clear instructions to find your home and provide a telephone number to avoid unnecessary delays. Ambulance crews are well trained at dealing with the practicalities of labor and ensuring that you reach the hospital safely — indeed, they can even be relied upon to deliver your baby at home or in the ambulance if the need arises.

Make certain that you know which entrance to the hospital you should use when you get there and the exact directions to the maternity unit — many hospitals may use a different entrance to the maternity unit at night for security reasons.

ADMISSION TO THE HOSPITAL

Always try to warn the hospital that you are on your way so that they can prepare for your arrival. Your midwife or physician will meet you at the maternity unit. After looking through your medical notes, a nurse or your doctor will check your temperature, pulse, blood pressure, and urine (for protein and glucose) and will palpate your abdomen to establish the presentation of your baby and listen to the

ARRIVING AT THE HOSPITAL

Let the hospital know
in advance if you
think you are in labor
so that they can prepare
for your arrival.

fetal heart. She will also be assessing your contractions and she will ask you questions about the pattern of activity you have noticed in your uterus thus far, whether your water has broken, and if you need pain relief at this time. The answers to these questions and the results of the abdominal examination may suggest that you need to have an internal examination in order to assess the dilation of your cervix. If you have prepared a written birth plan, this will also be discussed with you at this time.

The findings will be recorded in your medical records and, if you have started to dilate (more than 2.5–5cm) and are contracting regularly, you are considered to be "in labor." Most maternity records include a partogram or labor curve — a section with a graphical record of how your labor is progressing over time (*see* p.303).

What happens next will depend on your nurse or midwife's assessment and how your maternity unit is arranged. Some units have early labor rooms in which you will stay through much of your labor, until you are transferred to the main delivery unit just before your baby is born. Other maternity units prefer to admit you directly to a room where you will stay for the duration of labor and delivery. Whatever happens, your partner will be welcome to stay with you if this is what you want.

If you are not in labor

If your contractions are weak and irregular and your membranes are still intact, an internal examination may not be necessary although you and your midwife or doctor will probably conclude that a careful assessment of the cervix will help decide the next step. If you are not in labor and your midwife or doctor is certain that both you and your baby are well, they will want to discuss with you whether you would prefer to remain in the hospital for observation, or whether you can safely return home to wait for your labor to become established. The decision will depend on many factors, including how your pregnancy has been so far, your past obstetric history, how anxious or apprehensive you are feeling, and how close you live to the hospital. There is no need to feel embarrassed if your arrival at the hospital ends up being a false alarm — these are very common, particularly with first babies, and you cannot possibly be expected to know when labor has really started.

MANAGING A SUDDEN DELIVERY

IT IS UNCOMMON FOR A PREGNANT WOMAN TO HAVE LABOR THAT IS SO UNEXPECTED
AND SPEEDY THAT SHE HAS TO DELIVER HER OWN BABY. HOWEVER, HERE IS SOME PRACTICAL
ADVICE IN CASE YOU DO FIND YOURSELF IN THIS SITUATION.

Try to remain calm. This is always easier said than done, but having a panic attack will only make the situation more difficult to handle. Hopefully, your birth partner will be with you, but if this is not the case, then try to contact a neighbor or friend who is nearby and can provide you with immediate practical help and support.

Call emergency services (911) and request an ambulance. Explain what is happening to you and also ask them to contact your midwife or doctor. Ambulance dispatch centers and crews are well trained in talking women through labor and can assist you. Remember to keep your cell phone with you at all times.

Wash your hands and your vaginal area with soap and water if possible. Boil some water and collect plenty of towels or sheets. If you have time, cover the bed or the floor with plastic sheeting, blankets, sheets, newspapers, or clean towels and find a spare bowl that you can use to catch the amniotic fluid and blood. Then either get onto the bed or lie down on the floor.

If you feel the overwhelming urge to lie down, relax and start inhaling and blowing in short, controlled breaths. You may have practiced this in your prenatal classes and it will help prevent the baby's head from suddenly delivering.

If, despite your breathing, the baby's head starts to deliver before help arrives, reach down and place your hands on the baby's head at your vulva, applying gentle pressure to be sure the head emerges gradually, instead of popping out. When the baby's head has delivered, check with your fingers that there are no loops of umbilical cord around the neck and if there are, hook them under your finger and carefully over the baby's head.

Gently stroke the sides of the baby's nose downward and the neck and chin upward to help expel mucus and amniotic fluid from the nose and mouth.

Help has usually arrived by now, and the delivery of the baby's body can be aided by the ambulance crew or midwife. If you have to deal with this on your own, place your hands around the baby's head and apply firm pressure downward (never pull or jerk) to help deliver the first shoulder. Then gently sweep the head and first shoulder upward toward your pubic bone. This will allow the second shoulder to deliver and the rest of the body will then slip out easily and can be placed onto your abdomen. Wrap the baby in towels or blankets immediately to keep him warm.

Do not pull on the umbilical cord, but if the placenta delivers spontaneously, elevate it so that the blood drains into the baby. You can wait until professional help arrives to cut the cord, unless help is delayed.

The most important thing is for you and your baby to keep warm until professional help arrives.

"Try to remain calm. Having a panic attack will only make the situation more difficult to handle."

THE DELIVERY ROOM

It is a good idea to take advantage of maternity ward tours offered during your prenatal visits. These provide an opportunity to see the delivery rooms and ask questions about the procedures and equipment you are likely to come across during labor and delivery.

The delivery bed will be higher than your own bed for practical reasons. It can be raised and lowered electronically. The end of the bed will be detachable and there will be places for stirrups or IV poles to be attached.

The sphygomanometer is an instrument attached to a wide band of inflatable material that is placed around your upper arm to measure your blood pressure. Some are portable hand-held units, others are wall-mounted and the most modern are automatic machines on small trolleys.

Piped gas outlets and tubing in the wall above the bed are something that all hospital delivery rooms are equipped with. These deliver oxygen and via masks or mouth pieces.

The baby resuscitator is a high, movable crib with a platform covered by a mattress for your baby to lie on. The resuscitator is equipped with an overhead heater to keep the baby warm, a piped oxygen supply, and drawers containing equipment that the pediatrician may need. In addition, there will be a simple comfortable crib in the room for the baby to lie in after delivery.

Stirrups can be attached to special slots at either side of the delivery bed. These allow your legs to be raised and supported so you can be examined more thoroughly should you need to have forceps or vacuum delivery or if you

DELIVERY ROOM EQUIPMENT

An electronic fetal monitor will be used to measure the baby's heart rate and your contractions.

If labor is induced, a drug such as oxytocin will be administered by IV.

Every delivery room has a comfortable crib ready for the baby to be placed in after delivery.

require stitches after the birth. They are no longer routinely used for internal examinations during labor and are usually stored under the bed.

An IV pole will be attached to the delivery bed or it will be on wheels nearby. There are several situations when it will be essential for you to have an intravenous drip during labor:

• if you decide to have an epidural (*see* pp.311–15)
• if you are having labor induced (*see* pp.294–97)
• if you require drugs to strengthen your contractions (*see* p.304)
• if you are bleeding and the doctors need to have immediate access to your veins, to make sure they can restore your blood pressure if it drops.

Urinary catheters and bed pans are required in some circumstances during labor when you are unable to get to a bathroom.

FETAL MONITORING EQUIPMENT

As a medical student I remember an eminent obstetrician telling me that "traveling through the birth canal is the most dangerous journey a human being ever embarks upon." It is not surprising, therefore, that we spend a lot of time trying to monitor the progress of labor and the baby's ability to cope with it.

The simplest method of monitoring the fetus during labor and delivery is to listen with a fetal stethoscope (fetoscope), placed on the mother's abdomen. This short, hand-held, trumpet-shaped metal instrument used to be the only method of hearing the baby's heartbeat. Alternatively, a hand-held, battery-operated Doppler ultrasound machine can be used at regular intervals.

Electronic fetal monitoring (EFM) measures the baby's heart rate continuously and also the frequency and strength of the uterine contractions and displays the information on a paper printout or tracing. A healthy baby has a baseline heart rate of 120–160 beats per minute, which is continuously changing by 5 to 15 beats — this is described as "good variability." Lack of variability between contractions will alert your midwife or doctor to the possibility that the baby is not coping well with the stress of labor. Similarly, a low baseline heart rate of 100 beats per minute or less or a high heart rate over 160 beats per minute are further signs of possible distress. However, the most useful information gained from the fetal heart tracing is how the baby's heart rate responds to the stress of the contracting uterus.

There are two types of electronic fetal monitoring: external and internal. External EFM is completely noninvasive. Two small devices are strapped to your abdomen with soft belts — one picks up the fetal heart beat; the other measures the intensity and duration of each contraction. They are linked by

"It is a good idea to take advantage of maternity ward tours offered during your prenatal visits."

THE HAND-HELD DOPPLER
This battery-operated device is used by midwives to listen to babies' heartbeats during normal hospital labors or home births.

EXTERNAL ELECTRONIC FETAL MONITOR *This noninvasive device is used to measure the baby's heart rate and the strength of the uterine contractions.*

wires to the electronic fetal monitor and their findings are also displayed as flashing numbers on the front of the machine. In most labors, external monitoring is required only intermittently, and there is no need for the woman to be confined to her bed.

Internal EFM is used when the tracing of the baby's heart rate is difficult to pick up or when there is clear evidence of fetal distress and the medical team need to know exactly what is happening. The fetal heart tracing obtained is more accurate than the one produced by an external monitor. A small electrode is clipped to the baby's head (or bottom if the baby is breech) and linked up to the electronic fetal monitor. This clip can be applied only if the cervix has dilated to 2.5cm or more and your water has broken or been artificially ruptured. A belt around your abdomen holds the pressure transducer that measures your uterine contractions. Alternatively, a fluid-filled catheter is inserted into your uterus to gauge the pressure of the contractions.

Electronic fetal monitoring was adopted widely and enthusiastically when it was first introduced in the 1970s and was used by some hospitals, either intermittently or continuously, during childbirth for almost all women. However, recent studies have shown that its routine use in labor significantly increases the chance of unnecessary interventions for supposed "fetal distress" and does not actually improve the outcome for the baby during a normal uncomplicated labor.

FETAL BLOOD SAMPLING

If the EFM print-out shows signs of fetal distress, your doctor or midwife may suggest that a fetal blood sample (FBS) be taken. A sample of blood is taken from the baby's scalp and the pH (acidity/alkalinity) is measured in a special machine. The more acidic the reading, the more likely it is that the baby lacks oxygen and, therefore, that intervention is needed. In order to obtain the blood sample, you will need to be examined internally with your legs raised in stirrups.

If measurements confirm that the baby is distressed, the best course of action will depend on how far advanced you are in labor. Obviously, if you are only dilated a few centimeters, it will be necessary to deliver you by emergency cesarean section to avoid delay. However, if you are dilated nearly 10cm or in the second stage of labor, it is often possible to achieve a vaginal delivery more quickly than an abdominal one, albeit with the help of forceps or vacuum extraction in some cases. If the baby is not distressed, it is likely that you can continue safely with a vaginal delivery.

YOUR BIRTH PARTNER'S ROLE

It serves no purpose to be judgmental as to whether or not the father should be present at the birth of his child. Watching someone you care about go through the pain and physical trauma of labor and birth is difficult and some men decide that they don't want to be there, however much they love their partner. That said, it is undoubtedly true that the man who attends the birth of his child will witness an extraordinary event that he will remember for the rest of his life. In addition, he will be able to share it with the mother-to-be and that common experience will often strengthen the bond between them. Encourage your partner to do what feels right for him.

The most important things a birth partner can do are, first, know what the mother-to-be wants and, second, know what is going on during the labor and delivery. The first can only be achieved if the two of you have had detailed discussions, and the second is probably best achieved by your partner attending the partner's prenatal preparation session (there is usually at least one class) and reading the labor chapter in this book.

YOUR PARTNER The most important thing your partner can do is make sure he is fully informed before the birth so you can rely on him for support as your labor progresses.

Laboring women have different needs—some want physical reassurance such as massaging, hand-holding, and wiping sweat from their faces. Others need emotional reassurance and verbal encouragement. Your partner will have to be prepared for all eventualities and accept that you might want physical closeness one minute and not want him anywhere near you the next. It is also important for your partner to try not to let his fear or anxiety show.

Gathering information

A major part of your partner's role will involve liaising with the medical staff. There may be instances when something occurs that you do not fully understand. This is where your partner can really help, by asking for clarification to make sure you understand the medical reasons for a particular procedure. He needs to be prepared to ask questions about what is happening in a nonconfrontational way and to gather information so you are both kept fully informed and can participate in any medical decisions that need to be made.

INDUCING LABOR

WHEN LABOR IS INDUCED IT IS BROUGHT FORWARD ARTIFICIALLY, BEFORE IT HAS STARTED OF ITS OWN ACCORD. INDUCTION MAY BE NECESSARY IF THE MOTHER OR HER BABY NEED TO BE DELIVERED PROMPTLY AND IT IS UNLIKELY TO HAPPEN SPONTANEOUSLY.

"...there is no such thing as a textbook induction and it is difficult to predict how things will go."

Induction may be used for women who have never shown any signs of going into labor and for a few whose water has broken but who fail to start contractions within 24 hours. It is important to understand that having labor induced does not usually involve a single intervention being performed at a specific time. Being induced is a process and is likely to necessitate a complex set of interventions and interactions, the exact nature of which will be dictated by the events that occur during labor. Hence there is no such thing as a textbook induction and it is often difficult to predict how things will go. This is why most midwives and doctors are hesitant to recommend induction unless there is a really good reason to do so.

Induction rates vary considerably between different countries, different maternity units, and even between individual obstetricians in the same unit. The rate is influenced by many factors, but particularly by the complexity of the pregnancy and the individual obstetrician's perception of what circumstances may place the mother or the fetus at risk.

Overall, nearly 70–80 percent of inductions result in a vaginal delivery, but the procedure increases the risk of an assisted delivery with either forceps or vacuum extraction (see p.352–55). The best chances of a successful induction are when the mother has had a previous vaginal delivery, her cervix is ripe, the baby is of average size, and the head is engaged in a normally sized pelvis.

INDICATIONS FOR INDUCTION

The absolute indications for induction are that the baby would be better cared for in the outside world than in the womb, or that the mother's health demands that the pregnancy end promptly. All other indications are relative and will frequently include a mixture of fetal and maternal considerations.

There are many reasons why an induction may be considered:

• **Fetal**—when prenatal monitoring suggests that the baby's growth has slowed down or stopped or there are signs that the baby is distressed in utero. This may include a reduction in fetal movements or volume of amniotic fluid and is usually because the placenta is no longer functioning properly. Other fetal indications for induction arise if the baby has been affected by maternal rhesus isoimmunization (*see* p.128 and p.424) or the mother has diabetes mellitus, which places the baby at increased risk in the last few weeks of pregnancy (*see* p.408). Similarly, if the baby is known to have an abnormality that will require surgery immediately after delivery, it is safer for the baby to be delivered when all of the necessary expertise is readily available. The decision to induce depends on balancing the risks of delivering a baby prematurely with those of leaving it in utero. However, with modern neonatal expertise, most babies delivered at or after 28 weeks survive without serious problems.

• **Maternal** — severe preeclampsia, poorly controlled diabetes, preexisting kidney, liver, or heart disease, and autoimmune disorders may require induction.

• **A combination of fetal and maternal indications** — many of the fetal and maternal indications listed above can lead to the decision that induction is the best way of ensuring the welfare of both mother and baby. However, preeclampsia and maternal diabetes are the most frequent combined indications for induction, together with premature rupture of the membranes.

• **Post-maturity** — most units offer induction to women whose pregnancies are prolonged past 41 weeks because it reduces the risks of unexplained stillbirth and other late-pregnancy complications, without increasing the cesarean section rate.

BISHOP'S SCORES

If an induction is being considered, most maternity units use a Bishop's score table to make an objective assessment as to whether or not the cervix is favorable for induction. Your midwife or doctor will perform a vaginal examination and cervical dilation, measuring length, consistency, position, and the station that the fetal head has reached in the pelvis (*see* p.302), which are given a score of 0 to 3. Total scores of 5 or more are considered favorable for induction because the cervix is ripe.

SCORE	CERVICAL STATE				
	Dilation (cm)	Length (cm)	Consistency	Position	Station of head
0	Closed	3	Firm	Posterior	-3
1	1 – 2	2	Medium	Middle	-2
2	3 – 4	1	Soft	Anterior	-1
3	5+	0			0

METHODS OF INDUCTION

WHEN THE DECISION IS MADE TO INDUCE LABOR, THE METHOD USED WILL DEPEND ON WHETHER THIS IS A FIRST OR SUBSEQUENT PREGNANCY, THE PRESENCE OF A PREVIOUS UTERINE SCAR, WHETHER OR NOT THE MEMBRANES ARE INTACT, AND THE STATE OF THE CERVIX. IT IS UNUSUAL TO PLAN AN INDUCTION IF THE BABY IS NOT IN A CEPHALIC PRESENTATION (*SEE* P.268) AND THE HEAD IS NOT WELL, OR NEARLY, ENGAGED.

You will be admitted to the labor unit and your midwife or doctor will examine you and monitor the baby's heart rate with an EFM recording to make sure there are no signs of fetal distress (*see* p.291). The examination will start with one of them palpating your abdomen, confirming the longitudinal lie and cephalic presentation, and assessing the degree of engagement of the head (*see* p.302). Your midwife or doctor will then perform a gentle vaginal examination and use the Bishop's scoring system (*see* p.295) to assess the state of your cervix.

A favorable cervix is critical if the induction is to be successful.

PROSTAGLANDIN GEL OR PILLS

The hormone prostaglandin occurs naturally in the uterine lining and stimulates the uterus to start contracting. If your cervix is unfavorable, your midwife or doctor will suggest putting some synthetic prostaglandin pills or gel into the vagina to help ripen it. A second vaginal dose of prostaglandins may be needed about six hours after the first and some women require

further doses to ripen the cervix sufficiently. From a practical point of view this is often best done overnight, in the hope that the woman will wake up refreshed the next morning and will either start to go into labor or be better prepared to undergo the next part of the induction process. In pregnancies that have been straightforward, this can be carried out on the prenatal ward, but if recognized risk factors are present, the woman will be moved to the main delivery unit for this procedure.

After each insertion the baby will be monitored electronically for 30 minutes, but as long as the fetal heart tracing is normal, intermittent monitoring can then be used (*see* p.291). As soon as contractions start, another period of electronic monitoring will be advised.

AMNIOTOMY (AROM)

When the cervix is dilated (2.5–5cm) it is usually possible to artificially rupture the membranes easily by

SWEEPING THE MEMBRANES

Before deciding on a date for a formal labor induction, it is likely that your midwife or doctor will suggest attempting to sweep the membranes. The doctor or midwife will perform a vaginal examination and gently insert one or two fingers through the cervix and literally sweep them around its circumference. This often helps start the contractions because it releases prostaglandins from the cervix. It can be a little uncomfortable and often results in light bleeding or a "show." However, it is completely safe and is often an effective way of stimulating early labor contractions.

inserting a long, thin plastic hook into the vagina and through the cervix to break the delicate membranes and allow the amniotic fluid to start draining away. This releases further prostaglandins, which help establish regular uterine contractions. In some inductions, no further interventions are required after an AROM (artificial rupture of membranes) has been performed because the uterine contractions become well established in a relatively short period of time. However, when this is not the case you will need to move to the next part of the induction process—an oxytocin drip.

OXYTOCIN

Oxytocin is a hormone that is produced by the pituitary gland in the brain and causes the uterine muscle to contract. Oxytocin is given via an intravenous drip that is inserted into a vein in your lower arm. The oxytocin drug is injected into a sterile bag of fluid (usually a mixture of salt and sugar solutions), which is then attached to a drip stand. The starting dose is always small and is gradually increased until effective uterine contractions have been established, usually defined as three moderate to strong contractions occurring every 10 minutes. The quantity of oxytocin you receive is carefully measured by a special machine or infusion pump

attached to the drip. This allows the dose to be adjusted up or down, depending on the progress of your labor and, most importantly, how the baby responds to the uterine contractions.

Because uterine contractions that are induced by oxytocin can be strong and start suddenly before the baby has been exposed to more gentle uterine activity, there is a greater risk of the baby becoming distressed. Of course, this potential problem is frequently aggravated by the underlying reasons for which the induction is being performed. For example, if the baby needs to be delivered because of poor growth, then its reserves may already be lower than a baby who is normally grown and going through spontaneous labor. For this reason, once the oxytocin infusion has started, you will need to be monitored continuously with an electronic monitor (see pp.291–92).

You may find it useful at this point to read the section on the latent phase of labor (see p.298), where I explain the prolonged period of uterine activity usually needed before normal contractions become strong enough and regular enough to dilate the cervix effectively.

OXYTOCIN *The drug is administered via an intravenous drip inserted into a vein in your hand or lower arm.*

Once you have understood these points, I think it becomes much easier to appreciate why an induction that requires an oxytocin drip often results in an apparently lengthy and more painful labor. Labor is not really longer but there is a lot of catching up to do to reach the point when the cervix starts to dilate. Furthermore, the induced contractions may appear to be more painful because you have not experienced the gradual increase in uterine activity that occurs in the latent phase of spontaneous labor. This is one of the reasons why most maternity units suggest that you have an epidural anesthetic if you are induced and why the epidural is often inserted before the oxytocin drip is turned on.

"A favorable cervix is critical if the induction is to be successful."

ESTABLISHED FIRST STAGE

THEORETICALLY, THE FIRST STAGE OF LABOR STARTS WHEN REGULAR UTERINE CONTRACTIONS BECOME ESTABLISHED AND ENDS WHEN THE CERVIX IS DILATED 10CM. THIS FIRST STAGE CAN FURTHER BE DIVIDED INTO THREE PHASES: THE LATENT PHASE, THE ACTIVE PHASE, AND THE TRANSITION PHASE.

THE LATENT PHASE

During the latent phase of the first stage of labor, uterine activity starts with usually mild and irregular contractions. For many women, these contractions feel like menstrual period cramps or backache and are usually not seriously distressing. This early activity changes the cervix from being thick and barrel-shaped, about 1in (2cm) in length, into a much thinner, softer, shorter structure.

Although you may not be aware of the mild contractions spreading down your uterus, they are thinning the lower part of the uterus and cervix, drawing them up over the baby's head (if that is the presenting part) like a glove. This process is called effacement and needs to occur before the cervix can open up or dilate. The latent phase can last for eight hours (sometimes more for first-time mothers), but if you have had several children it is usually much shorter — indeed you may not even realize that something has started to happen.

The hormones secreted during the last few weeks of pregnancy help soften the cervix in preparation for labor, but dilation in the first stage can only be achieved by the onset of progressively stronger uterine contractions. Hence, in the latent phase, the mild contractions usually occur every 15 to 20 minutes, lasting for no more than 30 to 60 seconds.

FIRST STAGE PHASES

As the first stage of labor unfolds, the cervix effaces and dilates. It changes from being a structure that is firmly closed to one that is dilated 10cm and able to allow the baby's head, or other presenting part, to pass through.

THE LATENT PHASE *The cervix thins (effaces) and begins to stretch and open.*

THE ACTIVE PHASE *Contractions are stronger as the cervix dilates.*

THE TRANSITION PHASE *The cervix is fully dilated and ready for the baby to descend.*

Rest assured that if you find the pain you are experiencing in the latent phase distressing, you will be offered relief. However, until active labor has started, your midwife and doctor will probably recommend an injection of morphine rather than an epidural (*see* pp.308–23). This is because they will want to encourage you to stay upright and active for as long as possible, rather than confining you to a bed, in order to allow gravity to play its part in helping you reach the active phase.

THE ACTIVE PHASE

Technically, the active phase is said to have started when the cervix has dilated to about 3cm and uterine contractions have become more regular and rhythmical. Your midwife will be able to judge if you have reached the active phase based on what your uterine contractions are like, rather than what has happened to your cervix.

As the first stage progresses to the active phase, the contractions will become more noticeable around the center of your tummy and will be accompanied by a hardening and tightening of the uterine muscles that you can feel with your hand. Uterine contractions are painful because the uterus is a massive muscular organ and requires enormous amounts of energy to work efficiently. During a contraction, the blood vessels in the walls of the uterus are compressed and the muscle becomes short of oxygen, resulting in the release of chemical substances that mediate pain. These are washed away in the recovery period between contractions.

"...the uterus is a massive muscular organ and requires enormous amounts of energy to work efficiently."

The other thing to remember about contractions is that they slightly reduce the oxygen supply to your baby, because blood vessels in the uterus that are supplying the placenta are also compressed. As a result, your baby's heart rate may slow down at the peak of a contraction. This will be carefully monitored as your labor progresses (*see* pp.291–92) to make sure your baby is not getting too tired or distressed.

Changing contractions

As you enter the active phase of labor, your contractions will change in nature. First, they become stronger and more painful. Second, instead of being concentrated in the lower part of the uterus, they now begin at the top and spread downward through the entire uterus. This allows the baby's head (or other presenting part) to be pushed against the cervix, since the priority now is to get the cervix opened to a 10cm diameter. Your contractions will occur every

"...the baby's head and shoulders must descend deep into the pelvic cavity before the second stage of labor starts."

10 to 15 minutes, then every five minutes, then every two minutes, the timing being calculated from the start of one contraction to the start of the next.

By the end of the active phase, each contraction will last about 60 to 90 seconds, so there will be little time for rest in between. As they get stronger, you will feel as if you are being gripped around the abdomen by a tight band as the uterine muscles harden and tighten. During each contraction, the pain will usually start slowly, rise to a peak lasting about 30 seconds and then subside.

From 4–10cm the cervix usually goes through the most rapid phase of dilation, after which there may be a deceleration. Cervical dilation is not the only marker of progress, however; it is important for the baby's head and shoulders to descend deep into the pelvic cavity before the second stage of labor.

The total length of the active phase of the first stage varies because it is determined by whether or not this is your first baby. In a first labor, you are likely to dilate at about 1cm per hour, whereas if you have already had one or more babies you may dilate considerably faster.

Rupture of the membranes

In 15 percent of term pregnancies, the membranes rupture spontaneously (SROM) before labor starts and, in the majority of these cases, contractions and progressive cervical dilation follow within 24 hours. This leaves 85 percent of pregnancies in which the water is still intact when labor commences. In most cases, the membranes will rupture spontaneously as labor progresses but occasionally, and usually in very fast or precipitate labors, the baby will be delivered still surrounded by the amniotic sac.

Some obstetric units have a policy of artificially rupturing the membranes (AROM) when strong contractions have become established and cervical dilation has reached 4–5cm. This is because amniotomy or AROM causes the release of prostaglandins, which help speed up uterine contractions. It also removes the fluid cushion surrounding the baby's head, which means that more effective pressure is exerted on the cervix, further encouraging the progress of labor. Having said that, if your labor is progressing normally, there is no need to have an AROM if you feel strongly about not wanting any interventions.

If your labor has been induced (*see* pp.294–97) or needs to be augmented because the progress is slow (*see* p.304), you may be advised to have an AROM. The AROM will first help labor progress. It will also facilitate the monitoring of your progress because labors that are not completely straightforward need to be watched closely to make sure the baby does not become distressed. If the FHT (fetal heart tracing) has any unusual results, your midwife or doctor will probably suggest that the amniotic sac be ruptured in order to attach an electronic monitoring clip to the baby's head (*see* p.292). One of them will also inspect the amniotic fluid and check that there is no meconium staining present, which would suggest that the baby has already been exposed to stress.

AROM is usually a painless procedure (*see* pp.296–97) if you are already partially dilated. There are a few situations where AROM is not advisable, for example, if you go into premature labor. In such a case, it is always best to leave the amniotic fluid intact for as long as possible, since it protects and cushions the fragile premature baby during labor and delivery (*see* p.341).

THE TRANSITION PHASE

This is the name given to the interlude that sometimes, but not always, occurs during the final phase of the first stage of labor. This phase is marked by the cervix being fully dilated, and, characteristic of the second stage of labor, you experience the intense urge to push. At this point, the second stage of labor is fully underway.

The transition phase can last a few minutes or continue for an hour or more. For some women it can be the most difficult part of their labor because they already feel exhausted by the hours of contractions they have experienced. The contractions will be intense, coming every 30 to 90 seconds and lasting for 60 to 90 seconds. Hence there is very little time between them and many women feel frightened that they have completely lost control of what is happening. In some ways this is true, since the labor has developed a momentum of its own and there is no stopping until the baby is delivered. The good news is that this is not far off, so try to think of the transition phase as a very positive sign that the end of your labor is in sight.

"...think of the transition phase as a positive sign that the end of your labor is in sight."

Wanting to push

Some women experience an intense urge to push during the transition phase before the cervix is fully dilated. If you start pushing when the cervix is 8 or 9cm dilated, it will develop into a thick, swollen ring around the top of the baby's head, instead of the paper-thin pliable membrane that will allow the head to descend and slip past it. If you do develop the urge to push before you reach full dilation, your midwife or nurse will show you how to pant or take short shallow breaths when you are having contractions, to try to prevent you from breathing too deeply and bearing down. She may also suggest that you change to a position that takes the pressure of the baby's head off your cervix (such as on hands and knees with your bottom raised), since an upright position will encourage the urge to bear down. Alternatively, if you have an epidural in place, it may be a good idea to have a small increase in dosage at this point so that full dilatation and further head descent can be achieved before you start to do your pushing.

EXAMINATIONS IN LABOR

The onset of labor depends on the cervix starting to dilate, but progress in labor requires both continued cervical dilation and descent of the baby through the pelvic birth canal. There is no absolute size of baby or pelvis that can guarantee good progress during labor, nor is there a magical number of strong contractions that can predict a swift and smooth delivery. This is why it is so important for your midwife or doctor to perform an abdominal examination as well as a vaginal/internal examination whenever she is assessing your progress.

How often you are examined during labor will depend on many different factors, not least of which is how long or short your labor lasts. At each

ENGAGEMENT AND STATIONS

Now that you are in labor, it is important to assess how far the baby's head has descended into the pelvis. By definition, engagement means that the largest diameter of the head has entered the pelvic brim, which means that no more than two fifths of the head will be palpable in the abdomen. The less head that can be felt on examination, the better the progress of labor is likely to be. You will have a vaginal examination to identify how many centimeters your cervix is dilated and the level that the leading part of the head has descended within the pelvis. The levels are referred to as stations, which are best thought of as imaginary horizontal lines drawn through the pelvis at centimeter intervals. When the head first enters the pelvic brim it is said to be at –5 station. When the tip of the head reaches the middle of the pelvic cavity it is at zero station. When it reaches the vaginal opening it is at +5 station.

THE DESCENT *The position of the head is described according to where it is in cm above (-) or below (+) the ischial spines (the narrow part of the pelvis).*

LABOR CURVES

THE BEST WAY OF MONITORING THE PROGRESS OF LABOR IS TO USE A LABOR CURVE.
THIS IS A LARGE CHART CONSISTING OF VARIOUS GRAPHS ONTO WHICH ALL OF THE
OBSERVATIONS MADE DURING LABOR ARE ENTERED.

Your personal details will be noted at the top of the labor curve along with any special instructions or reminders to the midwives and doctors. Underneath this are several graphs recording the fetal heart rate, the number of contractions you are having in each 10-minute interval, your temperature, blood pressure, pulse, and the results of any urine tests. If you need pain relief or an oxytocin drip, the dosages and the timing of these drugs will also be recorded on the chart.

The most useful part of the labor curve is the graph of your cervical dilation and the station that the fetal head has reached, which the midwife or doctor will plot at each assessment. This shows at a glance how labor is progressing and will quickly identify any delays. Indeed, most labor curve graphs have bold black lines already drawn on them showing the anticipated curved pattern of cervical dilation from 0 to10 cm. The ideal curve for first-time mothers moves along and up the graph toward the 10cm mark more gradually, whereas the curve for mothers who have already had a baby is shorter and sharper. The ideal curve for head descent will move along and down the graph. Every labor will not follow these guidelines exactly, but if progress is slow (the entries are appearing significantly to the right of the ideal progress line), then interventions are likely to be needed. The earlier this is recognized, the better.

No. 00842758	LAST NAME DOE	FIRST NAME JANE
Parity 0+0	Age 25	Date Sept. 2, 2004
LMP Nov. 22, 2003	EDD Aug. 29, 2004	
Duration of Labor 12 HRS.	*Duration of Ruptured Membranes* 2 HRS.	

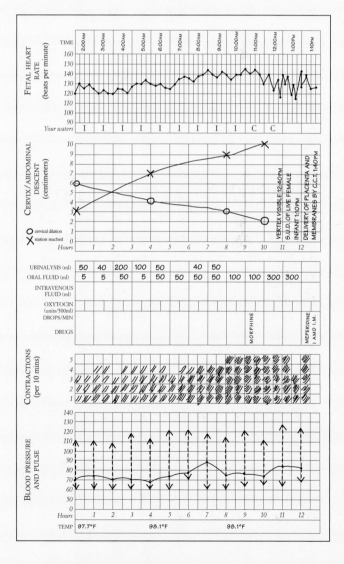

PROGRESS OF THE FIRST STAGE

Good progress is achieved by a combination of three important P factors:

▶ **the power**—strong uterine contractions that effectively dilate the cervix

▶ **the passenger**—a baby that can fit through the mother's pelvis and is in a good position for an easy exit

▶ **the passage**—a pelvis that is sufficiently roomy to allow the baby to pass through it.

All three of these P factors are relative to each other, and the progress of your labor will depend on how they interact with each other.

"...in the vast majority of pregnancies, the lie will be longitudinal and cephalic"

examination, the midwife or doctor will palpate your abdomen and confirm the lie and presentation of the baby (*see* p.268). In the vast majority of pregnancies this will be longitudinal and cephalic, hence the rest of this section on progress in labor assumes that this is the case. If you have a breech presentation or transverse or oblique lie at the onset of labor, you will find details about how these labors are managed on pp.356–59 and p.429.

AUGMENTATION OF LABOR

If the progress of a spontaneous labor begins to slow down, it may become necessary to accelerate or augment it. Using a labor curve is the best way of deciding when augmentation should be started. If the contractions are satisfactory but the membranes are intact, then an artificial rupturing of the membranes (*see* p.300) may be all that is needed to speed things up. If the contractions are weak, infrequent or irregular, and your water has already broken, then an oxytocin infusion will be started to strengthen and regularize the contractions. As with an induction (*see* pp.294–97), the dose is small to begin with and then gradually increased, aiming for about three to four moderately strong contractions every 10 minutes.

Continuous monitoring will be needed to make sure that the baby does not become distressed and a further examination will be carried out about two hours after augmentation. Usually this shows that there has been some progress in the cervical dilation or descent of the baby's head, in which case the oxytocin infusion will be continued until the next examination in two hours' time. Observations will be added to the labor curve (*see* p.303), and the curve of cervical dilation should appear normal. Occasionally, however, if there is no progress after three or four hours, doctors will be asked to reassess you and may advise delivery by cesarean section.

PROLONGED LABOR

PROLONGED LABOR IS USUALLY DEFINED AS LASTING LONGER THAN 12 HOURS
AFTER THE MOTHER IS RECOGNIZED AS BEING IN LABOR. IT COMPLICATES FIVE
TO EIGHT PERCENT OF ALL LABORS AND IS MUCH MORE COMMON IN FIRST-TIME
MOTHERS THAN THOSE WHO HAVE HAD A BABY BEFORE.

Labor becomes prolonged when the cervix is unable to dilate or because the
baby fails to descend through the birth canal or rotate into the optimal position
for a straightforward delivery. In reality it is often a combination of factors, since
dilation, descent, and rotation are all interdependent. Cephalopelvic
disproportion, fetal or maternal obstruction, inefficient uterine activity, and
occipito-posterior presentations are usual causes of prolonged labor, and they
are often closely interlinked.

CEPHALOPELVIC DISPROPORTION

Cephalopelvic disproportion (CPD) means that the baby's head is too large for
the mother's pelvis. It is a relative term, since a different-sized baby might slip
through the same pelvis easily. For first-time mothers, CPD may be suspected if
the head has not entered the pelvic brim at term. Further clues will be obtained
by looking at the mother's height and shoe size — if she is less than 5ft (150cm)
tall and wears size 7 shoes or smaller, she may have a small pelvis that will make
a vaginal delivery difficult or impossible.

In cases where there is a strong suspicion of cephalopelvic disportion
prenatally, doctors will often advise a cesarean section to avoid exposing the
fetus to a prolonged and difficult labor. On the other hand, if the head has
entered the pelvic brim and the mother wants to deliver vaginally, she may
choose to have a trial of labor. If this is attempted, progress will be carefully
monitored using a labor curve (see p.303). If progress is poor, then plans will be
made for an abdominal delivery.

In second or subsequent pregnancies, the head does not always enter the
pelvis until the onset of labor, so predicting CPD may be more difficult. A
careful review of previous labors and the birthweight of the babies may provide
useful clues. Some doctors may suggest an X-ray or CT scan to assess the exact
dimension of the mother's pelvis, although this is rarely used in current practice.
The reality is that however restricted or capacious the bony measurements may
be, the only way of knowing whether or not the baby's head will pass through
the pelvis is by monitoring labor as it progresses.

"The only way of knowing whether or not the baby's head will pass through the pelvis is by monitoring labor as it progresses."

OBSTRUCTED LABOR

This is usually the end result of a poorly managed or neglected labor in which CPD or a malpresentation, such as a shoulder or transverse lie (*see* p.429), has been missed. Other causes include pelvic masses in the mother, such as a uterine fibroid (*see* p.422), an ovarian cyst or a kidney transplant, or a congenital abnormality in the baby, such as hydrocephalus (*see* p.419). Happily, I can tell you that obstructed labor is a rare event these days, since most causes will be identified before you go into labor.

In a first labor, the uterus contracts strongly to try to overcome the obstruction and then may become inactive. However, if an obstruction occurs in a second labor, the uterus more commonly continues to contract strongly, leading to the development of a contraction ring in the uterus that is known as a Bandl's ring. The upper part of the uterus becomes thick and short and the lower part becomes progressively stretched and thinner. In this situation, urgent intervention with delivery by cesarean section is needed in order to prevent the uterus from rupturing (*see* p.427).

INEFFICIENT CONTRACTIONS

Labor will progress normally only if your uterine contractions are efficient and move downward through the entire uterus. When they fail to do so, labor usually becomes prolonged. The inefficient uterine activity can be under- (hypo) or over- (hyper) active and develops in 5 percent of first labors and about one percent of all labors. Underactivity — called uterine inertia — often responds to stimulation with oxytocin (*see* p.297) unless disproportion or another type of obstruction is present. Overactivity — also called incoordinate uterine activity — is when the various parts of the uterus contract independently. These contractions fail to dilate the cervix efficiently and are often very painful. Now that epidural anesthesia is used so widely, the severity and exact location of the mother's pain in labor can be difficult to monitor. For this reason, a labor curve is useful in identifying the different types of inefficient uterine activity. If slow cervical dilation persists and the cervix fails to dilate by more than 2cm over a period of four hours, accompanied by poor head descent, then plans will need to be made for delivery by cesarean section.

"Labor progresses normally only when your contractions are efficient, moving down through the entire uterus."

OCCIPITO-POSTERIOR PRESENTATION

Labor and delivery are more likely to be swift and uncomplicated when the baby is in the occipito-anterior position (OA, *see* p.270) — the back of the baby's head (the crown or occiput) is toward the mother's front (anterior). When the baby is in the occipito-posterior (OP) position its face is pointing forward and the back of its head is pressing against the mother's back (sacrum) with the baby's spine lying on top of the mother's spine. In this position it is more difficult for the baby to flex its neck and chin because the baby's bony crown is pushed up against the bony maternal sacrum, and, consequently, a larger than normal proportion of the head is presenting. This may prolong the labor and it often results in the mother experiencing more pain and discomfort in her lower back. This is why occipito-posterior positions are sometimes referred to as backache labors.

To take the pressure off your lower back, try getting down on your hands and knees, sitting with your legs crossed in front of you and leaning forward, or rocking your pelvis. Alternatively you may find that a vigorous massage of the painful area is helpful. One of the best ways of encouraging rotation of the baby's head is to stay upright and mobile for as long as possible. If you need to lie down, then adopt a position that will encourage internal rotation (your midwife will advise you). Always avoid lying flat on your back because in this position the complete weight of your baby will be pressing down on your spine and lower back.

Rotating the baby

Just over 10 percent of babies are in a posterior position at the start of labor (*see* p.270), so this is not an uncommon problem. In the majority of these cases the babies tend to rotate themselves into an anterior position before the end of the first stage, but labor invariably gets off to a slower start and the progress is often more painful and protracted, which is very tiring for the mother.

When the baby is in the OP position both epidural anesthesia and labor augmentation are often required during labor and, not surprisingly, maternal exhaustion and fetal distress are frequent complications. If the baby fails to move into the anterior position by the beginning of the second stage, the midwife or doctor will probably suggest increasing the dosage on your epidural (to prevent any urges to push), changing your position to encourage further rotation, and letting you rest for an hour or so. If the baby is still OP or transverse (*see* p.270) after this, it may be necessary to rotate the baby into the occipito-anterior position with forceps or the vacuum extraction to achieve a smooth delivery. When this proves to be unsuccessful, the only remaining option for delivery is an emergency cesarean section.

OCCIPITO-POSTERIOR
In this position the back of your baby's head is toward your back, with its spine pressing against yours.

are better to use. Also, having something in your mouth that you can bite on hard can be very helpful in the middle of a strong contraction.

For many women, nitrous oxide is most helpful in the early stages of labor. Some women manage using only nitrous oxide throughout, whereas others find they need an additional form of analgesia to cope with strong contractions or during the second stage of labor. I am sure that part of the benefit of using gas and air during the first stage is that it forces you to concentrate on your breathing technique, which helps you feel more in control of the situation and can also provide a degree of pain relief.

Although nitrous oxide readily crosses the placenta, it is eliminated both from your body as well as from your baby's body very rapidly, causing no adverse effects. You do not have to worry that your baby will be affected.

SYSTEMIC ANALGESIA

Systemic pain relief affects the whole body. Opioids, especially morphine and fentanyl, are frequently used in labor. Meperidine, which is known by the brand name Demerol, has also been widely used but is now less commonly administered. These drugs are all members of the family of narcotic (opiate) drugs, which literally means that they induce drowsiness as well as reducing pain. Opioid analgesics relieve pain by stimulating specific receptors in the brain and spinal cord so that the pain messages that are relayed to the brain by the nervous system are dulled. These are the same receptors that are used by endorphins — our body's naturally occurring analgesics.

Morphine is administered quickly and easily by injection, usually into a muscle either in your upper thigh or buttocks or, alternatively,

intravenously, and you will feel its effects within 15 to 20 minutes. The pain relief will wear off after three to four hours, when you will need to have a repeated dose.

Morphine tends to be used when an analgesic is required early in labor, as it acts over several hours. When an analgesic is only required toward the end of the labor, intravenous fentanyl is more likely to be given, as it offers quick pain relief but does not have such long-lasting effects.

Problems with morphine

Although it can perform an important role, morphine has its disadvantages as a labor analgesic because the dosages that are required for effective pain relief can also result in the mother becoming overly sedated. This can occasionally lead to breathing difficulties and low oxygen levels in the mother between contractions. Morphine can also be accompanied by additional side effects, such as nausea, vomiting, indigestion, and delayed gastric emptying, and many mothers tell me that they dislike morphine because it makes them feel out of touch with what is happening during labor.

The other disadvantage of morphine is that it rapidly crosses the placenta into the baby, in whom it can cause drowsiness. As the baby becomes sedated, there is often a reduction in the baseline variability on the fetal heart tracing that is displayed on the electronic fetal monitoring machine (*see* p.291), which makes interpretation of the fetal heart trace difficult. In addition, when morphine is administered close to delivery, the baby tends to be born with lower Apgar scores (*see* p.375) and, consequently, is more likely to require an injection of naloxone in order to help reverse the effect of the morphine.

REGIONAL ANESTHESIA

A variety of regional anesthetics can be used to block the pain associated with labor, delivery, and the completion of the third stage of labor. All of these depend on blocking nerve fibers by injecting them with local anesthetic drugs.

The type of regional anesthetic used depends on the procedure. For example, epidurals can be used throughout labor and all types of delivery, whereas spinal blocks are usually reserved for cesarean sections or manual removal of the placenta. Similarly, if used alone, a pudendal or cervical block will only provide sufficient analgesia for simple forceps or vacuum extraction deliveries.

EPIDURAL BLOCKS

A good epidural block will numb all sensation in your abdomen and stop you from feeling painful uterine contractions. This method of pain relief involves significant medical resources and can be offered routinely in hospitals that provide 24-hour anesthetic coverage in the labor ward. When you are admitted, tell your obstetrician or midwife that you might want to have an epidural so she can alert the anesthesiologist that he or she may be needed at a later stage.

How epidurals work

Your spinal cord is covered by a thick membrane or sheath, which is called the dura, and is further protected by the bony vertebral column that surrounds it (*see* diagram, p.313). The epidural space lies between the bony vertebral column and spinal cord.

The nerve fibers that control your contraction pains pass out of the spinal cord, pierce the dural sheath, and cross through the epidural space before passing between the vertebrae to enter your abdomen. The anesthetic drugs injected into this epidural space penetrate the nerve fibers and block your pain pathway.

If the dosage of anesthetic drug is high, some of the motor nerve fibers that control your legs and bladder will also be blocked, which will make your legs feel quite heavy and difficult to move, and you may no longer be able to tell when your bladder is full.

WHEN ARE EPIDURALS USEFUL?

▶ At your request: to help with painful uterine contractions in first or second stage of labor
▶ Multiple pregnancy
▶ Premature labor
▶ Prolonged labor: posterior positions; inefficient/irregular uterine contractions; suspected cephalopelvic disproportion following induction or augmentation of labor (*see* p.304)
▶ Instrumental delivery: vacuum extraction or forceps
▶ Breech delivery
▶ Elective cesarean section – unless there are specific contraindications (*see* p.362)
▶ Emergency cesarean section – unless there are contraindications or insufficient time
▶ Perineal repairs/episiotomies – where extensive suturing is required

EPIDURALS

▶ **Will the procedure be painful?**

Since the skin of your back is numbed with local anesthetic before the epidural needle is inserted, it is unusual for you to feel anything other than mild discomfort.

▶ **What happens if the epidural does not work?**

If the local anesthetic solution spreads unevenly in the epidural space, you may find that an area of your abdomen or a patch of your thigh is not effectively blocked. Occasionally, the block is only on one side of your body. However, these problems can be quickly resolved by the anesthesiologist, who will adjust the position of the catheter and may ask you to change your position to ensure that the drugs reach all of the nerve fibers evenly. Rarely, the epidural does not "take" and in this situation your anesthesiologist will probably decide to reinsert it.

▶ **I have had a previous back injury. Will I be able to have an epidural?**

The answer to this will depend on the nature and severity of the previous back injury. But generally speaking, it is unusual for an existing back injury to make an epidural out of the question. The most sensible thing

to do is to arrange to meet with one of the obstetric anesthesiologists during the prenatal period so that you can be offered advice regarding the best form of analgesia.

▶ **Can the epidural catheter damage my spine?**

It is extremely rare for the catheter to move inside your spine. If this did happen your caregivers would notice it quickly, since the area of numbness would move to a higher or lower level, which they will fix immediately. It is virtually impossible for an epidural to damage your spinal cord or paralyze you.

▶ **Will I be able to push my baby out in the second stage?**

The answer to this is yes, you should be able to, but it will be more difficult with an epidural. This is because you cannot feel your contractions and will not experience the strong urge to push that accompanies second-stage contractions. You will also be less able to judge where to direct your pushing efforts. However, your nurse, midwife, or obstetrician will help by telling you when the contractions are occurring and between the two of you, you can find a way of using them effectively. The other way of dealing with the

second stage is to let the epidural wear off slightly, so that when you start pushing, you are aware of your contractions and more importantly, you have a better idea of where in your perineum you should be aiming for.

▶ **Am I more likely to have an operative delivery?**

There is a widely held belief that epidurals increase the likelihood of a vacuum, forceps, or cesarean delivery because the woman is less likely to be able to push in the second stage. My personal view is that an experienced midwife or doctor, working with a motivated mother who really wants to deliver vaginally, can usually manage any uncomplicated delays in labor and achieve a normal vaginal delivery.

▶ **Will my baby be affected?**

None of the anesthetic drugs in your epidural will cross the placenta, so your baby will be unaffected by them. However, the epidural may occasionally cause a fall in your blood pressure, which, if sudden or sustained, could result in fetal distress. This is one of the reasons why EFM is routinely performed in women laboring with an epidural.

Preparing for an epidural

If you choose to have an epidural, your midwife or doctor will explain the procedure to you and the anesthesiologist will answer any questions you may have and will obtain your verbal or written consent to proceed.

You will be asked either to lie on a bed on your left side with your legs bent forward or to sit up on the bed and lean forward, stabilizing yourself by leaning your arms on a table. Lying down is usually more comfortable if you are already contracting strongly, whereas the upright position may be the best choice if you are having the anesthetic inserted before an elective cesarean section. Lying on your left side prevents the weight of your uterus from pressing on the major veins in your pelvis, which could make you feel light-headed and reduce the blood supply to your baby during the 20 to 40 minutes it will take to set up the epidural.

You will need to lie or sit very still during this time, but the anesthesiologist will interrupt the procedure each time you have a contraction and wait until it is over. If you have not needed an intravenous fluid drip before now, one will be inserted in your non-writing arm before the procedure starts and an infusion of fluid, usually dextrose-saline, will be started. This ensures that your blood pressure does not drop suddenly when the epidural block starts to work (*see* p. 315).

Your lower back (lumbar region) will be cleaned with antiseptic, sterile covers placed over the rest of your back and legs to reduce the risk of infection, and local anesthetic injected over the site chosen to insert the epidural to numb your skin and minimize your discomfort. It is unusual for the procedure itself to be painful.

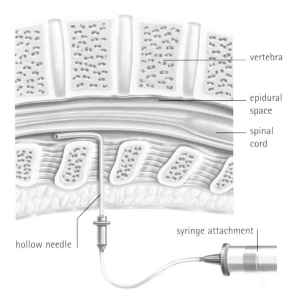

vertebra

epidural space

spinal cord

syringe attachment

hollow needle

INSERTING AN EPIDURAL *A hollow needle is inserted into the epidural space, leaving the spinal cord and its protective dural sheath untouched.*

The procedure

The anesthesiologist will carefully insert a fine hollow needle between two vertebral bones in the lumbar region of your lower back and from there, into the epidural space (*see* above). To check that the needle is in the right place, a small quantity of anesthetic will be injected. If this numbs your abdomen satisfactorily, a thin hollow plastic catheter will be threaded through the hollow needle and positioned into the epidural space. The needle is then removed and a protective bacterial filter is attached to the end of the catheter.

The long length of catheter outside your body will be led up your back and over your shoulder and taped onto your skin. This prevents the catheter from becoming dislodged and allows you to move around and receive small doses of pain relief throughout labor. The first dose of anesthetic will then be injected through the catheter and you will experience a cold sensation like an ice cube running down your lower spine as the drugs reach the spot.

The anesthesiologist and midwife will check your blood pressure immediately, then every 10 minutes for the next 30 minutes, and at regular intervals afterward. An electronic trace of the baby's heart (FHT) will also be performed during this period. In most maternity units, continuous fetal monitoring is advised after an epidural has been inserted, but in an otherwise normal labor intermittent EFM monitoring may be possible. Your abdomen will quickly go numb, but epidural anesthesia that is deep enough to allow a painless operative delivery, such as cesarean section or forceps, takes longer to develop — usually 20 to 30 minutes.

Conventional epidurals also block the nerve fibers that control your bladder. As a result, you will not be aware of developing a full bladder and, consequently, will find it very difficult to urinate on your own. In order to overcome this, a urinary catheter will be gently inserted into your urethra to drain your bladder continuously or intermittently. If mobile epidurals are available in your maternity unit, you will probably be able to urinate without the need of a catheter.

Once your epidural is working effectively, it can be increased regularly to maintain your pain relief. This is usually needed every three to four hours, but the exact timing will depend on each individual's needs and the progress of labor.

Mobile epidurals

Some hospitals have introduced mobile epidurals which use lower doses of drug to block the pain fibers but leave the motor fibers controlling your leg movement relatively unaffected. As a result the woman is usually less numb from her knees down and can be more mobile and benefit from gravity that may help the progress of her labor. She is also less likely to need a urinary catheter to empty her bladder. Another advantage of a mobile epidural is that, since the low-dose increases are usually needed every hour, the analgesia can be tailored more accurately to suit the stage of labor. However, mobile epidurals are not available everywhere.

When an epidural may not be possible

There are few absolute contraindications to having an epidural. They can be summarized as situations where the introduction of the needle could result in a blood clot (hematoma) or abscess (collection of pus) forming and placing pressure on the spinal cord. These are potentially very serious

PREPARING FOR AN EPIDURAL
Sterile covers are placed over your back and then a local anesthetic is injected.

complications, which could lead to paralysis. In reality, they are uncommon, but both inherited and acquired bleeding disorders can put you at risk. Similarly, if you have been taking large doses of anticoagulant drugs (for example, because you have suffered a thrombosis during pregnancy — *see* p.423), an epidural may not be recommended for you.

It is very rare for a pregnant women to have an infection in her lower back, but occasionally it may result from chronic tuberculosis or osteomyelitis (a serious infection of the bone pulp). In these situations, the risk of introducing an infection that could cause an abscess in the epidural or dural space will mean that epidurals and spinal anesthesia are not options.

MEDICAL COMPLICATIONS OF EPIDURALS

HYPOTENSION (low blood pressure)

A fall in your blood pressure is a common side effect of epidurals, usually most marked with the first dose. This is because in addition to blocking pain fibers, the anesthetic drugs also block some of the nerve fibers that control the size of the blood vessels in your pelvis and legs.

▶ As a result, these blood vessels dilate and the blood will tend to pool in them, reducing the volume of blood returning to your heart and head.

▶ This can cause a reduction in the blood flow through the placenta, which in turn reduces the oxygen supply to your baby.

▶ This is why the anesthesiologist will always take the precautions of inserting an intravenous drip before inserting the epidural and checking your blood pressure regularly after the first and subsequent doses of drug are injected. Meanwhile, your doctor or midwife will be monitoring your baby on the EFM machine.

HEADACHES

Headaches are a well-documented side effect of epidurals, but in reality they affect only a small percentage of women.

▶ Severe post-epidural headache is usually the result of accidental puncture of the membrane covering the spinal cord as the needle is being inserted into the epidural space.

▶ The pain is caused by the leakage of small quantities of spinal fluid, which results in traction or pulling of the membranes around the brain. It tends to be relieved by lying down.

▶ Similarly, some mothers report a slight tingling or numbness in one of their limbs and some also suffer from back pain.

▶ I do want to emphasize that, although this all sounds frightening, symptoms are only temporary and nothing to worry about.

▶ All these side effects will disappear, most within hours of the birth, some up to a few weeks later.

BACKACHE

Whether or not epidurals are a genuine cause of long-term backache is a fiercely debated topic in obstetric medicine. There are studies that say that it is and others that conclude that postnatal backache is more likely to be related to preexisting backache, rather than the use of epidural anesthetics during labor.

▶ Poor posture and strain on your sacroiliac joints is almost inevitable in the latter stages of pregnancy and during delivery, but many mothers forget the discomfort they experienced prenatally and blame their postpartum backache on the epidural.

▶ Interestingly, recent reports suggest that the use of low-dose mobile epidurals, which allow the mother to remain upright during labor, may reduce the chances of her experiencing postpartum backache.

SPINAL BLOCK

Much of the general information that I have already offered about epidural blocks also applies to spinal regional anesthetics. The principles in pain relief are the same — namely to block nerve fibers that conduct pain from the pelvic organs. The difference with a spinal block is that instead of trying to avoid piercing the dural sheath (in the case of an epidural), the anesthesiologist deliberately passes the needle through the epidural space and punctures the dural membrane to inject anesthetic drugs into the fluid surrounding the spinal cord.

Over recent years, spinal blocks have become increasingly popular for cesarean sections and emergency obstetric procedures because they are very quick to take effect — the pain relief is almost instantaneous, whereas an epidural will require 20–30 minutes. However, the spinal block is a one-shot technique and lasts for about an hour, possibly two, so it is not a useful method of pain relief throughout labor. Many anesthesiologists favor a combined spinal and epidural approach for cesarean sections. The spinal block offers instant pain relief and the insertion of an additional epidural catheter allows the delivery of small doses of analgesic drugs in the post-operative period.

PUDENDAL BLOCK

This is a injection of local anesthetic into the vaginal tissues surrounding the left- and right-sided pudendal nerves (these supply sensation to the lower half of the vagina). A good pudendal block will markedly reduce pain in the vagina and perineum during the second stage of labor, but it has no effect on the pain of uterine contractions. Therefore, a pudenal block is usually reserved for low, uncomplicated lift-out forceps or vacuum extraction deliveries when the mother has been given no other method of pain relief. The pudendal block will last long enough to perform the delivery of the baby and repair the episiotomy or any vaginal or perineal tears that may have occurred.

Since the area that needs to be injected is deep within the vagina, the pudendal needle is quite long and thick. A pudendal anesthetic will have no effect on the baby and can be used in combination with morphine or nitrous oxide. Although it is usually inserted by a doctor, there is no need for an anesthesiologist to be present. Hence, pudendal blocks are more commonly used in low-risk delivery units that do not have a 24-hour anesthetic service available.

PARACERVICAL BLOCK

This injection of local anesthetic is inserted into the sides of the cervix toward the end of the first stage of labor in order to block the nerve fibers from transmitting the discomfort of cervical dilation. Since a paracervical block takes effect immediately, it is occasionally useful for an emergency forceps delivery.

"Over recent years, spinal blocks have become increasingly popular for cesarean sections and emergency obstetric procedures because they are very quick to take effect."

GENERAL ANESTHESIA

Although over the past 20 years epidurals have become increasingly popular for deliveries by cesarean section, to the extent that they have virtually replaced general anesthesia, a general anesthetic is still sometimes used for abdominal delivery.

HAVING GENERAL ANESTHETIC

All the technical preparations for the operation will be undertaken while you are wide awake in the operating room. Your birth partner will be asked to leave when as you are about to become unconscious. You will be asked to breathe deeply from an oxygen mask for several minutes to increase your oxygen levels, and to lie on the operating table on your left side, which further improves the oxygen supply reaching the placenta.

Only when everything is absolutely ready will the anesthesiologist ask you to inhale the drugs to put you to sleep. This will be followed immediately by the insertion of an endotracheal tube (airway) into your mouth and down your throat, to ensure that oxygen can be delivered to your lungs and to prevent you from regurgitating food or fluid from your stomach. Further drugs to relax your abdominal muscles will be given intravenously and the surgeon is then able to perform the operation very quickly, delivering the baby in a few minutes, before significant amounts of the anesthetic drugs have crossed the placenta.

Overall, you will be asleep for about 45 to 60 minutes. It takes a lot longer to stitch the tissue layers back into place and make sure that the bleeding is under control than it does to open up the uterus and deliver the baby.

REASONS FOR USING A GENERAL ANESTHETIC

MATERNAL REQUEST

Acute fear of needles, backache, the operative procedure (if a cesarean section is planned), or a previous traumatic delivery are all valid reasons for a woman to request a general anesthetic.

OBSTETRIC INDICATIONS

Extreme emergencies, such as severe placental abruption or cord prolapse, are situations where the baby's life is at risk unless delivery is performed immediately. Severe bleeding may prompt the anesthesiologist to perform a general anesthetic, or even convert your regional block to one, because he or she will be better able to stabilize your cardiovascular system. Many favor a general anesthetic for women with an anterior placenta previa (see p.427).

MATERNAL INDICATIONS

Women with heart disease may be best delivered with the help of a general anesthetic. Similarly, there are pregnant women with such severe abnormalities of their spine (such as curvature of the spine or spina bifida) that it is technically too difficult to insert a regional anesthetic.

Coagulation problems following maternal infection, hemorrhage, or preeclampsia can make it unsafe to insert a regional block because of risk of bleeding into the epidural subarachnoid space (see diagram, p.313).

NONPHARMACOLOGICAL PAIN RELIEF

There are various ways in which pain can be reduced without using any drugs, although you should understand that their effectiveness varies and what might help one woman could prove totally ineffective for another.

Broadly speaking these methods of pain relief can be divided into two main groups:
• methods involving the use of equipment or expert practitioners including acupuncture, hypnotherapy, reflexology, transcutaneous electrical nerve stimulation, and water births
• natural methods for use by yourself or with a birth partner including breathing and relaxation, massage, aromatherapy, and homeopathy.

TRANSCUTANEOUS ELECTRICAL NERVE STIMULATION (TENS)

The TENS machine is a battery-operated device, connected by wires to small electrodes that are attached to both sides of your lower back by four adhesive pads. It works by conducting a small electric current through your skin to stimulate the production of endorphins (your body's own natural analgesics), which in turn help block the pain impulses carried by your nerves to your brain. The advantages of TENS are that you remain free to walk around, carrying the handheld control box, and you are in complete control of the frequency and strength of the electrical current. The TENS will not affect your baby in any way. It cannot be used while you are in water, so you will need to take it off while having a relaxing bath, or if you have chosen to have a water birth. Check with your maternity unit to see if they make TENS machines available; if not, you may be able to rent one from another source.

CHILDBIRTH EDUCATION CLASSES

The three most common types of childbirth education classes — Lamaze, Bradley, and Dick-Read — vary greatly but the philosophy behind all three is the same: that the pain of childbirth is increased by fear and tension. All three classes teach the mother breathing exercises and other physical conditioning and encourage the participation of the father in the birthing process, acting as coach. A new approach combines the techniques of Dr. Dick-Read with hypnotherapy.

BREATHING EXERCISES
The most popular methods of natural pain control involve breathing exercises and other physical conditioning.

ACUPUNCTURE

Acupuncture is another method of stimulating your body to produce endorphins. Instead of electrical currents, firm finger pressure or fine needles are applied to specific points on your body by a trained acupuncturist.

The theory behind acupuncture is based on the age-old Chinese belief that a life force called "chi" flows through the body and that medical disorders occur when there are imbalances in this life force. The balance is restored when the "chi" is unblocked by the insertion of fine needles into key areas of the body. Many women find acupuncture helpful during pregnancy to treat symptoms such as morning sickness, headaches, allergies, indigestion, backache and emotional disturbances including depression. It can be a very effective method of pain relief both before and during labor.

If you want to explore this option, you will need to find an acupuncturist who has experience in treating women in labor and is prepared to attend your labor at home or come into the hospital with you.

HYPNOTHERAPY

Hypnotherapy works by suggestion. To relieve the pain of labor this means that you will need to be hypnotized into believing that you can control the pain of your contractions and, as a result, will be less troubled by them. There are several ways to achieve this, but they will all require careful preparation and plenty of practice before you go into labor.

You can hire a hypnotherapist to attend your labor, or you could arrange to have your partner trained to help hypnotize you. Self-hypnosis is a further possibility, but I suspect that for most women, with all that is going on during labor, this

may be more difficult to achieve than anticipated. Nonetheless, hypnosis has been shown to be an effective method of pain relief in labor, may reduce the length of labor, and can be a useful tool with which to improve your emotional state both during and after delivery.

REFLEXOLOGY

In reflexology, gentle pressure or massage is applied to specific points on the feet. This stimulates nerve endings, which helps relieve problems in other parts of the body. During pregnancy, reflexology can be used to help ease backache, general aches and pains and, in combination with more orthodox medical remedies, treat problems such as high blood pressure and gestational diabetes. Some therapists believe that attending regular reflexology sessions during pregnancy allows you the option of using this as a method of pain relief during labor. It is also claimed that reflexology can help the progress of labor by making the uterus contract more efficiently and the cervix dilate faster. If you decide to explore this option, you will need to spend some time with a therapist during pregnancy and make sure that both you and your partner learn exactly where and how to massage the trigger points on your feet during labor.

WATER AND WATER BIRTHS

There is no doubt that immersion in water can relieve pain, particularly in the early stages of labor. The warmth of the water helps relax your muscles and the buoyancy of the water also supports your body, thereby relieving some of the pressure of the baby's head pressing down in your pelvis. Provided that your membranes have not ruptured, you can enjoy sitting in a warm bath either at home or in the maternity unit, for as long as you like during the early stages of labor.

I should mention here that most water-assisted births do not actually take place under water in the birthing pool. Even if you spend most of the first and second stage of labor in the water, most midwives will prefer you to be on "dry land" when the baby is actually born. This is quite simply because they will want to ensure that they have maximum access to you and your baby in the final critical stages of the delivery and also because not all midwives are experienced in supervising water births.

WATER BIRTH *Immersion in water is undoubtedly a valuable method of pain relief, particularly in the early stages of labor.*

In the past, fears were expressed that delivering a baby under water might lead to problems with him inhaling water into the lungs as the first breath is taken. This is unlikely to happen if the baby is brought to the surface quickly, since the umbilical cord continues to deliver a good supply of oxygen for several minutes after the birth, providing it is not cut.

The other concern is that the mother's body temperature may rise if she remains immersed in warm water for a long period of time. This will result in the baby developing a high temperature and increased heart rate, which could lead to hypoxia (lowered oxygen levels). This is why your midwife will be checking your temperature regularly and will advise you to leave the birthing pool if your temperature increases by more than 1.8°F (1°C) during labor or delivery.

BREATHING AND RELAXATION

There is no doubt that we all feel pain more acutely when we are tense or frightened. By learning how to relax and breathe properly, you will feel much calmer and as a result, will be in a much better position to cope with the labor. The breathing and relaxation techniques that you have been taught in your prenatal classes will be put to good use during the last few weeks of pregnancy and particularly when you are in labor. Try to spend a few minutes each day practicing inhaling deeply and exhaling slowly. It is a good idea to enroll your partner's help here, so that you can rely on someone else to remind you of these simple but important principles when you need them most.

In the early stages of labor, you will need to concentrate on breathing in and out slowly as each contraction starts. The secret is to close your eyes

BIRTH STORY

MURIEL, 31, HAS ONE DAUGHTER, TWO YEARS AND ONE MONTH OLD
SECOND BABY KILLIAN, BORN 39 WEEKS + 5 DAYS, WEIGHT 7LB (3.1KG)
LENGTH OF LABOR FROM FIRST CONTRACTION: APPROXIMATELY 12 HOURS

My first baby, Maela, *had been born at home — on dry land. For our second baby, we were planning to have another home birth but this time with the added benefit of a birthing pool. About three days before my due date, I felt a few contractions in the evening. They were quite strong but didn't last very long. The next day, when I took Maela to her day care, I told the staff that I would have the baby that night. I had a strong feeling that labor would start for good that evening — which it did.*

Right from the start, *the contractions felt strong, although manageable. As I was still breastfeeding Maela in the evenings, I fed her hoping she would sleep soundly through the night and this increased the strength of the contractions.*

They were coming every four minutes at that stage and I needed to concentrate on breathing and relaxing. My husband, Steve, started to get the birthing pool ready but we decided not to fill it until Margaret, my midwife, said it was OK to get in.

At about 11pm, *I phoned to tell her that my labor had started and she came around to see how I was doing. I was pleased to see her because I wanted to get into the pool, so I asked her to do an internal examination and it turned out*

that I had not dilated at all but my cervix was fully thinned. Margaret stayed for a little while, then went home. She had told me not to get into the birthing pool, so I had a bath instead and felt it did help a bit. We were taking the contractions one at a time

and trying to accept them or even welcome them (not very successfully). At about 3:30am, I did a self-examination since I am a prenatal instructor. I thought I had reached about 4cm dilation so Steve phoned Margaret again and she arrived at 4am. This time she let me get into the pool and I finally felt I was where I should be to give birth.

The contractions *were coming thick and fast and by 7am I wanted to push. I was in a half squatting position in the pool. The contractions had changed and I could feel the baby's head coming down. Margaret told me to look at her and pant. Our little baby was coming.*

I grabbed the tiny body, *brought it to the surface and held our little boy's head out of the water. We got out of the pool and I then felt the placenta being delivered. Margaret asked me to cut the umbilical cord myself, which I did. It felt wonderful to at last be holding my newborn baby boy.*

> "I grabbed the tiny body, brought it to the surface, and held our little boy's head out of the water."

MASSAGE *This provides a great opportunity for your partner to become physically involved in helping you cope with your labor. Encourage him to master the art of giving a good massage while you are pregnant.*

and inhale calmly through your nose, imagining that the breath is filling every part of your body. Concentrate on relaxing all of your muscles as you do so. Then, exhale slowly through your mouth, this time imagining that you are drawing out and exhaling the pain of your contraction. You may have been taught visualization techniques in your prenatal classes. The principle here is to focus on an image or visit a place in your mind that you find calming and soothing in order to take your mind off the pain. This is a sort of hypnosis and works better for some women than others.

As the contractions become more intense, you will probably find that you need to take shorter breaths, in groups of two or three, since strong

contractions make it difficult to keep up the slow breathing rhythm. At this stage you need to remember that breathing out is the most important part, since the breathing in will take care of itself if you are breathing out properly. My best tip here is to imagine that you are blowing wind through trees and that every breath needs to reach a spot about 12in (30cm) away. I often find that if I sit on the bed beside a woman in strong labor and ask her to ensure that every outward breath hits my nose, that she gets the hang of the new rhythm very quickly. Once achieved, it is easy to get her partner to take up the same position and encourage her to continue breathing out in the same way.

MASSAGE

A good massage is always relaxing and when you are in labor, it can really help relieve backache. If your baby is lying occiput-posterior with his spine closest to your spine and sacral bones, you will be particularly glad to have someone massage your lower back, preferably in slow, firm circular movements just above the cleft of your buttocks.

In addition to the physical comfort this provides, I think that it is also a source of emotional comfort. The fact that someone else is with you and helping you cope with the discomfort or pain helps reduce the feelings of isolation and fear that being in an unknown situation always engenders.

Asking your birth partner to extend the massage to your shoulders, neck, face, forehead, and temples will further help relieve tension and anxiety, enabling you to feel more relaxed during labor. Make sure that the person doing the massage warms his or her hands and removes any jewelry. Using scented oils or creams will help the hands slide easily over the skin.

AROMATHERAPY

In aromatherapy, essential oils are used to soothe and relax the body. It is thought that the scented oils trigger the nervous system to produce natural endorphins and that this helps reduce tension and alleviate some of the pain.

During early labor, the diluted oils can be absorbed through your skin when combined with massaging or by adding them to your bath or birthing pool. Alternatively, you can inhale them from a burner or vaporizer, which gently warms the oils producing a soothing, scented atmosphere.

If you wish to use aromatherapy during labor, you will need to take the oils and the vaporizer with you to the maternity unit. Check beforehand that all of the oils you are planning to use are suitable for use in pregnancy.

HOMEOPATHY

There are a wide variety of homeopathic or herbal remedies that can be used during labor to help relieve stress and discomfort. However, it is important to ensure that you obtain specialized advice about the types of herbs that are suitable and the doses that should be used. Remember, too, that you need to consult with your midwife or doctors about anything you are taking when you are in labor.

MY PRACTICAL TIPS TO HELP WITH LABOR PAINS

Here is a selection of practical tips and thoughts that I hope will come in handy on the big day. I was given them by a close friend and have since shared them with many of my patients.

▶ Labor is like walking a tightrope. The aim is to stay balanced and on the rope.

▶ Therefore, one step at a time, one contraction at a time.

▶ Don't think about how much further you have to walk. No one can tell you how much longer it will be before you give birth.

▶ Concentrate on getting through the next contraction with your breathing techniques.

▶ Don't think about how much pain you may be in in three contractions' time, just think about getting through your next "step" on the tightrope.

▶ Levels of pain vary along the tightrope and are unpredictable. What you are going through now could be better or worse in half an hour's time, so there is no point in worrying about it.

▶ Each contraction gets you one step closer to the end of the tightrope – the birth of your baby – so there is a very good reason to keep going.

▶ You should try to stay fed and hydrated in order to keep your energy levels up.

▶ Aim to find ways of distracting yourself in order to help take your mind off the pain.

▶ Find different positions that help you relieve your pain.

▶ Above all, try your best to stay as relaxed as possible. Tension increases pain.

▶ If you want pain relief, ask for it sooner rather than later and do not hesitate to request a stronger dose of morphine or an increase to your epidural, if you need it.

You may find it helpful to write out a list of your own reminders or practical coping tips for labor and delivery, which you can then pack in your hospital bag with your birthing plan to be sure that they are close by when you need them, or just in case your mind goes totally blank in the middle of your labor.

THE SECOND & THIRD STAGES

The second stage of labor begins when your cervix is fully dilated and ends with the birth of your baby. This is followed by the third stage, when the placenta and membranes are delivered. You will probably feel tired as you enter these phases, but knowing that the end is in sight will, I hope, spur you on through these final stages.

During the second stage of labor your baby is forced through your birth canal by uterine contractions that are now stronger and more frequent, occurring every two to four minutes, and lasting for 60–90 seconds. At this stage, you will probably feel as if you are contracting continuously and that labor has taken on a momentum of its own, which it has. There is now no stopping normal labor until the baby has been expelled from the birth canal. In first labors, the second stage may last for two to three hours, although the average length of time is one hour. In second or subsequent labors, the second stage usually lasts for about 15–20 minutes but can be much quicker and the baby may start to crown before the mother and her midwife recognize that she has entered the second stage.

The third stage of labor — the delivery of the placenta — usually lasts about 10 to 20 minutes, but can be shorter or longer, depending on whether the delivery is actively managed or the placenta is left to expel spontaneously (*see* p.333).

SOMEONE TO LEAN ON

Your partner has an important role during the second and third stages of labor. He will be able to support you physically as you work hard to push your baby out, as well as being able to tell you what he can see as the baby's head emerges. He can also give you invaluable verbal encouragement and reassurance as you both experience the birth of your baby.

"...during the second stage you will probably feel as if you are contracting continuously and that labor has taken on a momentum of its own, which it has."

THE SECOND STAGE OF LABOR

FOR MOST MOTHERS, THE FIRST INDICATION THAT THEY HAVE COMPLETED THE TRANSITION PHASE AND ENTERED THE SECOND STAGE OF LABOR IS THAT THEY DEVELOP A STRONG URGE TO PUSH OR BEAR DOWN. HOWEVER, IT IS IMPORTANT TO REFRAIN FROM PUSHING UNTIL THE MIDWIFE OR NURSE CONFIRMS THAT YOU ARE FULLY DILATED.

"When it is time to start pushing, it is vital that you work as a team with your midwife or nurse."

Once your midwife or nurse confirms that you are fully dilated and that it is time to start pushing, it is vital that you work as a team with her. Remember that the uterine contractions are going to continue involuntarily and what you now need to do is add the force of your voluntary pushing efforts to help expel the baby. Listen carefully to what the midwife or nurse tells you to do.

The idea is to push as much as you can as each contraction peaks and rest in between them. As each uterine contraction starts, you need to take a deep breath, hold it, brace your feet and push downward to force the baby lower into the pelvis. It is important that you contract your diaphragm and abdominal muscles and push down into your pelvis — not into your tummy, which won't help the baby's head descend at all. Try to visualize what is actually happening and where you are pushing. The effort needs to be directed specifically into the vagina and rectum, rather than vaguely "somewhere down there." Ideally, try not to hold one long breath, which can end up depriving you of oxygen and making you feel light-headed. During a good contraction you will probably be able to take three separate breaths and achieve three good pushes.

Knowing when to push

If you have had an epidural, the dose increases will hopefully be timed so that the effects are beginning to wear off by the time you begin the second stage. This means you will be aware of the contractions but will not be in pain. If you are totally numb as a result of the epidural, your midwife will alert you to the start of each contraction, although you may well learn quite quickly to recognize them because you will feel your uterus tighten when you place your hand on your abdomen. Furthermore, you and your partner will also be able to see from the electronic fetal monitor printout when the contractions are beginning and ending. However, I think it is best for you to concentrate on breathing and pushing and leave your partner and midwife or nurse to prompt you when to start and stop. At the end of each contraction try not to relax too quickly — the baby will not continue to move forward unless you relax slowly.

COPING WITH THE SECOND STAGE

TRY TO FIND A COMFORTABLE POSITION THAT IS REASONABLY UPRIGHT. BY THIS STAGE IN LABOR MOST WOMEN FIND THAT THEY WANT TO BE SUPPORTED ON A BED, ALTHOUGH SOME WILL PREFER TO SQUAT OR USE A BIRTHING STOOL. THE MORE UPRIGHT YOU ARE, THE MORE YOU WILL BE HELPED BY GRAVITY AND THE QUICKER YOUR BABY WILL BE BORN.

Many women worry about sounding or looking ridiculous during the second stage of labor. This is not the time to worry about appearances; it is the time to do what feels natural and comfortable for you. If that means grunting and making a lot of noise while you are pushing, that's fine. Similarly, it is pointless feeling worried or embarrassed that you may pass some stool or urine toward the end of the second stage. This is very common and you need to remember that your midwife and doctor have seen it all before.

Interestingly, once they have reached the second stage of labor, most women lose many of their inhibitions and cease being self-conscious. The combination of concentration and instinct take over and there is no time to think about anything other than doing what is necessary to push the baby out.

The other thing that surprises many women in labor is that, compared to some of the late first-stage contractions, the ones in the second stage often seem more bearable. I think this is because you are now actively participating in the labor and this helps dispel some of the tension caused by painful contractions. Although the pushing is hard work, you will feel a sense of satisfaction as each push brings the birth of your baby closer. Knowing that the finishing line is in sight boosts your energy reserves.

POSITIONS FOR SECOND STAGE

SITTING UPRIGHT *Supported by pillows, try to relax your back between contractions.*

KNEELING *A helper on each side supports you, or kneeling on all fours may be more comfortable.*

SQUATTING *This opens the pelvis wide and uses gravity to help push the baby out.*

EPISIOTOMIES AND TEARS

IDEALLY YOU WILL GIVE BIRTH WITHOUT NEEDING AN EPISIOTOMY OR ENDING UP WITH A PERINEAL TEAR. HOWEVER, SHOULD THE NEED ARISE AT THE TIME OF DELIVERY, CAREFUL CONSIDERATION WILL BE GIVEN AS TO WHICH IS LIKELY THE BETTER OPTION FOR YOU. EACH HAS ITS ADVANTAGES AND DISADVANTAGES SO FIND OUT AS MUCH AS YOU CAN ABOUT YOUR HOSPITAL'S POLICY ON EPISIOTOMIES AND PERINEAL TEARS DURING THE PRENATAL PERIOD.

EPISIOTOMIES

An episiotomy is a deliberate incision made in the stretched perineum and vagina to prevent uncontrolled tearing of the mother's tissues as the baby's head is delivered. It used to be thought that an episiotomy not only prevented extensive tears of the perineum but also the development of vaginal prolapse in later life. Since the evidence for the latter is now doubtful, episiotomies are no longer performed routinely.

There are, however, several situations when an episiotomy may be advisable:
▸ tight perineum in a first or subsequent labor
▸ large baby
▸ fetal distress that requires immediate delivery
▸ forceps or vacuum delivery
▸ to protect the head of a premature baby
▸ to protect the baby's head in a vaginal breech delivery (however, most breech babies are delivered by cesarean section).

If you have strong views about episiotomies – either that you want to avoid one at all costs or that you positively want to have one – you should make this clear to your doctor or midwife early in labor.

THE PROCEDURE

If your midwife or doctor judge that you need an episiotomy, they will ask your permission before they perform it. They will then swab down the skin area with antiseptic solution and give you a local anesthetic in your perineum unless you have an active epidural in place.

There are two methods of making the incision, either with a J-shaped mediolateral cut angled away from the vagina and rectum, or with a midline cut straight down from the bottom of the vagina toward the rectum. Both types of incision are made with scissors and because the perineum is tightly stretched, almost paper thin, at the time the cut is made, the bleeding is usually minimal. The advantage of a mediolateral

episiotomy is that it keeps the incision well away from the rectal area. This is particularly relevant if a forceps delivery is anticipated because this may extend the cut. The midline episiotomy avoids several blood vessels and is usually easier to repair, but if it extends during the delivery, it is more likely to tear into the rectum.

Once the baby and placenta have been delivered, your midwife or doctor will repair the episiotomy with stitches. They will probably suggest that your legs be placed in stirrups to make the repair easier. You will be given another dose of anesthetic to make sure you feel no pain during the procedure.

The episiotomy will be sutured in layers, ensuring that all of the tissues are brought together properly to repair the vagina and perineum. The sutures may be interrupted or continuous and either external or buried below the skin. Whatever type is used, they all dissolve and do not need to be taken out.

COMMON CONCERNS

The most common concerns about episiotomies are how much they will hurt afterward and how long they will take to heal. The reality is that they are painful, particularly on the second or third day after the birth, when the stitches often feel tight and uncomfortable. This is the result of the body's natural healing response, which inevitably causes swelling of the traumatized tissues.

Much relief can be obtained from placing ice packs against the episiotomy area and using an inflated rubber ring to sit on. However, the vagina has an excellent blood supply and most cuts will heal in one to two weeks as long as the area is kept as clean and dry as possible. Regular bathing with warm water will help relieve discomfort. It is not necessary

"...make your views on episiotomies clear to your midwife early in your labor"

to add disinfectant solutions and it is important to avoid highly perfumed soaps and oils, which can irritate the healing wound.

In the long run, most women do not have problems with the episiotomy scar but some experience continuing perineal pain, which can be a source of distress, particularly when it causes problems with sexual intercourse. Massaging the scar tissue with emollient or estrogen creams can help make the tissues more supple, and Kegel exercises will usually help improve the situation. If the discomfort continues, advice should be sought regarding further surgery.

PERINEAL TEARS

There are four degrees of perineal tear.

▶ **First degree**: these are minor tears to the vaginal skin around the entrance to the vagina. Most will heal well without any sutures.

▶ **Second degree**: the posterior vaginal wall and perineal muscles are torn but the anal sphincter muscles remain intact. Most will require several sutures to restore the anatomy of the muscles and more superficial tissues.

▶ **Third degree**: the anal sphincter muscles are torn but the mucous lining of the rectum remains intact. These need careful repair to ensure that the muscle layers are realigned.

▶ **Fourth degree**: the anal sphincter muscles are torn to the extent that the rectal mucosa is opened. Considerable skill is required to repair a fourth degree tear because the apex of the tear must be secured to prevent the development of a rectovaginal fistula (a persistent opening between the vagina and the rectum). These tears are uncommon, occurring in only one percent of births. They usually follow forceps or vacuum extraction delivery for a first baby, persistent occipitoposterior positions, or the delivery of a baby weighing more than 9lb (4kg).

EPISIOTOMY CUTS

MEDIOLATERAL *The cut is angled down and away from the vagina and the perineum into the muscle.*

MIDLINE *The cut is performed straight down into the perineum, between the vagina and anus.*

THE THIRD STAGE OF LABOR

THE THIRD STAGE OF LABOR INVOLVES THE DELIVERY OF THE PLACENTA AND MEMBRANES. THE MINUTES AFTER BIRTH ARE INVARIABLY AN EMOTIONAL TIME AND YOU AND YOUR PARTNER WILL PROBABLY BE AWARE ONLY OF THE FACT THAT YOU ARE FINALLY CUDDLING YOUR NEW BABY.

CUTTING THE CORD

CUTTING THE CORD *This is a straightforward procedure. If your partner would like to do it, let your midwife or doctor know in advance.*

Many women request that the baby be placed on their tummy immediately after delivery to start the bonding process. The cord will still be attached at this point and will continue to pulsate for one to three minutes. Unless the baby has been distressed during the delivery and is in need of prompt attention from the neonatologists, there is no hurry to clamp and cut the cord. Indeed, it is a positive advantage to wait for a few minutes, since a significant amount of blood will drain from the placenta into the baby (babies have a relatively small total blood volume), most of it in the first 30 seconds after the birth and the remainder in the next two to three minutes.

The midwife will place two clamps in the middle of the long umbilical cord, 1–2in (3–5cm) apart, to prevent bleeding from the baby at one end and from the placenta at the other end. She will then cut the cord between the two clamps, or your partner can cut it. Later on, the cord will be trimmed further and a plastic clip will be attached to the stump near your baby's umbilicus. Over the next few days this bit of remaining cord will shrink and the plastic clamp will either fall off or be removed, leaving the baby with a little knot of tissue at the umbilicus, or belly button, that will soon disappear.

DELIVERY OF THE PLACENTA

Having cut the cord, the next thing your midwife or doctor will do (in addition to checking your baby) is make sure that the placenta is delivered correctly and promptly. After the baby is born, continuing uterine contractions and the shrinking of the uterus considerably reduces the size of the placental bed. The placenta buckles inward, tearing the blood vessels and attachments to the uterine wall. This results in a small hemorrhage behind the placenta which further helps it separate from the uterus. The process starts as soon as the baby is born and is usually complete in five minutes. However, the placenta is usually retained within the uterus because the membranes take more time to strip away from the uterine wall. Once this placental separation has occurred, the uterine muscular wall clamps down on the blood vessels in the placental bed and encourages the formation of clots in the torn ends, reducing further blood loss.

Traditional management

When the placenta and membranes are allowed to separate from the uterus on their own and no attempt is made to deliver them until clear signs of separation are seen, this is described as traditional management of the third stage of labor. These signs include a gush of blood (the retroplacental hemorrhage), which is followed by contractions that make the fundus of the uterus rise in the abdomen. There is also a lengthening of the umbilical cord that is visible outside the vagina and you will experience an urge to bear down, which is a clear sign that the placenta has separated and that the uterus is trying to expel it into the vagina. When these events have occurred (which generally take about 20 minutes), the midwife or doctor will place her hand above your pubic bone in order to hold the uterus in place, and will ask you to give a short push while she gently pulls the umbilical cord and encourages the separated placenta to leave the vagina, followed by the membranes and the retroplacental blood clot. The midwife or doctor will then massage the uterus firmly to help contract it further and prevent any more bleeding. Further massaging of the uterus may be needed at regular intervals during the first hour after the birth to keep it firmly contracted.

"...you can speed up the natural process by placing your baby at your breast..."

If you would prefer not to have medical intervention in the third stage, you can speed up the natural process and try to avoid heavy bleeding by placing your baby at your breast and encouraging breast feeding as soon as possible. Suckling stimulates the release of oxytocin, which causes your uterus to contract and the placenta to separate from the uterine walls. Making sure that your bladder is empty will also help deliver the placenta promptly.

Active management

The reason why many maternity units advise active management of the third stage is because bleeding after the delivery of the baby and placenta can be torrential. Indeed, postpartum hemorrhage (*see* p.335) remains the most important cause of maternal death worldwide. During the prenatal period, your midwives will have discussed the third stage with you and explained that active management involves giving you an injection of oxytocin in your thigh muscle as soon as the baby's head and first shoulder have delivered. Oxytocin helps firmly contract the uterus, separate and start to expel the placenta and membranes, and then maintain the uterine contraction without any relaxation for about 45 minutes. Having waited for the uterus to firmly contract, your midwife or doctor will place a protective hand above your pubic bone in order to prevent the uterus from being pulled downward when the umbilical cord is gently pulled. This process is called controlled cord traction (CCT) and it usually results in prompt delivery of the placenta and membranes. If undue force is used at this stage it can lead to uterine inversion — the uterus is literally turned inside out.

YOUR PHYSICAL RESPONSE

Immediately before or after the delivery of the placenta, it is common for mothers to experience strange physical reactions in response to the enormous effort of giving birth. You may find yourself shivering and shaking uncontrollably and your teeth chattering violently, as if you have suddenly been exposed to extreme cold. This response is frequently accompanied by intense nausea. Since you are likely to have an empty stomach at this point, this will probably amount only to retching of bile and watery fluids. Rest assured that these reactions are completely normal and common. Your midwife will not be surprised, having seen them many times before, and will help you and your partner deal with them.

CHECKING THE PLACENTA AND MEMBRANES

As soon as the placenta and membranes are delivered, they will be checked to make sure that they are complete. A healthy term placenta weighs about 1lb 2oz (500g), measures about 8–10in (20–25cm) in diameter, and looks like a spongy disk. Any unusual appearances will prompt your midwife or doctor to send it to the pathology laboratory for analysis. In the vast majority of cases, the placenta will be unremarkable and, after weighing it and recording all the observations in your notes, it will be disposed of by the hospital. You may want to look at this extraordinary lifeline before it is discarded.

FETAL SURFACE *This smooth side of the placenta has blood vessels radiating out from the umbilical cord.*

WHEN PROBLEMS ARISE

Occasionally, complications can arise during the third stage of labor.

A retained placenta is one that remains within the uterus over 30 minutes after delivery of the baby. About one percent of deliveries are complicated by this and it is more likely to occur after very premature births because the umbilical cord is thinner and may snap more easily during cord traction. Since a retained placenta is often associated with postpartum hemorrhage, prompt action is needed to remove it. This is usually done in the operating room.

Early (primary) postpartum hemorrhage (PPH) is defined as the loss of about one pint (500ml) of blood from the uterus or vagina within 24 hours of delivery of the baby. Approximately six percent of deliveries are complicated by a PPH, but it is more likely to follow a prolonged labor or a forceps, vacuum extraction, or cesarean delivery. The incidence of PPH has fallen over the last 50 years because of improved awareness of the situations that are likely to cause it and either preventive management or prompt treatment when it occurs. Active management of the third stage of labor is probably the most important preventive measure responsible for the reduction, but prenatal

"...active management of the third stage has contributed to the reduction in PPH."

diagnosis of placenta previa (*see* p.427), improved anesthetic techniques, and the realization that prolonged or difficult labors are more likely to lead to a PPH have also contributed to the reduction.

When a serious PPH does occur, strict labor ward protocols, involvement of senior obstetricians and anesthesiologists, improvements in intensive care, readily available blood transfusions, better antibiotics, and a major reduction in the number of women who become severely anemic during pregnancy has meant that the number of maternal deaths has reduced significantly.

Late (secondary) postpartum hemorrhage is defined as any sudden loss of blood from the uterus or vagina, regardless of the volume of blood, from 24 hours to six weeks after the delivery. Late PPH occurs in 1 in 50–200 births, and is usually caused by retained pieces of placenta or membranes in the uterus. These frequently become infected when they are left in the uterine cavity and the inflammation that accompanies the infection further contributes to the bleeding. Usually the mother complains of feeling ill with pain and tenderness in the lower abdomen and develops a temperature and a smelly vaginal discharge. The problem needs to be identified quickly and treated with antibiotics. The removal of the retained tissues under general anesthetic is also usually required to resolve most late PPHs.

WHEN HELP IS NEEDED

Although all women and their caregivers hope for a
full-term pregnancy and an uncomplicated delivery,
when events make this difficult or impossible, extra
medical help will be needed to provide safety to both
the mother and baby. If this should happen to you,
being aware of what can occur during labor and birth
and the possible outcomes will help you make
informed decisions along the way.

CONTENTS

PREMATURE LABOR

339 Causes of premature labor

340 Signs of premature labor

341 Giving birth to a premature baby

342 Problems your baby may encounter

343 After the birth

MULTIPLE BIRTHS

345 Delivering twins

346 Vaginal delivery of twins

349 Birth story

ASSISTED DELIVERIES

352 Vacuum extraction

354 Forceps delivery

356 Breech births

358 Birth story

CESAREAN BIRTH

362 Elective or emergency sections

365 What to expect in the operating room

PREMATURE LABOR

Around 10 percent of births in Canada are classified as premature because they occur before 37 weeks. However, thanks to the enormous advances that have been made in neonatal care over the past 10 years, babies born after 30 weeks who have not had serious complications in utero are unlikely to experience major long-term developmental problems.

The most important thing to remember here is that the longer a healthy normal baby stays in utero and the greater its birth weight, the lower the chances of the baby experiencing problems after delivery and the shorter the time that he or she will have to spend in an intensive care baby unit. The chances of survival without handicap for a baby born at 23 weeks is only one percent, but with the passage of each week, the chance of survival improves significantly, so that at 26 weeks nearly one quarter will survive unharmed and by 30 weeks the risk of handicap is very small. This is the reason every effort will be made to keep your baby in utero for as long as possible, provided there are no problems that suggest it would be better cared for in the outside world. It is also important to understand that only about 1.5 percent of premature births occur before 32 weeks, and below 28 weeks the figure is less than 0.5–1 percent.

Much time is spent in prenatal clinics trying to identify those pregnant women who are at greater risk of going into premature labor. In the Journey section of this book I have included many mentions of the possible symptoms that may help you, your midwife, and doctor to recognize that you are at risk of delivering your baby prematurely.

CAUSES OF PREMATURE BIRTH

There are many reasons for premature delivery, but despite the research to try to predict why a pregnant woman might go into premature labor or why her membranes may rupture weeks before the due date, we are still unable to prevent the vast majority of preterm births. Indeed, we do not know exactly what triggers labor itself, let alone what the exact mechanisms are that set this trigger off too early. One theory focuses on the role of hormones secreted by the baby, the mother, or the placenta, while another indicates that the levels of a

"...every effort will be made to keep your baby in utero for as long as possible..."

specific protein that is present in the vagina and cervix will increase markedly when a woman is about to go into labor. It appears that infection plays a part in 20–40 percent of all premature births, and if you have already had a premature baby but there was not a clear medical reason for the early birth, then statistically you are more likely to have another premature birth.

However, babies sometimes have to be delivered early for medical reasons. These include preeclampsia, high blood pressure, diabetes, placental insufficiency, placental abruption, and bleeding from placenta previa (*see* pp.425–27). If you have already had a preterm baby as a result of any of the above, doctors will keep a close eye on you to try to avoid the same thing happening again.

SIGNS OF PREMATURE LABOR

If your water breaks before 37 weeks or you experience abdominal pain or vaginal bleeding or you start to develop uterine contractions, you should contact the labor ward and make sure that you are promptly examined by a midwife or doctor. They will check whether your uterus is contracting and the baby's position and then perform an internal examination to assess the cervix, determine the presenting part, and check that the umbilical cord has not prolapsed (*see* p.429). They will also be looking for signs of infection, now that the protective membranes have gone. If there is a significant risk of infection, they will want to induce or augment uterine contractions with an oxytocin drip (*see* p.297) to deliver your baby as quickly as possible. Sometimes you will need to deliver by cesarean section, especially if you or your baby are showing signs of distress, the presentation and lie of the baby are not optimal, or the cervix is very unripe.

You must also call the labor unit at once if your water has not broken but you think you are getting contractions, or if you have had a show. You will almost certainly be advised to go to the hospital, after which you will be monitored closely and advised to have complete bed rest. You may also be given the drug ritodrine or magnesium sulfate intravenously. Ritodrine (which works very much like the albuterol inhalers used by people with asthma) relaxes the uterus and helps stop contractions.

If your membranes are intact and your contractions are only mild, then bed rest, with or without drugs, may halt the beginning of labor, even if your cervix has begun to dilate. You will be able to go home as soon as your contractions have ceased, although you will need to take it easy for the remainder of the pregnancy and avoid having sex.

However, if contractions are well established it is difficult, even with the use of drugs, to delay delivery by much more than 48 hours. Even this short time

"If your membranes are intact and your contractions mild, bed rest may halt the beginnings of labor..."

can be of critical importance for your baby. It allows you to be transferred to a hospital with a NICU and gives time for a dose of prenatal steroids to be given to you to help mature your baby's lungs (*see* p.342). Before 34 weeks, the advantages of the baby remaining in utero are usually greater than those of being delivered, so you may be advised to take one of the drugs mentioned earlier, in an attempt to stop or reduce the uterine contractions. However, none of the tocolytic drugs (those used to help stop contractions) currently available can be thought of as reliable once it has been triggered to start early in pregnancy.

GIVING BIRTH TO A PREMATURE BABY

If doctors cannot halt your labor, then, for all intents and purposes, you will go through a normal delivery as long as your baby does not show signs of distress, in which case a cesarean section will be done. The good news is that your labor is likely to be a little shorter than that for a fattened-up, full-term baby. The head will be just that little bit smaller and this can make all the difference between needing an episiotomy and having just a little minor tearing or nothing at all. Despite this, doctors may decide to use forceps (and therefore do an episiotomy) to protect the baby's head as it descends the birth canal, because a premature baby's skull will be softer than that of a full-term baby. You will probably be advised to avoid morphine as a means of pain relief, because this can slow down an already fragile baby in its attempt to move down the birth canal and it causes problems after delivery because the respiratory system is depressed.

> "...a preterm labor is likely to be shorter than that for a fattened-up, full-term baby."

It is unlikely that you will be allowed to attempt a vaginal birth if your baby is breech, even if you are already in labor, because this will be considered too risky (*see* p.356), so a cesarean section will be done instead. Similarly, if you have developed a medical condition, such as placental abruption, bleeding from the placenta, or preeclampsia, vaginal delivery will be too dangerous for your premature baby and a cesarean section will be advised.

If your premature baby is delivered vaginally, you will be attended by a pediatrician as well as by a midwife and an obstetrician. Immediately after the birth, the baby will be assessed and given help breathing if necessary. Depending on the degree of prematurity, you may have the opportunity to hold your baby briefly before he is taken to the NICU. If your hospital does not have a dedicated NICU, you will either have been transferred to the nearest suitable maternity unit before the actual delivery, or your baby will be transferred there in a special ambulance immediately after the birth.

PROBLEMS YOUR BABY MAY ENCOUNTER

Most healthy babies born at or before 35 weeks will need help from a neonatal intensive care unit (NICU) because they are likely to experience breathing difficulties and require help with feeding. The breathing problems result from the fact that their lungs are not yet sufficiently developed and elastic enough to breathe unaided.

As discussed in the Journey section (*see* p.231) the fetal lungs continue to develop more tiny airways and alveoli well into the third trimester of pregnancy and only start to produce surfactant from about 26 weeks. This detergent-like substance coats the developing alveoli, allowing them to remain open and available for oxygen exchange after birth. When there is little surfactant present, the lungs are rigid and collapse down easily, which makes every breath the newly born premature baby takes more difficult. This is why a mechanical ventilator is often needed to push the air into and out of the immature lungs, and the neonatal doctors may suggest spraying some artificial surfactant into the baby's lungs. After 35 weeks there is usually enough surfactant available to make full ventilation unnecessary, although your baby may require some little tubes placed in his nose for a short time to ensure that sufficient oxygen is readily available.

If you have to be delivered at or before 35 weeks, you will be given an injection of steroids (usually betamethasone) to speed up the production of surfactant in the baby's lungs. The steroids need 24 to 48 hours to reach their full effect, so in cases of threatened preterm labor, the doctors will always try to

IN SAFE HANDS *Don't be alarmed by the equipment you encounter in the intensive care unit. The machinery and tubes are there to monitor your preterm baby and to help her breathe and feed until she is able to do so for herself.*

delay the delivery for enough time to allow the steroids to work. Similarly, your baby's sucking reflex is poorly developed before 35 weeks (*see* p.231) and the digestive system is often too immature to cope with large liquid feedings. This is why many premature babies need to be tube fed with small quantities of milk (preferably expressed breast milk) at frequent intervals. They soon get used to larger meals and I often find myself telling anxious mothers who have a baby in the NICU that when their baby can deal with 2fl oz (60ml) of tube feeding every three to four hours, she is likely to be discharged from the NICU very soon. This is a clear indication that she will now be capable of suckling on her mother's breast or from a formula milk bottle.

AFTER THE BIRTH

Rest assured that, although the birth of a premature baby is invariably very high-tech, it is vital to assemble all the machines, equipment, and staff to make sure that your baby is given the best care possible at this delicate stage in her life. The medical staff attending the birth will be well aware of how upsetting the whole situation usually is for parents—particularly first-time parents with no previous experience in childbirth—and they will do their best to make things easier for you. They will take a photograph of your baby within minutes of birth, so that you can put it beside your bed and get to know your baby's face. They will also give you all the time you need to ask questions, both during and after the birth, and will do everything in their power to reassure you and to explain the situation clearly to you.

EXPRESSING MILK
A positive way of getting involved with helping care for your premature baby is to express milk. You will be providing her with the best nutrition available.

On pages 404 and 405, I provide more detailed information on caring for premature babies, particularly during their stay in the NICU. Remember, though, that however distressing the early days and weeks can be, the vast majority of premature babies go on to become strapping toddlers who are every bit as healthy as their full-term peers.

My daughters were delivered by emergency cesarean section after I went into premature labor at 33 weeks. They were both a reasonable size for twin babies of their gestational age and had not had any problems prenatally. Nonetheless, they both needed assistance with breathing and feeding and were in the NICU for four weeks. The pediatricians were very careful to carry out numerous checks on them before they allowed me to take them home. It took only a month or two for them to catch up in their growth to singletons who were carried to term and if you could see them now (they are taller and heavier than all of their classmates), you would be reassured that premature twins grow up able to cope with just about anything.

MULTIPLE BIRTHS

The number of twin and triplet pregnancies has increased over the last 10 to 20 years and currently some three percent of all deliveries in Canada are multiple births. This rise is mainly due to the wider availability of assisted fertility treatments, which increase the chances of more than one egg being fertilized at the time of conception. Another important factor is that more women are embarking on pregnancies later in life, and rising maternal age increases the incidence of nonidentical (dizygotic) twin pregnancies.

Multiple pregnancies are at greater risk of a variety of complications, in particular premature delivery, fetal growth restriction, preeclampsia, anemia, placenta previa (*see* pp.423–28), and twin-to-twin transfusion syndrome (*see* p.346). Furthermore, the incidence of cerebral palsy is dramatically higher for multiple births compared to singletons. As a result, prenatal care for mothers with a multiple pregnancy is more closely monitored and the delivery is usually planned in a hospital unit where emergency help is always available.

Even if the pregnancy has been uncomplicated, 50 percent of twins will be born prematurely, before 37 weeks, and these babies are more likely to need help from an NICU. This is because they tend to be smaller than singleton babies and, irrespective of their actual birthweight, also behave less maturely than singletons and often require some assistance with breathing and feeding during the first few days or weeks of their lives.

TRIPLETS *The three babies visible in this scan will be delivered in a hospital unit where emergency help is readily available.*

DELIVERING TWINS

The main concern in a vaginal twin birth is the delivery of the second twin. Even if the first baby is head down and the labor starts spontaneously and progresses smoothly, there is no way of knowing how the second twin will cope with the mechanics of a hasty descent through the birth canal until the first twin has been delivered. No woman wants to go through labor and the vaginal delivery of her first twin, only to be told that she needs to undergo an emergency cesarean section to deliver her second baby. As a result, an increasing number of twin and all triplet (and higher number) pregnancies are now delivered by cesarean section. This may be an emergency procedure if the labor is very premature or if complications develop, or an elective procedure because the risks of a vaginal delivery are generally considered to be too great. If there are no maternal or fetal reasons to perform the elective cesarean section sooner, delivery should be delayed until 37–38 weeks to avoid neonatal respiratory problems. A cesarean delivery of twins is likely to be planned when:

- the mother requests this rather than vaginal delivery
- the first twin is not presenting head first
- placenta previa is diagnosed on an ultrasound scan
- intrauterine growth restriction (*see* p.428) is identified
- the birthweight of the second twin is estimated to be 1lb (500g) greater than that of the first
- one or both of the twins has a physical abnormality
- twin-to-twin transfusion syndrome is present. This disorder in the blood supply to identical twins only affects monochorionic pregnancies and has serious consequences because the blood vessels in the shared placenta favor one twin over the other — early delivery is usually required to save the life of the smaller twin.
- the babies are conjoined or Siamese twins. An attempt to separate them surgically may be attempted after delivery, depending on which organs they share.

Labor may be induced for twin pregnancies in which the first twin is cephalic at 37–38 weeks, since many women find the discomfort of late twin pregnancy difficult to deal with. Complications are also more likely to develop after this date. Recent studies have shown there is no significant increase in the rate of emergency cesarean section or reduction in the likelihood of delivering a healthy baby if labor is induced at 37 weeks.

VAGINAL DELIVERY OF TWINS

If you are planning a vaginal delivery for your twins, you will be carefully reviewed in the early stages of labor, to ensure that nothing has happened since the last clinic visit to suggest the plan should be revised. The labor ward staff will monitor both babies and will also perform an ultrasound to check their sizes and positions. If you have a scar in your uterus from a previous cesarean section or surgery, a vaginal delivery may be possible if the first twin is presenting cephalically.

Since there will need to be a lot of people on hand during a twin delivery (one or more obstetricians, an anesthesiologist, two midwives, and two pediatricians), you will be cared for in a larger than normal delivery room equipped to carry out emergency procedures. You will most probably have an epidural anesthetic so an emergency cesarean can be carried out without delay at any stage. A good epidural block is particularly important during the second stage of labor when external or internal manipulation to turn the second twin into a cephalic lie or a breech extraction may be required.

During labor, continuous electronic fetal monitoring (*see* p.292) is advisable and attaching a scalp clip to the first twin ensures that the tracings from the abdominal monitor on the second twin can be read without confusion. The first stage of labor is often a little shorter than for a singleton. If progress is slow, this is usually seen as an ominous sign prompting cesarean delivery. The use of oxytocin to augment labor is rarely considered to be the best option. The second stage of labor, before the delivery of the first twin, is essentially the same as for a single baby, but there will always be an anesthesiologist and obstetrician present in addition to the midwives and pediatricians. Immediately after the delivery of the first twin, the umbilical cord is clamped in two places (near the baby and at the end of the cord leading to the placenta) to prevent the transfusion of placental blood away from the second twin, who may remain in utero for some time.

"The first stage of a twin labor is often a little shorter than for a singleton."

Delivery of the second twin

The obstetrician will now palpate your abdomen to establish the lie of the second twin. If it is transverse, gentle external pressure will be applied to achieve a longitudinal lie (the baby lying parallel to your spine), and the midwife or nurse will be asked to maintain this position by gentle manual pressure.

If there is any uncertainty as to whether the presentation is cephalic or breech, a quick ultrasound scan can be performed. External cephalic version (turning a baby from presenting breech to head first, *see* p.271) for a breech presentation of a second twin is uncommon practice because it often results in further complications, which may then necessitate an emergency cesarean section. A smooth assisted breech delivery (*see* pp.356–59) is preferable.

There are no strict rules as to how long the second stage for twin two should be allowed to continue, but if delivery cannot be achieved within 30 minutes it is highly likely that an emergency cesarean section will be needed. Because the uterine contractions frequently diminish after the delivery of the first baby, most obstetricians will already have an oxytocin infusion in place and this will be started as soon as a longitudinal lie has been confirmed, in order to help drive the presenting part of twin two into your pelvis.

Ideally, the membranes around your second baby are left intact until the baby has descended further through your cervix and into the vagina, which helps prevent the cervix from closing. If the membranes rupture and there is a delay in the delivery, the obstetrician will insert a hand into your vagina and up into your uterus to guide the head downward (toward the helping hands of a pair of forceps or a vacuum extractor) or grasp hold of the breech or legs and assist the vaginal delivery. Occasionally, it may be better to perform an internal version or manipulation in the uterine cavity, turning a breech presentation through 180 degrees, but more usually the delivery continues as an assisted breech (*see* pp.357–59). Because of the limited experience of modern-day obstetricians, the incidence of cesarean section for twin two has increased.

Third stage of a twin birth

Active management of the third stage of labor (*see* p.333) is especially important in twin births since the risk of postpartum hemorrhage is higher because the uterus is more distended. As soon as your second twin is delivered, the doctors will increase the oxytocin infusion and you will be given an intramuscular injection of methylergonovine maleate or ergonovine. The infusion may need to be continued for some time after the delivery to make sure that your uterus remains contracted.

TWIN BIRTHS *These can be more complicated than singleton births, but they are also very special with the end result invariably being the safe delivery of two perfect babies.*

Twin births are special. I speak here as a mother and an obstetrician, having been blessed with twin daughters. Since the birth is not always straightforward and often involves babies that are premature and small for dates, pediatricians will monitor them carefully and will not hesitate to admit them to the NICU if they have any concerns. This is distressing and alarming for parents, but do remember that in the vast majority of cases this is a short, almost routine visit and the outcome is a happy one. Rest assured that the pediatric staff will keep you fully informed about your babies' progress and will be anxious to reunite them with you as soon as possible.

Support for the parents of multiple pregnancies is important, and detailed information and practical support to help them prepare for caring for their babies is best started in prenatal classes. After the birth, joining a local twin club will offer the great advantage of being put in touch with experienced parents who are undoubtedly one of the best sources of advice for others in the same situation (*see* p.438).

BIRTH STORY

DEBORAH, 32, FIRST PREGNANCY

NICHOLAS AND PATRICK, BORN 37 WEEKS + 5 DAYS,

NICHOLAS WEIGHED 5LB (2.25KG), PATRICK WEIGHED 7LB (3.15KG)

I discovered *I was carrying identical twins at my 12-week scan and, after I recovered from the shock, I found that my pregnancy progressed well. I was seen regularly by my consultant from 28 weeks onward and was told there was no reason why I could not attempt a vaginal delivery.*

My 36-week scan showed that the babies were growing well. But the following scan, at 37 weeks + 4 days, showed that one twin had stopped growing. This was because, like all identical twins, the babies were sharing a placenta but had separate amniotic sacs. In other words, they were monochorionic but diamniotic twins. The scan took place at 4pm and I was immediately scheduled for a cesarean section the following morning. There was no question of inducting a vaginal birth, especially since the consultant could see from the scan that one baby was lying transverse. Nobody could know what would happen during labor. My biggest fear all along had been that I might have one baby vaginally, only to end up with a cesarean section for the second twin. My top priority was to have both babies safely and it didn't matter to me how they came out. I had been present at my cousin's vaginal birth and I couldn't see what was so appealing about all that pain. As a result, I was very happy at the prospect of the cesarean section.*

The birth itself *was very straightforward and calm. My*

> "My top priority was to have both babies safely and it didn't matter how they came out."

husband was in the operating room with me, and both babies came out without any problems. Little Nicholas was born first and it turns out he had been cephalic and very much ready to come out. But he was the one who had stopped growing. Patrick was lying transverse, with one hand nonchalantly behind his ear, and he was born five minutes later. I don't think he felt like leaving his warm home. I asked to see the placenta: Nicholas' side was all crusty and dried up, while Patrick's was red and healthy. It was clear what had happened and I'm so grateful that the doctors spotted the problem and were able to act on it at once.*

The staff *were fantastic, although I was more or less sent out of the hospital after four days because they were short on beds.*

After two months, I have learned to be very organized. I breastfed for one month but it was very difficult, so I now bottle-feed and the twins almost sleep through the night. Nicholas' weight is catching up with his younger, heavier brother and I feel blessed to have them both in such good health.

ASSISTED DELIVERIES

The term assisted or instrumental delivery can sound rather frightening and I want to remind you that the vast majority of babies are still delivered vaginally without any need for assistance or medical intervention. However, if labor has been prolonged or the second stage is not progressing smoothly, it may be necessary to assist the vaginal delivery with the use of instruments such as forceps or a vacuum extractor.

It is important to understand that the aim of an assisted delivery is to guide the baby out of the birth canal with the help of your uterine contractions pushing the baby from above. The forceps or vacuum equipment are not designed to pull the baby out on their own. Most assisted deliveries are performed by an experienced obstetrician but, in some units, senior midwives have received special training and are able to perform vacuum extraction deliveries and low lift-out forceps. For either a forceps or a vacuum extraction, your doctor or midwife will request that you are in the lithotomy position with your legs supported by stirrups so that they have maximum visibility and access to your baby during the delivery. Whether or not you need an episiotomy will depend on individual circumstances and considerations (see pp.330–31). Most forceps deliveries will require an episiotomy but if you are having a vacuum extraction you may not need one.

EFFECTS OF INSTRUMENTAL DELIVERIES

Babies born by assisted vaginal delivery often bear the marks of the instruments after the birth, but don't worry because these usually disappear within a few days. After a vacuum extraction, there will always be a swelling on the scalp where the suction cup was placed and this can sometimes lead to extensive bruising and may even cause the baby to become jaundiced. With forceps, the skull or face may be bruised and appear slightly misshapen at the sites where the blades were placed. However, it is important to remember that a baby's skull is designed to cope with being put under pressure or compressed in some way during the birth, so these instruments are highly unlikely to pose any serious threat to your baby's long-term well-being.

"...a baby's skull is designed to cope with pressure during birth..."

VACUUM EXTRACTION

THE USE OF THE VACUUM EXTRACTOR HAS BECOME INCREASINGLY POPULAR OVER THE PAST FEW YEARS AND, IN MANY OBSTETRIC UNITS, THIS IS NOW THE INSTRUMENT OF CHOICE FOR ASSISTED VAGINAL DELIVERIES, VIRTUALLY REPLACING THE USE OF FORCEPS.

HOW THE VACUUM EXTRACTOR WORKS

Vacuum extraction equipment essentially consists of a cup made of metal or plastic that has a chain or a handle. The cup is attached to a tube, which connects with suction apparatus. The cup is positioned over the crown (occiput) of the baby's head and is held firmly against the scalp while a vacuum is gently built up, using a hand or electrical pump. This sucks some of the scalp tissue into the cup and the swelling that develops on the baby's head effectively produces a firm attachment.

"...the vacuum extractor is often the instrument of choice for assisted vaginal deliveries..."

When suitable vacuum pressure has been achieved, the edges of the suction cup are checked to ensure that no maternal tissues have been trapped. Traction is applied by pulling on the chain or plastic handle attached to the cup, while the mother bears down during a contraction. Once the head has crowned, the vacuum is released and the cup is removed. After allowing time for the baby's head to rotate externally, delivery of the shoulders and body proceeds as normal. The principle of vacuum extraction is that the line of traction should follow the mother's pelvic curve, since this is the pathway of least resistance for the baby's head as it descends through her birth canal.

ADVANTAGES AND DISADVANTAGES

The greatest advantage of the vacuum is that, if the baby's head is not directly in the occipito-anterior position, it can still rotate automatically as it descends through the maternal pelvis. Hence it is easier for the diameters of the head to negotiate the various diameters of the maternal pelvis (*see* p.328). Other important advantages of the vacuum extractor are that, unlike the use of forceps, it does not increase the diameter of the fetal head. As a result, there is less risk of damage to the vagina and perineum compared to a forceps delivery and some women may not require an episiotomy. In addition, the requirements for pain relief are usually less, although, in an ideal world, an effective regional block should always be in place before an instrumental vaginal delivery is attempted.

The disadvantage of the vacuum is that the delivery tends to be slower, because time is required to set up the equipment and achieve good pressue and also because the cup can become dislodged. However, in experienced hands, a good vacuum application pressure can usually be developed in about two minutes, about the same as the gap between contractions during the second stage of labor. If careful attention is paid to the positioning of the cup, the number that become dislodged is reduced and the number of smooth, swift vacuum deliveries increases.

If the baby's head has not been delivered after three or four good contractions, or after the cap has been in place for a total of 15 minutes, an alternative means of delivery needs to be considered.

POSSIBLE COMPLICATIONS

Although maternal complications after vacuum delivery are uncommon, fetal complications, including superficial scalp injuries, bruising, and bleeding into the head, can occur even after an apparently simple procedure but are more likely when the cap has become dislodged or the delivery is prolonged. A scalp swelling is always present after a vacuum extraction and is usually more extensive when a metal cup has been used. It invariably subsides in a few days with no harmful effects.

Superficial scalp injuries occur in about 12 percent of vacuum deliveries and again it is rare for them to lead to any long-term complications. However, cephalohematomas (a collection of blood beneath the top layer of the skull bones) develop in about six percent of vacuum extractions. The hematomas usually resolve by themselves within two weeks but, if they are extensive, may cause jaundice in the baby and presumably result in a nasty headache.

Bleeding into the head (intracranial hemorrhage) is uncommon (about 1 in 300–400 cases) but is potentially extremely serious. However, recent studies have shown that this figure is no greater than the figure for babies delivered by forceps or emergency cesarean section during labor, suggesting that the abnormal labor is the cause of the problem rather than the vacuum application itself.

VACUUM EXTRACTION

The cup is attached to the baby's head and a vacuum is built up within it. Then, synchronized with the mother's contractions, the baby is helped down the birth canal.

FORCEPS DELIVERY

FORCEPS HAVE BEEN USED BY OBSTETRICIANS FOR NEARLY 400 YEARS. UNTIL THE LATTER HALF OF THE 20TH CENTURY, CESAREAN SECTION WAS A DANGEROUS OPERATION AND FORCEPS PREVENTED MANY MOTHERS AND BABIES FROM SUCCUMBING TO LIFE-THREATENING EVENTS DURING DELIVERY.

Now, thanks to the enormous medical advances that have been made in anesthesia and the routine availability of antibiotics, blood transfusion, and adult and neonatal intensive care units, cesarean section is a relatively safe procedure and, as a result, the potential complications of a difficult forceps delivery are considered to be a greater threat to the mother and her baby.

There are three types of forceps: lift-out, straight traction, and rotational. Forceps deliveries can be described as high, mid, low and outlet, depending on where the baby's head is positioned in the pelvic cavity when the forceps are applied. High-cavity forceps deliveries are no longer performed because of the significant risk of causing maternal and fetal damage.

Lift-out (outlet) forceps are used to lift the baby's head out when the scalp is visible at the mother's vulva, which means that the entire baby's head has already reached the pelvic floor and is distending the vagina but the perineal muscles are holding it back. They are only appropriate if the baby's head is positioned directly occiput anterior (*see* p.270) or slightly rotated to the left or right. An injection of local anesthetic into the perineal tissues or the pudendal nerve (*see* p.316) may be all that is needed for a lift-out forceps delivery. An episiotomy is not always necessary.

Straight traction forceps are longer and are used for low- and mid-cavity deliveries when the baby's head has engaged and descended to more than 2cm below the ischial spines (low) or just above this station (mid-cavity). (*See* p.302 for diagrams of stations and head descent). The forceps lock together easily to form a protective cradle around the baby's head. At the height of a contraction, the operator applies gentle downward traction. The head descends

FORCEPS DELIVERY *The curved blades of the forceps are inserted one at a time and cradled around the baby's head. They are then used, in time with your contractions, to help draw the baby down the birth canal and deliver it.*

with each pull even if it slips backward again between contractions. Delivery is usually achieved with three good contractions and moderate traction, but if there is no obvious head descent by this time it suggests that there may be a degree of disproportion present and the decision as to whether to proceed with a vaginal delivery should be reviewed. Because the forcep blades take up additional room in the vagina, an episiotomy is often required to prevent uncontrolled perineal tearing as the baby's head stretches the perineum. An epidural or spinal block should be used for this type of forceps delivery to make sure the mother does not experience pain or discomfort when the blades are inserted and during the traction, delivery, and subsequent repair of the perineum.

"...forceps have prevented many mothers and babies from succumbing to life-threatening events..."

Rotational forceps are used to turn the baby's head in the mid-cavity from a transverse or occipito-posterior position to direct occipito-anterior. Following this downward traction on the long handles of the forceps allows the smooth descent of the baby's head and the delivery is then completed similar as with straight forceps. The application of rotational forceps requires considerable skill and experience and this type of delivery is likely to be carried out in an operating room, if any difficulties are encountered, a cesarean section can be performed immediately. It is essential for the mother to have an effective epidural or spinal block in place, not just for the delivery, but also afterward so that her vagina and cervix can be carefully examined for any potential tears or damage that the rotational forceps may have caused.

FORCEPS OR VACUUM EXTRACTION?

Despite the current trend favoring use of vacuum over forceps, there is still debate as to which is the best method of instrumental delivery. It is generally thought that the use of the vacuum results in less damage to the mother's vagina and perineum. On the other hand, the vacuum may be more traumatic for many babies compared to a smooth forceps delivery, because it leaves a swelling on the baby's head where the cup was placed.

There are pros and cons to each type of instrument, and I think it is more useful to consider the two methods as complementary, designed for different circumstances, rather than rivals to each other. The final choice should be determined by the circumstances that have led to the need for an attempted instrumental vaginal delivery and the experience and skills of the individual who performs the delivery.

BIRTH STORY

NATHALIE, 34, HAS ONE DAUGHTER, FOUR YEARS OLD

SECOND BABY ENZO, BORN 40 WEEKS + 4 DAYS, WEIGHT 8LB 6OZ (3.8KG)

LENGTH OF LABOR FROM START OF CONTRACTIONS: 21 HOURS

My 34-week scan *had shown the baby to be transverse but at subsequent examinations I was told he had turned and was cephalic, although his head never engaged, even at term. The day before my labor started, I remember a doctor getting me to feel the baby's bottom high up in my abdomen.*

My labor started *at around 1am with regular, period-like cramps that were generally perfectly bearable, so much so that I was able to get some sleep. By midday, the cramping stopped completely and only started again at around 3pm. I decided to go shopping with my husband for some last-minute food items, even though the contractions were now coming every 10 minutes or so. At 5pm I had a show, so I called the hospital*

but was told to wait until the contractions were longer and closer together. By 5:30, my water broke; the contractions were coming every five minutes and were more painful so we left soon after for the hospital.

A midwife examined me on arrival *and, palpating my abdomen, remarked on how hard the place was where the baby's bottom should be. I was taken to a delivery suite and waited while things progressed. At around 7pm, a doctor came and did a scan and revealed that in fact the baby was breech. What we had assumed was his firm little bottom had obviously been his head. We were shocked. He explained to us what a breech vaginal birth entailed and informed us of the risks, and left us to digest the information. By now the*

contractions were very strong and I was still using only gas and air.

At 8pm, a new doctor came in, *did an internal examination, and told us we needed to hurry up and make a decision since I was already dilated 3cm. He strongly advised me to have a cesarean because the baby was big. Not only were we really disappointed but we were still coming to terms with the turn of events. Soon after, we agreed to a cesarean delivery, simply because I did not want to risk my baby's health for the sake of misguided hesitation and stubbornness.*

Enzo was finally born at 10pm *and, although the birth itself went fine, I had to be given morphine regularly for the first couple of days. I was frustrated and depressed not to be able to look after him properly because of the pain from the incision. I was also exhausted, partly because of the inevitable noise on the ward. After three days, I discharged myself, knowing I would get more rest (and better food!) at home.*

"...the doctor explained in detail to us what a breech vaginal birth entailed and informed us of the risks..."

vaginal breech delivery is that it should not be hurried and there should never be any pulling or tugging of the baby, just guidance and gentle rotation as the baby emerges.

Delivering the head

If all is going well, the weight of the baby's body will help with the remainder of the delivery, encouraging the neck to be well flexed, which results in the head being best positioned to be smoothly and safely delivered. If the baby's neck remains extended, with the face looking upward into the uterine cavity (called star gazing) it is highly likely that problems will develop in delivering the "after-coming head." The baby's head is the largest part of its body and when the neck is extended an even wider diameter is presenting to the cervix, which may not yet have been fully dilated by the delivery of the buttocks, trunk, and shoulders. Performing a cesarean section in this situation is traumatic for everyone concerned. This is why everyone involved in your delivery will have been careful to heed earlier signs that a breech labor may not be progressing well and will advise changing to an abdominal delivery if it is thought the "after-coming head" is in danger of getting stuck at the last moment.

On a positive note, if all continues to go well, your obstetrician will now gently sweep the baby's body upward, over your pubic bone, and may insert a finger into the baby's mouth and gently pull downward, further flexing the head and helping it emerge smoothly. At this point, it is often best to apply a pair of lift-out forceps to the breech baby's head to guide it out in a controlled manner as it escapes the constrictions of the lower part of the birth canal. As you will now realize, several pairs of hands are needed to deliver a breech baby vaginally and an episiotomy is usually performed.

VAGINAL OR CESAREAN BREECH DELIVERY

During the last few years, several studies have been published that have changed many obstetricians' views about the best way to deliver a baby that is presenting by the breech. They conclude that cesarean section is the optimal way to deliver a full-term breech baby in a first-time mother, if attempts to turn the baby (*see* external cephalic version, p.271) have failed. However, some 10 percent of women with a breech presentation who are scheduled for a cesarean section will deliver vaginally because labor starts earlier than expected and is already well advanced when they arrive at the hospital. In addition, a small number of women will find themselves in an advanced stage of labor before it is realized they have a breech baby — the undiagnosed breech.

DURING A BREECH DELIVERY

The baby's buttocks are delivered first, followed by the legs. The baby then turns so that the shoulders can be delivered. The baby's weight draws the head down and the legs are lifted to allow safe delivery of the head.

CESAREAN BIRTH

I am very conscious of the fact that most prenatal classes, pregnancy books, and publications focus most of their attention on what labor will be like. Yet, in reality, a sizable percentage of women (at least one in five births in Canada) now deliver their babies by cesarean section and this is why I have included a detailed account of what you can expect to happen if you turn out to be one of them.

Despite the marked increase in the numbers of babies that are born by cesarean section, there are many individuals, both men and women, who continue to view this mode of delivery as the poor relation in childbirth. Indeed, some people feel that it is the method of last resort. Of course, these people are entitled to have their own viewpoint, but my concern is that all too frequently this leaves some women who have needed to have a cesarean delivery feeling that they have in some way failed or not done their part in natural childbirth.

I feel strongly that pregnant women should not be subjected to pressure or disapproval about the way their baby is delivered. There is no way that even the most experienced midwife or doctor can accurately predict what will happen to a woman in labor, so to suggest that, "if all else fails you will have to be subjected to a cesarean section" is, in my opinion, not only insensitive but also unkind. Every labor is different, and it is impossible to consider yourself a failure when you have successfully nurtured a baby in your womb for nine months and then delivered a healthy baby into the outside world. If cesarean sections allow more women a guarantee of going home with healthy babies, then this mode of delivery has to be a good thing and quite the opposite of "failed." I really do believe that the route by which you deliver your baby is of secondary importance, just as long as both of you are safe.

A cesarean section may be performed electively — meaning that this method of delivery was decided before labor started — or it may be an emergency procedure carried out after labor has already began. Of course, the operation itself is exactly the same, whether it is performed electively or as an emergency, but the underlying reasons for the cesarean section may be different.

"...women should not be subjected to disapproval about the way their baby is delivered."

ELECTIVE OR EMERGENCY SECTIONS

THERE ARE A WIDE VARIETY OF REASONS WHY A CESAREAN SECTION MAY BE ADVISED OR CHOSEN. IT IS IMPORTANT TO REMEMBER THAT ONLY A FEW OF THESE ARE ABSOLUTE INDICATIONS; MOST ARE RELATIVE, DEPENDING ON INDIVIDUAL LABOR AND CIRCUMSTANCES.

"...elective cesarean sections are performed when a vaginal birth is considered potentially risky..."

Most "elective" cesarean sections are performed when there are existing medical reasons to indicate that a vaginal birth is potentially risky, for the mother and/or her baby. That is not to say that a vaginal birth cannot be attempted, but in the opinion of the mother and her prenatal caregivers, cesarean section is the safer option. This may be the case when the baby is presenting breech or in another position which may make vaginal delivery difficult, if you have a placenta previa, if you are expecting twins or more, if you are suffering from an illness such as kidney, lung, or heart disease or diabetes, or if you have developed preeclampsia or severe high blood pressure in pregnancy.

The term "emergency" cesarean section may sound as if the baby needs to be delivered in a matter of minutes, if not seconds, in order to avoid a catastrophe. Very occasionally this is the case, but more often it means that it has become obvious to everyone involved that a cesarean section is required in the next hour or so.

The indications for an emergency cesarean section are dependent on many complex factors, which include unpredictable events that occur in labor, such as prolapse of the umbilical cord or signs of fetal distress, maternal and medical perceptions of the progress of that labor, and practical considerations such as the staffing and expertise available to achieve the safe delivery of a healthy baby.

SAFETY OF OPERATIVE DELIVERIES

Cesarean section is now considered to be a relatively safe procedure. When complications develop they are almost always due to the fact that the cesarean is performed under emergency circumstances or because of an underlying maternal or fetal problem. Thanks to the medical advances in anesthetics, antibiotics, blood transfusion, and adult and neonatal intensive care facilities, the risks for the mother have become a secondary consideration in the vast majority of cases, and the risk of physical damage to the baby during the delivery is small.

However, any surgical procedure is associated with a degree of risk and there are factors that significantly increase the risk associated with cesarean section. When the pregnant woman is seriously overweight, a smoker, has a

THE RISE IN THE RATE OF CESAREAN SECTIONS

THE NUMBER OF CESAREAN DELIVERIES HAS INCREASED DRAMATICALLY OVER THE LAST 10 TO 15 YEARS AND I THINK THE MOST USEFUL WAY TO UNDERSTAND THIS CHANGE IS TO CONSIDER THE CONTRIBUTING FACTORS.

ADVANCES IN GENERAL MEDICAL CARE

Advances have allowed some women with medical problems that were previously thought to preclude them from having children to now get pregnant and, with specialized help, remain healthy during pregnancy. However, an underlying medical disorder may make a planned cesarean section the safest way to deliver the mother and her baby. Similarly, mothers-to-be who develop severe diabetes or preeclampsia may require early delivery by cesarean section to protect their health.

ADVANCES IN OBSTETRIC CARE

Prenatal and intrapartum (labor) care have become so much more sophisticated. The routine availability of ultrasound scanning has resulted in our being able to identify many mothers and babies who are likely to experience problems in labor, before they are exposed to serious complications. The widespread introduction of regional anesthesia (see pp.311–16) for cesarean deliveries needs a special mention here, since it allows the woman to remain conscious throughout the operation, supported by her partner, and avoids the significant risks of a general anesthetic. There are three other obstetric reasons that have contributed to the increase in the cesarean section rate. The first is that the number of babies born prematurely has risen significantly over the last decade. Second, the increase in the numbers of older women giving birth makes an additional contribution to the cesarean section rate, since these women experience more complications during labor. Third, the use of high-cavity obstetric forceps in the second stage of labor has virtually disappeared over the last five to 10 years, and an emergency cesarean section is usually performed instead.

SOCIAL CHANGES, VIEWPOINTS, AND PERCEPTIONS

The views that pregnant women now hold about the way in which they would prefer to deliver their babies have also made a significant contribution to the increased rate of cesarean sections. Many of the women I meet in prenatal clinics have already developed clear views about the method of delivery they want. Some are passionate about achieving a vaginal delivery. Others are equally clear that they want to be delivered by cesarean section. Most recently, the trend for celebrity mothers to opt for a cesarean section (invariably in the private sector), because they want to dovetail their baby's birth into a busy work schedule, has resulted in the procedure being perceived as a fashionable option or the must-have accessory in childbirth.

MEDICOLEGAL CONSIDERATIONS

On some occasions when complex vaginal deliveries have resulted in babies suffering brain damage or other physical injuries, expensive and lengthy legal cases have followed. Inevitably, this leaves doctors more likely to err on the side of caution when there is choice to be made between a cesarean section or a complicated vaginal delivery.

If this is an elective cesarean you will probably walk into the operating room and lie down or sit on the operating table, ready for the epidural/spinal anesthetic to be inserted (*see* p.313). If you are already in labor, you will be wheeled into the operating room on your delivery room bed and, once in the room, you will be transferred onto the operating table. Looking around the room, you will see lots of pieces of equipment, much of it on mobile stainless-steel trolleys. There will be an anesthetic machine at the head of the operating table you are lying on, covered in instruments, monitors, dials, cylinders of different types of gases, and drawers full of useful bits and pieces.

"...the anesthesiologist will do everything possible to make you feel at ease and to explain what is going on, so you are sufficiently relaxed."

There will be a baby resuscitation cart in the room, equipped with an overhead heater to keep him/her warm, a piped oxygen supply, and lots of drawers containing equipment that the pediatrician may need. As you lie down, the nurse or midwife will be opening up sterile packs of instruments onto several carts that will be moved into position beside the operating table when they are needed. The walls of the operating room will be covered by open shelves containing sterile packs of instruments, gloves, gowns, syringes, needles, swabs, and sutures.

CESAREAN ANESTHESIA

Once in the operating room, the anesthesiologist will insert an intravenous drip into your arm so that you can receive fluids during the operation, and start to perform the epidural or spinal block. It is common at this stage for women to get anxious about the whole situation. Some start to hyperventilate and feel light-headed and nauseous. Others start to shake with nerves, not necessarily at the prospect of the operation, but more at the thought of the needle going into their spine. They can also worry about the anesthetic not working properly and being in pain during the operation. Let me reassure you on all these fronts. The anesthesiologist will be used to the physical signs of anxiety and, if you let him or her know you are feeling faint, you will be given oxygen through a mask. Any obstetric anesthetist will be skilled at inserting the needle, with or without maternal shakes. Indeed, they will do everything possible to make you feel at ease and to explain what is going on, so you are sufficiently relaxed throughout.

If you are having an elective cesarean, the anesthetic will take effect in a few minutes but the positioning of an additional epidural catheter (to provide you with pain relief after the operation) will take further time, usually around

20 minutes. If you are having an emergency cesarean section, you may already have an epidural in place, in which case you will need only an increased dose of anesthetic, which usually requires only a few minutes to take effect. As for the idea of the epidural or spinal block not working properly, the anesthesiologist will make sure that it is 100 percent successful by making a few checks: he or she will assess your sensation above and below the skin line where the anesthetic has been introduced and will only be satisfied that you are properly anesthetized when you confirm that you cannot feel below the line.

FINAL PREPARATIONS

When the anesthetist is confident that you are completely pain-free, a urinary catheter will be placed into your bladder. This has a dual purpose. First, it makes sure that your bladder remains empty during the operation and does not get in the way of delivering your baby. Second, because it will be left in for 24 hours or so after the operation, it will eliminate the need for you to get out of bed and struggle to the bathroom during those first few uncomfortable hours after the operation.

The next thing to happen is that your pubic hair will be shaved away from the site of the planned skin incision. Your abdomen will be thoroughly cleaned with an antiseptic solution and sterile sheets will then be draped over your upper abdomen and legs, leaving just the space where the incision will be made uncovered. The top end of the sterile sheets near your head will be hooked up to the anesthesiologist's drip stands to form a screen, so that you will not have to see what is going on during the operation, unless you tell the midwife that you want to be able to watch.

CESAREAN DELIVERY

Once everything is in place, the doctor will make an incision through the skin on your lower abdomen, at the top of where your pubic hair used to be, so that the scar will be mostly hidden once the hair has grown back. Incisions vary slightly in shape and length but, generally speaking, they are about 8in (20cm) long and are either straight or slightly curved, like a smile. The surgeon will then cut through several layers of fat, fibrous, and muscular tissue before making an incision into the lower part of the uterus.

Once the uterus is opened, the membranes will be ruptured (if they have not already done so) and amniotic fluid will come pouring out. For practical reasons, most of the fluid will be suctioned away before delivering the baby, so that all of the sterile sheets, not to mention the surgeon's clothes and feet, are

CESAREAN INCISION

The cut will be made just above the line of your pubic hair (bikini line). When the incision heals, the scar is very discreet.

not completely soaked with fluid. The surgeon will then check the exact position of the baby's head and insert a hand into the uterus, around the top of the head, and gently disengage it from the pelvic brim, in order to deliver the head through the uterine incision. This is often a tight fit and the assistant surgeon may be asked to apply some pressure at the top of the uterus to help the delivery. Sometimes small forceps will also be required, particularly if the baby's head is in an awkward position.

If this is an emergency performed during the second stage of labor, it may even be necessary for another assistant to examine you vaginally and help push the baby back up the birth canal, to deliver the head smoothly through the incision. This may seem a bit alarming to the parents, but I promise you that it is not dangerous for the baby. As the head gently emerges from the uterus, the baby's mouth and nose are immediately suctioned to clear the mucus and then the shoulders, followed by the trunk, are delivered very quickly.

FIRST CUDDLE *Your newborn baby will be handed to you to cuddle while the surgeon stitches together the layers of tissue that were cut to reach the uterus.*

AFTER THE BIRTH

Most babies have started crying and protesting before their legs are free of the uterine cavity. Indeed, the baby positively bursts into the world during a cesarean section. The cord is clamped and cut and the baby is then free — to be shown to the expectant parents for a first kiss and then quickly wrapped in towels to dry the fluid and prevent her from becoming cold. It is very likely that the midwife or pediatrician will choose to move the baby to the warmed rescusitation machine for a short time, in order to check her breathing and heart rate, clean all the vernix off her face and body, and perform the Apgar scores (*see* pp.375–76). They will then bring the bundled baby over to you and your partner to cuddle, unless of course there is a problem that necessitates moving the baby to the neonatal intensive care unit (NICU). If this is necessary, you will still be shown your baby beforehand.

Many partners choose to move in front of the screen so they can watch the delivery and take photographs of the birth. Others will want to remain shielded from the view of the operation and the delivery. For the mother, the cesarean delivery will be a strange and sometimes rather amusing experience. There won't be many times in your life when you have no sensation of pain but are conscious of the fact that someone is rummaging around your tummy.

Once the baby has been delivered, the anesthetist will give the mother an intravenous oxytocin drip to maintain the contraction of the uterus and help deliver the placenta. Just like in a vaginal delivery, active management of the third stage of labor helps reduce bleeding from the uterus or placental bed (*see* p.333). The placenta will be carefully checked to make sure it is complete. Meanwhile, the surgeons will clean the uterine cavity before starting to repair the uterine incision with one or two layers of stitches. They will then start to stitch up all the layers of tissue that were cut through to reach the uterus, using soluble stitches, and finishing with the skin stitches or staples. The skin stitches or staples will be removed during the next three to five days.

> "...the procedure takes about one hour, of which only five minutes involves the delivery of your baby."

From the time the anesthetic is given to the time when the stitching is complete, a cesarean will take around one hour, of which only five minutes involves the actual delivery of your baby. The rest of the time is taken up by anesthetizing you and stitching you up afterward.

CLASSICAL CESAREAN SECTIONS

A classical section, in which the uterine incision is made vertically into the muscles in the upper segment of the uterus, is now performed only rarely. This is because horizontal lower segment incisions are preferred for most cesarean deliveries, since the uterine muscle heals better and the skin incision also heals more quickly and is less unsightly. However, there are occasionally reasons to perform a classical incision, most usually for a premature baby of less than 30 weeks, when the lower segment may be so narrow and poorly developed that trying to deliver a fragile and already compromised baby through such a small aperture will undoubtedly lead to physical trauma for that baby.

When a baby is in a transverse lie and the membranes have ruptured it may be impossible for the surgeon to manipulate the baby to deliver through a lower segment incision without risking serious trauma to the uterus or baby. Similarly, when the lower segment cannot be approached easily because of large uterine fibroids or dense adhesions from previous surgery, it may prove necessary to perform a classical uterine incision. Because the risks of uterine rupture in a subsequent labor are high, individuals who have undergone a classical section will be advised not to have a trial of vaginal delivery for future pregnancies.

LIFE
AFTER
BIRTH

YOUR NEWBORN BABY

The busy hours you spent in labor and giving birth
are often followed by a brief period of reflective
calm. The staff who have been involved in your
delivery seem to melt away and you and your
partner are left to marvel at and savor the arrival
of your beautiful new baby. It is an emotional time
– after nine months of anticipation, you now meet
the tiny new person you have created together.

CONTENTS

THE HOURS AFTER BIRTH

378 Adaptations at birth

379 How your newborn looks

THE FIRST SIX WEEKS

384 Your physical recovery

390 Your emotional recovery

394 First days and weeks at home

396 Feeding your baby

400 Family adjustments

403 The six-week postnatal check

404 Caring for a premature baby

THE HOURS AFTER BIRTH

Most term babies will take their first breath or gasp within 30–60 seconds of the head emerging from the birth canal and before the umbilical cord is cut. This gasp is stimulated by the light and colder temperature of the delivery room compared to that of the environment inside the uterus. It is an extraordinary event: the baby's chest is often still trapped in the pelvic cavity. Nevertheless, this first gasp is usually strong enough to inflate the lungs.

As your baby takes his first breath, your midwife or doctor will ensure that his upper airway is clear by suctioning mucus and amniotic fluid from the mouth and nose. Once the baby's cord has been cut, the lack of oxygen supply from the mother acts as further stimulus to establish breathing on dry land.

Successful inflation of the baby's lungs is achieved by the presence of surfactant in the alveoli or air sacs. Surfactant determines the stability of the lungs after birth by lowering the surface tension in the alveoli, thereby allowing efficient gas exchange. Without enough surfactant, the alveoli become completely airless at the end of each breath and the baby then has to struggle against the continuing high surface tension to draw in the next breath. Just after birth, the baby's breathing rate increases, the nostrils flare, expiratory grunting is noted, and the tissue between the ribs is pulled in with each breath. This is respiratory distress syndrome and occurs in 1 in 100–200 of all deliveries, but is usually mild. Premature babies frequently require help with breathing since they often have insufficient surfactant in the alveoli of their lungs and may need surfactant to reduce the surface tension (*see* p.342).

APGAR SCORES

The doctor or midwife will assess your baby's overall condition one minute after birth and again after a five-minute period of observation, using the Apgar scoring system. This is a simple and highly effective tool developed by an American doctor, Virginia Apgar, after whom it is named. The maximum score is 10, two points for each of the signs that are assessed: skin color, breathing, heart rate, muscle tone, and reflexes (*see* table, p.376). In black or Asian babies

"...your baby's overall condition will be assessed using the Apgar scoring system."

APGAR SCORING SYSTEM

Apgar score	2	1	0
Skin color	Pink all over	Body pink; extremities blue	Pale/blue all over
Breathing	Regular, strong cry	Irregular, weak cry	Absent
Pulse/heart rate	Greater than 100 bpm	Less than 100 bpm	Absent
Movements/muscle tone	Active	Moderate activity	Limp
Reflexes after given certain stimuli	Crying or grimacing strongly	Moderate reaction or grimace	No response

the color of the mouth, palms of the hands, and soles of the feet is checked. A score of seven or more at one minute indicates a baby in good condition, a score between four and six usually means that the baby will need help to breathe, and a first score of less than four means that resuscitation and life-saving procedures are required. At the five-minute assessment, a score of seven or more indicates a good prognosis and a lower score will require careful monitoring of the baby.

Apgar scores provide an excellent short-term diagnosis of the baby's well-being immediately after birth. However, they are of little help in assessing a baby's long-term development, so don't worry if your baby's first score is low because it invariably picks up by the second assessment. Even if this is not the case, it is unlikely that your baby will have any serious long-term problems.

MEASUREMENTS AND IDENTIFICATION

While the Apgar scores are being performed, your midwife will be busy cleaning off the blood and fluids from your baby's skin. The body temperature of newborns falls by 1.8–2.7°F (1–1.5°C) immediately after birth because they rapidly lose heat from their wet skin and also because they have a relatively large surface area to body weight. This is why it is so important to dry babies as soon as possible after delivery and make sure that they are warmly wrapped.

Next, your midwife or nurse will weigh your baby, measure the head circumference and body length, and attach plastic identification bracelets to the wrists or ankles with your name and the baby's hospital number and date of birth. It is essential that your baby can be clearly identified before leaving the delivery room so that there is never any confusion or baby mix-up fears at a later date. The baby's crib will also be labeled clearly and some maternity units take footprints from the baby that are then attached to the baby's notes.

PHYSICAL CHECKS

In addition to assessing your baby's condition with the Apgar scoring system, your midwife or doctor will carry out a preliminary check to make sure that your baby has no obvious physical abnormality. They will look at the baby's face and tummy, listen to the heart and lungs with a stethoscope (a newborn baby's heart rate is normally about 120 beats per minute), turn him over and look at his back, run their fingers down his spine, check that his anus is open, note whether he has or has not urinated, and count the number of fingers and toes present. At a later date, a pediatrician will check your baby again and perform a more thorough physical examination before you go home (see p.387). It is common practice to give all newborn babies a few antibiotic eye drops in order to prevent inflammation or infection of the eyes (conjunctivitis) from developing after the journey through the birth canal. After all of the checks have been completed, your warmly wrapped baby will be handed over so that you can start to get to know him.

"...your midwife or doctor will carry out a preliminary check that your baby has no obvious physical abnormality."

VITAMIN K

This vitamin is present in food, especially in liver and some vegetables. Vitamin K is essential because it helps blood clot and prevents internal bleeding. However, newborn babies receive very little vitamin K because they are fed entirely on milk. Added to this, their livers, which are responsible for producing other essential blood-clotting substances, are relatively immature and, as a result, they run a small risk of developing vitamin K deficiency bleeding (VKDB) or hemorrhagic disease of the newborn. Consequently, the Canadian Paediatric Society (CPS) recommends that all babies receive vitamin K supplements soon after birth. There are two alternative methods of administering vitamin K to your baby:

• by injection — one dose of intramuscular vitamin K prevents VKDB in virtually all babies. A single dose may be given to your baby by the midwife or nurse soon after birth.

• by mouth — oral vitamin K is as effective as intramuscular injections, but only if repeated doses are given. Two doses are administered in the first week to all babies regardless of whether they are breastfed or bottle-fed. Breastfed babies are advised to have a third dose at one month of age.

Formula milk is fortified with vitamin K, and as a result bottle-fed babies are at an even lower risk of VKDB. However, the advantages of feeding with breast milk over formula are considered to far outweigh the marginal increase in the risk of VKDB.

ADAPTATIONS AT BIRTH

THROUGHOUT PREGNANCY, YOUR BABY RECEIVES A CONTINUOUS SUPPLY OF OXYGEN AND NUTRIENTS FROM THE PLACENTA, WHICH ALSO REMOVES ALL THE BABY'S WASTE PRODUCTS. WITHIN A FEW MINUTES OF DELIVERY, YOUR NEWBORN HAS TO CHANGE FROM BEING COMPLETELY DEPENDENT ON THE PLACENTA TO TAKING INDEPENDENT CONTROL OF THE ENTIRE METABOLISM.

The first thing is that your baby's lungs need to receive blood to oxygenate and pass to the left side of the heart to pump to all of the body organs. In utero, 90 percent of the blood supply by-passed your baby's lungs because there was no need to oxygenate it and hence the right side of the heart and the pulmonary (lung) vessels were at a higher pressure than the left side. Thus, the blood returning to the heart was either shunted directly from the right to the left side through a hole (the foramen ovale) between the two upper chambers (atria), or passed via the lower right chamber of the heart (ventricle) into the pulmonary artery. Because of the high pressure in the lungs, most of this blood was forced to flow into a duct, the ductus arteriosus, which diverts blood into your baby's aorta to reach the rest of his body.

As your baby takes a first breath and fills his lungs with air, the pressure in the pulmonary blood vessels falls and the ductus arteriosus closes, which results

CIRCULATION BEFORE AND AFTER BIRTH

BEFORE BIRTH *the baby's blood supply is shunted from the right to the left side of the heart through the foramen ovale.*

AFTER BIRTH *the blood supply passes through the lungs where it receives oxygen and begins to circulate around the body.*

in all of the blood from the right ventricle entering the lungs to receive oxygen. From the lungs, this massive increase in blood flow passes to the left side of the heart, ready for pumping around his body. At the same time the flow of blood to the right side of the heart is reduced as the vessels in the umbilical cord start to constrict. As the pressure on the left side of the heart increases and the pressure on the right side decreases, it is no longer possible to shunt blood through the foramen ovale, which closes over like a flap. The baby now has an "adult" blood circulation (*see* diagram).

After all these cardiovascular changes are in place, your infant's liver receives much larger quantities of blood. As a result, the liver can start to metabolize the food or glycogen stores that it has built up over the last eight weeks of intrauterine life in order to meet the energy needs of the first few days of life until feeding becomes established.

The body temperature of most newborn infants falls by 1.8–2.7°F (1–1.5°C) after birth (*see* p.376). Term babies have laid down brown fat which they can now use for heat production without even needing to shiver.

HOW YOUR NEWBORN LOOKS

MANY COUPLES ARE SURPRISED BY THE APPEARANCE OF THEIR NEWBORN BABY. THEIR NEWLY DELIVERED INFANT CAN BE A FAR CRY FROM THE CHERUBLIKE INDIVIDUAL DEPICTED IN MAGAZINES. BUT IT WILL ONLY TAKE A FEW DAYS FOR THE BLEMISHES AND VISIBLE SIGNS OF THE TRAUMAS OF DELIVERY TO DISAPPEAR.

The first glimpse of your baby will arouse all sorts of different emotions, not all of which are necessarily positive.

All babies are born with blue eyes and the final color of their eyes may not be evident until the baby is six months old. The eyelids will probably look puffy — another consequence of the pressure effects of labor. Your baby may squint or appear to be cross-eyed for several months after birth, but this is rarely anything to worry about. Your baby's focus is poorly adjusted at birth but when you hold him at about 8in (20cm) from your face, he will be able to see you and start to understand the details of your face.

The head often appears pointed or cone-shaped after a vaginal delivery, particularly if the labor was prolonged. This is because the bones of the skull overlap to allow the head to be subjected to pressure and progress smoothly during the descent through the bony birth canal. Within a week, your baby's skull will have returned to its normal shape. Sometimes the pressure also causes

"All babies are born with blue eyes. The final color may not be evident until the baby is six months old ..."

YOUR BABY'S HEAD *This may appear cone-shaped or pointed for a few days after a vaginal delivery.*

AT BIRTH *Your baby may be covered by a thick greasy vernix which has protected his skin from the watery environment of the womb.*

swelling on the sides of the face and if forceps or a vacuum extractor were needed, there may be some bruising on the face or scalp. You will notice a soft rectangular area on the top of the head (the anterior fontanelle) where the baby's skull bones have not met together. This will not close completely until about 18 months of age.

Some babies are born with a thick coating of white greasy vernix caseosa, which has protected their skin from the watery environment in the womb. Others will have none or just a few residual patches. Some midwives will clean it off the baby's skin soon after the delivery while others will leave it on to fall off or rub off in the next few days. Most newborn babies have quite blotchy skin, not just because of the rigors of labor but also because it takes some time for the circulation to the arms and legs to become well established. Dry, flaky areas of skin on the arms and legs are common. In the uterus, your baby was covered in fine, downy lanugo hair. At birth, some babies have lots of it left on the scalp and shoulders, whereas others have none. Any that remains rubs off during the next week or two. Small white spots on the face, called milia or milk spots, are very common. They are caused by blocked sebaceous glands that lubricate the skin. They will disappear quickly after delivery. The color of your baby's scalp hair at birth may change over the next few months.

Some babies are born with long fingernails, and the problem with this is that they tend to lead to scratches on the face and elsewhere as the baby starts to explore his own body. Avoid cutting your baby's young nails with scissors, which can damage the nail beds. Instead, nibble the nails off gently and painlessly in your mouth. Placing protective mittens on your baby's hands will help prevent further scratches from developing.

Birthmarks are skin blemishes caused by clusters of small blood vessels under the surface of the baby's skin. They do not usually require any treatment. Caucasians are commonly born with pink skin patches (called stork bites) on the nose, eyelids, forehead, base of the skull, and under the hairline on the neck. Most of them disappear within a year. Strawberry birthmarks (nevi) start off as small red dots on the skin and may continue to increase in size for a year after birth. The majority of them have disappeared by the age of five years. Most babies with dark skin tones have birthmarks called Mongolian spots. These are blue-gray patches of skin on the back or the buttocks. They are completely harmless and usually fade away in the first couple of years. Port-wine stains are large reddish purple skin marks usually found on the baby's face and neck. Since these are permanent birthmarks you may wish to seek expert advice from a skin specialist.

Babies of both sexes frequently have swollen breasts at delivery and may even leak a little milk. This is entirely normal and is a result of the mother's pregnancy hormones that take time to clear from the baby's body. The swelling and milk secretions will subside in a few days. Both girls and boys frequently have swollen genitals at birth. Again, this is the result of maternal hormones engorging the tissues and will settle down quickly. In girls, high estrogen levels produced by the placenta can also cause the womb lining to become thickened while they are still in utero. If this is the case you may notice that your baby daughter experiences some vaginal bleeding after delivery (like a light period) as the thickened womb lining breaks down. It will only last for a day or two and is nothing to worry about. The testes of a baby boy may still be in the groin at birth but usually descend without complication at a later date.

PUTTING YOUR BABY TO YOUR BREAST

While you are holding your new baby it is a good idea to try putting him to your breast because the hormones oxytocin and prolactin are produced when the nipple is touched or stimulated. Oxytocin helps the uterus contract, so even if you are planning to bottle-feed, it is useful to put your baby to the breast just after the delivery. Prolactin makes the milk come in and, although you will be producing only colostrum for the first few days, the sooner you get the milk or "let-down" reflex working, the better. The idea immediately after delivery is simply to get the baby used to being on the breast, so don't worry if he does not seem to be very interested in feeding immediately. Most term babies already have a sucking or rooting reflex (*see* p.387), so when you touch the corners of their mouths with a finger or the nipple, they will turn to the stimulus and attempt to suckle.

Term babies already have food reserves built up when they are born. Many women feel anxious if their baby does not start to feed immediately but the truth is that babies are often more interested in sleeping after labor and delivery. However, premature babies need to be given small bottle or drip feedings of expressed milk or formula during the first 24–48 hours of life because they have less reserves and the sucking reflex is rarely developed before 35 weeks of gestation.

FIRST FEEDINGS *These help your baby get used to the idea of breastfeeding as well as stimulating the release of hormones, causing the uterus to contract.*

THE FIRST SIX WEEKS

After nine months of anticipation, excitement, and probably some apprehension, you and your partner can now start the next stage of this journey as you discover and explore your roles as parents. This section of the book will guide you through the first few weeks of your life after your baby's birth.

During this period of enormous change, you will inevitably experience a huge range of emotions. You will feel wonder and awe at the tiny person you have created and will be fascinated as you get to know the little quirks of her personality. You may also feel overwhelmed by her vulnerability and complete dependency on you.

In addition, you will be recovering from the physical effects of giving birth, as well as adjusting your relationship with your partner as you learn to accommodate your new family member. Coming to terms with the practical aspects of caring for your baby can also be challenging, especially when you still have your usual household chores to do as well.

ADJUSTING TO CHANGE

At times it may seem like there are a lot of balls in the air to juggle and the pressure on women not to drop any of those balls is probably greater than it has ever been. It seems that this is made worse by the media coverage of celebrity mothers who, within 10 minutes of having their babies, are zipped back into their size 6 jeans, starring in their next blockbuster movie, and at the same time, seem able to be the perfect mother. Faced with these sorts of images, many "normal" women dare not own up to having a difficult time during the first few weeks of parenting.

Becoming a mother is a time of great joy for both you and your partner but it is also a time when the parenting learning curve is steep. I hope that by being honest with you about what life after birth can be like, you will realize that all the physical and emotional changes you are experiencing are very common, and regardless of whatever you are doing, or not doing, with your baby, you are still going to be a great mother.

"...many women dare not own up to having a difficult time in the first few weeks of parenting."

YOUR PHYSICAL RECOVERY

THE POSTPARTUM PERIOD IS THE SIX WEEKS FOLLOWING THE BIRTH OF YOUR BABY. HOW YOU RECOVER PHYSICALLY WILL DEPEND ON A VARIETY OF FACTORS, INCLUDING THE TYPE OF LABOR AND DELIVERY YOU HAD, YOUR GENERAL STATE OF HEALTH, AND YOUR DOMESTIC SUPPORT AND SOCIAL CIRCUMSTANCES.

"After pains are uterine contractions caused by the hormone oxytocin..."

Here, I will discuss the most common physical aftereffects of labor and delivery and some of the problems that can arise.

As your uterus starts to shrink back to its prepregnant state in the first few days after the birth, you will have a very heavy bloody vaginal discharge, called lochia. Lochia is made up of blood, mucus, and tissue debris, all of which needs to be expelled from the uterus. You will need extra-thick sanitary pads for the first few days and disposable panties because the blood loss is likely to be heavy. The flow usually calms down after the first week and the color of the blood gradually changes from bright red to brown.

After pains are the period-like pains that many women experience after delivery, particularly if they are breastfeeding. They are uterine contractions caused by the hormone oxytocin, which encourages the uterus to shrink back down into the pelvis more quickly. Since oxytocin is released when the baby suckles at the breast, it is common for women to experience after-pains or pass some small blood clots while they are breastfeeding. After-pains should last only a few days after the delivery, but if they are making you feel uncomfortable ask your midwife or doctor for a suitable form of pain relief. Depending on the type of delivery you have had and the extent of your discomfort, you can choose from injections, pills, or rectal suppositories.

Some degree of breast engorgement is almost inevitable as the milk starts to come into your breasts. The breasts become swollen, hard, and sore, and this normal inflammation commonly raises your temperature slightly. Fortunately, the problem usually resolves spontaneously in a day or two as breastfeeding becomes established (*see* p.398).

If you have stitches they will become tighter as the skin surrounding them swells and the wound starts to heal. This can make sitting down uncomfortable. Sitting on a rubber ring helps during the first few days since this avoids any direct pressure being placed on the perineum. Similarly, placing ice packs or local anesthetic creams and sprays on the perineum can help. You may also find that urinating produces a burning or stinging sensation as the urine flows directly over the wound. If possible, try to stand up or crouch over the toilet with your legs as wide apart as possible to help direct the flow of urine straight into the toilet. Gently wash the area with a cool sponge or washcloth afterward and pat your wound dry. Many women tell me that using a hair dryer on a cool setting to dry the perineum is helpful. Bidets are a real bonus at this time, since you can bathe your perineum with soothing warm water while urinating.

The bladder undergoes a particularly stressful time during labor and delivery, which can result in difficulties urinating. If this happens, you may need to have a catheter inserted into your bladder to rest the muscles and allow them to regain their normal tone. The physical trauma of delivery can also encourage the development of a bladder infection. Prompt treatment with antibiotics and drinking plenty of water usually resolves the problem.

Many women fear that opening their bowels for the first time after the delivery will be a painful experience. Rest assured that your stitches are unlikely to burst open even if you do find that you are straining. To help prevent constipation, start drinking plenty of fluids (ideally water) as soon as possible and eat plenty of high-fiber foods such as cereals, fresh fruits and vegetables, and dried fruits. Gentle exercise will also help.

POSTNATAL EXERCISES

It is important to perform Kegel exercises (see p.165) after a vaginal delivery, particularly if you had a long, drawn-out labor, that will have stretched the muscles considerably. Make sure you do these exercises for a short time on a regular basis. Try setting yourself the target of doing them by lunchtime every day, for example, which is much better than doing lots of them once a week. You can start by doing a few pelvic squeezes the day that you give birth, then gradually build up your regular exercise program.

After giving birth, you can also use deep breathing to tone your lower back and abdominal muscles.

KEGEL EXERCISE *Pull in and tense your pelvic floor muscles as if you are holding back urine, hold for a few seconds then relax gradually. Repeat 10 times.*

ABDOMINAL STRETCH *Lie on your back with your hands clasping your bent knees. Breathe deeply, pulling your abdominal muscles inward and upward as you exhale.*

Toning your abdomen as quickly as possible after the birth is probably a key concern. If you had a vaginal delivery, you can try gentle abdominal exercises during the first few weeks after delivery. If you had a cesarean delivery you may be advised to wait until after your six-week checkup. My view is that you can try some gentle exercises after a cesarean delivery as long as they do not make you feel uncomfortable.

AFTER A CESAREAN SECTION

"Most women will need strong analgesia for the first 48 hours after a cesarean section."

The lochia is frequently less heavy after a cesarean section because the surgeon usually cleans out the uterine cavity before stitching up the walls of the uterus, thereby removing blood clots, pieces of membrane, placenta, and other debris. Nonetheless, you will have lochia for several weeks and may pass small blood clots and experience some after-pains when breastfeeding.

Most women will need strong, effective analgesia for the first 48 hours after the operation. Some hospitals offer patient-controlled analgesia (PCA) —hand-held pumps that allow you to give yourself small doses of intravenous morphine through an IV drip. Pain relief can come in the form of further intramuscular injections of morphine (which may leave you feeling rather hazy), rectal suppositories (which enter the blood stream quickly and are effective at numbing the pain while leaving your head clear), or pills. Pills are the slowest-acting form of pain relief and are usually more suitable after the first couple of days.

Any person who has an abdominal operation and subsequently requires bed rest is at risk of developing thrombosis (*see* p.423). Pregnant women have additional risk factors because of their hormonal status and the fact that they have been carrying a heavy weight pressing on their pelvic and lower leg veins for many months. Your midwives and doctors will be encouraging you to get up and move around as early as possible after your cesarean section. If your first attempt to stand up and walk leaves you feeling dizzy, just remember that in a few hours you will feel much stronger. The more active you are in the first few days, the shorter your overall recovery time will be.

Your abdominal wound will be covered by a sterile dressing that usually remains in place for about 48 hours. You may not realize what type of stitches or clips have been used to close the skin layer until one of the midwives or doctors takes down the dressing to inspect the wound. Staples or clips are usually removed on about day three, whereas individual or continuous sutures are usually left in place until about day five. It is rare for the removal of the skin sutures to cause much more than a little discomfort, but if any problems are anticipated you will be given some pain relief beforehand.

EARLY POSTNATAL CHECKUP

BEFORE BEING DISCHARGED FROM THE HOSPITAL, BOTH YOU AND YOUR BABY WILL UNDERGO A POSTNATAL CHECKUP. MANY HOSPITALS PREFER TO HAVE A PEDIATRICIAN CHECK YOUR BABY, BUT IN SOME UNITS SPECIALLY TRAINED SENIOR MIDWIVES PERFORM THIS TASK.

Your midwife or doctor will want to know how much lochia you are passing, whether you are having any problems urinating or defecating, and how you feel emotionally. They will measure your temperature, pulse, and blood pressure, examine your breasts, check that your uterus is well contracted, inspect your perineum, and make sure your calves are not tender or swollen. Your hemoglobin level will be measured and you will be given iron tablets if it is low. You will be offered a rubella vaccination if you are not already immune. Your midwife will make sure that you have enough analgesics to take home with you. She will also discuss your plans for contraception as the majority of women ovulate since six to eight weeks after giving birth, even if they are still breastfeeding.

Your baby's physical condition will be reviewed by examining her head, eyes, skin, limbs, breasts, and genitals. The heart and lungs will be carefully listened to with a stethoscope. Her hips will be checked for any signs of dislocation (clicky hips) by gently bending the legs

upward and then rotating the hips outward. The abdomen will be gently palpated to exclude enlargement of any organs such as the liver or spleen and the baby's spine will be carefully checked to confirm that all of the vertebrae are complete. Your

midwife or doctor will also look for more generalized problems, such as signs of infection, jaundice (see p.388) or low blood sugar. They will check your baby's temperature, skin color, and muscle tone, and look for evidence of lethargy or irritability.

YOUR BABY'S REFLEXES

Newborn babies have several important reflexes which will be tested during the discharge examination:

STARTLE REFLEX *Your baby's arms and legs will stretch out when her head is allowed to flop backward.*

ROOTING REFLEX *Her head will turn toward a finger stroking her cheek, her mouth open ready to suck.*

GRASP REFLEX *Your baby's fingers and toes will be able to grasp your finger very strongly.*

STEPPING REFLEX *When supported under the armpits your baby makes stepping movements.*

Your scar will appear red and raised at this stage and will also be tender to the touch. You may find it helpful to place a soft pad over it when you are dressed. However, the wound does not need to be covered all the time, and indeed being exposed to the air will help it to heal more quickly. It is also perfectly safe to have as many long soaks in the bath as you like — the warmth of the water can be very soothing. Always dry the wound gently with a clean towel.

You may find that the skin around the scar becomes dry and itchy after about a week — gently rubbing in emollient cream helps relieve this. The area of skin around the wound may be numb because the nerves that innervate the skin have been cut. This superficial numbness is normal and tends to continue for several months while the nerves grow back. Another cause of concern is that the upper edge of the scar tends to be rather bumpy and sometimes overhangs the lower edge when you are standing upright. Once, again this is normal and just reflects the fact that the surgeon cut through several muscle layers and these take time to knit together again and provide a flat muscular wall.

NEONATAL JAUNDICE

Jaundice is common in newborns because the excess red blood cells that the baby required in utero have to be broken down and eliminated. A yellow pigment called bilirubin is produced and needs to be processed by the liver before it can be excreted. When the bilirubin levels are high, the pigment is deposited in the skin and the whites of the eyes, which then appear yellow.

Physiological jaundice is very common, occurring in as many as 60 percent of all newborns, particularly premature babies because their livers are immature. The yellow discoloration affects the skin and is visible within 24 hours of birth. The jaundice usually peaks at day four and disappears without treatment within 10 days. However, if the levels of bilirubin become very high there is a risk that the pigment will be deposited in the brain causing permanent damage (called kernicterus). To prevent this, heel prick samples will be taken to monitor bilirubin levels in your baby's blood. If they reach a certain threshold ultraviolet light or phototherapy will be given for a few hours every day. The UV light breaks down the bilirubin in the skin, which can then be excreted in the urine without needing to be processed by the liver. You will be encouraged to feed regularly, since the calories and fluid intake will also help resolve the problem. As soon as the bilirubin levels fall below the threshold levels, the phototherapy will be stopped.

Breast-milk jaundice affects about five percent of breastfed babies who remain mildly jaundiced for up to 10 weeks, probably because hormones in the breast milk interfere with the liver's ability to break down bilirubin. The jaundice is not harmful and disappears if bottle-feeding is started, but there is no need to stop breastfeeding if your baby is otherwise well. After two to three weeks your doctor will order blood tests to confirm that your baby's liver and thyroid function are normal. (For pathological jaundice see p.434.)

LEAVING THE HOSPITAL

The length of your stay in the maternity unit will depend on the type of birth you have had. It can range from a few hours (six hours after giving birth is usually the earliest a woman will be allowed home) to more than a week if you have experienced complications. The average stay in the hospital is one to two days after a normal vaginal delivery, and five days after a cesarean section.

How long you stay in the hospital is an individual decision. It is important to remember that the purpose of you being in the maternity unit is to get advice and help you look after your newborn baby and also make sure that you make a fast recovery from labor and delivery. If you have opted to go home as soon as possible, make sure that you feel confident about how to change a diaper and bathe your baby and have talked to the midwives about obtaining practical help with feeding after you have left the hospital.

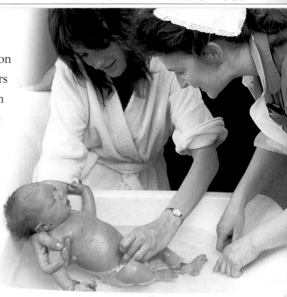

BATHING TECHNIQUES
Learning how to give your baby a bath during your hospital stay will prepare you for when you get home.

The hospital will notify your own doctor that you are about to be discharged from the maternity unit with your newborn baby and will provide details of your baby's postnatal progress and any concerns or problems that have occurred or may need special attention during the next few weeks. Your baby will have a heel prick blood test, usually before you two leave the hospital, to exclude phenylketonuria (a rare metabolic disorder) and thyroid deficiency. The tiny sample of blood is obtained by pricking your baby's heel and applied to a card and sent to a laboratory for analysis.

On the road

If you are returning home by car, law requires that your baby travels in a special infant car seat that needs to face the rear of the car. If you have a passenger-side airbag in the front, your baby seat must be fitted into the back seat of the car. Wrap up your baby warmly, because newborn babies are not good at maintaining or regulating their body temperature. As a rough rule of thumb, they should wear one more layer than you, plus a suitable hat and mittens in winter, or a sun hat in summer.

If you have had a cesarean section, you technically should not drive for a few weeks because, due to your abdominal wound, you are less capable of making a sudden stop. For this reason, you are more likely to cause an accident or injure a third party.

YOUR EMOTIONAL RECOVERY

THE DRAMATIC CHANGES IN HORMONE LEVELS THAT OCCUR IMMEDIATELY AFTER THE BIRTH OF A BABY FREQUENTLY RESULT IN EMOTIONAL PEAKS AND VALLEYS. SO DON'T BE SURPRISED IF, DURING THE FIRST FEW DAYS AND WEEKS, YOU FIND YOURSELF BURSTING INTO TEARS FOR NO OBVIOUS REASON.

TIME FOR ADJUSTMENT

The days and weeks following the birth of your baby are ones of major adjustment. Allow yourself time to get to know your baby and to adapt to your new responsibilities.

Giving birth is an enormous achievement and most women will feel physically and emotionally exhausted. Instead of being able to catch up on much needed sleep and recover from the events in peace and quiet, you now find yourself on call day and night for your new baby. The realization that you are completely responsible for this helpless new human being hits you. These are powerful and difficult emotions to deal with, particularly for first-time mothers, and it is not at all surprising that they leave you feeling vulnerable and weepy. Let me reassure you that these feelings and responses are entirely normal and also temporary. They will start to subside in the next few days or weeks as your hormone levels become more stable and you adjust to the new demands and responsibilities of being a parent.

BONDING

Many new mothers I talk to are worried about whether they are bonding well with their newborn baby. I firmly believe that there is no right or wrong way to get to know and learn to love your baby. Some women fall immediately and unconditionally in love with their newborn, whereas others will be so shell-shocked by the delivery that it may take some time to adjust to the fact that they have just become a parent. Just because the so-called bonding process starts a little more slowly, this does not mean that they are going to be bad mothers or that their baby will suffer in the future. Please do not fall into the trap of feeling guilty or inadequate if this is the case for you. You will bond with your baby in your own time and unnecessary anxiety and distress can be avoided if you keep reminding yourself of this fact.

Another common problem in the early postpartum period is that many women strive for "imaginary perfection" as soon as they reach home and subsequently feel distressed and frustrated when they realize that this is virtually impossible to achieve. The reality of your new lifestyle is that it will be unpredictable. Young babies rarely understand how to fit in with your perception of an ideal daily routine and it will take time and patience to reach some sort of acceptable compromise.

BABY BLUES

The demands of an infant are endless and often tedious and many women, especially when they have their first child (less so with subsequent children), suddenly find that they are left, literally, holding the baby. In the past, women were surrounded by an extended network of female relatives who helped out when a new baby arrived (and continued to do so throughout the subsequent years). Today, women are much more isolated and, until they have made a few friends locally, they often have to struggle by themselves.

The vast majority of women experience some degree of the "baby blues" in the week following the birth of their baby. The baby blues usually start around day four or five, just when your breast milk is beginning to come in, and you are feeling physically uncomfortable. However well prepared you may think you are for the postpartum period and no matter how many people have warned you about what is likely to happen, the baby blues will invariably hit you by surprise. You are expecting to continue to feel euphoric and exhilarated that you have successfully delivered a healthy baby, but suddenly and inexplicably you find yourself weeping uncontrollably. I think the most disturbing aspect for most women is that they are powerless to do anything about these extraordinary surges of emotion.

The period of baby blues usually disappears naturally within a couple of weeks. You start to recover physically, your hormone levels settle down, and you learn to look after your baby and find ways to make sure that you are not left coping on your own. Yet, for some mothers, these feelings of mild depression do not improve and postpartum depression can ensue.

POSTPARTUM DEPRESSION

Exactly how many women suffer from postpartum depression has always been difficult to establish. Depending on who you ask, the answer could be anything from 5 to 20 percent of all women during the first year of their baby's life. I am sure that this uncertainty is because many women feel ashamed by their feelings of distress and are reluctant to reveal the problem and ask for help. It is also because family, friends, doctors, and midwives are not very good at recognizing that early baby blues has now developed into a more serious problem.

SIGNS OF DEPRESSION

If you are experiencing some of the following feelings, you may be suffering from postpartum depression:

▶ overwhelming fatigue, disturbed sleep and, early-morning wakening
▶ persistent anxiety and low self-esteem
▶ lack of concentration
▶ weepiness
▶ dry mouth, appetite loss, constipation
▶ loss of libido
▶ rejection of your partner

FIRST DAYS AND WEEKS AT HOME

NOW THAT YOU ARE AT HOME WITH YOUR TINY BABY, ALL SORTS OF ANXIETIES MAY START TO SURFACE. REMEMBER THAT BABIES ARE A LOT TOUGHER THAN THEY LOOK. SHORT OF ACCIDENTALLY DROPPING HIM, THERE IS NOT MUCH YOU CAN DO THAT WILL ACTUALLY HARM YOUR BABY.

GRANDPARENTAL ROLE

Accept any offers of help that come your way. Grandparents in particular are often enthusiastic supporters as you adjust to your new life.

During the first few weeks, try to find someone to do the household chores, particularly those that involve lifting, carrying, or bending, since you will need your energy to care for the baby. The more help you can get, the quicker your recovery will be. You also must be sure that your return home does not result in your house becoming a coffee shop. Family and friends want to see the new baby, but make sure that they pull their weight when they visit.

If a home care nurse is offered under your medical insurance coverage, take advantage of it. Your nurse will visit you the first few days after delivery to check how you and your baby are progressing. She gives you and your baby a thorough examination to make sure you are both doing well and will assess your recovery, checking for signs of infection, including newborn jaundice. The nurse will also make sure your milk is coming in for breastfeeding and that your baby is latching on successfully.

Pace yourself

Many women find that once they have returned home they don't feel like venturing out again for some days. For many women, caring for a newborn baby takes up all of their time and waking thoughts and the last thing they want to do is expose themselves to the fast pace of life beyond the front door. This is an entirely normal reaction and my advice is to aim to do only what you feel like doing so that you can recover from the birth and get to know your baby in your own time.

During the next few months you will experience interrupted sleep and are likely to become tired as you provide round-the-clock care for your baby. Pace yourself from the beginning. Instead of trying to do the housework while your baby is sleeping (he will sleep an average of 16 hours a day) use the time to get some rest and much-needed sleep for yourself.

COMMON CONCERNS ABOUT YOUNG BABIES

UMBILICAL CORD

The stump of the umbilical cord usually stays in place for about 10 days after birth, during which time it should be washed and carefully dried on a daily basis to avoid infection. Special powders and wipes are available from your midwife or local pharmacy to speed up this drying process, which will help the stump simply fall off, leaving the tummy button in its place.

VOMITING

Young babies frequently bring up some of their feeding, particularly when they are trying to get rid of gas. This is nothing to worry about unless the vomiting is forceful and occurs after every feed (see pyloric stenosis p.434) in which case you should talk to your doctor or pediatrician.

TRAPPED GAS

Trapped gas gives rise to abdominal cramps and pain and not surprisingly the baby cries and is difficult to settle after a feeding. If simple measures such as placing your baby against your chest and massaging his back in order to encourage the gas to escape do not work, then ask your pediatrician to recommend some medication that will ease your baby's discomfort.

LOOSE STOOLS

Your baby will pass meconium (a sticky green-black mixture of bile and mucus) for the first few days, following which the stools will turn yellow-brown. Breastfed babies commonly pass looser stools than bottle-fed babies, but if your baby starts to pass watery green stools it is likely that he is suffering from diarrhea. Young babies can quickly become dehydrated and this needs to be treated immediately. Give your baby some cool, boiled water. If he has constant diarrhea, develops a dry mouth, and a sunken anterior fontanelle, contact your doctor at once.

DIAPER RASH

The ammonia in urine irritates the baby's sensitive skin, so it is not surprising that most babies experience a degree of diaper rash, even if their diapers are changed regularly. However, diaper rash can be exacerbated by perfumed toiletries, creams, and wipes that are not hypoallergenic. It is best to wash your baby's bottom with water and nonperfumed baby soap and gently pat it dry. Zinc- and sulfur-based barrier creams applied to the reddened area encourage the skin to heal and help protect against further irritation.

STICKY EYES

This is usually due to a mild eye infection called conjunctivitis. It is common immediately after delivery when blood or other fluids may have come into contact with the eye. Gently wiping each eye with a fresh piece of cotton soaked in cool, boiled water usually resolves the sticky eyes, but if the problem continues your pediatrician will prescribe an antibiotic eye cream.

FACIAL SPOTS

The small white spots (milia) that many babies are born with usually disappear in a few weeks without any treatment. If they become infected and red, bathe them in cool, boiled water before applying an antiseptic cream.

Contact your doctor immediately if your baby:

▸ is vomiting continuously
▸ is passing watery green stools
▸ is very lethargic
▸ is irritable and feeding poorly
▸ starts to wheeze or develops a cough
▸ is breathing very quickly, very slowly, or irregularly
▸ develops a high temperature
▸ shows signs of an infection or skin rash

FEEDING YOUR BABY

MOST WOMEN HAVE DECIDED BEFORE THE BIRTH WHETHER THEY WANT TO BREASTFEED OR NOT. THE DECISION IS A PERSONAL MATTER AND I BELIEVE THAT WOMEN SHOULD NOT BE MADE TO FEEL INADEQUATE IF, FOR WHATEVER REASON, THEY CHOOSE TO BOTTLE-FEED FROM THE BEGINNING.

However, it is important to be aware that you can offer your baby significant long-term health benefits by breastfeeding, even if it is only for a few weeks. Breastfed babies are likely to experience fewer infections and less likely to suffer allergies than bottle-fed babies. Furthermore, breastfeeding for a minimum of two months is thought to reduce a woman's risk of developing breast cancer later in life. On a practical note, breastfeeding requires no bottles or sterilizing equipment and can be undertaken at any time and in any place.

BREASTFEEDING

When a baby sucks on a nipple and areola (the brown skin around the nipple) two things occur. First, the mother's pituitary gland (at the base of the brain) is stimulated into releasing the hormone prolactin that produces milk. Secondly, the pituitary gland also releases oxytocin, which stimulates the alveoli to contract and forces the milk into the milk ducts and toward the nipple. This process is called the let-down reflex.

MILK PRODUCTION

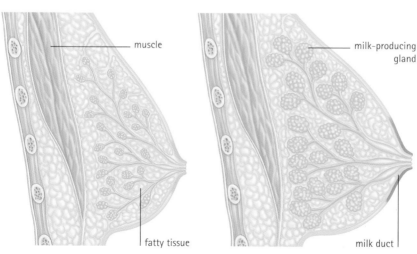

muscle

milk-producing gland

fatty tissue

milk duct

BEFORE PREGNANCY

DURING BREASTFEEDING

STRUCTURE OF THE BREAST

Your breast is made up of a mixture of adipose (fatty) and secretory tissue. Each breast contains about 15–25 lobes and each lobe is drained by a milk duct that leads to the nipple. The lobes are made up of individual alveoli (sacs) that swell up and contain the milk.

For the first few days after the birth, your breasts will produce only small quantities of colostrum (about 3–4 teaspoonfuls daily). This is a concentrated clear yellow secretion which provides your baby with all the water, protein, and minerals required until you are producing proper milk. Colostrum also contains high levels of maternal antibodies and a substance with natural antibiotic activity called lactoferrin, which helps combat infection. If, for any reason, your baby is not with you in the days immediately after the birth, try to express some colostrum and ask that it be given to your baby.

Your breasts start to produce white breast milk in increasing quantities from about day three onward. Breast milk contains fat, carbohydrate, protein, and other nutrients in exactly the right proportions to ensure the healthy growth of your baby. After the milk comes in, you may find you are feeding up to a dozen times over 24 hours. Soon, you will build up to around 20 minutes per feed every two to four hours.

LATCHING ON *Your baby should have all of your nipple and as much of the areola as possible in his mouth, which then forms a tight seal. As he squeezes the nipple against the roof of his mouth milk will be drawn out.*

HOW TO BREASTFEED

When breastfeeding, the whole areola should be in your baby's mouth in order for him to "latch on" and feed correctly. If he is latched on correctly, he will have his mouth wide open and you should feel a suction effect over the whole area. His top lip is turned upward and creased over and you will see his ears and jaw moving rhythmically as he sucks. If he is not latched on correctly, start again. Do not leave him to suck on just your nipple as it will become sore and cracked. Your baby should empty one breast at each feeding to ensure he gets both the dilute and thirst-quenching foremilk and the thicker, more nutritious hindmilk.

It is essential to be comfortable when you are feeding. Support your back properly and put a pillow under your baby so you are not bending down. Your baby should lie facing you, rather than just with his head turned toward your breast. You can also try lying down with your baby alongside you.

EXPRESSING BREAST MILK

You can express your milk by hand or with a breast pump, although expressing by hand can take longer. Breast pumps have a funnel that you place over your areola, forming an airtight seal. Pumps can be either hand- or battery-operated. Before starting to express you will need to use the bottle sterilizer that comes with the breast pump. You can keep the milk in the refrigerator for up to 24 hours or freeze it in a sterile freezer bag, where it will keep for up to six months.

BREASTFEEDING

Q&A

▶ **My breasts are very engorged and painful. What should I do?**

When the milk starts to come in, between the third and fifth day after delivery, it is common for the breasts to swell and become engorged due to over-production. Finding yourself with a fever and swollen, rock-hard breasts can be a painful experience, but it is entirely normal and usually settles down within 24 hours or so. As your baby starts to feed regularly your body will adapt to producing the right quantities of milk needed to nourish him.

If you develop breast engorgement, it is essential that you drain the milk from your breasts regularly to prevent the milk from seeping into the surrounding breast tissue, which can lead to mastitis (see breast infection pp.432–33). There are several things you can do to drain swollen breasts and prevent severe engorgement.

• Feed your baby a little and often so that your breasts are drained regularly.

• Express a little milk before you start to feed – this will soften the nipple and will help your baby latch on.

• Even if you have a cracked nipple, you must try to drain that breast – try using a nipple shield or express milk regularly from it.

• If your baby is not feeding very well, express the milk and either store it or discard it. Milk production works on a supply-and-demand basis, so if you do not empty a full breast regularly, future production will be poorer.

▶ **How can I cure blocked ducts?**

If a red, tender patch develops on the breast, you have a blocked milk duct. This is extremely common, but to prevent it from developing into mastitis:

• start each feeding from that breast, because your baby's suction is strongest at the beginning of a feeding

• place a warm washcloth or a cold compress inside your bra over the red patch

• feed your baby on all fours, so that your breasts hang down directly over him – this allows the breast to drain much more quickly

• express milk from that breast to help clear the blockage

▶ **My nipple is cracked and really sore. What should I do?**

Try to keep feeding on that breast to avoid engorgement. If necessary, express milk from that side while your nipple recovers and feed your baby from the other side. After a feeding, smear a little milk or saliva on the nipple and let it dry naturally. Expose your breasts as much as possible to the air and change breast pads after each feeding to help your nipples heal.

▶ **I don't think my baby is putting on as much weight as he should. What can I do?**

Breastfed babies often put on weight at a slower rate than bottle-fed babies and the growth chart you will be shown at the health center gives a wide spectrum for so-called "normal" weight. If your doctor is worried about your baby's weight gain ask yourself the following questions:

• Are you eating enough? Successful breastfeeding requires an extra 500 calories per day, 1,000 for twins, for your body to produce enough milk.

• Are you drinking enough? Plenty of fluids are needed to aid milk production. Add an extra two pints a day of water to your normal intake.

• Are you resting enough? If you are tired your milk supply will be lower.

If you have breastfeeding problems seek advice from your midwife, lactation consultant, or doctor or contact an organization such as the La Leche League of Canada (see pp.436–38).

BOTTLE-FEEDING

Bottle-feeding does offer some advantages, the least being that your partner can help feed your baby. Infant formula feeds are made with cow's milk (soy ones are available if your baby develops an allergy to cow's milk). They are fortified with essential vitamins and minerals and are a close imitation of human milk.

If, like many women, you breastfeed first and then switch to bottle-feeding, the switch should be gradual, starting with one bottle a day, so that your baby gets accustomed to the nipple and to the taste of formula milk. This way, you will also prevent your breasts from becoming engorged. If you have been able to express breast milk into a bottle while breastfeeding, you should find the switch to formula relatively effortless. If your baby complains, it can sometimes help if someone other than you offers the bottle.

If you bottle-feed your baby from the start, you will probably find that your milk does not come through very strongly and gradually dries up. Formula-fed babies invariably need fewer feedings a day and wake less during the night. This is because cow's milk forms a much more solid curd, which takes longer to digest, hence the tendency for formula-fed babies to go longer between feedings.

It is important to be hygienic and organized when bottle-feeding. Wash the bottles thoroughly and use boiled water to mix the formula. You can make up to 24-hours' worth of bottles in advance and store them in the refrigerator. Bottle-fed babies need to drink additional water since formula is not as thirst-quenching as breast milk. Once again, cool, boiled water is best.

The temperature of formula milk is a matter of habit, with some babies happy to drink cold milk straight from the refrigerator. If you do warm it up, always test it on the inside of your wrist and, if you heat it up in a microwave, shake the bottle to mix the formula before testing the temperature.

BURPING YOUR BABY

Breastfed babies take in very little air during a feeding, particularly once they have learned to latch on correctly. Bottle-fed babies, on the other hand, tend to take in more air — their mouths form a less airtight seal around a nipple — so may need more burping. The two main positions for burping a baby are over the shoulder and sitting on your lap. When your baby is sitting on your lap, make sure that the head does not slump down. The esophagus (feeding pipe) needs to stay relatively straight in order for the air to escape easily. Rub rather than pat your baby's back and place a cloth under your baby's chin to catch any milk that is brought up with the burp. Some babies swallow more air than others and you will eventually work out the most effective way to deal with this.

BURPING YOUR BABY

Sit him on your lap using one hand to support his neck and prevent his head from slumping down while you use your other hand to firmly rub his back.

FAMILY ADJUSTMENTS

HOWEVER MUCH YOU VOWED — AS MANY FIRST-TIME PARENTS DO — THAT YOUR BABY WOULD NOT CHANGE YOUR LIFE, REALITY WILL BE VERY DIFFERENT. HAVING A FIRST BABY CAUSES AN ENORMOUS EMOTIONAL, PRACTICAL, AND FINANCIAL CHANGE IN YOUR LIVES.

PARTNERS

BEING A DAD *Allow your partner to be as involved as possible in the care of his new baby — even if his way of doing things is slightly different to yours.*

Fathers are often overlooked during the adjustment period after the birth because the baby and mother are usually receiving most of the attention. Yet your partner is probably feeling physically tired, too, and is expected to be supportive and understanding of you and appear delighted by the demands that a new baby has suddenly placed on his lifestyle. The key thing here is to make sure that you both clearly communicate your individual needs.

Do try to get your partner involved in the care of the new baby, since this will help him understand some of the difficulties that you may be experiencing and prevent him from feeling excluded. This will probably require you to step back a bit and allow him to do things in his own way, even if this is slightly different from how you do them. Try to resist the temptation of continually criticizing his diaper changing or dressing technique. Babies are very adaptable and the last thing you want to do is undermine your partner's ability to look after his baby.

Your partner may find that he ends up feeling physically distanced from you during the first few weeks, particularly if you are breastfeeding. It is not difficult to understand how this can become another source of resentment. You are locked into a close relationship with your new baby and seem to have an endless supply of cuddles and kisses for him, but not enough energy left for anyone else. It is easy for your partner to start feeling neglected. This situation will change in time, but recognizing that your partner may need some reassurance that he is not going to be permanently left out in the cold is an important consideration and one that you need to make sure you convey.

RESUMING YOUR SEX LIFE

SEX IS AN ISSUE THAT IS RARELY DISCUSSED OPENLY BY NEW PARENTS OR THEIR

DOCTORS. HOWEVER, IT IS ESTIMATED THAT MORE THAN 50 PERCENT OF COUPLES

HAVE NOT RETURNED TO THEIR PRE-PREGNANCY LEVELS OF SEXUAL ACTIVITY ONE YEAR

AFTER THE BIRTH OF THEIR FIRST CHILD.

This fact suggests that it is common for couples to experience a significant change in desire, frequency, and the quality of their sexual relationship at this time. There are many factors that could account for this change. An appreciation of the most likely reasons may help you and your partner discuss and hopefully improve the situation.

▶ **Many mothers are so exhausted** by birth and by the continuous demands of their baby that the only thing they are interested in doing in bed is sleeping until the next time their baby wakes them.

▶ **An episiotomy scar** (or perineal tear) can make penetrative sex painful for weeks after the birth.

▶ **Vaginal dryness** is a consequence of breastfeeding (the result of high levels of prolactin and low levels of estrogen) and can make sex painful.

▶ **Some women feel unattractive** to their partner because they have gained weight during pregnancy, because their lactating breasts leak milk as soon as they are touched, or because they now have a large red abdominal scar after having a cesarean delivery.

▶ **Women often feel unsupported**, lonely, worried, or taken for granted after having a baby, all of which can result in a lack of libido. Postpartum depression is much more common than most people realize (see p.391) and mothers may experience symptoms for up to a year following the birth, which will invariably have an adverse effect on their sex lives.

▶ **Men, too, can suffer a temporary loss of desire**. This may simply be caused by fatigue, or the fact that they are adjusting to their new role as a father, but it may have a more deep-rooted cause. For example, some men now view their partner more as a mother than a lover, or they feel distressed having witnessed their partner's difficult vaginal delivery and the pain she suffered.

It is important to understand that you are not unusual or alone if you find your desire for sex has deserted you in the weeks or months after birth. It is also important that you discuss the physical or emotional problems you are experiencing with your partner at the earliest opportunity. You will both need to be open with each other to prevent resentment and anger from further complicating a sensitive and potentially explosive situation.

Most couples will find that they are better able to cope with the situation if they receive regular reassurances that they are still loved and valued. Staying in regular physical contact, albeit only with cuddles and kisses, during the first months after the birth can help reinforce the fact that this is not a permanent state of affairs.

Eventually, you will resume your sex life but it may take time and it may not be with the same frequency. However, many couples discover that the change in their relationship and lifestyle results in a greater level of sexual intimacy in the long term.

SIBLINGS

The arrival of a new baby in the house can be an unwelcome shock for other young children, who may find it difficult to accept the permanence of this new situation. Preparing a child psychologically and trying to involve him in the practical preparations for the arrival of the baby can be helpful. Friends and family can also ease the situation by bringing a little gift for siblings as well as for the new baby, playing with them, or taking them out for a day trip.

In the weeks following the birth, try to provide as much continuity as possible in the lives of other siblings so that they don't feel that family life now revolves completely around the new baby. Keep up with playgroups and after-school activities, invite their friends to play and, in particular, try to continue the normal bedtime routine — including reading a story — whenever possible.

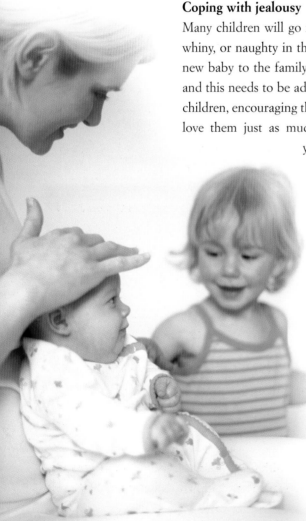

NEW ARRIVAL In the weeks following the arrival of a new addition to the family, try to involve older siblings as much as you can.

Coping with jealousy

Many children will go in for attention-seeking behavior by being more clingy, whiny, or naughty in the early weeks. There is no doubt that the addition of a new baby to the family frequently causes feelings of jealousy in other siblings and this needs to be addressed rather than swept under the carpet. With older children, encouraging them to talk about their feelings and telling them that you love them just as much as before will help reassure them. However, with younger children it is likely that plenty of extra cuddles and some time spent alone with you each day will also be needed. Your partner and close family friends can really help by looking after the new baby for you while you offer your other children some individual and much-needed attention.

Don't be surprised to hear your young children talk about putting the baby in the trashcan or returning him to the hospital or back into mom's tummy. You also need to be aware of the fact that it is common for young children to "accidentally" attempt to harm the new baby, by pinching or hitting him, when they think your back is turned. These are all entirely normal and predictable responses and I can assure you that your older children will come around to loving their new sibling in time. Nevertheless, you do need to take the precaution of never leaving your baby unattended with a young child in the room.

THE SIX-WEEK POSTNATAL CHECK

YOU AND YOUR BABY WILL GO TO YOUR DOCTOR OR PEDIATRICIAN ABOUT SIX WEEKS AFTER THE BIRTH. THIS PROVIDES AN OPPORTUNITY FOR YOU TO TALK ABOUT ANY CONCERNS YOU HAVE ABOUT YOURSELF OR YOUR BABY.

Your baby's check will involve a full physical examination together with an assessment of his developmental progress since birth, including:

- growth — size, length, and weight, which will be plotted on a growth chart
- head circumference and assessment of the anterior and posterior fontanelles
- eyes, ears, and mouth (sight and hearing will be formally assessed at later visits)
- heart, chest, and breathing
- abdominal organs and genitals
- hip alignment and stability
- reflexes — degree of head control, grasp reflex, and muscle tone.

In addition to asking you questions about your baby's general well-being, feeding, and toilet habits, the health clinic staff will explain the recommended times for your baby's vaccinations. If you have concerns about these, talk to your doctor or pediatrician or obtain up-to-date information from the Canadian Paediatric Society (*see* p.436). Although many scary stories relating to vaccinations have now been refuted and new vaccination programs promise even greater safety, there are still babies at risk as a result of mothers deciding against some vaccinations.

Your examination will make sure that you have fully recovered from delivery.

- Your blood pressure will be measured
- Your urine will be tested to check if there is protein or blood present.
- You will be weighed and advised about diet if necessary.
- Your breasts and nipples will be checked.
- Your abdomen will be examined to check that the uterus is well contracted and if you had a cesarean section, the scar will be examined.
- A pelvic examination will be performed if you had an episiotomy or perineal tear to check that the vagina has healed and that you have no pain or discomfort. After a cesarean section or complicated vaginal delivery, an internal examination will be carried out to check that the uterus is well contracted, not tender, and that you have no vaginal bleeding or discharge.

Now is the time to discuss any problems you may have with pain, bleeding, bowels, or bladder. You will also be reminded to think about contraception.

THE HEAD CIRCUMFERENCE *of your baby will be noted.*

YOUR BABY'S HEART RATE *and breathing will be monitored.*

HIS DEGREE OF HEAD CONTROL *will be checked.*

CARING FOR A PREMATURE BABY

AROUND 10 PERCENT OF BABIES ARE BORN BEFORE THE 37TH WEEK AND ARE CLASSIFIED AS BEING PREMATURE. MANY OF THESE BABIES, ALTHOUGH SMALLER THAN A FULL-TERM BABY, CAN BE CARED FOR LIKE A NORMAL NEWBORN AND DO NOT NEED ANY SPECIAL CARE. A FURTHER TWO–THREE PERCENT OF BABIES ARE BORN AT TERM BUT WITH A LOW BIRTHWEIGHT RELATIVE TO THEIR GESTATIONAL AGE AND NEED SPECIAL CARE.

Generally speaking, any baby whose birthweight is less than 3lb (1.5kg), either because they are premature or small-for-dates, will be taken to the Neonatal Intensive Care Unit (NICU). Other premature babies may be above this weight but may have other problems. Usually, they simply need more time to grow or for their lungs to mature so that they can breathe unaided.

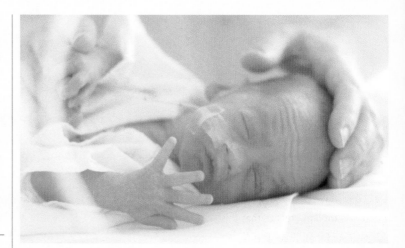

TOUCH IS VERY IMPORTANT *Studies have shown that cuddling and touching premature babies can help them gain weight and grow.*

NEONATAL INTENSIVE CARE UNIT

This special unit cares for vulnerable babies in the best possible environment. The unit protects your baby from infection by limiting access to all but essential people – medical staff, parents, and the immediate family of the baby. There is also a high ratio of caregivers to babies. While in the unit the babies are constantly monitored to make sure any problems are dealt with immediately. The staff always encourage parents to participate in the care of their baby and they take care to explain what is going on so that the parents understand and feel involved. Additionally, all NICU's have counselors for parents to talk to and many have baby feeding advisers to help with breastfeeding.

If your baby is taken to an NICU, she may well be placed in an incubator and attached to various monitors and wires. She may be ventilated to enable her breathing. The first visit to an NICU is invariably a shock for parents. It is difficult to see your tiny baby lying helplessly in an incubator, surrounded by high-tech machinery and a tangle of wires. The medical staff will always be on hand at this time to reassure you and provide answers to any questions you might have. They will show you how to express milk and feed your baby, how you can stroke her inside the incubator, and will encourage you to talk to her. In addition, even the smallest baby can usually be cuddled, so they will help you take your baby out of the incubator.

Gradually, you will learn how to care for her, including changing her diaper, giving her a bath, and helping with her feedings. Once she is stronger and no longer ventilated, you will be able to spend as long as you want holding her. There are no visiting hours in an NICU — parents can spend as much time as they want with their babies.

COPING EMOTIONALLY

One of the major hurdles to overcome when your baby spends more than a few days in special care is the realization that you will be going home without her. This can be a severe blow, particularly if you are leaving behind a very premature or sick baby. Yet, it is vital not to feel guilty — although I realize that this is easier said than done. It is unlikely that anything you have done has actively contributed to the premature birth and you can be sure that your baby will now receive the best care available to enable her to thrive and go home as soon as possible.

When you go home make the most of this opportunity to regain your strength and make the emotional and practical adjustments to having a baby that you and your family were perhaps not able to do because of the unexpected early birth.

Furthermore, you do not have to stay at the hospital every waking hour, particularly if you have other children. This could lead to feelings of resentment on their part once the baby is back home. The time that your new baby spends in the hospital can be a useful adjustment period for other children, and although you may not be spending more than a few hours a day with your baby in the NICU there is not a shred of evidence to suggest that this will negatively impact your ability to love your child.

GOING HOME

Generally speaking, a baby will go home when she is able to feed fully, either with breast milk or formula; she weighs at least 4lb 7oz (2kg) and gaining weight; she is more than 34 weeks gestation; and she maintains her own body temperature.

When the time to go home is imminent, many units ask the mother to come in and stay for at least one night in the bedrooms available for this purpose. This gives mothers the confidence to look after their baby once they are back home.

Premature babies are usually home within two to three weeks of the time they were due. By then, unless there is an underlying health problem, the baby should be treated as any full-term newborn. She should be given plenty of cuddles to make her feel secure and it is unlikely she will display any differences in behavior from a full-term infant.

The stages of development and weight gain of a premature baby are calculated from the date that the baby was due. By the time she is two years old, she will have caught up developmentally and physically with full-term children.

LOOKING AFTER A SPECIAL CARE BABY

BABY CARE *You will be encouraged to care for your premature baby, including changing her diapers.*

MAKING CONTACT *There are many ways to interact with your baby while she is in the incubator.*

CONCERNS AND COMPLICATIONS

EXISTING MEDICAL CONDITIONS

This section includes most of the disorders that I encounter on a day-to-day basis and those that I am asked about most frequently. If you know that you have a medical condition or are diagnosed with one in pregnancy, it is important to make sure that you get specialized medical help.

Epilepsy

If you suffer from epilepsy, it is particularly important that you are under close medical supervision when you are trying to become pregnant and during the pregnancy itself. Some antiepileptic drugs (particularly sodium valproate and carbamazapine) can cause abnormalities in the baby, such as heart and limb defects, mental retardation, CLEFT LIP AND PALATE, and are best changed to a different type of drug. Your doctor will advise you of the best drug to be taking and, once you are pregnant, will arrange for you to have a specialist ultrasound scan to detect any fetal abnormalities. Pregnancy can change the way antiepileptic drugs are metabolized in the body and you may need a higher dose to ensure that you do not have a seizure. Some antiepileptic drugs may reduce your folic acid levels and hence you need to take high-dose folic acid supplements before becoming pregnant and during the first 12 weeks of pregnancy to minimize the risk of having a baby with a neural tube defect such as SPINA BIFIDA.

Any seizure in a pregnant or postpartum woman needs to be carefully assessed to establish whether it is due to epilepsy or eclampsia. Breastfeeding is safe, although some drugs (phenobarbital and primidone) may have a sedative effect on the infant.

Diabetes

There are two types of diabetes in pregnancy: preexisting diabetes mellitus and GESTATIONAL DIABETES (pregnancy induced). Diabetes mellitus affects 3 percent of the population and since pregnancy usually exacerbates the disorder, specialized prenatal care is needed to minimize the maternal and fetal complications associated with diabetic pregnancy. Women with preexisting diabetes mellitus should aim for optimal control of their blood sugar levels before they become pregnant, since hyperglycemia at conception and during the period of embryogenesis increases the risk of miscarriage and may cause major fetal abnormalities including cardiac, skeletal, and neural tube defects. High-dose folic acid supplements should be prescribed for all diabetic women planning to become pregnant and continued until they reach the second trimester. A careful search for fetal abnormalities will be performed at the 20-week ultrasound scan.

Careful control of the mother's sugar levels should be maintained throughout pregnancy because maternal glucose, but not insulin, crosses the placenta. If your diabetes is usually managed with oral hypoglycemic drugs you will probably need to change to insulin injections. The additional demands of pregnancy make it more difficult to accurately control your blood sugar levels on oral drugs alone, since they are long-acting, less predictable than insulin, and cross the placenta. Maternal hyperglycemia prompts the secretion of additional insulin from the fetal pancreas, resulting in macrosomia (big babies), polycythemia (too many red blood cells), poor lung maturation, and problems for the newborn including hypoglycemia, respiratory distress syndrome, jaundice, and poor temperature control. Babies exposed to high and low blood sugar levels in utero are at risk of intrauterine death and stillbirth. Fetal growth and well-being will be assessed regularly. It is important to remember that babies of some diabetic mothers are growth restricted.

Women with diabetes are more prone to developing pregnancy-induced hypertension, preeclampsia, polyhydramnios, and urinary tract and vaginal candida infections. A combination of careful dietary measures and regular adjustments of the mother's insulin dosage is usually needed to maintain stable blood sugar levels in later pregnancy. You will be shown how to check your own blood sugar levels and you will also be asked to check your urine regularly for ketones. The timing of delivery, which should be performed in a unit with neonatal facilities, will be dictated by the presence or absence of fetal and maternal complications. Most women will require intravenous insulin infusions during labor and delivery.

Asthma

Some 3 percent of pregnant women will have symptoms of asthma, which may be missed because most pregnant women develop a degree of breathlessness. Asthma is often triggered by allergies to foods, chemicals, dust, pollen, and smoke, or it follows a viral chest infection. If possible, pregnant women should avoid exposure to these triggers. It tends to improve in pregnancy due to the increased production of maternal cortisone. Inhaled steroids and bronchodilator drugs have no effect on the fetus, but women who require oral steroids during pregnancy have a greater risk of developing PREECLAMPSIA and having a baby with INTRAUTERINE GROWTH RESTRICTION (IUGR). During labor and delivery, which need to be covered with IV steroids, epidural is

the best option for pain relief. Breastfeeding reduces the risk of the baby developing future allergies (atopy).

Inflammatory bowel disease

Inflammation of the small intestine (Crohn's disease) and large intestine (ulcerative colitis) usually causes profuse diarrhea, with blood and mucus in the stools, and is accompanied by severe abdominal pain. These symptoms may improve during pregnancy as a result of increased maternal steroid hormone levels. You will be advised not to get pregnant until your symptoms are controlled so that the amount of steroid medication needed is minimal during pregnancy. Vaginal delivery is preferable since women with this disease are at greater risk of postoperative complications.

Heart disease

Maternal heart disease during pregnancy is uncommon but potentially serious and should always be cared for in units with specialist expertise. Rheumatic heart disease used to be the most likely underlying cause of heart disease in pregnant women, but today this is rare. However, there are now a significant number of women of childbearing age who underwent surgery for congenital heart disease as a child. The dramatic improvement in the life expectancy of these women has allowed many of them to now be requesting help to achieve successful pregnancies of their own. Detailed

management is beyond the scope of this book but preventing sudden blood loss, controlling blood pressure, and ensuring that the second stage of labor is short, and that delivery is covered by antibiotics are all important issues.

Essential hypertension

Preexisting high blood pressure (essential hypertension) needs to be under good control when you are planning to become pregnant. The risk of developing PREECLAMPSIA (toxemia) and other severe problems such as kidney damage are greater if your blood pressure is high at the start of your pregnancy. Some of the antihypertensive drugs are not suitable for use in pregnancy, so you should talk to your doctor about your plans to become pregnant well in advance, or as soon as the pregnancy test is positive.

Renal disease

Occasionally renal disease presents for the first time during pregnancy, triggered by the extra filtering load placed on the kidneys and additional problems of HIGH BLOOD PRESSURE and PREECLAMPSIA. Women with existing renal disease need to understand that pregnancy can result in a marked deterioration in their renal function and an earlier requirement for dialysis. If the disease is progressive it is best to embark on pregnancy sooner rather than later. In relapsing disease it is better to aim for a remission before getting pregnant. Prepregnancy counseling should include advice on the risks of various medications to the fetus and the woman's fertility, the need for early medical care, and a possible change in medication, strict blood pressure control, and details of the obstetric problems that may be encountered (premature delivery, preeclampsia, IUGR). Women with good kidney transplant function can usually achieve a successful pregnancy with specialist help. Immunosuppressive drugs do not significantly increase the risk of fetal abnormalities but early delivery by cesarean section is common. Women with transplants should also be warned that they run an increased risk of an episode of graft rejection after pregnancy.

These pregnancies need careful team management by renal physicians and obstetricians.

Autoimmune disorders

Improved medical care for women with autoimmune or connective tissue disorders has led to an increase in the number of women embarking on pregnancy. Systemic lupus erythematosus is a multi-system disease that may affect the kidneys, skin, joints, nervous system, blood, heart and lungs. Maternal symptoms may deteriorate during pregnancy and postnatally and if the mother carries anti Ro or La antibodies, the fetus is at risk of congenital heart block and neonatal lupus. In antiphospholipid syndrome, the presence of cardiolipin antibodies or lupus anticoagulant leads to RECURRENT MISCARRIAGE,

late pregnancy complications and an increased risk of maternal THROMBOSIS. Treatment with aspirin and heparin significantly improves pregnancy outcome. Women with systemic sclerosis are at risk of serious pregnancy complications if they have heart, lung or kidney involvement. Rheumatoid arthritis usually improves during pregnancy but frequently relapses in the postpartum period. Pregnancies complicated by connective tissue disease require specialist prenatal care by a multi-disciplinary team, since the risks of PREECLAMPSIA, IUGR, ABRUPTION and prematurity are increased and may be exacerbated by the steroid medication that many of these women need to continue taking during pregnancy.

Thyroid disease

If you suffer from an under- or over-active thyroid it is unlikely that you will get pregnant until your thyroid function is controlled. Women with thyroid disease need careful supervision during pregnancy because alterations in their thyroid function can be masked by the symptoms of pregnancy. If you are taking drugs for your thyroid, your doctor may advise you to switch to another type when you become pregnant and the doses may need to be altered as pregnancy progresses. Hypothyroidism in the baby results in cretinism (a severe form of mental retardation), which is why all babies in Canada are screened during the first week of life (*see* p.389).

Acne

Although acne is not serious, some drug treatments for acne (such as the vitamin A analog Accutane and tetracyclines) can cause serious abnormalities in the unborn baby and should be discontinued before you try to conceive. If you find yourself pregnant unexpectedly, don't be alarmed — just stop the treatment immediately.

Psychiatric disorders

Mental health problems affecting pregnant women can be divided into psychotic and depressive illnesses. Schizophrenia affects 1 in 1,000 individuals and presents problems for pregnant women since people with schizophrenia are usually single, socially isolated, and likely to be heavy cigarette, alcohol, and drug users. The effect of antipsychotic drugs on the fetus, the capacity of the woman to give informed consent for procedures, and the likelihood that she will relapse postpartum all have serious safety implications for mother and baby. These problems are increasing because modern-day antipsychotic drugs no longer reduce fertility. Women with serious depression often experience a deterioration during pregnancy or the postpartum period, which is worsened if their medication is withdrawn or reduced suddenly. Postpartum depression may be better understood today (*see* p.391), but preexisting psychiatric disease in pregnant women remains stigmatized and poorly treated.

INFECTIONS AND ILLNESSES

I am regularly asked by pregnant women about the possible effects of an infectious illness on their own health and that of their baby. Common illnesses such as colds and flu are unlikely to cause harm (*see* pp.32–33) but others can have damaging effects. Information on these is provided here.

Chickenpox

Chickenpox is caused by varicella zoster virus and is transmitted by droplets spread at the time of face-to-face contact. The incubation period is between 10 and 21 days, during which a fever usually develops along with an itchy rash of watery blisters that burst and crust over in a few days. An individual with chickenpox is infectious for 48 hours before the blisters appear until they crust over. Chickenpox is so contagious that 90 percent of children have had it before they reach adolescence and a first infection during pregnancy is rare (3 per 1,000).

If you develop your first chicken-pox infection in the first eight weeks of pregnancy it is unlikely to cause a miscarriage, but if you catch it between eight and 20 weeks your baby may develop the congenital varicella syndrome with abnormalities affecting the limbs, eyes, skin, bowel, bladder, and brain, together with growth problems in later pregnancy — but the risk is small (1–2 percent). Between 20 and 36 weeks your baby will not be affected but the virus will remain in the body and may show up as shingles in the first years of life. However, if you develop chickenpox after 36 weeks

and up to 21 days after the delivery, your baby may develop chickenpox. This may be a severe infection (neonatal chickenpox) if it starts within five days of delivery or within the next three weeks, because the newborn baby's immune system is not mature enough to deal with the virus. These complications can be avoided if the problem has been identified and your baby is given a special antibody injection called ZIG (zoster immune globulin), which reduces the severity of the attack if it is administered before symptoms appear. The antiviral drug acyclovir may reduce the symptoms if it is started within 24 hours of the rash appearing.

If you think that you have been exposed to chickenpox, your doctor will arrange a blood test to establish your immunity. If there is any uncertainty, your baby will be given a ZIG injection at the time of delivery.

Rubella

Ninety percent of pregnant women are immune to rubella because they have been previously infected or vaccinated as children (part of the MMR program — measles, mumps, rubella). Of the 10 percent of susceptible women, only a few will be infected for the first time in

pregnancy but this has serious implications for the fetus, who may develop congenital rubella syndrome. Rubella infection is spread by breathing infected air particles and maternal symptoms develop two to three weeks after exposure — a rash of flat pink spots on the face and ears, which then spreads to the trunk accompanied by pain and swelling of the joints, together with fever and swollen lymph glands. Infected individuals can infect others for one week before symptoms begin and for a few days after they have passed.

If you develop a rash in pregnancy, your doctor will take a blood sample to establish whether you have rubella infection and will repeat the test two weeks later to see whether you have developed an antibody response. If rubella is confirmed before 12 weeks your baby has an 80 percent risk of congenital abnormalities ranging from eye cataracts, deafness, heart defects to learning difficulties. Between weeks 13 and 17, a primary rubella infection may cause deafness in the baby. After 17 weeks there is no risk to your baby. Babies born with congenital rubella may have a low birthweight, skin rash, enlarged liver and spleen, and jaundice and may remain contagious for months.

Parvovirus

The symptoms of infection with parvovirus B19 are similar to rubella (German measles) but may be so mild that they go unrecognized. Parvovirus is spread by droplets (coughing and sneezing) and contact with fomites (substances that absorb infectious particles, such as bedding, clothes, and carpets). It does not cause congenital abnormalities and most infections during pregnancy are followed by healthy live births. It is not common during pregnancy but can cause late miscarriage and intrauterine death which is usually associated with FETAL HYDROPS.

Cytomegalovirus (CMV)

CMV is one of the herpes viruses and is so common in young children that 50 percent of adults have been infected before the age of 30 years. The infection often goes unnoticed but may cause a vague flulike illness with sore throat, mild fever, aching limbs, and fatigue. It is usually acquired by close physical contact or from infected blood, urine, saliva, mucus, or breast milk.

Only a few susceptible women will experience a primary CMV infection during pregnancy and among these women the chance of transmitting the virus to the baby is about 40 percent. These babies are at risk of congenital CMV, which may result in mental retardation and hearing, sight, and developmental problems but the number of affected babies is small. Currently, there is no treatment to stop or reverse the effects of congenital CMV but new antiviral drugs are being investigated. Since CMV is the most common infectious cause of mental retardation in Canada, the search for a vaccine is ongoing. At-risk groups (hospital, laboratory, and nursery workers) need to take simple aseptic precautions, such as handwashing, when pregnant.

Toxoplasmosis

Most of the population is immune to toxoplasmosis due to a previous infection, which may have been so mild that the symptoms of a flulike illness with low-grade fever and swollen glands went unnoticed. Infection for the first time during pregnancy is rare (1 in 2,000) but can cause serious problems for the baby. During the first three months of pregnancy the risk of the baby becoming infected is low but the risk of injury is high and includes early or late miscarriage and live-born babies with severe neurological problems (HYDROCEPHALY, cerebral calcification, and damage to the eyes). Near the time of delivery, the baby is more likely to become infected, but congenital toxoplasma infection is less likely to cause neurological damage.

Typically, pregnant women are not routinely tested for toxoplasmosis but if a blood test suggests that a woman is infected she will be offered antibiotic treatment to reduce the risk of transmission to the baby and may need to undergo cordocentesis (*see* p.143) to establish whether the baby has been infected. Some women opt for termination of pregnancy if this is confirmed.

Tuberculosis

TB infection used to be extremely rare in pregnancy since the prevalence of pulmonary (chest) TB in developed countries is low and in underdeveloped countries more widespread disease involving the pelvis frequently led to infertility. However, increasingly mobile populations have resulted in a significant number of pregnant women with pulmonary TB. Individuals with HIV infection are more susceptible to infection with TB due to alterations in their immune response. Active TB in the first half of pregnancy is usually treated with isoniazid antibiotic, but after 20 weeks it is safe to use rifampicin. If the mother's TB is inactive at the time of delivery, the baby needs to be vaccinated with BCG, does not need to be isolated, and can be breastfed.

Listeria

Listeria is a food-borne bacteria. Infection during pregnancy is uncommon but can have serious consequences for the baby including late miscarriage and intrauterine death. During pregnancy women have lowered resistance to listeria, which multiplies rapidly in the placenta. Typically the mother experiences a brief flulike illness with malaise, nausea, diarrhea, and abdominal pain. Penicillin antibiotics are a rapid cure but the best way to avoid problems during pregnancy is to take careful measures to prevent any exposure to infection (*see* above).

Streptococcus B infection

Between 5 and 30 percent of women carry this normal gut bacterium in their upper vagina. Most have no symptoms although it can produce a discharge or urinary tract infection. If the infection is present during labor the baby may be affected. Only 1 percent of at-risk babies develop strep B infection by swallowing or inhaling vaginal secretions, but this neonatal infection can be fatal. Classically, signs of septicemia and meningitis develop some two days after birth. Premature babies are at greater risk of infection particularly if the mother's membranes are ruptured. Prenatal screening for strep B is usually done at the first prenatal visit and between 35–37 weeks of pregnancy. However, if you have had a previously affected baby or threaten to go into premature labor you will be offered testing since the use of IV antibiotics during labor and four hours before the delivery is the best way to protect the baby from neonatal infection.

Sexually transmitted diseases

HERPES

There are two types of herpes infection. Type 1 (HSV1) causes cold sores of the mouth or lips. Type 2 (HSV2), known as genital herpes, causes painful ulcers of the vulva, vagina or cervix. If a mother develops her first genital herpes infection near the time of delivery, there is a 10 percent risk that the baby will

become infected during the delivery. The consequences of this can be severe, including herpes encephalitis or meningitis, which is why cesarean section is advised and after delivery the baby will be given antiviral drugs. Following her primary infection the mother produces antibodies which will protect a future fetus but do not prevent her from suffering further attacks. It is currently standard practice to perform a cesarean section on pregnant women who have secondary genital herpes infection in order to reduce the risk of transmission of the virus to the newborn.

GONORRHEA

Gonorrhea is a highly contagious bacterial infection that usually affects the cervix but may be present in the urethra, rectum or throat. It is often accompanied by CHLAMYDIA, TRICHOMONAS, and SYPHILIS infection. Unprotected sex with an infected individual leads to transmission of the infection in 90 percent of cases. The infection may be asymptomatic or accompanied by vaginal discharge, pain, and urinary discomfort. It is an important cause of pelvic inflammation, which damages the fallopian tubes, leading to ECTOPIC PREGNANCY and infertility. Infection during pregnancy is associated with premature rupture of membranes and preterm delivery. The risk of postpartum pelvic inflammatory disease and systemic spread (painful joints and skin rash) is increased. The diagnosis is best made from culture of cervical swabs and effectively treated with penicillin antibiotics. Although

the baby is not at risk of infection during pregnancy, exposure to the organism during delivery may cause neonatal conjunctivitis and occasionally a septicemia requiring intensive treatment.

CHLAMYDIA

The bacteria *Chlamydia trachomatis* is the most common STD in Canada. Although 40 percent of infected men have symptoms such as penile discharge, testicular inflammation, and urinary discomfort, only 15 percent of infected women have symptoms such as vaginal discharge, pelvic pain or urinary problems. Even when there are no symptoms, infection may be present in the vagina, cervix, uterus, anus, urethra or eyes and can have serious consequences. Silent damage to the fallopian tubes increases the risk of ectopic pregnancy and may lead to infertility. If present at the time of delivery, 40 percent of babies will become infected. Chlamydia is the leading cause of neonatal conjunctivitis (eye infection) which may result in blindness or neonatal pneumonia. Early diagnosis is important because the infection can be effectively treated with antibiotics.

SYPHILIS

Syphilis infection is carried by the bacterium *Treponema pallidum*. It is not common in pregnant women, but the incidence is increasing in some ethnic groups and damage to the baby can be prevented by early treatment with penicillin. This is why all pregnant women undergo screening for syphilis infection at their initial prenatal visit. In the primary stage of infection, an ulcer (chancre) appears, which is similar to herpes but less painful and lasts three to six weeks. Untreated, the infection progresse in a few months to secondary syphilis with fever, an itchy rash, swollen glands, weight loss, and fatigue. Without treatment, tertiary syphilis develops some years later with damage to the brain, nerves, and many other body organs. The impact of syphilis during pregnancy is that the bacteria can penetrate the placenta after 15 weeks and infect the fetus. Seventy percent of infected women will transmit the infection to the fetus. If the fetus survives the initial infection, it will be in the second stage of the illness at birth. In 30 percent this will result in stillbirth and in a further 30 percent the baby will be born with congenital syphilis and suffer from fits, developmental delay, skin and mouth sores, infected bones, jaundice, anemia, and microcephaly. A single dose of penicillin usually cures the maternal infection and prevents fetal infection. At birth the baby will be given further antibiotics if necessary. Diagnosing syphilis should prompt an additional search for chlamydia, gonorrhea, HIV, and hepatitis B and C infections.

HIV INFECTION

HIV infection is most commonly transmitted through sexual contact, the use of contaminated needles or infected blood and blood products. In Western countries most cases of HIV infection are found in homosexual/bisexual males and heterosexual drug abusers. In central London the prevalence of HIV infection in pregnant women is less than 1 percent but in some African countries the prenatal prevalence is higher than 40 percent.

Becoming pregnant does not appear to affect the health of an HIV-infected woman but has serious implications for her baby. Approximately 20 percent of HIV-infected newborn babies develop AIDS in the first year of life and die before four years of age. Many of the remainder have developed AIDS before the age of six. Routine prenatal screening and treatment of HIV-positive pregnant women can dramatically reduce the risk of transmission to the baby and development of full-blown AIDS in the mother thereby improving her long-term survival. HIV transmission to the baby can be reduced from 20 percent to 2 percent by treating positive pregnant women with a combination of antiretroviral drugs during the last few months of pregnancy, delivering the baby by elective cesarean section, avoidance of breastfeeding, and actively treating the newborn baby.

Sadly, the majority of pregnant women with HIV live in countries where the high cost of drugs and medical interventions excludes them from obtaining life-saving treatment.

TRICHOMONIASIS

This infection is caused by the organism *Trichomonas vaginalis*, which inhabits the urinary tract and vagina and is frequently accompanied by chlamydia and gonorrhea. It may be symptomless or cause a thin, frothy, yellow-green vaginal discharge with a fishy smell, together with inflammation and pain in the vagina and urethra. Infection during pregnancy is occasionally responsible for pneumonia in the newborn baby. The diagnosis can be made on a cervical smear or vaginal swab. Infections should be treated with metronidazole antibiotic, which is safe to use in late pregnancy and during breastfeeding.

BACTERIAL VAGINOSIS

This is a common cause of vaginal discharge, affecting 10–20 percent of women, but may be symptomless. The discharge is usually thin, grey-coloured and nonitchy, with a strong fishy odour. It is diagnosed by the presence of clue cells on a vaginal smear test. In pregnancy, the altered hormonal environment in the vagina is less acidic, favoring the growth of the many organisms that are present in bacterial vaginosis.

BV infection during pregnancy has been strongly linked with late miscarriage and premature birth. Although treatment with clindamycin or metronidazole antibiotics clears the infection in a few days, recurrence in pregnancy is common. Screening and treating all infected pregnant women has not reduced the preterm birth rate. It appears that pregnant women with a history of premature delivery are particularly susceptible to this infection and may benefit from regular screening and antibiotic treatment when the infection is present.

FETAL ABNORMALITIES

Congenital abnormalities are present at birth and are often due to genetic causes. Others are acquired as a result of environmental factors during pregnancy or occur for no known reason. You will find more on how these abnormalities develop in the prenatal test section (*see* pp.134–43).

CHROMOSOME ABNORMALITIES

These abnormalities are due to a fault in the baby's complement of 23 pairs of chromosomes, because there are too many, too few, or one chromosome is abnormal. The most common chromosomal disorder, Down syndrome, is discussed in detail on page 147.

Trisomies

PATAU SYNDROME (TRISOMY 13)
In Patau syndrome, which occurs in 1 in 10,000 live births, three copies of chromosome 13 are present. The majority of affected babies miscarry early in pregnancy, but of the 20 percent that are liveborn, most die within a few days of birth. Those that survive have severe mental handicap. Microcephaly and severe facial abnormalities, too many fingers and toes, EXOMPHALOS and HEART AND KIDNEY DEFECTS are characteristic and are usually identified during pregnancy on ultrasound scan.

EDWARD SYNDROME (TRISOMY 18)
In Edward syndrome, three copies of chromosome 18 are present; this occurs in 1 in 7,000 live births. The physical malformations include INTRAUTERINE GROWTH RESTRICTION (IUGR), strawberry-shaped head, CHOROID PLEXUS CYSTS, HEART AND KIDNEY DEFECTS, DIAPHRAGMATIC HERNIA, EXOMPHALOS, low-set ears, small receding jaw, shortened limbs, clenched hands, and feet with a curved sole described as "rocker bottom," all of which may be seen on the 20-week scan. The integrated screening test (*see* p.138) will identify 60 percent of babies with Edward syndrome. Severe mental retardation is usual and most of these babies die within the first year of life.

Triploidy (69XXY or XYY)

The presence of an extra set of 23 chromosomes, called triploidy, may result from an egg being fertilized by more than one sperm or the fertilized egg not dividing. It occurs in 2 percent of conceptions, but these pregnancies usually miscarry (20 percent of all chromosomal miscarriages are triploidies). When the extra set of chromosomes comes from the father, the embryo does not develop but the placental tissues grow rapidly in an uncontrolled manner and the pregnancy rarely continues beyond 20 weeks (*see* HYDATIDIFORM MOLES p.422). When the extra set comes from the mother, the pregnancy may continue into the third trimester. Although the placenta is normal, the fetus usually has severe asymmetrical growth retardation. Triploidy is not influenced by maternal age.

Translocation

Translocation occurs when a piece of one chromosome becomes attached to the end of another. Individuals with a balanced translocation appear normal because the normal chromosome counteracts the effect of the abnormal one. If he or she becomes a parent, there are three possible outcomes: the baby may have normal chromosomes; it can inherit the balanced translocation; or it may inherit an unbalanced translocation, which invariably leads to miscarriage or a severe abnormality in the baby. Translocations may be reciprocal or Robertsonian and are a cause of RECURRENT MISCARRIAGE. New translocations can arise that are not inherited from either parent.

Sex chromosome abnormalities

TURNER SYNDROME (45XO)

This occurs in 1 in 2,500 live-borns; one of the two X chromosomes is completely missing. These girls have normal intelligence, but their growth is seriously affected, and they have no menstrual periods and are therefore infertile. Other physical characteristics are webbing of the neck and cubitus valgus (a wide carrying angle at the elbows). A high percentage of fetuses with a single X chromosome miscarry or are identified by prenatal diagnosis. Abnormalities detected on ultrasound include cystic hygroma (a large fluid-filled sac behind the neck), CARDIAC DEFECTS, particularly coarctation of the aorta, HYDROPS FETALIS, and horseshoe kidneys. Turner syndrome can also exist in mosaic form, meaning that the girl has two different cell lines — 46XX and 45XO. If her egg cells contain a normal set of chromosomes, she will not necessarily be infertile.

KLINEFELTER SYNDROME (47XXY)

When boys have an extra X sex chromosome, it is known as Klinefelter syndrome and occurs in 1 in 1,000 live births. In adult life these men tend to be tall with a reduced head circumference and lower intelligence level but are not usually considered mentally retarded. Men with Klinefelter syndrome are infertile and more susceptible to autoimmune disease, malignancy, and cardiovascular disease in adult life.

TRIPLE X (47XXX)

Women with an extra X sex chromosome have normal fertility and there is a wide variation in mental capacity. Some may have lower intelligence than normal, but rarely suffer from mental retardation. This occurs in 1 in 1,000 live births.

SUPERMALES (47XYY)

Some boys have an extra Y chromosome. They have normal appearance, mental development, and fertility. In adult life they have an increased incidence of language and reading difficulties, hyperactivity, and impulsive and aggressive behavior. This occurs in 1 in 1,000 live births.

Dominant genetic disorders

FAMILIAL HYPERCHOLESTEROLEMIA

More than 60 million people suffer from this genetic disorder, although men tend to be more severely affected than women. High blood cholesterol levels and narrowing of major blood vessels lead to heart attacks at an early age and fatty skin deposits around the eyelids. In parents who have a history of early heart disease, blood from their baby's umbilical cord can be tested for high cholesterol levels at birth. This allows the diagnosis to be made at birth and offers the possibility of preventative lifestyle measures to reduce the severity of the disease.

HUNTINGDON'S DISEASE

This dominant disease affects 1 in 20,000 and has an insidious onset in middle life, starting with

personality changes and progressing to uncontrolled movements, aggressive sexual behavior, and dementia. Huntington's disease has full penetrance so that children of an affected parent have a 50 percent risk of the disease, which never skips a generation. Affected individuals and their families often try to hide the early onset of symptoms but the sufferer is usually only too aware of the problems lying ahead. Recent linkage studies show that the abnormal gene is on chromosome 4 and analysis of fetal DNA obtained from CVS samples provides accurate prenatal diagnosis and prediction of late onset disease. Genetic counseling for affected families is essential.

Recessive genetic disorders

TAY-SACHS DISEASE

This is a fatal recessive disorder common in Ashkenazi Jewish families and French Canadians. It is caused by a deficiency in the enzyme hexosaminidase A, which results in fatty material being deposited in the nerve cells of the brain. Babies with the disease appear normal at first but by six months have started to develop progressive motor weakness and mental disability. The child becomes blind, deaf, and unable to swallow, and suffers increasingly severe fits before dying at the age of three to five years. Carriers of the disease can be identified by a simple blood test before or during pregnancy. If both parents are carriers, there is a 25 percent chance in each pregnancy of their having an affected baby. Amniocentesis or chorionic villus sampling will be offered to confirm the diagnosis. Because there is no treatment for this disease, many couples choose to terminate an affected pregnancy.

CYSTIC FIBROSIS

This is the most common recessive genetic disease in Caucasians, affecting 1 in 2,500 live births. The disorder is due to an abnormality in sodium transport, which makes the secretions of the lungs, digestive system, and sweat glands too thick and sticky. Mucus accumulates in the lungs, leading to severe chest infections and since the pancreas and liver are also affected, the normal flow of digestive enzymes in the gut is compromised. This causes malnutrition if lifelong daily enzyme supplements are not started promptly. The severity of the disease is variable, ranging from death in the first year of life to poor health in middle age. Regular physical therapy can help improve the lung problems. Males with cystic fibrosis are infertile, due to blockage of their sperm transport tubes (vas deferens).

One in 22 Caucasians are carriers for the most common gene mutation responsible for CF (DF508), which is located on chromosome 7, making it possible to screen prospective parents and undertake prenatal diagnosis on DNA samples from a fetus at risk of the disease. However, there are many different mutations in the CF gene and current screening techniques can only identify 85 percent of carriers.

Carrier detection for CF is offered to Caucasians and individuals with a history of CF, partners of identified CF carriers, parents of a fetus with echogenic bowel detected on ultrasound scan, and sperm donors. It is important that couples who undergo screening receive detailed genetic counseling and are aware of the limitations of the tests.

PHENYLKETONURIA (PKU)

This recessive genetic disease is present in 1 in 14,000 births. It is caused by a defective gene that results in a deficiency of the enzyme that converts the essential amino acid phenylalanine into tyrosine. The buildup of high levels of phenylalanine in the bloodstream is toxic to the developing brain. If a special diet with low phenylalanine is started in the first few weeks of life the irreversible brain damage and learning disabilities can be avoided. All babies are tested for PKU after birth (*see* p.389).

SICKLE CELL ANEMIA AND THALASSEMIA

If you are of Mediterranean or African origin, you will be offered a special electrophoresis test of your hemoglobin to determine whether you have sickle cell or thalassemia traits (*see* p.424). If you carry the sickle cell trait, it is important that your partner's sickle cell status is established early in your pregnancy, because there is a chance that your baby could inherit a double dose of the trait and develop full-blown sickle cell disease. This leads to severe anemia, infections, pain, and

eventually heart and kidney failure. Similarly, if you carry the A or B thalassemia trait, you will need to arrange for your partner to be tested, too. A baby with full-blown thalassemia suffers from severe anemia and iron overload, leading to multiple organ failure. If both parents are sickle cell carriers they may choose to undergo an invasive test such as amniocentesis or chorionic villus sampling to find out whether the baby has inherited the disease. Prenatal diagnosis is also offered when both parents carry the alpha or beta thalassemia trait.

Sex-linked genetic disorders

DUCHENNE'S MUSCULAR DYSTROPHY (DMD)

This is the most common sex-linked disorder and affects 1 in 4,000 boys. He may appear normal in infancy, but, between the ages of four and 10 years, loses his ability to walk due to muscular weakness and is usually confined to a wheelchair soon after. Identifying female carriers of DMD used to depend on finding increased blood levels of the muscle enzyme creatinine kinase. This was an unreliable test and most couples carrying a male fetus were therefore offered a termination of pregnancy. The DMD gene has now been identified. In approximately two-thirds of families, a deletion is present on the short arm of chromosome X. Hence most female carriers can be identified before pregnancy. Prenatal diagnosis can also be performed on fetal DNA samples during pregnancy, to establish whether the baby is affected by DMD.

HEMOPHILIA

This X-linked recessive disorder affects 1 in 10,000 males and is due to a deficiency in blood coagulation factors that makes the blood clot too slowly. There are two types of hemophilia. The most common is hemophilia A, in which low levels of factor VIII are present. In hemophilia B (also called Christmas disease), there is a deficiency in factor IX. The symptoms of both are prolonged bleeding from wounds and into joints, muscles, and other tissues following minor trauma. The severity of the disease depends on how little of the clotting factor is present in the blood.

Today, both hemophilia A and B can be treated by injections or transfusions of plasma containing the missing clotting factors and, with medical help, sufferers can hope to lead a more normal life. This emphasizes the importance of identifying which type of hemophilia is present. Since carrier females may have normal or low levels of the clotting factors, diagnosis was unreliable before DNA testing became available. In families with a history of hemophilia, female carriers can now be accurately identified before pregnancy and fetal DNA testing during pregnancy can establish whether a male baby is affected.

FRAGILE X SYNDROME

This X-linked disorder is the most common form of inherited mental retardation (1 in 1,500 males and 1 in 2,500 females). Mental impairment is variable in carrier females, but DNA testing to confirm the suspected diagnosis of Fragile X or carrier status is now possible. Genetic counseling should be offered to all women and their families with a history of mental retardation, since as many as 1 in 200 women carry the gene mutation.

OTHER CONGENITAL ABNORMALITIES

This section includes fetal abnormalities for which there is no known specific genetic cause although some, such as neural tube defects, tend to run in families. The list includes most of the abnormalities that sometimes become apparent on ultrasound scans.

Neural tube defects (NTDs)

These are one of the most common and serious congenital abnormalities. In the absence of prenatal screening about 1 in every 400 babies will be affected. The embryonic neural tube fails to close properly during the first four weeks of pregnancy, resulting in incomplete development of the brain and spinal cord and varying degrees of permanent neurological damage. The most severe forms are anencephaly (the skull bones are incomplete and the brain is underdeveloped) and encephalocoele (brain tissue projects through a hole in the skull). These babies are rarely liveborn. In spina bifida (myelomeningocoele) the spinal cord is not protected by the bony spinal column and may be closed (covered by protective membranes) or open (no covering membranes). The degree of paralysis, weakness, and sensory disability is variable and can range from a wheelchair existence and complete lack of bladder and bowel function to mild walking difficulties. However, babies with open spina bifida are often severely handicapped, requiring frequent surgical procedures and prolonged hospitalization. The majority of severe cases develop HYDROCEPHALUS, resulting in mental retardation and learning difficulties. The mildest form of NTD is spina bifida occulta, a lesion in the lowest part of the sacral spine that usually goes unnoticed and is present in 5 percent of healthy babies. Prenatal screening for open spina bifida has been greatly improved by routine ultrasound scanning. In addition to the bony defect in the vertebral column, most babies with a myelomeningocoele have scalloping of the frontal skull bones (the lemon sign on an ultrasound scan) and a cerebellum that looks more like a banana than the normal dumbbell-shaped structure. Closed spina bifida has a better prognosis because the defect is more easily treated surgically after delivery, but is more difficult to detect prenatally.

Spina bifida can run in families, but 95 percent of these babies are born to women with no family history. It is linked to poor diet and the risk of recurrence is 1 in 20 after a previously affected baby. Taking folic acid supplements for three months before pregnancy and during the first trimester prevents 75 percent of cases. Women with a previous NTD or on antiepileptic medication should take high doses of folic acid before conception (see p.51).

Hydrocephalus

This condition (often referred to as water on the brain) is caused by too much cerebrospinal fluid. It is usually due to a blockage in the circulation of the fluid or because of an over-production or reduced absorption of the fluid. Hydrocephalus is often associated with SPINA BIFIDA or follows a brain hemorrhage in a premature baby. If the problem is present before birth it can be seen on an ultrasound scan. As the head swells, the brain tissue is compressed, the skull bones become thinner, the sutures of the head widen, and the fontanelles bulge. After delivery, if the hydrocephalus is due to a blockage it may be possible to insert a tube to drain the fluid from the ventricles of the brain into the abdominal cavity or heart. Occasionally, the hydrocephalus is inherited as a sex-linked recessive disorder in males and these families need genetic counseling.

Microcephaly

In these babies the bony skull and brain size are smaller than average. The babies are nearly always severely intellectually impaired. Recognized causes include rubella infection in the first trimester, CYTOMEGALOVIRUS, TOXOPLASMOSIS and SYPHILIS infections, severe irradiation, and maternal heroin and alcohol addiction. A few cases are inherited as a recessive genetic disorder. Often no obvious cause can be found.

Choroid plexus cysts (CPC)

These cysts in the ventricles of the baby's brain are usually bilateral and seen in as many as 1 percent of all 20-week screening ultrasound anomaly scans. Most CPCs are now thought to be benign structures and usually disappear by 24 weeks. However, since they are associated with TRISOMY 18, detailed counseling will be needed to help parents decide whether they should expose their pregnancy to the risk of an invasive diagnostic test.

Gut abnormalities

DUODENAL ATRESIA
In this disorder, the small gut between the bottom of the stomach and ileum is absent and is usually diagnosed by the double bubble sign on ultrasound scan (bubble 1 is the normal stomach, bubble 2 results from the duodenum being unable to empty into the lower gut, which can also cause POLYHYDRAMNIOS). The blockage can be resolved by surgery

immediately after delivery, but in one-third of cases this abnormality is associated with Down syndrome.

ESOPHAGEAL ATRESIA
In this disorder the tube between the throat and stomach is partially absent, leading to vomiting and excess dribbling immediately after delivery. It is often associated with a fistula (passage) between the esophagus and trachea (windpipe). Hence POLYHYDRAMNIOS and the double bubble sign may not be evident on ultrasound scans. If a fistula is present there is a serious risk of food entering the lungs and choking the baby. Esophageal atresia requires immediate surgery and sometimes multiple operations, but responds well to surgical correction if it is an isolated problem.

HYPERECHOIC FETAL BOWEL
If the bowel is seen to be very echogenic (white streaks) on an prenatal ultrasound scan, this may be secondary to a major chromosomal abnormality, CYSTIC FIBROSIS, bowel obstruction, fetal infection, or GROWTH RESTRICTION. It can also occur in entirely normal fetuses.

Diaphragmatic hernia

This serious congenital abnormality affects 1 in 3,000 babies and can be diagnosed on the 20-week ultrasound scan. The muscular diaphragm separates the contents of the chest (heart and lungs) from the abdomen (liver, stomach, spleen, intestines). If a defect occurs in the development of the diaphragm, varying amounts of these abdominal organs can herniate into the chest cavity. In about 50 percent of fetuses there are associated chromosomal abnormalities, genetic syndromes and other structural abnormalities. At birth the baby will need immediate intensive care and ventilation before undergoing multiple surgical operations to replace the abdominal organs and reconstruct the diaphragm. In utero surgery may be attempted in specialist centers to give the affected lung a better chance of developing normally.

Abdominal wall defects

OMPHALOCELE (EXOMPHALOS)
Omphalocele occurs in 1 in 5,000 babies and is due to a defect in the abdominal wall underneath the umbilicus, through which varying amounts of small bowel and liver protrude covered by the peritoneal membrane. Most of these babies are identified on ultrasound scan during pregnancy and some 50 percent have associated chromosomal, cardiac, or bladder abnormalities. Karyotyping (chromosome analysis) and ultrasound scans are needed to assess the problem. If it is an isolated defect, surgical correction after birth has a good prognosis, although it may require multiple operations.

GASTROSCHISIS
In this condition loops of bowel protrude through the abdominal wall defect and are not covered by peritoneum. In most cases the abnormality is isolated and there is no increased incidence of

chromosomal abnormalities. The abdominal wall defect is usually small and can be repaired easily. Early delivery is usually planned.

Cardiac abnormalities

Structural heart disorders are the most common severe congenital abnormality in newborn babies, affecting 8 per 1,000 live births. They are an important cause of perinatal and childhood death. The incidence of cardiac abnormalities is increased in babies who are premature, have Down syndrome, are infected with RUBELLA virus or who have mothers with congenital HEART DISEASE, DIABETES, EPILEPSY, or families with a history of cardiac abnormalities. In 30 percent of babies with a cardiac defect another structural abnormality is found and in 20 percent a chromosomal disorder is present.

Many heart defects can be diagnosed on ultrasound scan during pregnancy. This is why the 20-week anomaly scan routinely aims to obtain a view of the four chamber heart. If an abnormality is suspected, further scans will be arranged. The option of fetal karyotyping (chromosome analysis) should be offered to parents since the results may influence the plan for management at the time of delivery. Some cardiac lesions may require immediate surgical correction, whereas others can be dealt with later on.

SEPTAL DEFECTS
These "holes in the heart" account for 50 percent of all congenital heart

defects. A hole in the septum (wall) dividing the two upper (atrial) or the two lower (ventricular) chambers of the heart, results in oxygenated and deoxygenated blood being mixed instead of separated. An atrial septal defect may result in few symptoms, but ventricular septal defects give rise to a loud heart murmur, and since the heart has to pump harder, it becomes enlarged. Untreated, the problem can be very serious particularly when complicated by CYANOSIS (blue baby).

CYANOTIC DEFECTS (BLUE BABY)
These disorders account for 25 percent of all congenital heart disease and require expert surgical and medical care. The outlook is often poor, depending on the severity of the lesion. In Tetralogy of Fallot (one of the most common forms of complex congenital heart defects), there is a large septal defect, abnormal aorta, and narrowing of the pulmonary valve. When the aorta and pulmonary artery are connected the wrong way around most of the blood receives no oxygen from the lungs and any oxygenated blood is sent back to the lungs rather than being pumped around the body.

PATENT DUCTUS ARTERIOSUS
Ten percent of cases of congenital heart disease are caused by failure of the duct between the heart and lungs to close after birth. This is more common in premature babies. The duct usually closes on its own given time but may require indomethacin drug treatment and occasionally surgery.

HYPOPLASTIC LEFT HEART

This is present in 10 percent of babies with congenital heart disease. The left side of the heart is so under-developed that when the ductus closes at birth, the baby cannot obtain oxygenated blood. This condition is often fatal and when diagnosed prenatally, parents may choose to terminate the pregnancy.

Hydrops fetalis

This is present in a wide variety of fetal, maternal and placental disorders. It is diagnosed on prenatal ultrasound scan when widespread accumulation of fluid in the body leads to edema of the skin and effusions (pools of fluid) around the heart, lungs, and abdominal organs. Immune hydrops occurs in severe RHESUS SENSITIZATION (see p.128). Nonimmune hydrops may be seen with fetal chromosomal, heart, lung, blood, and metabolic disorders, some congenital infections, and malformations of the placenta and umbilical cord. The overall outlook is poor, with a mortality rate of 80–90 percent depending on the cause. Despite investigations, including invasive fetal testing, the abnormality remains unexplained in one-third of cases.

Renal abnormalities

The fetal kidneys and bladder are visible at the 20-week scan. Severe renal problems are usually accompanied by OLIGOHYDRAMNIOS or reduced amniotic fluid because urine production is compromised.

POTTER SYNDROME

The fetal kidneys are absent (agenesis) or poorly formed and the lungs are underdeveloped as a result of the lack of amniotic fluid. The baby usually has facial abnormalities including widely spaced eyes, down-turned nose, low-set ears, and a small jaw. At birth, no urine is passed and the baby dies within a few hours from respiratory failure. The problem is rare but more common in boys.

HYDRONEPHROSIS

Enlarged kidneys are identified on ultrasound scan in 2 percent of all fetuses during the second trimester. They are usually due to narrowing or blockage of one or both of the ureters. When isolated, the finding is often insignificant. However, it may be associated with chromosomal abnormalities, in particular Down syndrome. Severe hydronephrosis leads to kidney damage due to the pressure of retained urine on the normal kidney tissue and may need to be drained by inserting a ureteric shunt to prevent kidney failure.

POLYCYSTIC KIDNEYS

This is a recessive genetic disorder with variable expression. Some fetuses will appear to have normal kidneys on prenatal ultrasound scan and present with renal failure as a teenager. Others will be found at the 20-week anomaly scan because of absent liquor and grossly enlarged kidneys. Adult polycystic kidney disease is a dominant genetic disease which can present in utero with enlarged cystic kidneys. One of the parents usually has kidney cysts.

FETAL SURGERY

A few fetal abnormalities may be amenable to corrective treatment before birth. These procedures are only undertaken in specialist units by pioneering fetal surgeons. The most successful techniques to date are those that involve inserting needles or fine tubes through the mother's abdomen and into the uterine cavity or the fetus under ultrasound guidance. Intrauterine blood transfusions may be needed for severe Rhesus incompatibility, and drugs to correct irregularities of the fetal heartbeat or destroy life-threatening tumors can be directly injected into the fetus. Occasionally, fetal tissue samples may need to be obtained to make the diagnosis of a rare genetic disorder.

Other examples of ultrasound-guided fetal surgery are the insertion of drainage tubes into severe cases of HYDROCEPHALUS or HYDRONEPHROSIS.

Open fetal surgery is experimental and is usually only considered in situations where there is nothing to lose. The mother's abdomen is opened and an incision in the uterus is made to gain access to the fetus and conduct the surgery. Great care is taken to keep the baby warm, replace the amniotic fluid, and avoid damaging the placenta. Even if the surgery can be successfully performed, the baby remains at risk of premature labor, infection, and leakage of amniotic fluid. Diaphragmatic hernias and fetal tumors may be treated in this way.

PROBLEMS IN PREGNANCY AND LABOR

Although the majority of pregnancies and births are straightforward, there are inevitably instances when something does not go according to plan. Some of the problems that you may encounter are summarized here with information on the up-to-date methods of managing and treating them.

Ectopic pregnancy

An ectopic pregnancy develops outside the uterine cavity. This occurs in about 1 in 50 pregnancies. Although some ectopics "miscarry" without complication (tubal miscarriage), there is a risk that the pregnancy may continue to grow and rupture through the walls of the fallopian tube. The vast majority of ectopic pregnancies occur in the fallopian tubes, but occasionally they may be found on the ovary or in the abdominal cavity.

The general symptoms are the same as those of early pregnancy, accompanied by a positive pregnancy test and lower abdominal pain, which almost always starts before any vaginal bleeding has occurred. If your doctor suspects an ectopic pregnancy you will be sent for an ultrasound scan. This will show that there is no pregnancy sac within the uterine cavity, although the lining of the uterus may be thickened. The ectopic may be removed by surgery. More and more hospitals are developing the expertise to do this by laparoscopy, avoiding the need for an open operation. If the ectopic has not ruptured and the hormone HCG levels are low, treatment with methotrexate may be possible.

Hydatidiform mole

Hydatidiform moles are the most common type of placental tumor. There are complete moles and partial moles. Complete moles are rare in Caucasian women (1 in every 1,200–2,000 pregnancies), but are much more common in women from Southeast Asia.

Moles are derived entirely from the cells of the father, due to an accident that occurs at the time of fertilization. No embryo is present in the pregnancy sac, but the placental tissues develop rapidly in an uncontrolled fashion, resembling a bunch of grapes on an ultrasound scan. Persistent bleeding and severe nausea are often associated with the presence of these moles, and the size of the uterus is usually larger than would be expected for the menstrual dates. A complete mole may develop into an invasive cancer in a small percentage of cases, so specialist treatment is needed.

Partial moles are more common and usually mimic the appearance of an inevitable or incomplete miscarriage. The partial mole contains a fetus/embryo which has three sets of chromosomes instead of two (TRIPLOIDY). The placental cells swell and proliferate but not to the same degree as occurs in a complete mole. A partial mole may be distinguished from a miscarriage only when the pathologist examines the tissue removed from the uterus.

Fibroids

Fibroids are benign growths of the uterine muscle wall and can vary in size from a small pea to a large melon. What causes them to develop is not understood, but they tend to run in families and are more common in African-American women. Most pregnant women will have no problems with their fibroids, but if the embryo implants over a fibroid protruding into the uterine cavity the risk of early miscarriage is increased.

Fibroids usually increase in size during pregnancy because of the high estrogen levels and increased uterine blood supply. If they undergo red degeneration (the fibroid's blood supply is cut off, causing it to turn red and die), late miscarriage or premature labor may result. Large fibroids distorting the uterine cavity may lead to abnormal presentations and positions. Occasionally, fibroids obstruct the birth canal, preventing a vaginal delivery, but they usually shrink in size after delivery.

Incompetent cervix

The cervix usually remains tightly shut and sealed with a plug of mucus throughout pregnancy. An incompetent cervix starts to shorten and open during the fourth or fifth month of pregnancy, exposing the membranes to the risk of rupture and miscarriage. The condition is uncommon and may be caused by damage to the cervix during a previous labor, cervical operation, or termination. If you are diagnosed with an incompetent cervix, you may be advised to have a cervical cerclage or suture in your next pregnancy, which sews the cervix closed until the end of the pregnancy. The thread is usually cut a few weeks before term to allow a normal vaginal delivery.

Venous thromboembolism

Women are more likely to develop a blood clot or thrombosis in a pelvic or leg vein during pregnancy and the postnatal period. This is due to increased levels of clotting factors and decreased levels of anticoagulant factors that protect women from uncontrolled uterine bleeding during pregnancy and after the delivery. Venous thromboembolism (VTE) occurs in less than 1 per 1,000 births, but there are several important risk factors that increase the likelihood of VTE in pregnancy. These include age over 35 years, immobility, smoking, obesity, operative delivery, previous VTE, family history of VTE, severe varicose veins, PREECLAMPSIA,

dehydration, SICKLE CELL DISEASE, maternal illness, and infection.

The thrombosis usually starts in the deep veins of the lower leg but may have extended up into the femoral or pelvic veins before it is detected. The danger is that part of the blood clot may break off and be swept off into the lungs where it blocks one of the major blood vessels. This is called pulmonary embolus (PE) and although the incidence is only about 1 in 6,000 births, it is potentially very serious. Any pregnant woman with signs of a DVT or PE should be started on anticoagulation treatment as a matter of urgency even before the diagnosis is confirmed.

The signs of a DVT are pain and swelling in the calf or thigh muscles, with localized redness and tenderness of the leg – inability to put your heel to the ground when walking is diagnostic. Once the DVT is proven, an elastic compression stocking should be fitted and you will be confined to bed with your leg elevated until fully heparinized and until the leg stops being tender.

The symptoms of a pulmonary embolus are shortness of breath, chest pain, coughing up blood, faintness, collapse, together with all the signs of a DVT. A chest X-ray and examination may show evidence of a PE and a ventilation perfusion scan of the lung and bilateral Doppler ultrasound leg studies should be undertaken urgently since two-thirds of deaths from PE occur within the first two to four hours. Women with a proven PE will be given warfarin treatment after delivery for three to six months.

Obstetric cholestasis

This is a rare condition but can lead to complications in late pregnancy, including stillbirth. The main symptom is severe itching without a rash, usually most intensely on the palms of the hands and soles of the feet, caused by bile salts being deposited under the skin. A small percentage of women become jaundiced. The lower levels of bile leads to a reduction in the absorption of vitamin K, which increases the chances of mother or baby bleeding.

Ursodeoxycholic acid treatment helps reduce the itching and liver function abnormalities and vitamin K tablets improve blood clotting. You will also be advised to have an induction of labor at 37–38 weeks to reduce the risks of late pregnancy complications.

Anemia

The red cells in your blood contain hemoglobin (a complex of four protein chains attached to iron), which carries the oxygen around your body. During pregnancy it is common for women to become mildly anemic, because the hemoglobin levels fall due to the demands of the growing baby and also because of the increased fluid content of the mother's blood, which "dilutes" the hemoglobin level. Your hemoglobin is measured on several occasions during the prenatal period. If your levels are low (less than 100mg/dl) you will look pale, feel tired, breathless, or faint and require iron and folic acid supplements. Mild iron-deficiency anemia in pregnancy is not harmful to the baby, who will carry on helping itself to all the iron it requires from your stores. If the hemoglobin levels do not improve after three or four weeks of treatment, further blood tests will be performed to check for rarer causes of anemia. Occasionally, it may be necessary to give injections of iron or even a blood transfusion.

SICKLE CELL ANEMIA

Sickle cell anemia (*see* p.417) is an inherited abnormality in the production of the protein chains that make hemoglobin. This results in a change in the shape of the red blood cells produced making it more difficult for them to navigate around the blood vessels smoothly. As a result they are easily damaged. The breakdown of the damaged cells results in hemolytic anemia. Cell debris clogs up the blood vessels leading to strokes, infection, and pain in the bones, limbs, chest, or abdomen. Pregnant women with sickle cell disease are at constant risk of a sickle cell crisis. This can be life-threatening for the mother and compromises placental function and fetal growth. They need to be cared for in specialized centers.

THALASSEMIA

The thalassemias (*see* p.417) are another group of inherited hemoglobin abnormalities. Alpha thalassemia is common in Southeast Asia, whereas beta thalassemia is usually found among people living around the Mediterranean or in the Middle East, India and Pakistan. Carriers of the trait are likely to develop more severe anemia during pregnancy. Beta thalassemia major results in severe anemia and a life-long problem of trying to get rid of the excess iron in the circulation. This is why iron supplements should never be given to thalassemics although folate treatment is often prescribed.

ABO incompatibility

ABO incompatibility may occur in babies with blood type A, B or AB born to mothers with blood type O. Type O women routinely have antibodies to blood types A and B, but they are too large to cross the placenta. However, during pregnancy a few fetal red cells will enter the mother's circulation and stimulate the formation of a smaller sized anti-A or B antibody, which may cross back to the baby's circulation and attack the baby's red cells. If many red cells are destroyed this will lead to jaundice after birth, which may need treatment with phototherapy or an exchange transfusion.

Maternal red cell antibodies

At the prenatal booking visit your blood group is checked and the presence of any atypical antibodies to your red blood cells is noted and you will be given a special card with details of them which should be shown to your prenatal caregivers. Red cell antibodies usually develop as a result of a previous blood transfusion or pregnancy, but can occur naturally. They are not related to any illness or infection and are not harmful to your health. However, it is important to know about these antibodies during pregnancy, because if you need a blood transfusion other blood groups as well as ABO and rhesus have to be taken into account during the cross matching. In addition, red cell antibodies may occasionally attack the baby's red blood cells leading to jaundice (see ABO incompatibility).

Rhesus disease

The rhesus factor is present on the surface of red blood cells. It is made up of three paired parts – C, D and E – of which D is the most important because it can lead to rhesus isoimmunization (*see* p.128). About 85 percent of Caucasian people carry the D antigen and are known as rhesus D positive, while the 15 percent who lack it are rhesus negative. If you are Rh-negative, problems may arise if you are carrying a baby who is Rh-positive because there is a risk that you could develop antibodies that can cross the placenta and attack and destroy the baby's red blood cells. Although this is rarely a problem in a first pregnancy, you may develop antibodies as a result of exposure to your baby's Rh-positive blood during delivery, which can cause problems in a subsequent pregnancy.

Rhesus disease can largely be prevented by giving injections of anti-D to Rh-negative women during pregnancy and after delivery (*see*

BLOOD PRESSURE PROBLEMS

Uncontrolled high blood pressure in pregnancy can result in serious problems for both mother and baby. The most common form is pregnancy induced hypertension — PIH (preeclampsia or toxemia), but women with preexisting hypertension or hypertension due to kidney disease are also at risk.

PREECLAMPSIA

preeclampsia or pregnancy-induced hypertension (PIH) complicates 5–8 percent of all pregnancies. Most cases are mild and usually occur in first-time mothers during the second half of pregnancy, and are resolved soon after the birth. Severe cases can occur earlier in pregnancy. Others may not arise until you are in labor or make a first appearance only after delivery with little warning.

Pregnant women are checked for symptoms of impending preeclampsia at every prenatal visit, during labor and after birth. The classical signs are raised blood pressure, peripheral edema (swelling of the hands, feet, and legs) and the presence of protein in the urine. The only cure for preeclampsia is delivery of the baby. However, if the baby is very immature, it may be possible to buy some more time for the baby to continue growing in utero by giving the mother treatment.

Mild preeclampsia may have no significant effect on the growth and well-being of the baby. However, when placental blood flow and function are reduced there is always the risk of the baby developing INTRAUTERINE GROWTH RESTRICTION (IUGR) and oxygen shortage (hypoxia). Regular ultrasound and Doppler blood flow monitoring of fetal growth in pregnancies complicated by preeclampsia is now common and plays an important role in deciding on the best time to deliver. In mothers with severe PIH, the baby is also at risk of premature delivery, placental abruption, and intrauterine death.

Normal blood pressure in a non-pregnant woman is less than 140/90mm of mercury. However, blood pressure measurements in pregnancy vary between individuals and at different stages of pregnancy. Hence it is more useful to compare the prenatal visit readings with the blood pressure measurements that are made at the first prenatal visit when assessing the risk of preeclampsia.

Mild PIH — the blood pressure (BP) rises to 140/100, with mild edema and clear urine. The woman usually feels well but may require oral antihypertensive treatment if the BP is consistently raised.

Severe PIH — the blood pressure (BP) exceeds 160/110 and heavy proteinuria is present. Sudden and intense swelling of the face and limbs may occur with marked weight gain. Immediate treatment is needed to lower the BP and prevent the onset of convulsions,, which usually requires intravenous antihypertensive and sedative drugs, followed by immediate delivery of the baby, generally by cesarean section.

The causes of preeclampsia are not clearly understood. There is no doubt that there is a genetic component since the problem tends to run in families. Preeclampsia is more common in first-time mothers, twin and diabetic pregnancies, and in women with preexisting hypertension or kidney disease. It also appears to be associated with poor maternal diet and vitamin deficiency. There are many features pointing to a disordered inflammatory response and increasing evidence to suggest that preeclampsia involves an abnormal response of the mother's immune system to the placenta and baby.

ESSENTIAL HYPERTENSION

Essential hypertension complicates 1–3 percent of pregnancies and is more frequent in women over the age of 35 years. It is defined as persistently raised blood pressure (BP) greater than 140/90 before 20 weeks and may be diagnosed before pregnancy or identified at the first prenatal visit. Most women will already be taking an antihypertensive drug and need to be supervised by a physician in order to modify the dosages during pregnancy.

ECLAMPSIA

The signs of eclampsia are coma and convulsions and usually occur at the final stage of severe untreated PIH or essential hypertension with superimposed PIH. Eclampsia is now rare in the developed world, although it remains a potentially life-threatening obstetric emergency for mother and baby, since all of the maternal blood vessels go into spasm leading to kidney, liver, and brain dysfunction together with a dramatic shortage of blood flow and oxygen to the fetus. Immediate measures are needed to sedate the mother's irritable brain, stabilize her blood pressure, and deliver the baby, which invariably requires cesarean section.

p.128) to mop up any Rh-positive fetal blood cells that may have entered your circulation and stop development of destructive maternal antibodies. However, if antibodies are detected in your early blood tests in a subsequent pregnancy, you will need specialist care during your pregnancy. You will be offered further blood tests every four weeks, and your baby will be monitored for signs of anemia or heart failure. Severely affected babies may need multiple blood transfusions in utero to allow the pregnancy to continue until it is safe to deliver. At birth the baby will undergo tests for hemoglobin, ABO, and rhesus blood grouping, bilirubin levels, and a Coombs test (which detects the maternal rhesus antibodies). Jaundice often develops in the first 48 hours of life, requiring immediate treatment.

Amniotic fluid problems

POLYHYDRAMNIOS

This excess of amniotic fluid usually becomes noticeable when the volume is greater than two litres. You will develop a tense abdomen through which it is difficult to feel fetal parts clearly and in severe cases, heartburn, breathlessness and abdominal discomfort develop particularly when the onset is sudden. Polyhydramnios can be caused by increased production of amniotic fluid because the placental surface is large (twins) or the fetal urine production is increased (poorly controlled diabetes). It may also result because a fetal malformation prevents the fetus from swallowing the fluid or absorbing it.

Polyhydramnios almost always occurs in pregnancies affected by HYDROPS, because the fetus develops heart failure or severe anemia, but in many cases no specific cause is identified. Polyhydramnios increases the risk of premature labor, CORD PROLAPSE and ABNORMAL PRESENTATIONS and may be relieved by amniocentesis to drain away some of the fluid.

OLIGOHYDRAMNIOS

A reduced amniotic fluid pool is most likely to be due to INTRAUTERINE GROWTH RESTRICTION (IUGR) or ruptured membranes, but can also occur in healthy post-mature pregnancies. The amount of amniotic fluid in late pregnancy is a good measure of fetal well-being; ultrasound measurements that show reduced fluid near to term usually prompt a decision to deliver the baby. Rarely, oligohydramnios is noted on the 20-week scan, which usually means that the fetus has an abnormality of the renal tract. Oligohydramnios in early pregnancy results in poor lung development and limb pressure deformities in the baby.

Gestational diabetes

Between 1 and 3 percent of pregnant women develop gestational diabetes (glucose intolerance). The risk is greater in women who are obese, over 30, have a history of gestational diabetes, large babies, or intrauterine death or stillbirth, or a family history of diabetes. During pregnancy the placenta produces hormones that block the effects of insulin.

This insulin resistance usually begins at 20–24 weeks and increases until delivery. If your pancreas cannot produce sufficient insulin to counteract this effect you will develop hyperglycemia (high sugar levels) and will be diagnosed as having gestational diabetes. You will be offered a glucose tolerance test between 24 and 28 weeks (see p.212). Most women diagnosed with gestational diabetes can be treated with dietary measures alone, but 10 percent will also require insulin treatment before the end of their pregnancy. Careful monitoring of the pregnancy by a multidisciplinary team consisting of a dietician, an obstetrician, and an endocrinologist improves the outcome for both mother and baby.

Gestational diabetes is not associated with an increased risk of miscarriage or congenital abnormality because the glucose intolerance starts later in pregnancy. However, later pregnancy complications are common because the fetal pancreas produces more insulin to cope with the high maternal sugar levels that readily cross the placenta. This may lead to abnormal presentations, macrosomia (fat baby), and POLYHYDRAMNIOS, all of which increase the risk of premature labor and complications during labor and birth. Hence you will be offered regular fetal growth scans and estimations of fluid volume and may be advised to undergo an induction of labor before term. Fifty percent of gestational diabetics will develop overt diabetes or high blood pressure in later life.

Antepartum hemorrhage

Antepartum hemorrhage (APH) is best defined as significant vaginal bleeding after the 24th week of pregnancy. Before this date the bleeding is called a threatened miscarriage. After 24 weeks the baby has a chance of survival, so it is particularly important to diagnose or exclude bleeding from the placenta (due to PLACENTA PREVIA or PLACENTAL ABRUPTION), which may require immediate delivery to protect you and your baby. Occasionally, the bleeding is from a cervical erosion or polyp. If you experience bleeding in pregnancy you and your baby need to be assessed in hospital immediately.

Placental abruption

In this condition the placenta starts to separate from the wall of the uterus. The underlying cause is often unclear, but it is more common in multiparous women, cigarette smokers, cocaine and crack users and women with poor nutrition, high blood pressure or thrombophilia (pro-clotting tendency). The bleeding that results may be "revealed" if some of the blood is able to escape from the uterus into the vagina or "concealed" when the blood is trapped between the wall of the uterus and placenta.

Placental abruption is invariably painful, because blood seeps into the muscles of the uterus, causing irritation and contractions. If you experience a minor abruption, the baby is not distressed and your own condition is stable, it may be possible for you to go home after a few days observation in hospital. If the bleeding is severe, the build-up of blood behind the placenta leads to severe pain and further detachment of the placenta. If on examination, the uterus feels "woody" and is tender to touch then an emergency delivery will be needed, usually by cesarean section.

Placenta previa

One in 200 pregnancies at term are complicated by placenta previa where the placenta is implanted in the lower segment of the uterus and lies in front of (previa) the presenting part of the baby. If the placenta completely covers the internal part of the cervix, the cervical os (complex previa), the only option for delivery is cesarean section. In minor degrees of previa (partial or marginal), where the baby's head is able to descend past the lower edge of the placenta, a vaginal birth may be possible.

It is common for the placenta to be low-lying at the 20-week scan. However, by 32 weeks, the lower segment of the uterus has started to extend downward and previously low-lying placentas now appear to be placed higher in the uterus. Placenta previa is responsible for 20 percent of cases of antepartum hemorrhage and is more common in multiparous women. The bleeding is characteristically painless, usually recurrent, and can be very severe, necessitating emergency delivery and a blood transfusion.

Abnormally adherent placenta

The placenta usually separates from the uterine wall some minutes after delivery. Occasionally it has invaded too deeply into the endometrial lining and the uterine muscle (placenta accreta — 1 in 1,500 births) or penetrates through the muscle wall to extend outside the uterus (placenta percreta — 1 in 2,500 births). In these cases, it cannot spontaneously separate and attempts to remove it manually may lead to postpartum hemorrhage (see p.335) and even UTERINE RUPTURE. Placenta accreta or percreta are more common in women with a placenta that has implanted in the lower uterine segment or who have a uterine scar. If surgical removal is not possible, the placenta will be left to slough off in time.

Uterine rupture

This usually follows an obstructed labor, inappropriate use of oxytocic drugs and the rupture of a previous cesarean section or myomectomy (fibroid) scar, but occasionally occurs before labor in women with a uterine scar. A classical cesarean section scar is far more likely to rupture during labor than a lower segment scar, which is why elective cesarean delivery before term is advised for these women. The rupture may be silent and painless, or be accompanied by severe pain and shock due to intra-abdominal bleeding together with acute fetal distress. Emergency hysterectomy may be required.

FETAL GROWTH IN PREGNANCY

INTRAUTERINE GROWTH RESTRICTION (IUGR)

In approximately 3–5 percent of pregnancies the baby suffers from growth restriction, which is also referred to as fetal growth retardation, small for dates, small for gestational age, or placental insufficiency. The best definition of IUGR is a baby whose birthweight is below the 5th centile for growth at that gestational age. IUGR is the third most important cause of perinatal mortality (after prematurity and congenital abnormalities). Consequently, trying to identify babies at risk of IUGR is part of routine prenatal care.

CAUSES OF IUGR

• General factors include racial variations, low socioeconomic status, high parity (many previous births), poor prenatal education, and a previous baby with unexplained IUGR.
• Maternal health issues include low maternal weight before pregnancy, weight gain of less than 22lb (10kg) during pregnancy, and poor nutrition. Smoking is an important and preventable cause of IUGR worldwide. Alcohol, amphetamines, heroin, and cocaine all have a powerful adverse effect on fetal growth. IUGR has a high risk of recurrence, suggesting that the problem runs in families.
• About 5 percent of IUGR babies have a chromosomal abnormality such as Down syndrome or a structural congenital abnormality of the heart, kidney, or skeleton. Symmetrical growth IUGR should always raise the suspicion of a fetal infection with RUBELLA, CYTOMEGALOVIRUS, SYPHILIS, or TOXOPLASMOSIS. Syphilis and toxoplasmosis can be treated with antibiotics during pregnancy to reduce the damage to the fetus.
• Any disorder that reduces placental function or blood flow will result in IUGR because the supply of oxygen and nutrients to the fetus is reduced. This may be due to abnormalities in the early development of the placenta or because the placenta becomes less efficient in later pregnancy following placental bleeding or abruption. Women with poor nutrition or an underlying medical disorder are more likely to develop placental insufficiency. IUGR develops in 20 percent of all twin pregnancies but is more likely in identical twins where there is a risk that one baby will receive a reduced share of the placental blood flow (see twin-to-twin transfusion syndrome, p.346).

SCREENING FOR IUGR

Awareness of the causes of IUGR and those mothers who are at greatest risk is an important part of screening for IUGR. Abdominal examinations will miss some 30 percent of babies with IUGR, and menstrual dates are inaccurate in at least 1 in 4 pregnancies. This is why a dating scan in the first trimester of pregnancy is such a useful baseline measurement, particularly in pregnancies that later become complicated. Sequential ultrasound scans during the second and third trimester of pregnancy (see p.214 and p.257) are the best way to identify fetal growth problems and will distinguish between symmetrical and asymmetrical IUGR.

If a fetal chromosomal abnormality or infection is suspected, the mother will be advised to have an amniocentesis or infective screen to confirm the diagnosis. The inclusion of Doppler blood flow measurements of the fetal cerebral, umbilical, and uterine vessels can help doctors assess the severity of the IUGR. Together with other tests of fetal well-being they will influence how the rest of your pregnancy is treated.

MANAGING AN IUGR PREGNANCY

If consecutive ultrasound scans show that your baby's growth has been static or that the fluid volume or blood flow to the baby is now reduced, it may be necessary to consider delivering your baby early. Of course, this will only be an option if your baby has reached a viable age and if your doctors feel that the baby would be better cared for in the outside world rather than being left in utero.

Babies with IUGR are more likely to develop fetal distress and asphyxia during labor and be born with low Apgar scores. In severe cases, an elective cesarean section may be the preferred method of delivery. Babies with moderate IUGR may require induction of labor, particularly when the amniotic fluid volume is reduced. If carefully managed, babies with mild IUGR are often delivered vaginally.

IUGR babies are more likely to experience postnatal complications and a pediatrician will be on hand at the time of delivery to assess the severity of the IUGR and the support that the newborn baby may require. IUGR babies usually catch up in growth after delivery unless the IUGR is due to a congenital abnormality or was very severe during early pregnancy.

Umbilical cord problems

CORD PROLAPSE

If the umbilical cord is positioned below the baby and the membranes rupture, the cord can slip or prolapse through the cervix. This occurs in 1 in 300 pregnancies and is more common in premature babies, breech presentations, transverse or oblique lies, and when there is POLYHYDRAMNIOS. Prolapsed cord is an obstetric emergency, because once exposed to cold air the umbilical blood vessels will go into spasm, cutting off the oxygen supply to the baby. Prompt delivery is needed.

CORD COMPRESSION

Mild, intermittent cord compression during a contraction occurs in about 10 percent of labors. The FHT may show signs of mild fetal distress, but usually the baby has sufficient energy stores to recover quickly from the temporary lack of oxygen. Cord compression is often seen in the second stage of labor, particularly when the cord is short or wrapped around the baby's neck. Cord compression is more likely to lead to fetal distress and asphyxia in a baby that is already at risk because of IUGR or post-maturity, particularly if OLIGOHYDRAMNIOS is also present.

SINGLE UMBILICAL CORD ARTERY

The cord usually contains three blood vessels: two arteries and one vein. However, in about 5 percent of babies only one artery and one vein are present, which may be detected on an ultrasound scan. In 15 percent of affected babies the abnormality is associated with other congenital abnormalities and IUGR, and consequently the finding will prompt further investigations. The condition is more common in twins.

VELAMENTOUS CORD INSERTION

When the cord runs through the membranes before entering the placenta (vasa previa) there is a risk that the vessels will be damaged when the membranes rupture, resulting in fetal bleeding. This condition is present in 1 percent of term pregnancies and is more common in twins.

Abnormal fetal lie and presentation

A transverse lie, an oblique lie, or a shoulder presentation is more common in women who have already had a baby because the uterus is more lax. These abnormal presentations are also associated with prematurity, multiple pregnancy, FIBROIDS, uterine malformations, POLYHYDRAMNIOS, and PLACENTA PREVIA. It may be possible to perform a gentle cephalic version (if placenta previa is not present) but the baby often returns to the previous presentation. In late pregnancy the risk of cord prolapse may require admission to the hospital, and delivery may have to be by cesarean section.

Face presentations occur in 1 in 500 deliveries, usually by chance but occasionally because the baby is anencephalic or has a swelling in the neck or shortening of the neck muscles. There is little point in trying to diagnose the problem before labor or in early labor, because the face presentation may resolve spontaneously when it passes through the pelvis. The labor is usually prolonged and the facial swelling can be severe and take several days to settle down.

Brow presentation is the least common (1 in 1,500 births) and most unfavorable of all abnormal presentations, since the presenting part is too broad to be delivered vaginally. It can be associated with fetal abnormalities, particularly HYDROCEPHALY.

Shoulder dystocia

This is an obstetric emergency because the head has already delivered but the shoulders do not follow because they are wedged in the pelvis. Swift action is required to prevent the baby from developing asphyxia. Placing the mother's legs in stirrups allows the midwife or doctor to apply firm downward traction on the baby's head and neck to encourage the anterior shoulder under the pubic symphysis. An extensive episiotomy, and pressure applied above the pubic bone by an assistant, helps the delivery. Shoulder dystocia is more common in obese and diabetic women, in babies weighing more than 9lb (4kg), and following a prolonged labor with good uterine contractions. If there is a history of shoulder dystocia an experienced obstetrician should always be present at the next delivery.

Miscarriage

Miscarriage — the spontaneous loss of a pregnancy before the fetus is able to survive outside the mother's uterus — is the most common complication of pregnancy. It occurs in 15 percent of recognized pregnancies but we now know that some 50 percent of fertilized eggs are lost, many of which never reach the stage of being visible on the ultrasound scan. The vast majority of random miscarriages occur early in pregnancy and are due to fetal chromosome abnormalities that are incompatible with further development. Miscarriage after 12 weeks of gestation is uncommon and affects only 1–2 percent of pregnancies.

Miscarriage is a process, not a single event, so if you experience vaginal bleeding or pain in pregnancy there are several possible outcomes. In a threatened miscarriage there is no obvious problem on ultrasound scan and the bleeding will stop after a few days or recur again, but the cervix remains closed. If the process continues and the cervix starts to open, usually accompanied by cramping abdominal pain, the miscarriage becomes inevitable. It may go on to be complete, in which case the uterus empties its contents entirely, or incomplete if some pregnancy tissues are left behind.

Removal of the remaining tissues using drugs or surgery to evacuate the uterus is usually advised to prevent hemorrhage and infection. Sometimes the pregnancy stops developing but there are no obvious signs of a problem (missed miscarriage) until an ultrasound scan demonstrates that the fetus has died (embryonic miscarriage) or there is no evidence of a fetal pole within the early pregnancy sac (anembryonic pregnancy), also known as a "blighted ovum."

The risk of miscarriage increases with maternal age and also if the woman has experienced previous miscarriages. Recurrent miscarriage — usually defined as three or more consecutive pregnancy losses — is uncommon, affecting only 1 percent of couples. Most couples who experience this distressing problem wish to undergo investigations sooner rather than later in order to establish whether or not they have an underlying cause for the repeated miscarriages.

In the majority of cases, no cause is found and these couples should be reassured that their prognosis for a successful pregnancy next time is excellent. Nonetheless, referral to that specializes in miscarriage is very valuable for these couples, since they will be offered the latest investigations and opportunities to participate in new treatment trials, not to mention gaining the psychological benefits of knowing that they have done all they can to help prevent the miscarriages recurring.

I cannot overstate the value of joining a research program if you have suffered recurrent miscarriages. Repeatedly, studies have shown that future pregnancy outcome is improved for women who are cared for in a specialized clinic by a dedicated team.

RECOVERY AND COUNSELING

Losing a baby at any stage in pregnancy can be a devastating experience. We all react to and deal with grief in different ways, but when it comes to pregnancy loss the stages of acute grief, mourning, and healing can be lengthy processes and there are no shortcuts that can be taken. The first stage invariably includes shock, disbelief, numbness, confusion, and sometimes denial. Next comes the angry stage, often complicated by guilt, despair, depression, and physical symptoms of anxiety, such as insomnia, poor sleep, and loss of appetite.

With time, acute grief gives way to a deep sadness and later will be replaced by feelings of mourning, regret, and yearning for the baby you have lost. Eventually, you will become resigned and accepting of what has happened although this never completely takes away the emotional pain, but you will be able to deal with it in a more controlled way. You will need support during the recovery period and this may come from many different sources: family, friends, the hospital medical team, your physician, other parents who have had similar experiences, local or national support groups. Most maternity units can put you in touch with specialist counselors who have experience in helping couples cope with the aftermath of early and late pregnancy loss.

Stillbirth and neonatal death

Stillbirth (SB) follows the death of a baby in utero after 20 weeks. It may be anticipated because a serious congenital abnormality was identified during pregnancy, but 50 percent of all SBs occur without warning.

The diagnosis may be suspected if the mother reports a lack of fetal movements. This can be confirmed on an ultrasound scan that reveals the absence of a fetal heart beat. Labor usually starts spontaneously a few days after the baby's death, but you may prefer to have labor induced at the earliest opportunity and occasionally some women may choose to deliver their baby by cesarean section. If delivery has not occurred within seven days you will be advised to undergo induction of labor, because after this time there is a risk that you could develop a serious blood-clotting abnormality if the fetal tissues remain in utero.

The risk of SB is increased in high-risk pregnancies. However, the SB rate has fallen dramatically as a result of improved maternal health, nutrition, and prenatal monitoring for problems such as high blood pressure, diabetes, growth restriction, cholestasis, and rhesus disease.

SB in labor is now rare (1 in 1,000), due to improved intrapartum monitoring, but it still occasionally follows a massive placental abruption. Even when a detailed postmortem is performed,

the cause of the SB is not always understood, which is particularly distressing for the parents.

Neonatal death (NND) is the loss of a baby within four weeks of birth and affects 3–4 per 1,000 babies, most of them dying within the first week of life. In 25 percent of NNDs the baby has either a severe genetic or chromosomal abnormality or a structural problem, most commonly affecting the heart. NND is also associated with early premature birth, and occasionally follows infection during pregnancy, or fetal distress and asphyxia during labor. If the baby dies after four weeks of life, it is called an infant death.

Sudden infant death syndrome (SIDS) — previously called crib death — is rare, affecting 1 in 1,600 babies, but is more common among premature babies, severely growth-restricted babies, boys, and multiple births.

Termination (early and late)

The decision to undergo a termination of pregnancy for a fetal abnormality is never an easy one (see p.138). If you find yourself in this distressing situation you will need some information about your options and what is likely to happen, and my patients tell me that this is a subject that most pregnancy books fail to include. Before 12 weeks of pregnancy the termination can be performed surgically or medically, but after 12 weeks it is usually safer to induce

labor using drugs and deliver the fetus vaginally. The surgical approach involves clearing out the uterus using suction under general anesthesia, which has the advantage of being quick and physically painless since the mother is unconscious. You should expect to have some vaginal bleeding for up to a week after the procedure and you will probably be given a course of antibiotics to prevent infection.

The medical approach involves a combination of two drugs; the first is a single dose of an oral progesterone antagonist (an anti-hormone tablet); the second is a prostaglandin, which is usually given vaginally 48 hours later. The prostaglandin can also be given orally, but this route can be associated with nausea and stomach upsets. The vaginal tablets are repeated at regular intervals until the termination is complete, the number of doses required being related to how far advanced the pregnancy is. However, vaginal bleeding and cramping abdominal pains usually start before or soon after the first vaginal tablet and in the majority of cases the fetus is expelled within 24 hours. You will be given painkilling drugs to help you cope with any discomfort and you can expect to have light vaginal bleeding for up to a week after the termination.

If it is suspected that some of the pregnancy tissues have been retained, you will be advised to have a surgical curettage under anesthetic, but in the vast majority of cases this will not be necessary.

CONCERNS AFTER BIRTH

The days and weeks after birth are often dogged with minor problems.
I have included general advice on many of these in Life After Birth
(*see* pp.370–405), so I am concentrating here on maternal complications
that may arise and also problems that may be present in newborns.

MATERNAL PROBLEMS

It is important to seek advice promptly if you notice symptoms of any
of the following conditions that sometimes occur in the days and weeks
after the birth. Most are only temporary and can be resolved speedily
with appropriate treatment, although a few may need specialist help.

Postpartum pyrexia

Postpartum or puerperal pyrexia
is defined as a rise in maternal
temperature to 100.4°F (38°C) or
more, from day 1 to day 10 after
delivery and is usually caused by
infection. Thanks to improved
hygiene, obstetric care, and infection
control in hospitals, the incidence of
postpartum infection has now fallen
to about 3 percent and is rarely life-
threatening. The most likely site
of infection is the uterine cavity
(endometritis) or perineum, but
urinary tract and breast infections are
also common. THROMBOEMBOLISM
may cause a postpartum pyrexia
and is more likely to develop after
a cesarean section, as are chest or
wound infections.

UTERINE INFECTION

Most cases are caused by infections
ascending from the cervix or vagina.
The organisms infect the placental
bed and any pieces of retained

placenta or membranes left in the
endometrial cavity. If the lochia
begins to smell offensive or you
start to develop lower abdominal
pain and tenderness, it is likely that
you have developed endometritis.
This is important to diagnose and
treat promptly to avoid complications
such as damage to the fallopian
tubes, resulting in future difficulties
becoming pregnant.

Your doctor will examine you
internally and take some vaginal
swabs for testing. If the examination
suggests that there may be tissues
left within the uterine cavity
(cervix partly open and the uterus
enlarged, tender, and boggy), you
will be started on a course of
antibiotics and advised to undergo
a uterine evacuation to remove the
tissues. Since no one wants to give
a woman who has just delivered a
baby a general anesthetic unless
absolutely necessary, an ultrasound
scan is often performed to confirm
the examination findings.

URINARY INFECTION

Urinary infections are particularly
common in women who have been
catheterized during labor or have
had a difficult delivery. Any rise in
temperature after delivery should
prompt your doctor or midwife
to send a sample of urine to
the laboratory to be tested and
antibiotics are usually started
immediately. It is important to
check that the urine infection has
been treated effectively by testing
another urine sample after the
treatment has been completed.

MASTITIS

Almost every mother develops some
degree of breast engorgement as the
milk starts to come into her breasts.
The breasts become swollen, hard,
and sore, and this commonly causes
a slight rise in her temperature.
Fortunately, the problem usually
disappears spontaneously in a day
or two as breastfeeding becomes
established. However, if you
become feverish and start to feel
sick, your breasts need to be
examined for signs of localized
or patchy redness and induration
(pitting hardness). This is called

mastitis and can be extremely painful because one of the milk ducts has become blocked and the stagnant pool of milk in the blocked duct can quickly become infected. The organism is usually a staphylococcus present on your or your baby's skin, which then enters a cracked or sore nipple and spreads into the breast tissues.

Caught early, mastitis responds promptly to antibiotics, mild analgesics, and keeping the breast milk flowing by continuing to breastfeed, or expressing the milk to relieve the pressure. However, if mastitis is not identified and treated quickly, it can develop into a full-blown breast abscess. In addition to feeling generally sick with a high temperature, you will have a hot firm lump in one of your breasts that contains pus, which will have to be surgically incized (opened) and drained in the hospital.

Perineal problems

Approximately 50 percent of women who give birth vaginally require some sort of stitching. If at any stage in the few weeks after the delivery your perineum starts to throb, appears inflamed, or produces any sort of discharge, consult your midwife or physician. You may have developed a wound infection, and this is usually treated simply and effectively with antibiotics. Sometimes it is judged best to remove one or two of the stitches to release the pressure in the inflamed area and make it easier to access the wound to clean it

thoroughly. Occasionally, after a traumatic vaginal delivery, a hematoma (collection of blood) can swell up in the walls of the vagina. This is removed surgically to relieve the pain, tie off the bleeding point, and keep infection from developing.

Some women continue to experience problems with their episiotomy or perineal wounds for several weeks, but there is no need to suffer in silence. Your physician and midwife will be able to make sure there is no sign of infection. They may suggest that you consider having some physical therapy using ultrasound to help relieve the discomfort. Your maternity unit will also be able to refer you to the obstetric physical therapists, who have expertise in helping women with postpartum problems involving the perineum, bowel, bladder, and vagina.

Stress incontinence

Women who have had a vaginal delivery often suffer mild, temporary urinary incontinence, because the bladder neck has been stretched and pulled downward by the pressure of the baby's head passing through the birth canal. Usually this manifests itself as stress incontinence, where urine seeps out when you laugh, cough, sneeze, or move quickly.

Kegel exercises will improve your ability to regain full bladder control — the sooner you start them, the quicker the benefits will be. However if, despite regularly performing these exercises, you are

still suffering from urinary or urge incontinence that disrupts your life (leaking persistently, unable to go out of the house because of the fear of accidents, or not being able to find a toilet quickly enough), then arrange for more specialized help through your physician.

Fecal incontinence

After a vaginal delivery, particularly those involving a prolonged second stage of labor and an extensive episiotomy or tear, some women may lose a degree of control over their bowels. This usually disappears soon after giving birth, with the help of some Kegel exercises. However, on the rare occasions when a woman develops full fecal incontinence and is simply unable to control her bowel movements, specialist help is needed, since it usually means that the anal sphincter and rectal skin have been torn.

Anemia

Symptomatic anemia after the birth may be due to acute blood loss (more common after prolonged labor, operative delivery, and postpartum hemorrhage) or because the mother's iron stores have been depleted during pregnancy because of poor nutrition, difficulties in absorbing iron, twin pregnancies, or several pregnancies in quick succession. A blood transfusion may be required in severe cases, but iron and folic acid replacement is usually sufficient. Treatment should be started promptly.

PROBLEMS IN BABIES

Most of these problems are detected only after birth, usually during the baby's checkups in the hospital and at six weeks. However, cleft lip and palate is sometimes seen on ultrasound and fetal alcohol syndrome may be suspected if your baby has growth problems during pregnancy.

Cerebral palsy

Cerebral palsy (CP) describes a range of abnormalities in movement, muscle tone, posture, speech, vision, and hearing in young children, caused by damage to one or more areas of the brain. CP affects 1 in 400 children and is more common in pregnancies complicated by premature delivery, IUGR, and infection. There are three types of CP depending on the area of the brain affected, and affected children usually have a combination of two or more types. There is no prenatal test that can detect cerebral palsy.

Fetal alcohol syndrome

Regular alcohol consumption during pregnancy may result in teratogenic (early) and toxic (later) damage to the fetus depending on how much alcohol is consumed. The main features of fetal alcohol syndrome (FAS) are INTRAUTERINE GROWTH RESTRICTION (IUGR), failure to thrive after birth, damage to the nervous system, and poor childhood growth. Attention deficit disorder, language delays, and mild to moderate mental retardation gradually become evident. The characteristic facial appearance includes microcephaly, flattened nasal bridge, underdeveloped middle of the face, short upturned nose, and thin upper lip. FAS affects about 1 in 500 babies in Canada, and is an important and preventable cause of learning difficulties.

Pathological jaundice

Occasionally, neonatal jaundice (*see* p.388) may be a sign of a more serious underlying condition such as anemia caused by blood group incompatibility, liver or thyroid disease, or an inherited enzyme disorder that weakens the red cells making them break down more readily. These rarer forms of jaundice are referred to as pathological jaundice and usually necessitate treatment with phototherapy and possibly even a blood transfusion. In severe cases, or when the baby is very premature, drugs to stimulate the liver to get rid of the excess bilirubin may be needed.

Cleft lip and palate

The development of the upper lip and palate (roof of the mouth) in the fetus involves the joining together of tissues in the midline of the face. When this is incomplete, as occurs in 1 in 750 babies, a split in the lip (harelip) and/or the palate results. The defect can be seen on prenatal ultrasound scans. Babies with a cleft palate may have difficulty feeding and are at risk of choking, because the absence of a bony roof to the mouth interferes with sucking and swallowing. Corrective surgery is done after birth. A cleft lip is usually closed at about three months but surgery to close the palate may be delayed until at least 12 months, to ensure it has developed fully.

Pyloric stenosis

This affects 1 in 500 newborn babies and is more common in boys. It is caused by thickening of the pylorus muscle between the bottom of the stomach and the small intestine. As food builds up, the stomach contracts strongly in an attempt to force food into the upper intestine. The problem starts soon after birth with persistent projectile vomiting during or right after a feeding. As a result, the baby becomes hungry and irritable, and quickly becomes dehydrated and loses weight. Pyloric stenosis is diagnosed by feeling the contracted muscle in an abdominal examination and confirmed with an ultrasound scan or barium swallow X-ray. Prompt surgery to loosen the muscle cures the condition.

Umbilical hernia

This is caused by a weakness in the muscles of the abdominal wall at the point where the umbilical cord entered your baby's abdomen. A small bulge around the baby's umbilicus containing a section of intestine is common, occurring in about 10 percent of all babies, with a higher incidence in African-American children. It usually closes up of its own accord in time.

Inguinal hernia

This weakness in the lower abdominal wall in the groin region is caused by failure of the inguinal canal to close after birth. It occurs in about 3 percent of newborn babies and is often bilateral. During pregnancy the testes of a baby boy pass through the inguinal canal to reach the scrotum. Although girls do not have testes, they do have an inguinal canal so they too are susceptible to hernias.

Hernias are more likely in premature babies, babies with CYSTIC FIBROSIS, and baby boys with UNDESCENDED TESTES. As long as the contents of the bulge can be pushed back into the abdominal cavity, there is little cause for concern. However, occasionally, a loop of intestine becomes trapped in the hernia, obstructing the bowel. These strangulated hernias are a surgical emergency and need to be dealt with promptly to save the bowel and repair the abdominal wall defect.

Hypospadias

This common abnormality is found in 1 in 500 baby boys. The external opening of the urethra is positioned on the underside of the penis instead of at the end. The penis may curve downward and the foreskin or prepuce appears hooded. Sometimes the urethral opening is far back in the scrotum or on the upper side of the penis (epispadias). Curative surgery is carried out at one year.

Undescended testes

This condition is found in 1 in 125 newborn boys. In 15 percent of cases both testes are undescended. The majority have descended spontaneously by nine months of age but if the problem persists after this time, your pediatrician may recommend a pediatric surgeon. If the testes remain undescended it can lead to testicular cancers, abnormal sperm production, and infertility.

Imperforate anus

The anus is closed, either because it is sealed by a thin membrane of skin over the external opening or because the passage between the rectum and anal canal has not developed (anal atresia). The baby's lower bowel becomes distended and swollen toward the end of pregnancy, which is visible on ultrasound scan. All babies are examined at the time of delivery and undergo immediate corrective surgery if necessary.

Dislocated hips

This congenital abnormality is identified in as many as 1 in 200 babies at the routine postnatal check (see p.387). It is more common in girls, in the left hip, in multiple pregnancies, and in babies that are born breech, or have another abnormality such as Down syndrome or a NEURAL TUBE DEFECT.

If the hip is dislocated, the hip joint is unstable and will make a clicking sound when the knees are bent up toward the hips and the legs rotated outward. The problem is usually curable with the use of orthopedic manipulation and splints to hold the hip in the correct position during the first few months of life. Occasionally surgery may be required.

Talipes

This is a condition in which the baby's feet are turned inward (equino varus) so that the soles are facing each other. Less commonly, the feet are turned outward (calcaneo valgus). Talipes can be diagnosed on ultrasound scan during pregnancy and often the problem runs in families.

The mildest form is caused by abnormal positioning of the feet during pregnancy and usually corrects itself during the first few months after birth. However, if the feet cannot be easily manipulated into the correct position, regular physical therapy will be required and the baby will probably need to wear corrective splints for many months to ensure that his walking develops normally. Very severe forms of talipes may necessitate surgical correction at various points over several years.

USEFUL ADDRESSES

Alberta Association of Midwives
Main Post Office Box 11957
Edmonton, AB T5J 3L1
Tel: (780) 425-5464
www.albertamidwives.com

Association of Midwives of Newfoundland and Labrador
CNS, 100 Forest Road
St John's, NL A1A 1E5

Association of Nova Scotia Midwives
PO Box 2722, Halifax CRO
Halifax, NS B3J 3P7

Asthma Society of Canada
130 Bridgeland Avenue, Suite 425
Toronto, ON M6A 1Z4
Tel: (866) 787-4050
Email: info@asthma.ca
www.asthma.ca

Autism Society Canada
Box 22017, 1670 Heron Road
Ottawa, ON K1V 0C2
Tel: (613) 789-8943
Email: info@autismsocietycanada.ca
www.autismsocietycanada.ca

The Breastfeeding Committee for Canada
Box 65114
Toronto, ON M4K 3Z2
Email: bfc.can@sympatico.ca
www.breastfeedingcanada.ca

Canadian Association of the Deaf
Suite 203, 251 Bank Street
Ottawa, ON K2P 1X3
Tel: (613) 565-2882
www.cad.ca

Canadian Association of Family Resource Programs (FRP Canada)
707-331 Cooper Street
Ottawa ON K2P 0G5
Tel: (866) 6-FRPCan
Email: info@frp.ca
www.frp.ca

Canadian Association of Midwives
6555 Chemin de la Cote-des-Neiges, Bureau 442
Montreal, QC H3S 2A6
Tel: (514) 807-3668
www.canadianmidwives.org

Canadian Child Care Federation
201-383 Parkdale Avenue
Ottawa, ON K1Y 4R4
Tel: (800) 858-1412
Email: info@cccf-fcsge.ca
www.cccf-fcsge.ca

Canadian Chiropractic Association
1396 Eglinton Avenue, West
Toronto, ON M6C 2E4
Tel: (416) 781-5656
www.ccachiro.org

Canadian Coalition for Immunization Awareness & Promotion (CCIAP)
400-1565 Carling Avenue
Ottawa, ON K1Z 8R1
Tel: (613) 725-3769 ext. 139 or 170
www.immunize.cpha.ca

Canadian Council of Food and Nutrition
3800 Steeles Avenue West,Suite 301A
Woodbridge, ON L4L 4G9
Tel: (905) 265-9124
Email: info@ccfn.ca
www.ccfn.ca

Canadian Council for Tobacco Control
192 Bank Street
Ottawa, ON K2P 1W8
Tel: (800) 267-5234
www.cctc.ca

Canadian Cystic Fibrosis Foundation
2221 Yonge Street, Suite 601
Toronto, ON M4S 2B4
Tel: (800) 378-2233
Email: info@cysticfibrosis.ca
www.ccff.ca

Canadian Diabetes Association
National Life Building
1400-522 University Aenue
Toronto, ON M5G 2R5
Tel: (800) 226-8464
Email: info@diabetes.ca
www.diabetes.ca

Canadian Down Syndrome Society
811, 14th Street N.W.
Calgary, AB T2N 2A4
Tel: (800) 883-5608
www.cdss.ca

Canadian Foundation for the Study of Infant Deaths
586 Eglinton Avenue East, Suite 308
Toronto, ON M4P 1P2
Tel: (800) 363-7437 (END-SIDS)
Email: sidsinfo@sidscanada.org
www.sidscanada.org

Canadian Hemophilia Society
625 Ave Président Kennedy, Suite 505
Montréal, QC H3A 1K2
Tel: (800) 668-2686
Email: chs@hemophilia.ca
www.hemophilia.ca

Canadian Institute of Child Health
Suite 300, 384 Bank Street
Ottawa, ON K2P 1Y4
Tel: (613) 230-8838
E-mail: cich@cich.ca
www.cich.ca

Canadian Medical Association
1867 Alta Vista Drive
Ottawa, ON K1G 3Y6
Tel: (800) 457-4205
www.cma.ca

Canadian Mental Health Association
8 King Street East, Suite 810
Toronto, ON M5C 1B5
Tel: (416) 484-7750
www.cmha.ca

Canadian Organization for Rare Disorders
151 Bloor Street West, Suite 600
Toronto, ON M5S 1S4
Tel: (877) 302-7273
www.raredisorders.ca

Canadian Paediatric Society
2305 St. Laurent Boulevard
Ottawa, ON K1G 4J8
Tel: (613) 526-9397
www.cps.ca

The Canadian Women's Health Network
Suite 203, 419 Graham Avenue
Winnipeg, MB R3C 0M3
Tel: (204) 942-5500
www.cwhn.ca

CHADD Canada
(Children and Adults with Attention Deficit/Hyperactivity Disorder)
Standard Life Postal Outlet
PO Box 43021
Edmonton, AB T5J 4M8
Tel: (866) 434-9004
www.chaddcanada.org

The College of Family Physicians of Canada
2630 Skymark Avenue
Mississauga, ON L4W 5A4
Tel: (800) 387-6197
www.cfpc.ca

College of Midwives of British Columbia
Suite 210, 1682 West 7th Avenue
Vancouver, BC V6J 4S6
Tel: (604) 742-2230
www.cmbc.bc.ca

College of Midwives of Manitoba
235-500 Portage Avenue
Winnipeg, MB R3C 3X1
Tel: (204) 783-4520
www.midwives.mb.ca

College of Midwives of Ontario
55 St. Clair Avenue West, Suite 812
Box 27
Toronto, ON M4V 2Y7
Tel: (416) 327-0874
www.cmo.on.ca

Dietitians of Canada
480 University Avenue, Suite 604
Toronto, ON M5G 1V2
Tel: (416) 596-0857
www.dietitians.ca

Doula C.A.R.E. (Canadian Association, Registry and Education)
Maple Grove Village
PO Box 61058
Oakville, ON L6J 6X0
Tel: (888) 879-3199
www.doulacare.ca

Health Canada
Address Locator 0900C2
Ottawa, ON K1A 0K9
Tel: (866) 225-0709
www.hc-sc.gc.ca

**INFACT Canada
(Infant Feeding Action Coalition)**
6 Trinity Square
Toronto, ON M5G 1B1
Tel: (416) 595 9819
www.infactcanada.ca

Infertility Awareness Association of Canada
2100 Marlowe Avenue, Suite 350
Montreal, QC H4A 3L5
Tel: (800) 263-2929
www.iaac.ca

La Leche League of Canada
Breastfeeding Referral Service
12050 Main Street W.
PO Box 700
Winchester, ON K0C 2K0
Tel: (800) 665-4324
lalecheleaguecanada.ca

Midwives Association of New Brunswick
PO Box 25023
Moncton, NB E1C 9M9
Tel: (506) 536-0709
www.manb-asfnb.ca

Midwives Association of the Northwest Territories
PO Box 995
Fort Smith, NT X0E 0P0
Tel: (867) 872-6253
www.canadianmidwives.org/
north_west.htm

Midwives Association of Nunavut
Rankin Birth Centre
Box 298
Rankin Inlet, Nunavut X0C0G0
Tel: (867) 645-8306 / 8305
www.canadianmidwives.org/
nunavut.htm

Midwives Association of Saskatchewan
2836 Angus Street
Regina, SK S4S 1N8
Tel: (306) 586-2241
www.canadianmidwives.org/
saskatchewan.htm

Motherisk
Hospital for Sick Children
555 University Avenue
Toronto, ON M5G 1X8
Tel: (416) 813-6780
www.motherisk.org

Multiple Births Canada
PO Box 432
Wasaga Beach, ON L9Z 1A4
Tel: (866) 228-8824
www.multiplebirthscanada.org

**Multiple Birth Families
Association**
PO Box 5532, Station F
Ottawa, ON K2C 3M1
Tel: (613) 860-6565
www.mbfa.ca

Muscular Dystrophy Canada
2345 Yonge Street, Suite 900
Toronto, ON M4P 2E5
Tel: (800) 567-2873
Email: info@muscle.ca
www.mdac.ca

**Pacific Post Partum
Support Society**
104-1416 Commercial Drive
Vancouver, BC V5L 3X9
Tel: (604) 255-7999
www.postpartum.org/
  supportgroups.html

Postpartum Support International
927 N. Kellogg Avenue
Santa Barbara, CA 93111
USA
Tel: (805) 967-7636
Helpline: (800) 944-4773
Email: psioffice@postpartum.net
www.postpartum.net

Public Health Agency of Canada
130 Colonnade Road
A.L. 6501H
Ottawa, ON K1A 0K9
www.phac-aspc.gc.ca

Public Health Agency of Canada
1015 Arlington Street
Winnipeg, MB R3E 3R2
www.phac-aspc.gc.ca

PHAC regional telephone numbers

Alberta: (780) 495-2651 or
  (780) 495-2754
Atlantic: (902) 426-2700
British Columbia: (604) 666-2083
Ontario: (416) 973-4389
Manitoba: (204) 983-2508
Northwest Territories: (780) 495-2651
  or (780) 495-2754
Nunavut: (416) 973-4389
Quebec: (514) 283-2306
Saskatchewan: (204) 983-2508
Yukon: (604) 666-2083

Smokers' Telephone Helplines
Alberta: (866) 332 2322
British Columbia: (877) 455 2233
Manitoba, New Brunswick, Nova
Scotia, Ontario, Saskatchewan:
  (877) 513-5333
Newfoundland/Labrador:
  (800) 363-5864
Prince Edward Island:
  (888) 818 6300
Quebec: (866) 527 7383

**The Society of Obstetricians and
Gynaecologists of Canada**
780 Echo Drive
Ottawa, ON K1S 5R7
Tel: (800) 561-2416
www.sogc.org

**Spina Bifida and Hydrocephalus
Association of Canada**
977-167 Lombard Avenue
Winnipeg, MB R3B 0V3
Tel: (204) 925-3650
Information Line: (800) 565-9488
Email: spinab@mts.net
www.sbhac.ca

**Thalassemia Foundation
of Canada**
338 Falstaff Avenue,
North York, ON M6L 3E7
Tel: (416) 242-8425
Email: info@thalassemia.ca
www.thalassemia.ca

INDEX

Page numbers in *italic* refer to the illustrations

A

abdomen
  abdominal wall defects, 420
  exercises after birth, 385, 386
  muscles, 171
  pain, 103, 113, 184, 191–2
  palpating, 241, 266
  prenatal checks, 119–20
  surgery, 117, 119–20
ABO incompatibility, 424
abortion, 116–17, 431
abscesses, 314, 315, 433
acetaminophen, 35
acne, 410
Active Birth Centre, 249
active phase of labor, *298*, 299–301
acupressure wristbands, 99
acupuncture, 319
adhesions, abdominal surgery, 120
adrenal glands, 232
adrenocorticotropic hormone
  (ACTH), 159
aerobic exercise, 54
after pains, 384
AIDS, 130, 414
air travel, 36–7, 63, 179, 251–2
alcohol, 29, 52, 100, 215, 223, 434
all-in-one suits, 225
allergies, 35, 116, 409
alpha-fetoprotein (AFP) test, 137,
  139–40
alveoli, 182, 203, 342, 375
ambulances, 287, 289, 341
amino acids, 43
amnio PCR, 143
amniocentesis, 136, 139, 140–3,
  142, 188–9
amnion, 95, *95*
amniotic fluid
  in first trimester, 109
  meconium in, 261–2, 286
  oligohydramnios, 234, 426
  polyhydramnios, 234, 426
  in second trimester, 154–5, 170, 182
  in third trimester, 204, 234
  twins, 21
  ultrasound scans, 175
  volume, 259
  water breaking, 239, 243, 284,
  286, 300–1
amniotic sac, 70, *71*, 95, *95*
  twins, 21, 125
amniotomy (ARM), 296–7, 300–1
anabolic steroids, 35
anemia, 423–4
  after birth, 433
  blood tests, 127, 213, 241
  causes of, 234–5
  iron and, 48
anaerobic exercise, 54
anesthetics
  dental care, 104
  general anesthetics, 308, 317
  regional anesthetics, 308, 311–16

analgesic drugs, 308, 309–10
androgens, 159
anencephaly, 140, 418
animals, safety, 33–4
ankles, swelling, 119, 266
announcing the news, 75–6, 114–15
antacids, 35, 49
anterior position, 268
antibiotics, 28, 35, 192, 216
antibodies
  antibody screen, 213
  blood transfusions, 117
  in breast milk, 262
  in colostrum, 397
  maternal red cell antibodies, 424
  Rhesus disease, 126, *128*, 128,
  424–6
anticoagulant drugs, 315
anti-D injections, 128, 213, 241
antidepressants, 392
antiemetics, 35, 99
antihistamines, 35, 177
antioxidants, 48
antiphospholipid syndrome, 410
anus
  hemorrhoids, 171, 217
  imperforate anus, 435
  perineal tears, 331
Apgar scores, 310, 368, 375–6
appendicitis, 34, 120, 192
areola
  breastfeeding, 396, 397
  changes in pregnancy, 73, 96,
  96, 156
arms (baby's)
  in first trimester, 70, *70*, 93, 94, 107
  in second trimester, 153–4, 167
aromatherapy, 323
aspirin, 35
assisted deliveries, 351–9
asthma, 35, 116, 409
asymmetrical growth restriction, 257
atosiban, 340
attitude of baby in uterus, 268
au pairs, 254–5
augmentation of labor, 304
autism, 176
autoimmune disorders, 410

B

baby *see* embryo; fetus; newborn
  baby; post-mature baby;
  premature baby
baby blues, 391
baby clothes, 224–5
back pain, 185
  epidurals and, 315
  localized backache, 243–4, *244*
  occipitoposterior presentation,
  307
  preventing, 193
  relieving, 218–19
bacteria
  food poisoning, 50
  infectious illnesses, 412–14
  urinary infections, 82
bacterial vaginosis, 414

Balaskas, Janet, 249
Bandl's ring, 306
barrier contraception, 28
Bart's serum test, 136, 137
bassinets, 228
bathing suits, 179
baths, 229
bearing down, *238*, 289, 302, 333
bedpans, 291
bedrest, 340
bedding, baby's, 228
beds
  delivery bed, 290
  getting out of, 193
belly button *see* umbilicus
betamethasone, 342
bile salts, obstetric cholestasis,
  242, 423
bilirubin, 388
biophysical profile, 256, 259
biparietal diameter (BPD), 125,
  125, 174
birth *see* delivery; labor
birth partners, 293, 325
  cesarean section, 365, 368
birth preference plan, 245–7
birthing center, 85, 88
birthing pools, 88, 250–1, *250*, 274,
  319–21, 320
birthing rooms, 88
birthmarks, 156, 380
Bishop's scores, induction of labor,
  295, 296
bladder
  after birth, 385
  in first trimester, 73
  infections, 82, 122, 385
  stress incontinence, 215, *215*, 243,
  433
  in third trimester, 206
blankets, 228
blastocyst, *15*, 20–1, 24, 69
blastomeres, 20
bleeding
  delivery of placenta, 333
  in first trimester, 102–3, 131
  on implantation, 74
  lochia, 384, 386
  nosebleeds, 160
  placental abruption, 191, 427
  show, 273, 284
  vaginal, 264
  vitamin K deficiency, 377
  and waters breaking, 286
  see also hemorrhage; periods
blinking reflex, 108
blood
  blood disorders, 117
  blood groups, 126, 424
  circulation in placenta, 111
  clots, 386, 423
  importance of iron, 48
  increase in volume, 72, 95–6,
  156–7, 170, 171, 185, 207, 234
blood flow scans, Doppler, 189,
  189, 257, *257*
blood pressure, 96, 171
  epidurals and, 315

blood pressure cont.
  monitoring, 78, 121, 160
  in third trimester, 207
  see also high blood pressure
blood sugar levels
  baby's, 242
  diabetes, 408–9
  dizziness, 103
  and morning sickness, 98
blood tests
  ectopic pregnancy, 81
  fetal, 188–9, 292
  in first trimester, 126–31
  pregnancy tests, 24–5
  serum screening tests, 136–9
  in third trimester, 212, 213, 241
blood transfusions, 126
  fetal, 143, 421
  risk factors, 117, 129
blood vessels
  adaptations at birth, 378–9, *378*
  mother's, 171, 207
blue baby syndrome, 35, 420
body image, 210–11
body mass index (BMI), 41
body temperature
  baby's, 203, 228
  mother's, 170, 208
  newborn baby, 374, 379, 389
  water births, 320
bonding, 332, 390
bones, baby's, 107–8, 167
bottle-feeding, 399
  equipment, 229, 276
bowel movements
  after birth, 385
  incontinence, 433
  in labor, 239
  newborn baby, 395
brain development
  in first trimester, 66, 69, 94–5
  in second trimester, 153, 181–2
  in third trimester, 205
  ultrasound scans, 174–5
bras, 104–5, *105*, 275
Braxton Hicks' contractions, 212,
  237–8, 264, 283–4
breast milk, 397
  expressing, *343*, 397
  leaking, 264
breast pumps, 397
breastfeeding
  after pains, 384
  antibodies, 262
  breast-milk jaundice, 388
  clothes, 275
  colostrum, 208–9, 264, 381, 397
  diet, 398
  feeding bras, 275
  implants and, 105
  let-down reflex, 381, 396
  newborn baby, 381, *381*, 396–8
breasts
  baby's, 167, 262, 381
  blocked milk ducts, 398
  cancer, 120
  changes in pregnancy, 96, *96*, 112
  engorgement, 384, 398, 399, 432

breasts cont.
  implants, 105
  mastitis, 398, 432–3
  menstrual cycle, 17
  milk ducts, 96, 105
  pregnancy bras, 104–5, *105*
  prenatal checks, 120
  signs of pregnancy, 73
  structure, *396*
  in third trimester, 208–9, 264
breathing
  in labor, *238*, 326
  newborn baby, 375
  pain relief, 320–2
  yoga exercises, 55
breathing problems
  asthma, 409
  premature babies, 182, 204, 341, 342, 375
  respiratory distress syndrome, 242, 375
breathlessness, 112–13, 184, 207, 242
breech presentation, 213, 234, 241, 268, *269*, 356
  breech births, 356–9, *359*
  cesarean section, 269–71, 357, 359
  multiple births, 347, 348
  premature birth, 340
  types of, 269–70
  vaginal delivery, 269, 271
brow presentation, 268, 429
brown fat, 169, 379
brucellosis, 34
burping babies, 399, *399*

C

cesarean section, 361–9
  breech births, 269–71, 357, 359
  emergency cesarean section, 317, 362, 368
  epidurals, 312, 314, 366–7
  general anesthesia, 317
  incisions, 367, *367*, 369
  multiple births, 345–8, 349
  post-mature babies, 272
  premature birth, 340, 341
  recovery from, 386
  rise in rate of, 363
  risk factors, 362–4
  scar, 364, 367, *367*, 388
  spinal block, 316
  stitches, 386
  versus vaginal delivery, 364
  wound, 386–8
caffeine, 35, 52
calcium
  in baby's bones, 107, 167
  in diet, 47, 48, 49
  supplements, 51
calories, 40, 223, 398
cancer, breast, 120
candidiasis (yeast), 177, 216
car trips, 36, 193, 389
car seats, 227, 276, 389
carbohydrates, 44
carbon dioxide, 111, 112–13
cardiac abnormalities, 420–1
cardiac scans, 189
carpal tunnel syndrome, 220
carriages, 226
cat humps, back exercise, *219*

catheters
  epidurals, 312, 313, 366
  urinary, 291, 314, 367, 385
cats, safety, 33–4
cells
  chromosomes, 22
  early pregnancy, 20–1, *20*, 69
  stem cells, 246
cephalic presentation, 213, 234, 241, 268
cephalohematomas, 353
cephalopelvic disproportion (CPD), 267–8, 305
cerebral palsy, 176, 345, 434
cervix, *17*, *18*
  active phase of labor, 299, 300
  augmentation of labor, 304
  bleeding, 131, 264
  breech presentation, 269, 359
  dilatation, 298, 299, 300, 303
  incompetent cervix, 423
  induction of labor, 295, 296–7
  inefficient contractions, 306
  latent phase of labor, 298
  mucus plug, 71, 284
  paracervical block, 311, 316
  premature birth, 188, 340
  prolonged labor, 305
  signs of pregnancy, 25, 72
  smear tests, 131
  "sweeping" membranes, 271–2, 296
  transition phase of labor, 301–2
checkups, postnatal, 387, 403
cheese, 44, 45
chemical hazards, 30, 63
chickenpox, 32, 127, 411
child benefit, 61
childbirth *see* delivery; labor
childcare, 252–5
childcare centers, 252–3
children
  and new baby, 277, 402
  telling about pregnancy, 105, 195–6
chlamydia, 127, 413
chloasma, 171, *171*
chloramphenicol, 35
chloroquine, 37
chocolate, 52
cholera vaccination, 37
cholesterol, familial hypercholesterolemia, 145, 416
chorion, 70, 95, *95*, *108*, 111
chorionic villi, 70, 95, *95*, 110, *111*, *154*
chorionic villus sampling (CVS), 136, 140, *141*
choroid plexus cysts (CPC), 419
Christmas disease, 418
chromosomes, 22
  abnormalities, 144–5, 415–18
  amniocentesis, 142
  chorionic villus sampling (CVS), 140, *141*
  FISH test, 143
  in ovum, 18
  serum screening tests, 136–7
cleft lip and palate, 144, 434
clinics *see* prenatal care
clitoris, 108
clothes
  for baby, 224–5
  breastfeeding, 275
  in first trimester, 132–3

clothes cont.
  in the hospital, 275
  maternity bags, 274, 277
  in second trimester, 163, 178–9
  sweat rashes, 177
  in third trimester, 220–1, 275
cocaine, 29
coccygeal pain, 243–4
coffee, 52, 100, 215
cold remedies, 35
cold sores, 413
colds, 33
colitis, ulcerative, 409
colostrum, 208–9, 264, 381, 397
color, eyes, 23, 182, 379
complementary therapies, 34
complete breech, 269, 356, *356*
computers, safety, 31
conception, 17–25
congenital abnormalities, 27, 144–7, 415–21
  family history, 117
  folic acid and, 51
  screening and diagnostic tests, 134–43
congenital varicella syndrome, 32
conjoined twins, 346
conjunctivitis, 377, 395
connective tissue disorders, 410
constipation, 172, 184, 187
  after birth, 385
  fluid intake and, 52, 187
  and hemorrhoids, 217
  laxatives, 35
contraception, 132
  after birth, 387
  failure of, 28
contractions
  active phase of labor, 299–300
  augmentation of labor, 304
  Braxton Hicks' contractions, 212, 237–8, 264, 283–4
  breathing techniques, 322
  delivery of placenta, 332–4
  fetal monitoring, 291–2, *292*
  induction of labor, 297
  inefficient contractions, 306
  latent phase of labor, 298
  onset of labor, 285–6
  pain, 299, 300
  premature birth, 340
  second stage of labor, 325–9
  transition phase of labor, 301
  see also pain relief
controlled cord traction (CCT), 334
coping strategies, 393
cord *see* umbilical cord
cordocentesis, 136, 143
corpus luteum, 18
cortisol, 159, 232, 261
cortisone, 409
coughs, 33
counseling
  after miscarriage, 430
  genetic, 146
cradle, 228
cramps, in legs, 217–20
cravings, 73, 100
cretinism, 410
crib death (SIDS), 228
cribs, 228, 276
Crohn's disease, 35, 409

crown rump length (CRL), 124–5
crowning, baby's head, 328, *328*
Cultural Warping of Childbirth (by Doris Haire), 86–87
cyanotic defects, 420
cycling, 54, 56, 165
cystic fibrosis, 145–6, 417
cystitis, 122, 192
cysts, ovarian, 306
cytomegalovirus (CMV), 412

D

dairy products, 45, 49
death
  crib death, 228
  miscarriage, 430
  neonatal death, 431
  postpartum hemorrhage, 333, 335
  safety of home births, 87
  stillbirth, 144, 183, 263, 431
  termination of pregnancy, 431
deep vein thrombosis (DVT), 220, 423
dehydration, 52, 99, 395
delivery, 325–31
  assisted deliveries, 351–9
  breech births, 357–9
  cesarean section, 361–9
  estimated date of (EDD), 78, 79, 116, 271
  multiple births, 345–9
  placenta, 325, 332–4
  positions, *327*
  sudden delivery, 289
  see also labor
delivery rooms, 290–1
dental care, 61, 104, 194
depression
  postnatal, 116–17, 391–3
  preexisting, 410
DHEAS, 232
diabetes, preexisting, 34, 117, 121, 408–9
  see also gestational diabetes
diagnostic tests, 134, 135, 140–3
diapers, 229, 276
diaper liners, 229
diaper rash, 276, 395
diaphragmatic hernia, 419–20
diarrhea, 192, 395
diathermy, 365
Dick-Read, Dr. Grantley, 248
diet, 39–52
  breastfeeding, 398
  in first trimester, 83
  in second trimester, 164–5, 184
  in third trimester, 223
dieting, 40
digestive system (baby's)
  fetal abnormalities, 419–20
  in first trimester, 69, 94
  in third trimester, 261
  ultrasound scans, 174
digestive system (mother's), 172, 187, 206
dilatation of cervix, 298, 299, 300, 303
discharges, vaginal, 120, 264
  infections, 215–16
  lochia, 384, 386
  show, 273, 284

discharges, vaginal cont.
  signs of pregnancy, 97
  see also bleeding
dislocated hips, 435
disposable nappies, 229
diuretics, 35
dizziness, 103–4, 177, 189–90
DNA, 22, 143, 145–6
doctors, 91
  prenatal care, 78–80, 85
  home births, 89
dominant genes, 22, 23
  genetic disorders, 145, 416
Doppler blood flow scans, *110*, 189,
  189, *257*, 257
Doppler sonicaid, 108, 161, 291, *292*
Down syndrome, 144, 147
  amniocentesis, 139, 140–3, *14*
  chorionic villus sampling (CVS),
    140, *141*
  nuchal fold translucency scan,
    123, 135, 136, 137, *137*
  risk of, 81, 147
  screening tests, 135–40
  structural markers, 176
dreams, 222
drinks, 52, 223
drip stands, *290*, 291
driving, 36, 193, 389
drugs
  analgesic drugs, 308, 309–10
  antimalarial drugs, 37
  for existing medical conditions,
    35, 82, 116, 408
  free prescriptions, 61
  induction of labor, 297
  for morning sickness, 99
  preventing premature birth, 340,
    341
  recreational drugs, 29, 116
  risks in pregnancy, 28
  termination of pregnancy, 431
Duchenne's muscular dystrophy
  (DMD), 146, 417–18
ductus arteriosus, 378–9, 420
duodenal atresia, 419

E
E-coli, 50
early (primary) postpartum
  hemorrhage (PPH), 335
ears (baby's)
  in first trimester, 93, 107
  in second trimester, *151*, 153,
    167–8, *168*
ears (mother's), blocked, 157
eclampsia, 425
ecstasy, 29
ectopic pregnancy, 25, *81*, 422
  abdominal pain, 103
  after fertility treatment, 74
  subsequent pregnancies, 80, 81
Edward's syndrome, 138, 139,
  144, 415
EEGs (electroencephalograms),
  181
effacement, cervix, 298
egg *see* ovum
ejaculation, 19
electronic fetal monitoring (EFM),
  290, 291–2

embryo, 8, 21, 66–71, 69–70
  see also fetus
emergency cesarean section, 317,
  362, 368
emotions
  after birth, 390–3
  on becoming pregnant, 25
  father's feelings, 76–7
  in first trimester, 73, 75–6, 101,
    114–15
  prelabor symptoms, 284
  premature babies, 405
  in second trimester, 172–3
  in third trimester, 210–11, 238–9,
    265
Employment Insurance Act, 59,
  60–61, 63
encephalocele, 418
endometritis, 432
endometrium, 17
endorphins, 310, 318, 319, 323
enemas, 239
engagement of baby's head, 262,
  263–4, *263*, 266–7, *267*, 283,
  302
engorgement, breasts, 384, 398,
  399, 432
entonox, 299, 309–10, *309*, 316
environmental hazards, 30–1
epidermis, 181
epididymis, *14*, 19
epidural block, 311–15
  breech births, 357
  cesarean section, 366–7
  contraindications, 314–15
  forceps delivery, 355
  induction of labor, 297
  medical complications, 315
  mobile epidurals, 314, 315
  multiple births, 346–7
  occipitoposterior presentation,
    307
  preparation for, 313
  procedure, 313–14, *313*, *314*
  second stage of labor, 326
episiotomy, 328, 330–1, *331*
  breech birth, 359
  forceps delivery, 330, 351, 355
  premature birth, 341
  problems, 433
  pudendal block, 316
  scars, 401
  stitches, 384–5, 433
equipment
  for babies, 226–9, 276
  delivery rooms, 290–1
  fetal monitoring, 291–2
  home births, 274
ergotamine, 35
erythromycin, 35
essential fatty acids, 44
essential hypertension, 409, 425
essential oils, aromatherapy, 323
estimated date of delivery (EDD),
  78, 79, 116, 271
esophageal atresia, 419
estriol, 137
estrogen
  and breast cancer, 120
  contraceptive pill, 28
  effects on baby, 262, 381

estrogen cont.
  in first trimester, 71, 73
  functions, 158
  menstrual cycle, 17–19
  and skin pigmentation, 156
  and uterine fibroids, 192
exercise, 39, 53–7
  back exercises, 219, *219*
  in first trimester, 83
  postnatal exercises, *385*, 386
  in second trimester, 165
  in third trimester, 223
exhaustion, 100–1, 113
exomphalos, 414, 420
expressing breast milk, *343*, 397
external cephalic version (ECV),
  241, 271, 347
eye drops, newborn baby, 377
eyes
  color, 23, 182, 379
  in first trimester, 93, 107
  newborn baby, 377
  in second trimester, *150*, 153,
    167, 182
  sticky eyes, 395
  in third trimester, 203, 231

F
face (baby's), 93, 107, *151*, 153
face (mother's)
  mask of pregnancy, 171, *171*
  swelling, 266
face presentation, 429
fainting, 103–4, 170, 177, 190
fallopian tubes, 17, *17*
  ectopic pregnancy, 25, 81, *81*, 422
  fertilization of ovum, 20
  ovulation, 18
  sperm's journey through, 19, *19*
familial hypercholesterolemia,
  145, 416
family history, genetic diseases,
  145, 146
family practitioner units, 85, 87, 88
family practitioners, 89, 91
family daycare, 253
fat
  in diet, 45
  weight gain in pregnancy, 40, 42
fat (baby's)
  premature babies, 169
  in second trimester, 153, 169
  in third trimester, 203, 261
fathers
  prenatal classes, 133, 221
  birth partner's role, 293, 325
  and cesarean section, 365, 368
  involvement with pregnancy,
    76–7, 114, 211
  and newborn baby, 400
  paternity leave, 60
fatigue
  dehydration, 52
  in first trimester, 73, 100–1, 113
  in third trimester, 209, 237
fears about labor, 273, 284
fecal incontinence, 433
feeding
  premature babies, *343*, 381
  see also bottle-feeding;
    breastfeeding

feet
  palmar erythema, 208
  reflexology, 319
  swelling, 35, 119
  talipes, 435
fertility treatment, 21, 117
fertilization, *15*, *16*, *19*, 20–1
fetal distress
  induction of labor, 294–5, 297
  monitoring, 292
  occipitoposterior presentation, 307
  premature birth, 341
  prolapsed cord, 356
  second stage of labor, 329
fetal monitoring
  breech births, 357
  and epidurals, 314
  equipment, 291–2
  multiple births, 347
  second stage of labor, 329
fetoscopy, 143
fetus, 8
  abnormalities *see* congenital
    abnormalities
  blood tests, 188–9
  fetal alcohol syndrome, 29, 52, 434
  fetal anomaly scan, 123, 136,
    173–6, *175*
  fetal blood sampling (FBS), 292
  fetal heart recordings, 258–9, *258*
  fetal pole, *80*, 81
  in first trimester, 92–5, 93–5,
    106–9, 107–9
  growth monitoring, 214, 256–7
  intrauterine growth restriction
    (IUGR), 214, 256–7, 428
  movements, 154, 168–9, 172, 186,
    190–1, 204, 233, 261, 273
  position in uterus, 204–5, 213,
    213, 234, 241, 268–71, *269–70*,
    306–7, *307*, 429
  in second trimester, *150–5*, 153–4,
    166–9, 167–9, *180–3*, 181–3
  in third trimester, *200–5*, 203–5,
    230–3, 231–4, 261–3
  viability, 183
  see also embryo; newborn baby
fevers, 33
fiber, in diet, 44, 48, 187
Fiberall, 187
fibroids, uterine, 191–2, 306, 422
fingernails
  baby's, 153, *183*, *200*, 231, 380
  mother's, 119
fingerprints, 181
fingers
  baby's, *67*, 93, 107
  swelling, 35, 119, 207, 266
first prenatal visit, 78–80, 115,
  116–17
first trimester, 8, 64–147
fish, in diet, 44
FISH (fluorescent in-situ
  hybridization), 143
flu, 33, *33*
flu remedies, 35
fluid retention, 35, 119, 207, 266
folic acid, 27, 46, 51, 408
follicle stimulating hormone (FSH),
  17
follicles, ovulation, 17–18
fontanelles, 380

food *see* diet
food aversions, 100
food cravings, 73, 100
food hygiene, 51
food poisoning, 50, 192
footling breech, 269, 356, *356*
foramen ovale, 378, 379
forceps delivery, 351, 354–5, *354*
  breech birth, 359
  and epidurals, 312, 314
  episiotomy, 330, 351, 355
  pain relief, 354, 355
  premature birth, 341
  pudendal block, 316
foreign travel, 37
forgetfulness, 160
formula milk, 377, 399
Fragile X syndrome, 146, 418
frank breech, 269, 356, *356*, 357
freckles, 156
free radicals, 48
friends, relationships with, 196
fructose, 44
fruit, 44, 48
fundus height, 160–1, 170, 184, 206,
  234, 240
fungal infections, 177

G

gas and air, 290, 309–10, *309*
gas, trapped, 395
gastroenteritis, 33, 192
gastroschisis, 420
general anesthetics, 308, 317
genetic disorders, 22, 144–7,
  415–18
  counseling, 146
  older mothers, 81
genetics, 21, 22–3
genital herpes, 413
genitals (baby's)
  in first trimester, 108
  newborn baby, 232, 381
  in second trimester, *150*, 167
germ layers, 21
German measles *see* rubella
gestational diabetes, 426
  glucose tolerance test, 212
  older mothers, 81
  in third trimester, 241–2
  urine tests, 121–2
  weight gain and, 184
ginger, for morning sickness, 99
glucose tolerance test, 122, 160, 212
glycosuria, 121–2
golf, 57
gonorrhea, 127, 413
grandparents, 255, 277
granulosa cells, 17
grasp reflex, *387*
growth monitoring, 214, 256–7
gum problems, 104, 157, 194
gut abnormalities, 419
Guthrie test, 389, 410
gyms, 54

H

hair (baby's)
  lanugo hair, 181, 203, 231, 261, 380
  in second trimester, 153
hair (mother's)
  dyes, 133
  hair removal, 163
  in second trimester, 185
handicaps, premature babies, 339
hands (baby's)
  in first trimester, *67*, 70, 93, 94
  in second trimester, 154
  in third trimester, *200*
hands (mother's)
  prenatal checks, 119
  carpal tunnel syndrome, 220
  palmar erythema, 208
  swelling, 35, 119, 207
harelip, 434
hats, 224, 225
hay fever, 35, 116
head (baby's)
  assisted deliveries, 351–5
  breech births, 359
  cephalopelvic disproportion
    (CPD), 267–8, 305
  crowning, 328, *328*
  delivery, 328–9, *328*
  engagement, 262, 263–4, *263*,
    266–7, *267*, 283, *302*
  in first trimester, 93, 107
  fontanelles, 380
  hydrocephalus, 306, 419
  newborn baby, 379–80, *380*
  occipitoposterior presentation,
    306–7
  in third trimester, 262
  ultrasound scans, 174–5
headaches, 177, 216–17, 315
Healthy Mothers, Healthy Babies
  Coalition, 249
hearing, baby's, 167–8
heart (baby's)
  adaptations at birth, 378–9, *378*
  cardiac scans, 189
  congenital abnormalities, 420–1
  Doppler blood flow scans, 257,
    257
  during contractions, 299
  in first trimester, 69, 70, 94,
    108
  monitoring, 258–9, *258*, 291–2,
    292
  newborn baby, 377
  in second trimester, 168, 182
  sonicaid machines, 108, 161
  in third trimester, 261
  ultrasound scans, 125, 174
heart (mother's)
  aerobic exercise, 54
  heart disease, 34, 409
  heart rate, 53, 95–6, 171
  palpitations, 242
heartburn, 35, 172, 184, 187, 283
heat rash, 221
height, and size of pelvis, 118
hematoma, vaginal, 433
hemoglobin
  anemia, 423–4
  blood tests, 126–7, 129, 213
  sickle cell anemia, 424
  thalassemia, 424
hemophilia, 146, 418
hemorrhage, 126
  prepartum hemorrhage, 427
  intracranial hemorrhage, 353

hemorrhage cont.
  postpartum hemorrhage, 333,
    335, 348
  retroplacental hemorrhage, 333
  see also bleeding
hemorrhagic disease of the
  newborn, 377
hemorrhoids, 171, 217
hepatitis, 117, 127, 129
herbal remedies, 34, 323
herbal teas, 52, 99
hernias
  diaphragmatic hernia, 419–20
  inguinal hernia, 435
  umbilical hernia, 434–5
heroin, 29
herpes, 412, 413
hiccups, 108, 181, 204
high blood pressure
  Doppler blood flow scans, 189
  eclampsia, 425
  effect on placenta, 110
  essential hypertension, 409, 425
  family history, 117
  older mothers, 81
  preeclampsia, 425
  pregnancy induced hypertension,
    171
hips, dislocated, 435
HIV, 117, 127, 130, 414
"hole in the heart," 420
home birth
  prenatal care, 78–9
  choosing, 84–7, 89
  preparations for, 274
homeopathy, 323
hormones
  baby's, 232
  breastfeeding, 381, 396
  and breathlessness, 113
  and circulatory system, 96
  contraceptive pill, 28
  and fatigue, 101
  fertility treatment, 74
  in first trimester, 21, 71
  functions, 158–9
  and gum problems, 104
  induction of labor, 296, 297
  and ligaments, 56
  menstrual cycle, 17–19
  and morning sickness, 98
  placenta and, 110
  pregnancy tests, 24–5
  and uterine fibroids, 192
horseback riding, 57, 165
hospitals
  admission to the hospital, 287–8
  prenatal care, 78–9, 85
  birthing pools, 88
  birthing rooms, 88
  choosing, 84–7, 88, 90
  delivery rooms, 290–1
  leaving the hospital, 389, 405
  neonatal intensive care units
    (NICU), 341, 342–3, 348, 404–5
  onset of labor, 285–6
housework, 209, 251, 394
human chorionic gonadotropin
  (HCG), 21, 71
  ectopic pregnancy, 81
  functions, 158
  and morning sickness, 98

human chorionic gonadotropin cont.
  pregnancy tests, 24–5, 74
human placental lactogen (HPL), 158
humidifiers, 160
Huntington's disease, 145, 416
hydatidiform moles, 422
hydrocephalus, 306, 419
hydronephrosis, 421
hydrops fetalis, 421
hygiene
  animals, 33–4
  food safety, 51
  foreign travel, 37
hyperechoic fetal bowel, 419
hyperemesis gravidarum, 99
hypnotherapy, 319, 322
hypoglycemia, 242
hypoplastic left heart, 421
hypospadias, 435
hypotension, epidurals and, 315
hypothalamus, 18
hypothyroidism, 410

I

ibuprofen, 35
identical twins, 21, *21*, 123, 125
identification bracelets, 374
illness
  during pregnancy, 32–5
  existing medical conditions, 34,
    82, 116, 408–10
  infectious illnesses, 411–14
immune system, 262, 410
immunizations
  flu, 33
  newborn baby, 403
  rubella, 32–3
  travel immunization, 37
imperforate anus, 435
implants, breast, 105
in-laws, relationships with, 194–5
in vitro fertilization (IVF), 21, 74,
  74, 146
incapacity benefit, 61
incompetent cervix, 423
incontinence
  fecal incontinence, 433
  stress incontinence, 215, *215*,
    243, 433
incoordinate uterine activity, 306
incubators, 404, *405*
indigestion, 35, 172, 184, 187, 283
induction of labor, 294–7
  diabetic mothers, 241–2
  indications for, 294–5
  methods of, 296–7
  multiple births, 346
inefficient contractions, 306
inertia, uterine, 306
infections, 411–14
  premature birth, 340
  puerperal pyrexia, 432
  urinary infections, 82, 122, 192,
    215, 432
  uterus, 432
inflammatory bowel disease, 409
influenza, 33, *33*
inguinal hernia, 435
inhalation analgesia, 309
inheritance, 22–3
inhibin A, 137

insulin, 408
integrated test, 135, 136, 138–40
internal examinations, 25, 120, 267
intestines, baby's, 94, 94, 108–9
intracranial hemorrhage, 353
intracytoplasmic sperm injection
 (ICSI), 74
intrauterine contraceptive devices
 (IUDs), 28
intrauterine growth restriction
 (IUGR), 214, 256–7, 428
iron
 anemia, 423–4
 dietary sources, 47, 48–9
 functions, 47
 supplements, 35, 49, 51, 127, 213
isometrics, 54
itching skin, 217, 242

J

jaundice
 neonatal jaundice, 388
 pathological jaundice, 434
jealousy, siblings, 402
jogging, 165

K

kernicterus, 388
ketones, 121
kick charts, 273
kicking see movements
kidneys (baby's)
 congenital abnormalities, 421
 in second trimester, 154
kidneys (mother's)
 in first trimester, 73
 infections, 82, 122–3, 192
 renal disease, 409–10
 in second trimester, 156
 urine tests, 121
Kitzinger, Sheila, 249
Klinefelter's syndrome, 145, 416
knee hug, back exercise, 219
knee squeezes, back exercise, 219
kneeling position, delivery, 327

L

labor
 active phase, 298, 299–301
 approaches to childbirth, 248–9
 augmentation of, 304
 birth choices, 84–9
 birth preference plan, 245–7
 breech presentation, 269, 271,
  356–9
 curves, 288, 303,304
 examinations in, 302–4
 first stage, 283–307
 induction, 294–7
 inefficient contractions, 306
 latent phase, 298–9, 298
 multiple births, 345–9
 obstructed labor, 306
 pain relief, 273, 308–23
 premature labor, 339–43
 prolonged labor, 305–7
 risk factors, 119
 second stage, 325–31
 signs of, 283–5

labor cont.
 starting, 273
 third stage, 325, 332–5
 transition phase, 298, 301–2
 trial of labor, 305, 357, 364, 369
 triggers, 339–40
 water births, 250–1, 250
 see also delivery
lactoferrin, 397
lactose intolerance, 43
Lamaze, Dr Ferdinand, 248
lanugo hair, 168, 169, 181, 203, 231,
 261, 380
laparoscopy, 34, 81
latching on, breastfeeding, 397
late (secondary) postpartum
 hemorrhage, 335
latent phase of labor, 298–9, 298
lateral position, 268
laxatives, 35, 187
Leboyer, Frederick, 248–9, 250
legs (baby's)
 in first trimester, 70, 70, 93, 94, 107
 in second trimester, 154, 167
legs (mother's)
 prenatal checks, 119
 cramps, 217–20
 deep vein thrombosis, 220, 423
 swelling, 35, 119, 207
 varicose veins, 131, 171, 235
let-down reflex, 381, 396
libido, 132, 172, 401
lie, baby's position in uterus, 213,
 213, 233–4, 268, 429
lift-out forceps, 354
lifting weights
 as exercise, 56–7
 safety, 63, 193
ligaments
 abdominal pain, 103, 113, 184
 relaxation of, 56, 185
lightening, 263
linea nigra, 156, 171, 171
lip, cleft, 144, 434
listeria, 50, 192, 412
lithotomy stirrups, 351
liver
 hepatitis, 129
 neonatal jaundice, 388
 newborn baby, 377
liver, in diet, 48–9
lochia, 384, 386
longitudinal lie, 213, 213, 233, 268
love, 105, 390
lungs (baby's)
 adaptations at birth, 378–9
 newborn baby, 375, 377
 premature babies, 341, 342
 in second trimester, 154, 182
 in third trimester, 203–4, 231–2, 261
lungs (mother's)
 pulmonary embolism, 423
 tidal volume increase, 112–13
luteinizing hormone (LH), 18

M

macrosomia, 241
malaria, 37, 129
malnutrition, 40
maloprim, 37
mask of pregnancy, 171, 171

massage, pain relief, 322, 322
mastitis, 398, 432–3
maternal red cell antibodies, 424
maternity allowance, 60–1
maternity bags, 274, 277
maternity leave, 59–62, 63, 220
maternity nurses, 252
maternity pay, 60, 63
maternity rights, 59–62, 115
mattresses, cot, 228
measles, 33
measurements, newborn baby, 374
meat, 43
meconium, 261–2, 286, 395
medical conditions, existing, 34, 82,
 116, 408–10
medical records, 115, 116–17, 131,
 162
medicines see drugs
mefloquin, 37
membranes
 amniotomy, 296–7
 delivery of, 333, 334
 multiple births, 347
 rupture, 239, 243, 284, 286, 300–1
 "sweeping", 271–2, 296
menstrual cycle, 17–19, 78
menstrual periods, 19, 21
 estimated date of delivery, 78, 79,
  116
 irregular, 74
mental handicaps, 147, 176
mental health problems, 116, 392,
 410
metabolism, 40
Metamucil, 187
microcephaly, 419
midwives, 85, 87, 91
 admission to the hospital, 287–8
 after birth, 394
 delivery pack, 274
 home births, 89
 hospital births, 90
 midwifery units, 88
 onset of labor, 285–6
 types of prenatal care, 85
migraine, 35, 216–17
milia, 380, 395
milk, drinking, 45
 see also breast milk; formula milk
milk ducts, blocked, 398
milk spots, 380, 395
minerals, 47, 48–9
miscarriage, 75–6, 183, 430
 after diagnostic tests, 140, 141, 143
 after surgery, 34
 air travel and, 36
 counseling, 430
 Down syndrome, 147
 exercise and, 53–4
 illness and, 32–3
 IUDs and, 28
 missed miscarriage, 430
 risk of, 102, 114, 131
 subsequent pregnancies, 80
 threatened miscarriage, 427, 430
mobile epidurals, 314, 315
moisturizers, 177, 177
moles, 156, 163
Mongolian spots, 380
monosomies, chromosome
 abnormalities, 144

Montgomery's tubercles, 96
mood swings, 101, 114
morning-after pill, 28
morning sickness, 83, 97–9, 113
morphine, 386
mosaic cells, 140, 142, 147
mouth, cleft lip and palate, 144,
 434
movements, fetal, 154, 168–9, 172,
 186, 190–1, 204, 233, 261, 273
MRI scans, 268, 269
multiple pregnancies see triplets;
 twins
mumps, 33
myotonic dystrophy, 145

N

nails see fingernails; toenails
naloxone, 310
names
 choosing, 196–7
 surnames, 197
nannies, 253–4
nausea
 and abdominal pain, 192
 after delivery, 334
 morning sickness, 83, 97–8, 113
navel see umbilicus
neonatal death (NND), 431
neonatal intensive care units
 (NICU), 341, 342–3, 348, 404–5
neonatal jaundice, 388
neonatologists, 91
nerves
 carpal tunnel syndrome, 220
 epidural block, 311
 sciatica, 243
nervous system (baby's)
 in first trimester, 94
 in second trimester, 153, 154,
  168–9
 in third trimester, 205
nesting instinct, 251, 284
neural tube defects, 146, 418–19
 folic acid supplements, 27, 51
 screening tests, 137, 138, 139–40
nevi, strawberry, 380
newborn baby
 adaptations at birth, 378–9
 after birth, 379–81
 Apgar scores, 375–6
 appearance, 379–81
 bottle-feeding, 399
 breastfeeding, 381, 381, 396–8
 breathing, 375
 congenital abnormalities, 415–21
 family adjustments, 400
 jaundice, 388
 measurements, 374
 postnatal check-ups, 377, 387, 403
 premature babies, 404–5
 problems, 375, 395, 434–5
 reflexes, 387
 vitamin K supplements, 377
 weight gain, 398
nipples
 baby's, 167
 breastfeeding, 396, 397
 cracked nipples, 397, 398
 and hormone production, 381
 nipple shields, 398

nipples cont.
piercings, 163
signs of pregnancy, 73, 96, *96*
starting labor, 273
nitrous oxide, 309–10
non-stress test (NST), 256, 258–9, *258*
nose, stuffiness, 157, 170
nosebleeds, 160
notes, 115, 116–17, 131, 162
nuchal fold translucency scan, 123, 135, 136, 137, *137*
nurseries, childcare, 252–3
nurses, maternity, 252
nutrition *see* diet

O

obesity, 41
oblique lie, 213, *213*, 233, 268, 429
obstetric cholestasis, 242, 423
obstetricians, 91
obstructed labor, 306
occipitoposterior presentation, *270*, 306–7, *307*
Odent, Michel, 249
oils, aromatherapy, 323
older mothers, 81, 144, 147
oligohydramnios, 234, 426
omphalocoele, 420
operating theatres, cesarean section, 365–6
opioids, pain relief, 310
orgasm, 19, 222
orthopedic belts, for back pain, 218, *218*
ossification, baby's bones, 107–8, 167
osteomyelitis, 315
osteopaths, 218
ovaries, *17*
baby's, 108, 167
fertility treatment, 74
ovulation, 17–19
overdue baby *see* postmature baby
overweight women, 41, 118
ovulation, 17–18, *18*
ovum (egg)
fertility treatment, 74
fertilization, *15*, *16*, *19*, 20–1
genes, 22
multiple pregnancies, 21, *21*
ovulation, 17–18, *18*
Oxford Non-stress Test (Sonicaid System), 258–9
oxygen
breathlessness, 112
hemoglobin levels, 126–7
metabolic changes, 72
placenta, 111
oxytocin
after pains, 384
augmentation of labor, 304
breastfeeding, 381, 396
breech births, 357
delivery of placenta, 333, 369
functions, 159
induction of labor, 297
inefficient contractions, 306
multiple births, 347
nipple stimulation, 273
second stage of labor, 329
third stage of labor, 333, 334

P

pain
abdominal pain, 103, 113, 184, 191–2
after pains, 384
contractions, 299, 300
episiotomy, 331
leg pain, 220, 423
rib pain, 184, 206–7
second stage of labor, 328
stitches, 384–5
see also back pain
pain relief, 273, 308–23
after cesarean section, 386
for after pains, 384
analgesic drugs, 308, 309–10
forceps delivery, 354, 355
general anesthetics, 308, 317
latent phase of labor, 299
nonpharmacological, 318–20
in pregnancy, 35
premature birth, 341
regional anesthetics, 308, 311–16
vacuum extraction delivery, 352
water births, 250
palate, cleft, 144, 434
palmar erythema, 208
palpitations, 171, 242
panting, in labor, 328
pants, 178
pantyhose, 178, 235
paracervical block, 311, 316
parasites, toxoplasmosis, 33–4, *33*
parental leave, 61
parentcraft classes, 194
parents, relationships with, 194–5
part-time work, 62
partners *see* fathers
parvovirus, 412
Patau's syndrome, 144, 415
patent ductus arteriosus, 420
paternity leave, 61
pathological jaundice, 434
pediatricians, 91
Peel report, 87
pelvic floor muscles
exercises, 165, 215, 331, *385*, 433
stress incontinence, 215, *215*
pelvis
cephalopelvic disproportion (CPD), 267–8, 305
engagement of baby's head, 262, 263–4, *263*, 266–7, *267*, 283, *302*
internal examinations, 120
ligaments, 56, 185
pelvic tilts, 219
size of, 118, 120
surgery, 117, 119–20
penicillin, 35
penis, 108, *150*, 167
hypospadias, 435
peppermint tea, 99
perineum
crowning, 328
episiotomy, 330–1, *331*
problems, 433
pudendal block, 316
stitches, 384
tears, 331
peritonitis, 120

pethidine, 299, 310, 316, 341
pets, safety, 33–4
phenylalanine, 417
phenylketonuria (PKU), 146, 389, 417
phototherapy, neonatal jaundice, 388
physical examinations, 117–20
pica, 100
piercings, 163
pigmentation, skin, 156, 171, *171*
pilates, 54
pill, failure of, 28
pillows, 228, 276
Pinard's stethoscope, 291, 296, 329
pituitary gland, 17, 18, 297, 396
placenta, 21, 110–11, *111*
abnormally adherent placenta, 427
cesarean section, 369
chorionic villus sampling (CVS), 140, *141*
delivery of, 325, 332–4
development of, 70, 95
functions, 110
hydatidiform moles, 422
low-lying, 169–70, 175
placenta praevia, 240, *240*, 241, 427
placental abruption, 191, 427
placental insufficiency, 257
post-mature babies, 262–3, 272
retained placenta, 335
in second trimester, 154, 169–70
sudden delivery, 289
in third trimester, 205, 262
twin-to-twin transfusion syndrome, 346
twins, 21, *21*
ultrasound scans, 175
platelets, 127
polio, 33, 37
polycystic kidneys, 421
polyhydramnios, 234, 426
port wine stains, 380
posterior position, 268–9, *269*
post-mature baby, 271–3
assessment, 272
induction of labor, 295
placenta, 262–3
skin, 261
postnatal checkups, 387, 403
postpartum depression, 116–17, 391–3
postpartum hemorrhage, 238, 333, 335
postpartum period, 384–405
posture, *164*
and back pain, 185, 193
Potter's syndrome, 421
preeclampsia, 425
effect on placenta, 110
fluid retention, 119, 207–8
older mothers, 81
signs of, 35, 240
subsequent pregnancies, 80
urine tests, 123
weight gain and, 184
pregnancy-associated protein (PAPP-A), 136, 137, 139
pregnancy discrimination law, 59
pregnancy-induced hypertension, 171
pregnancy tests, 24–5

preimplantation genetic diagnosis (PGD), 146
premature baby, 404–5
body fat, 169
breathing problems, 182, 204, 341, 342, 375
feeding, 381
handicaps, 339
labor, 339–43
neonatal jaundice, 388
older mothers, 81
predicting, 188
problems, 342–3
retained placenta, 335
rupture of membranes, 301
sucking reflex, 231
twins, 343, 345
viability, 8–9, 183
premenstrual symptoms, 17
prenatal care
blood tests, 126–31
first prenatal visit, 78–80, 115, 116–17
in first trimester, 115–31
maternity rights, 61
physical examinations, 117–20
screening tests, 134–43
in second trimester, 160–2, 173–6, 188–9
specialist care, 119, 256–9
in third trimester, 212–14, 240–2, 266–71
types of, 85, 87
urine tests, 121–3
prenatal classes, 77, 133, 194, 221
prepartum hemorrhage (APH), 427
presentation, baby in uterus, 213, 234, 241, 268–71, *269–70*, 306–7, *307*, 429
previous pregnancies, 116–17
progesterone and breathlessness, 113
and circulatory system, 96
contraceptive pill, 28
in early pregnancy, 21, 71
and fatigue, 101
functions, 158
menstrual cycle, 18–19
and morning sickness, 98
and urinary infections, 82
and uterine fibroids, 192
projectile vomiting, 434
prolactin
breastfeeding, 381, 396
effects on baby, 262
functions, 159
prolapse, cord, 269, 356, 429
prolonged labor, 305–7
prostaglandins
amniotomy, 297, 300
induction of labor, 296
in semen, 222, 273
"sweeping" membranes, 271–2, 296
termination of pregnancy, 431
prostate gland, 19
protein
in diet, 43–4
in urine (proteinuria), 78, 121, 122–3, 160
vegetarian diet, 49
psychiatric disorders, 116–17, 410
pubic symphysis dysfunction, 244

pudendal block, 311, 316
puerperal psychosis, 392
puerperal pyrexia, 432
pulmonary embolus, 423
pulses and grains, 44
pumps, expressing breast milk, 397
pushing
  delivery of baby, 326
  epidural block, 312
  transition phase, 301–2
pyelonephritis, 82, 122, 192
pyloric stenosis, 434

Q

quadruple test, 135, 137
"quickening," 154

R

rabies vaccination, 37
rashes, 177
  diaper rash, 276, 395
  heat rash, 221
  sweat rash, 177
recessive genes, 22, 23
  genetic disorders, 145, 416–17
recreational drugs, 29, 116
rectum
  episiotomy, 330
  perineal tears, 331
red blood cells
  ABO incompatibility, 424
  anemia, 234–5, 423–4
  baby's, 205
  blood tests, 213
  hemoglobin, 48, 126–7, 213
  increased volume of, 72, 156
  maternal red cell antibodies, 424
  neonatal jaundice, 388
  sickle cell trait, 129, 424
reflexes
  fetus, 108
  let-down reflex, 381, 396
  newborn baby, 387
  sucking reflex, 205, 231, 343, 381
reflexology, 319
regional anesthetics, 308, 311–16
relaxation techniques, pain relief, 320–2
relaxin, 56, 159
renal abnormalities, 421
renal disease, 409–10
reproductive system, 17
respiratory distress syndrome, 242, 375
rest, 193, 237
resuscitator, 290, 368
retroplacental hemorrhage, 333
Rhesus disease, 126, 128, 213, 241, 424–6
rheumatoid arthritis, 410
ribcage, 184, 206–7
ritodrine, 340
rooting reflex, 381, 387
rotating babies, 307
rotational forceps, 355
rubella (German measles), 33, 411
  congenital defects, 32
  cordocentesis, 143

rubella cont.
  screening for immunity to, 117, 127
  vaccination, 32–3
rupture, uterine, 364, 369, 427

S

sacroiliac pain, 244
safety, 27–37
  alcohol, 29
  complementary therapies, 34
  drugs, 29, 35
  environmental hazards, 30–1
  food hygiene, 51
  food poisoning, 50
  illness in pregnancy, 32–4
  smoking, 29
  travel, 36–7
  at work, 62–3
salbutamol, 271
saline drips, 313
salmonella, 50
salt, 49, 100
sanitary napkins, 384
saturated fats, 45
scalp injuries, vacuum extraction delivery, 353
scans see ultrasound scans
scars
  abdominal surgery, 119–20
  cesarean sections, 364, 367, 367, 388
  episiotomy, 331, 401
  subsequent labors, 346
schizophrenia, 410
sciatica, 243
screening tests, 134–40
scrotum, testes' descent into, 262
sebaceous glands, 380
second trimester, 8–9, 148–97
seizures, 408
self-employment, 62
seminal vesicles, 19
senna, laxatives, 187
septal defects, 420
serum screening tests, 136–8
sex
  after birth, 401
  in first trimester, 132
  in second trimester, 172
  starting labor, 273
  in third trimester, 222
sex of baby, 22, 108, 167, 175
sex chromosomes, 22
  abnormalities, 145, 416
sex-linked genetic disorders, 146, 417–18
sexually transmitted diseases, 117, 127, 413–14
shift work, 63
shoes
  for babies, 225
  and back pain, 193
  and pelvis size, 118, 305
shoulder dystocia, 429
shoulder presentation, 429
shoulders, delivery, 328, 329, 357
show, 273, 284
Siamese twins, 346
siblings
  and new baby, 277, 402

siblings cont.
  telling about pregnancy, 105, 195–6
sickle cell anemia, 129, 140, 145–6, 417, 424
sickle cell trait, 129, 417
single mothers, 77
sit-ups, 56
sitting posture, 193
skeleton, baby's, 107–8, 167
skiing, 57, 165
skin (baby's)
  birthmarks, 380
  in first trimester, 107
  neonatal jaundice, 388
  newborn baby, 380, 380
  post-mature babies, 261
  in second trimester, 153, 168, 169, 181, 183
skin (mother's)
  acne, 410
  prenatal checks, 119
  changes in pregnancy, 96–7, 96
  itching, 217, 242
  piercings, 163
  pigmentation, 156, 171, 171
  rashes, 177
  in second trimester, 185
  spider nevi, 96, 96, 119, 171
  stretch marks, 120, 162, 162, 217
  tanning, 163
skirts, 178
skull
  assisted deliveries, 351, 352
  fetal, 262
  fontanelles, 380
  newborn baby, 379–80
  see also head
sleep
  and back pain, 193
  fetus, 182
  in third trimester, 215, 236–7, 265
slings, 227, 227
smell, sense of, 73
smoking, 29, 110, 116
snacks, 83
Society of Obstetricians and Gynaecologists of Canada, 87, 436
soft drinks, 52
sonicaid, 108, 161, 291, 292
sperm, 14
  fertility treatment, 74
  fertilization of ovum, 15, 16, 19, 20
  genes, 22
  and sex of baby, 22
  sexual intercourse, 18–19, 19
spermicides, 28
sphygomanometers, 290
spider nevi, 96, 96, 119, 171
spina bifida, 144, 146, 418–19
  folic acid supplements, 27, 51
  screening tests, 138, 139–40
spinal block, 311, 316, 355
spinal cord
  baby's, 69, 94–5, 168
  epidural block, 311, 313
  ultrasound scans, 174
spinal exercises, 219, 219
sports, 54, 57, 165, 223
spots, newborn baby, 380, 395
squash, 57

squatting position, delivery, 327
squints, 379
standing
  posture, 164, 193
  safety at work, 62
star gazing, breech birth, 359
starchy foods, 44
startle reflex, 387
stations, engagement of baby's head, 302
statutory maternity pay, 60
stem cell collection, 246
stepping reflex, 387
sterilization, 28
sterilizing equipment, 229
steroids, 35, 120, 341, 342, 409
stethoscopes, Pinard's, 291, 296, 329
sticky eyes, 395
stillbirth, 183, 431
  chromosome abnormalities, 144
  post-mature babies, 263
stitches
  cesarean section, 386
  episiotomy, 330, 331, 384–5, 433
stomach, baby's, 108
stools, newborn baby, 395
straight traction forceps, 354–5
streptococcus B infection, 413
streptomycin, 35
stress incontinence, 215, 215, 243, 433
stretch marks, 120, 162, 162, 217
stretching exercises, back, 219, 219
strollers, 226–7
sucking reflex
  breastfeeding, 381
  in fetus, 108, 205, 231
  premature babies, 231, 343
sudden delivery, 289
Sudden Infant Death Syndrome (crib death), 228
sugar, in urine, 78, 121–2, 122, 160
sulfonamides, 35
suntans, 163
supermarkets, 416
support pantyhose, 131
surfactant, 203–4, 232, 261, 342, 375
surgery
  abdominal, 117, 119–20
  cesarean section, 361–9
  fetal, 421
  in pregnancy, 34
surnames, 197
sweat rashes, 177
sweating, 170, 177
swimming, 54, 56, 57, 165, 223
symmetrical growth restriction, 257
syphilis, 117, 127, 413–14
systemic lupus erythematosus, 410
systemic pain relief, 310
systemic sclerosis, 410

T

talipes, 435
tanning, 163
taste, sense of, 73
taste buds, baby's, 167
tattoos, 163

Tay-Sachs disease, 146, 416–17
tea, 215
    herbal teas, 52, 99
tears, perineal, 316, 331
teeth
    dental care, 61, 104, 194
    milk teeth, 93, 107, 167
telling people your news,75–6, 114–15
temperature see body temperature
tennis, 57
TENS (transcutaneous electrical
    nerve stimulation), 318
termination of pregnancy, 116–17, 431
testes (testicles)
    descent into scrotum, 262, 381
    development of, 108, 167
    sperm production, 19
    undescended, 435
testosterone, 159, 232
tetanus vaccination, 37
tetracyclines, 35
thalassemia, 129, 140, 145–6, 417, 424
thalidomide, 99
third trimester, 9, 198–277
threatened miscarriage, 427, 430
thrombosis
    after cesarean section, 386
    deep vein, 220, 423
    family history, 117
thumb-sucking, 181
thyroid disorders, 389, 392, 410
toenails, baby's, 231
toes, baby's, 107
toxoplasmosis, 33, 412
    avoiding, 33–4, 50
    congenital abnormalities, 33
    cordocentesis, 143
    screening for, 127
transcutaneous electrical nerve
    stimulation (TENS), 318
transition phase of labor, 298, 301–2
translocation, chromosome
    abnormalities, 145, 415
transverse lie, 213, 213, 233, 268,
    369, 429
travel, 36–7
    to the hospital, 287
    leaving the hospital, 389
    in second trimester, 179
    in third trimester, 251–2
trial of labor
    after cesarean section, 364, 369
    cephalopelvic disproportion, 305
    breech births, 357
trichomoniasis, 414
trimesters, 8–9
    first trimester, 64–147
    second trimester, 148–97
    third trimester, 198–277
triple test, 135, 136, 137
triple X, 416
triplets, 345
    cesarean section, 345–6
    conception, 21
    fertility treatment, 74
    growth of uterus, 112
triploidy, chromosome
    abnormalities, 144, 415
trisomies, chromosome
    abnormalities, 144, 415
trophoblast cells, 21
tubal ligation, 28

tuberculosis (TB), 117, 315, 412
Turner's syndrome, 144, 416
twins, 21, 21
    delivery, 345–9
    family history, 117
    fertility treatment, 74
    growth of uterus, 112
    lie in uterus, 233
    postpartum depression, 392
    premature babies, 343, 345
    twin-to-twin transfusion
        syndrome, 346
    ultrasound scans, 123, 125
    vanishing twin syndrome, 74
typhoid vaccination, 37

U

ultrasound scans
    after previous pregnancy
        problems, 80–1
    dating scan, 124–5, 125
    Doppler blood flow scans, 189,
        189, 257, 257
    fetal anomaly scan, 123, 173–6, 175
    fetal growth monitoring, 214, 256–7
    in first trimester, 102, 123–5, 123–5
    nuchal fold translucency scan,
        123, 135, 136, 137, 137
    pregnancy tests, 25
    safety, 31
    in second trimester, 188
    in third trimester, 241
    vaginal, 124, 188
ultraviolet light, neonatal jaundice, 388
umbilical cord, 110, 110
    around baby's neck, 328–9
    breech births, 356
    cord compression, 429
    cordocentesis, 143
    cutting, 332
    delivery of placenta, 333, 334
    in first trimester, 95
    multiple births, 347
    prolapse, 269, 356, 429
    retained placenta, 335
    single umbilical cord artery, 429
    stem cell collection, 246
    stump, 395
    sudden delivery, 289
    twins, 21
    velamentous cord insertion, 429
umbilical hernia, 434–5
umbilicus (belly button)
    baby's, 332, 395
    inversion, 234
underwear, 275
underweight women, 41
unsaturated fats, 45
urinary infections, 82, 122, 192,
    215, 432
urination
    catheters, 291, 314, 367, 385
    and epidurals, 314
    frequency of, 73, 96, 113, 215
    leaking, 215, 215, 243, 284, 433
    with stitches, 384–5
urine tests
    glucose tolerance test, 212
    pregnancy tests, 24
    for protein, 78, 122–3, 160
    for sugar, 78, 121–2, 122, 160

uterus, 17
    abnormally adherent placenta, 427
    after birth, 384
    after pains, 384
    baby's position in, 213, 213, 233–4
    blastocyst embeds in lining, 21, 74
    blood flow to, 53
    delivery of placenta, 332–4
    fibroids, 191–2, 306, 422
    in first trimester, 71–2, 95, 112
    infections, 432
    inversion, 334
    menstrual cycle, 17
    placenta previa, 427
    placental abruption, 427
    rupture, 364, 369, 427
    scars, 364, 369
    in second trimester, 156, 160–1,
        169–70, 184
    in third trimester, 206, 234, 240
    see also contractions

V

vacations, 36–7, 179
vaccination see immunizations
vacuum extraction (ventouse
    delivery), 351, 352–3, 353, 355
    and epidurals, 312
    pudendal block, 316
vagina
    baby's, 167
    bacterial vaginosis, 414
    bleeding, 264
    crowning, 328
    discharges, 97, 120, 215–16, 264,
        384
    episiotomy, 330–1, 331
    haematoma, 433
    infections, 215–16
    internal examinations, 25, 120,
        267
    perineal tears, 331
    pudendal block, 316
    signs of pregnancy, 25, 72
    ultrasound scans, 124, 188
vaginal delivery
    after cesarean section, 364
    breech births, 356–9
    premature birth, 340
    twins, 345, 346–8
    versus cesarean section, 364
vanishing twin syndrome, 74
varicose veins, 131, 171, 235
vas deferens, 19
vegan diet, 43, 49
vegetables, vitamin content, 48
vegetarian diet, 49
veins
    deep vein thrombosis, 220, 423
    spider nevi, 96, 96, 119, 171
    varicose veins, 131, 171, 235
velamentous cord insertion, 429
venous thromboembolism, 423
ventouse delivery see vacuum
    extraction
vernix caseosa, 169, 181, 203, 231,
    261, 380, 380
viability, premature babies, 183
video display terminals, safety, 31
viral illnesses, 32, 411–14
visualization techniques, 322

vitamins, 46–8
    supplements, 51
    vitamin A, 46, 48, 49, 51
    vitamin B complex, 46, 48, 49, 51
    vitamin C, 46, 48, 49
    vitamin D, 47, 48
    vitamin E, 47, 48
    vitamin K, 377, 423
vomiting
    and abdominal pain, 192
    morning sickness, 83, 98–9, 113
    newborn baby, 395
    projectile vomiting, 434
vulva
    signs of pregnancy, 72
    varicose veins, 235

W

walking, 54, 56, 56, 165, 235
washing baby clothes, 224–5
water, drinking, 52, 187, 223
water births, 250–1, 250, 319–21, 320
water, breaking, 239, 243, 284, 286,
    300–1
weight gain
    baby's, 231, 398
    mother's, 40, 42, 118, 170, 184, 223
weight training, 54, 56–7
weights, lifting, 63, 193
Wharton's jelly, 110
white blood cells, 127, 130
womb see uterus
work, 59–63
    chemical hazards, 30
    flexible work, 62
    maternity rights, 59–62, 115, 220
    part-time work, 62
    returning to, 63
    safety at, 62–3
wounds
    cesarean section, 386
    perineal, 433
wristbands, acupressure, 99
wrists, carpal tunnel syndrome, 220

X

X chromosomes, 22, 144–5, 146
X-rays, 30–1, 104

Y

Y chromosomes, 22
yeast infections, 131, 177, 216
yellow fever vaccination, 37
yoga, 54–6, 223
yolk sac, 67, 68, 70, 95, 95, 108

Z

zinc, 47, 48, 49
zygote, 20, 20

ACKNOWLEDGMENTS

Author's acknowledgments

Writing this book has been an exciting and rewarding challenge. It has had a lengthy gestation period, during which I have had the pleasure of working with some very talented individuals. I want to acknowledge their contribution and thank them for their expertise, guidance, encouragement, and practical support. There are too many to include each by name but some need a special mention. Maggie Pearlstine persuaded me to embark on the project and convinced me that it could, should, and would be written. Debbie Beckerman, author and mother of two young children, has devoted countless hours to ensuring that we included all the issues that other pregnancy books have not addressed. That she is now a close personal friend is an unexpected bonus. Esther Ripley has contributed more than editorial skills to the project. Her enthusiasm for the subject matter is only surpassed by her ability to remain calm, patient, and encouraging on every occasion that I was late meeting a deadline. Additional thanks to Angela Baynham, Liz Coghill, and the creative team at Dorling Kindersley. I am also grateful to my colleague May Backos, who read through the entire manuscript, to all my medical and midwifery colleagues at St, Mary's for their help and advice, and to the many patients who have so generously shared their feelings, thoughts, anxieties, fears, and triumphs with me over the years. I hope that I have done justice to their requests for a new pregnancy bible.

Without the support of my family, this book would never have got off the starting block, let alone reached completion. My husband, John, deserves special recognition. I consider myself very fortunate to be able to rely on the fact that he is always supportive, constructively critical, and tolerant, even when dinner is late yet again. A big thank you is also due to my twin daughters, who have remained extraordinarily good humored and understanding, despite my preoccupation. Clare and Jenny are a daily source of delight and wonder to me, which is without doubt, the inspiration and real reason for writing this book.

Publisher's acknowledgments

Thanks to the following for their editorial support:
Julia North, Katie Dock, Isabella Jones
Additional photography: Ruth Jenkinson
Additional illustrator: Debbie Maizels
Additional DTP design: Julian Dams, Grahame Kitto
Picture Research Administrator: Carlo Ortu
Additional Picture Research: Franziska Marking
Picture Librarian: Romaine Werblow
Proofreader: Constance Novis; Indexer: Hilary Bird

Picture credits

Most of the images in this book are of the embryo and fetus live in utero, pictured using endoscopic and ultrasound technology. When this has not been possible, images have been taken by reputable medical professionals as part of research or to promote educational awareness.

Dorling Kindersley would like to thank the following for their kind permission to reproduce their photographs: (abbreviations key: t=top, b=bottom, r=right, l=left, c=centre) **1: Prof. J.E. Jirasek MD, DSc.**/CRC Press/Parthenon; **2–3: Corbis**/Ariel Skelley; **5: Corbis**/LWA-Dann Tardif (br); **LOGIQlibrary** (tl), (tc), (tr); **6: Professor Lesley Regan** (tl) **7: Photonica**/Henrik Sorensen (br); **8: Science Photo Library**/Edelmann (tl); **9: Corbis**/Susan Solie Patterson (tr); **10–11: Getty Images**/David Oliver; **12: Mother & Baby Picture Library**/Ian Hooton (b); **13: Getty Images**/Bill Ling; **14: Science Photo Library**/D. Phillips (crb), Prof. P. Motta/Dept. Of Anatomy/University "La Sapienza", Rome (cla), VVG (clb); **15: Science Photo Library**/Edelmann (c), Prof. P. Motta/Dept. Of Anatomy/University "La Sapienza", Rome (cra); **The Wellcome Institute Library, London**: Yorgos Nikas (cfr); **16: Science Photo Library**/Richard Rawlins/Custom Medical Stock Photo; **18: Science Photo Library**/Prof. P. Motta/Dept. Of Anatomy/University "La Sapienza", Rome (br); Professors P.M. Motta & J. Van Blerkom (bl); **19: Science Photo Library**/D. Phillips (br); Dr. Yorgos Nikas (bl); **20: Science Photo Library**/Edelmann (tl), (cla), (clb), (cfl); **24: Mother & Baby Picture Library**/Ruth Jenkinson (tl); **26: Alamy Images**/Camera Press Ltd; **30: Getty Images**/Gibson (c); **31: Mother & Baby Picture Library**/Ian Hooton (br); **33: Science Photo Library**/CNRI (tr), Dr. Gopal Murti (cfr), Moredun Scientific Ltd (crb); **36: Bubbles**/Lucy Tizard (bl); **37: Mother & Baby Picture Library**/Ian Hooton (tr); **38: Mother & Baby Picture Library**/Ian Hooton; **44: Getty Images**/Tom Mareschal (bl); **46: Getty Images**/Chris Everard (bl); **Prof. J.E. Jirasek MD, DSc.**/CRC Press/Parthenon (br); **47: Alamy Images**/foodfolio (bl); **Science Photo Library**/Ian Hooton (tl), Tissuepix (br); **51: Getty Images**:/Anthony Johnson (br); **56: Mother & Baby Picture Library**/Ruth Jenkinson (tl); **57: Mother & Baby Picture Library**/Ruth Jenkinson (br); **58: Mother & Baby Picture Library**/Ian Hooton; **60: Getty Images**/Garry Wade (cla); **62: Mother & Baby Picture Library**/Ian Hooton (tl); **65: Getty Images**/Chronoscope; **66–71: Prof. J.E. Jirasek MD, DSc.**/CRC Press/Parthenon; **74: Science Photo Library**/Zephyr (bl); **75: Getty Images**/Peter Correz (tr); **76: Corbis**/Ariel Skelley (bl); **80: Professor Lesley Regan; 83: Mother & Baby Picture Library**/Ian Hooton (cfr); **84: MIDIRS**: (bl); **88: Mother & Baby Picture Library**/Ruth Jenkinson (bl); **89:**

The Wellcome Institute Library, London/Anthea Sieveking (tr); 90: Mother & Baby Picture Library/Ian Hooton (bl); 92: Prof. J.E. Jirasek MD, DSc./CRC Press/Parthenon; 94: Life Issues Institute (bl); Science Photo Library/Edelmann (bc), (br); Prof. J.E. Jirasek MD, DSc./CRC Press/Parthenon (tl); 96: Bubbles/Jennie Woodcock (cfl); 96: Mediscan/Medical-On-Line (clb;) 99: Getty Images/Ericka McConnell (tr); 100: Mother & Baby Picture Library/Ian Hooton (tl); 105: Mother & Baby Picture Library (tr); 106: Science Photo Library/Edelmann; 107: Science Photo Library/Edelmann (cra); 108: LOGIQlibrary (tl); 109: Science Photo Library/Edelmann (tr); GE Medical Systems (b); 110: LOGIQlibrary; 111: Science Photo Library/BSIP (cla); 115: Getty Images/Daniel Bosler (t); 118: Mother & Baby Picture Library/Ian Hooton (b); 121: Mother & Baby Picture Library/Ian Hooton (br); 123: Mother & Baby Picture Library/Eddie Lawrence; 124: LOGIQlibrary; 125: LOGIQlibrary; 126: Mother & Baby Picture Library/Ian Hooton; 137: Professor Lesley Regan (c), (cfr); 141: Professor Lesley Regan (cfr); 149: Mother & Baby Picture Library/Ian Hooton; 150: Getty Images/Steve Allen (l); Prof. J.E. Jirasek MD, DSc./CRC Press/Parthenon (b); 150–151: Getty Images/Ranald Mackechnie; 151: Prof. J.E. Jirasek MD, DSc./CRC Press/Parthenon (br); Life Issues Institute (tr); 152: Getty Images/Steve Allen; 153: Getty Images/Steve Allen (cr); 154: Science Photo Library/Professor P.M. Motta & E. Vizza (cfl), VVG (tl); 155: Science Photo Library/GE Medical Systems (b); Getty Images/Steve Allen (tr); 158: Science Photo Library/CNRI (bc); Edelmann (bl); 159: Alamy Images/Janine Wiedel (bc); Photonica/Henrik Sorensen (bl); 162: Bubbles/Angela Hampton; 163: Alamy Images/Camera Press Ltd; 166: Science Photo Library/Neil Bromhall; 167: Science Photo Library/Neil Bromhall (cfr); 168: Oxford Scientific Films (bl); Science Photo Library/Neil Bromhall/Genesisi Films (br); 169: Science Photo Library/Neil Bromhall (tr); 171: Science Photo Library/DR P. Marazzi (cfr); The Wellcome Institute Library, London (br) 172: Mother & Baby Picture Library/Ruth Jenkinson (b); 175: LOGIQlibrary (tl), (l); Professor Lesley Regan (c), (cfr); 176: Mother & Baby Picture Library/Ian Hooton (t); 177: Alamy Images/Camera Press Ltd (br); 179: Getty Images/Juan Silva; 180–183: Prof. J.E. Jirasek MD, DSc./CRC Press/Parthenon (tr); 185: Mother & Baby Picture Library/Ruth Jenkinson; 187: Corbis/Cameron; 189: LOGIQlibrary (tr); 190: Mother & Baby Picture Library (b); 193: Alamy Images/Bill Bachmann; 195: Powerstock/Super Stock (b); 196: Mother & Baby Picture Library/Dave J. Anthony (b); 197: Alamy Images/Dan Atkin (t); 199: Corbis/Jim Craigmyle; 200: LOGIQlibrary: (c), (l); Science Photo Library/Dr. Najeeb Layyous (b); 200–201: Getty Images/Jim Craigmyle; 201 LOGIQlibrary (tr), (br); 202: Life Issues Institute; 203: Life Issues Institute (crb); 204: Science Photo Library/BSIP, MARIGAUX (tl); 205: Life Issues Institute (tr); 205: Professor Lesley Regan (bl); 211: Mother & Baby Picture Library/Ian Hooton (tr); 218: Oppo; 221: Mother & Baby Picture Library/Ian Hooton; 223: Mother & Baby Picture

Library/Ian Hooton; 225: Alamy Images/Camera Press Ltd (t); 227: Corbis/Roy McMahon; 228: Getty Images/Ross Whitaker; 230: Science Photo Library/GE Medical Systems; 231: Science Photo Library/GE Medical Systems; 232: LOGIQlibrary (br); Science Photo Library/GE Medical Systems (bl); 233: Alamy Images/Nick Veasey X-ray (t); 236: Mother & Baby Picture Library/Ian Hooton; 243: Alamy Images/Stock Image; 246: Science Photo Library/Colin Cuthbert; 248: Science Photo Library/Mark Clarke; 249: Bubbles/Moose Azim; 253: Alamy Images/David Young-Wolff; 255: Powerstock/Jesus Coll; 256: Mother & Baby Picture Library/Caroline Molloy; 257: Professor Lesley Regan (ca), (cra); 260: Science Photo Library/GE Medical Systems; 261: Science Photo Library/GE Medical Systems (b); 262: Science Photo Library/GE Medical Systems (tl); 263: Science Photo Library/Mehau Kulyk (b); 265: Mother & Baby Picture Library/Ian Hooton (t); 271: Mother & Baby Picture Library/Ian Hooton (t); 277: Bubbles/Loisjoy Thurstun; 278–279: Alamy Images/SHOUT; 280: Corbis/Jules Perrier; 281: Alamy Images/plainpicture/Kirch, S; 282: Mother & Baby Picture Library/Ian Hooton; 284: Corbis/Anne W. Krause; 288: Mother & Baby Picture Library/Ruth Jenkinson; 290: Mother & Baby Picture Library/Moose Azim (bl); Science Photo Library/Brian Yarvin (bc); Getty Images/Photodisc Green (br); 293: Mother & Baby Picture Library/Ruth Jenkinson (br); 297: Mother & Baby Picture Library/James Fletcher (tr); 309: Mother & Baby Picture Library/Moose Azim (r); 314: Alamy Images/Janine Wiedel (bl); 318: Mother & Baby Picture Library/Ruth Jenkinson (br); 322: The Wellcome Institute Library, London/Anthea Sieveking; 324: Angela Hampton/Family Life Picture Library; 329: The Wellcome Institute Library, London/Anthea Sieveking (tr); 332: Mother & Baby Picture Library/Moose Azim (bl); 334: Science Photo Library/CNRI (ccb); 336: Corbis/Annie Griffiths Belt; 337: Alamy Images/Peter Usbeck; 342: Corbis/Tom Stewart (b); 343: Mother & Baby Picture Library (tr); 344: Corbis/ER Productions; 345: Professor Lesley Regan (r); 348: Mother & Baby Picture Library/Indira Flack (bl); 360: Alamy Images/Yoav Levy; 368: Alamy Images/Janine Wiedel (bl); 370–371: Getty Images/Kaz Mori; 382: Powerstock/Super Stock; 372: Alamy Images/plainpicture/Kirch, S (b); 373: Getty Images/Rubberball Productions; 374: Mother & Baby Picture Library/Moose Azim; 380: Alamy Images/Shout (cfl); Mother & Baby Picture Library/Ruth Jenkinson (tl); 381: Mother & Baby Picture Library/Ruth Jenkinson (br); 389: The Wellcome Institute Library, London/Anthea Sieveking; 390: Bubbles; 394: Corbis/Don Mason; 397: Getty Images/Roger Charity; 399: Bubbles/Loisjoy Thurstun; 402: Mother & Baby Picture Library/Ian Hooton; 404: Alamy Images/Janine Wiedel; 405: Alamy Images/Peter Usbeck (cbr); Science Photo Library/ Joseph Nettis (crb); 406–407: Corbis/Norbert Schaefer.

All other images © Dorling Kindersley
For further information see: www.dkimages.com